American Samurai

OTHER BOOKS BY WILLIAM LAREAU

CONDUCT EXPECTED: The Unwritten Rules for a Successful Business Career

THE INSIDE TRACK: A Successful Job Search Method

MILLENNIUM MANAGEMENT: Last Chance for American Business

American Samurai

WARRIOR FOR THE COMING
DARK AGES OF AMERICAN BUSINESS

by

William Lareau

NEW WIN PUBLISHING, INC.

Printing Code
    11, 12, 13, 14, 15

Library of Congress Cataloging-in-Publication Data

Lareau, William.
        American Samurai : warrior for the coming of the dark ages of
American business / by William Lareau.
    p.   cm.
    Includes bibliographical references.
    Includes index.
    ISBM 0-8329-0458-9 : $17.95
    1. Organizational effectiveness.   2. Career development.
3. Competition, International.   4. Industrial management—United
States.   I. Title.
HD58.9.L37 1991   90-19814
658—dc20   CIP

Dedicated to . . .

My Dad, Ernie, "Big Ernie" Lareau

Table of Contents

Introduction

American business is facing a crisis of incredible proportions. Unless we face some hard facts and deal with the coming disaster immediately, we will be lost as a world economic power. We will enter the Dark Ages of American business, unable to compete and cut off from world markets. We will be shunned among the economic giants. This book outlines the absolutely necessary minimum steps that must be implemented at once in order to assure our future economic survival.

America is headed for a drastic reduction in the quality of life as a direct result of the escalating inability of American business to be competitive in the rapidly changing international marketplace. No longer can intelligent workers hide their heads in the sand and simply go blindly along for the ride. They won't like the destination. Business life and careers from now on will be zero-sum games (there's only so much to go around), with a decreasing sum and more players. Those who act as if things haven't changed since the 1950s will be the losers. Our future demands a new work credo and a new American worker—a warrior who will battle to hold off the coming Dark Ages and lead us to rebirth as the preeminent world economic power.

An American Samurai knows what the score is and does what must be done to advance the cause of American industrial survival. The American Samurai is not the typical trusting emplyoee, a blindly led minion of big business who does what he or she is told and hopes that the "company" will take care of things. The American Samurai knows what American business needs and knows what must be done. The American Samurai fights for the changes that must be made, knowing that a failure to change the system dooms us all. Yet the American Samurai does not sacrifice his or her career in a futile attempt to lead resistant and irritated sheep out of the darkness. American Samurai bide their time, advancing their careers, doing what they must do to survive for themselves and their families, working quietly and secretly to improve the system, until they see that American business is beginning to awaken from the stupor of its ignorance. Then, and only then, will the American Samurai come out of hiding in numbers like Ninja springing from ambush, to work openly to put American business back on top again.

This book outlines what has happened to get us into the mess we are in, what is likely to happen over the next decade (the handwriting is on the wall for those few with clear vision who wish to read it), and what American business should be doing to reestablish competitiveness (and how to do this).

Finally, this book outlines the necessary survival tactics that thousands of American Samurai will have to practice so that their true spirit and beliefs will remain hidden from the stupid and vengeful managers who will protect the old system to its last day.

This book is different from any other that you've ever read. I'm not going to beat around the bush and make attempts to paint a pleasant, optimistic picture. There are many others who will gladly assist you in donning rose-colored glasses. We don't have time for that nonsense anymore. The situation is bleak, and we need to face facts and get moving. I'm not going to coddle you, and I'm not going to dump a lot of academic trivia on you. I'm going to give it to you straight. Read on and become an American Samurai.

American Samurai

1

We're Not Number One Anymore

This chapter is a test. If you pass the test, you're a candidate to enter training to become an American Samurai. If you fail the test, you're beyond hope and probably should concentrate on getting a management job in an industry such as automobiles or steel, where everybody is waiting to be killed off by the competition. The test works this way: if you are scared to death for the future of American industry after reading this chapter, you pass. If this chapter doesn't scare you, or if you don't believe it, you fail.

You need to appreciate how bad things are for two reasons:

1. If you don't accept that American business is in big trouble, you're not going to believe that drastic action, both for yourself and for the entire American business sector, is necessary. And if you don't believe that extreme measures are required, you'll be inclined to react in the typical American management mode—stick your head in the sand and ignore the problem and hope that somehow, somewhere, someone (else, of course) will take care of things.

2. This book is going to describe roles and behaviors for management and nonmanagement workers that are very different from those we have learned from observing and being part of traditional American business practices. The sorry shape we're in is a direct consequence of the failure of the existing system of management and business. If you have a clear picture of the economic devastation that this failed system has wrought, you'll understand the necessity for a complete transformation of American management.

American business is dying by the minute. There are some who try to squirm away from this unpleasant truth by pointing out that the size of our economy means that we're number one. They try to take comfort in the fact

1

that we still have the largest gross national product. Or they note that because we spend more money or generate more jobs than anyone else, we're still number one. Wrong.

These shoddy, transparent arguments are simply refusals to see the truth. Just because we're the biggest and *used* to be the king of the economic hill doesn't mean that we're number one now, any more than a failing, fat, punch-drunk heavyweight champion is the best simply because he's been fighting amateurs. American business is fat, overweight, slow, and failing fast. We won the title by beating up a bunch of skinny kids and sickly old men. But now we're facing the real thing—contenders that are leaner, meaner, smarter, faster, and hungrier than we are. We may still hold the title, but we're about to get our lights punched out by the ranked contenders.

The Bank of Japan estimated in 1987 that 20,000 to 30,000 American industrial workers lose their jobs each month as American companies close or cut back in the face of foreign competition. The situation is probably much worse than even those numbers indicate. The big industries such as cars and steel get most of the press when layoffs and plant closings hit, but we're being beaten in every area. For example, the American Apparel Manufacturers' Association reported in January 1990 that their industry saw jobs fall from 1.26 million in 1980 to 1.09 million in 1989—a loss of 251,000 jobs in 9 years. That's over 2300 jobs lost every month simply because our jockey shorts don't measure up to imports.

The data in Table 1-1, which shows that eight of the world's top ten largest publicly held companies were Japanese, was shocking when it first appeared in 1987. Now such information is commonplace. The reaction has become, "So, what else is new?" What else is new is that it's getting worse every day. If we want to survive as an economic power, much less recover the number one spot, we had better do more than furrow our brows and turn on the television set (made in Japan, of course) to escape reality.

Table 1-1.
The ten largest publicly held companies in
the world in 1987.*

1. Nippon Telegraph and Telephone (Japan)
2. IBM (U.S.)
3. Exxon (U.S.)
4. Sumitomo Bank (Japan)
5. Industrial Bank of Japan (Japan)
6. Tokyo Electric Power (Japan)
7. Nomura Securities (Japan)
8. Dai-Ichi Kangyo Bank (Japan)
9. Fuji Bank (Japan)
10. Mitsubishi Bank (Japan)

*Parade Magazine, November 22, 1987.

The situation hasn't gotten any better in the last 3 years. Table 1-2 lists the world's top 20 companies in terms of total market value. Thirteen of the 20 are Japanese (as are 43 out of the top 100). This is a pattern of almost complete domination. Whatever Japan is doing is working.

Table 1-2.
The world's top 20 companies in
total market value in 1990.*

Rank	Company name	Country	Market value (billions of dollars)
1.	Nippon Telegraph and Telephone	Japan	118.79
2.	IBM	U.S.	68.89
3.	Industrial Bank of Japan	Japan	67.71
4.	Royal Dutch/Shell Group	Neth/Britain	67.14
5.	General Electric	U.S.	62.54
6.	Exxon	U.S.	60.00
7.	Sumitomo Bank	Japan	55.81
8.	Fuji Bank	Japan	53.17
9.	Toyota Motor	Japan	50.54
10.	Mutsui Taiyo Kobe Bank	Japan	49.80
11.	Dai-Ichi Kangyo Bank	Japan	49.57
12.	Mitsubishi Bank	Japan	47.17
13.	AT&T	U.S.	46.96
14.	Sanwa Bank	Japan	45.60
15.	Tokyo Electric Power	Japan	41.68
16.	Philip Morris	U.S.	39.11
17.	Hitachi Ltd.	Japan	33.04
18.	Merck	U.S.	32.72
19.	Nomura Securities	Japan	32.54
20.	Long-term Credit Bank of Japan	Japan	32.44

*Business Week, July 16, 1990.

Much of the trade and industry data we're going to be looking at in this chapter shows Japanese domination of American industry. This may make it appear that I'm glorifying the Japanese culture as the ultimate culture. I'm not. As we'll see in later chapters, the Japanese have been successful because they're doing some very smart things. A comparatively small number of American companies such as Motorola and Xerox are using the same techniques (not always companywide) and being very successful, some even beating the Japanese at their own game. It's not the culture of the Japanese that makes them number one, it's the new business approaches they're using. It's these techniques I glorify, not the country or the culture of the people who use them.

The Japanese are now dominant in business because they started to aggressively use these new business techniques many years ago and have continued to implement them more comprehensively than any other country.

If it sounds now and then as if I'm frustrated about the Japanese beating us whenever and wherever they want, you're right. But not at the Japanese. I reserve my frustration for the leaders of American business for not having the motivation to apply what the Japanese have shown us is possible.

The most aggravating and humiliating aspect of this situation is that the United States first introduced the Japanese to the techniques that got them started along the road to world economic dominance. Most of our business leaders have been too shortsighted to pay attention to their own experts over the last 40 years, whereas the Japanese were not only paying attention, but learning, applying, and expanding upon the basic skills we taught them.

Evidence for the success of the different way of working that the Japanese are using is everywhere, in every industry. The top ten largest banks in the world are Japanese. You don't have to use a lot of imagination to figure out where the Japanese get their money. Our balance of trade each year in the last half of the 1980s has run from about minus 100 to minus 140 billion dollars per year (meaning that we're buying more foreign products than we're selling). Some of this is due to oil imports, but the largest share is the direct result of American products not being competitive with foreign products. Just for cars alone, we pay out nearly 50 billion dollars more per year than we bring in. In 1990 our deficit with Japan alone is running about 50 billion dollars per year for all products and services.

You've been hearing about these huge numbers for so many years now that they probably don't even register anymore. Let me translate them for you. Let's say that a typical worker in the automotive industry makes $40,000 per year in total pay (about $15.00 per hour with liberal overtime when there is demand for American cars) and that it costs another $25,000 per year per employee for benefits (pensions, medical insurance, vacations, sick days, etc.). We end up with a cost of $65,000 per year per employee. About 40% of the cost of a car is related to personnel costs of one kind or another (engineers to design it, labor to build it, managers to stand around and watch and executives to hide in offices and do magazine interviews, etc.).

Forty percent of 50 billion dollars in lost sales is 20 billion dollars. Dividing that by $65,000 equals 307,692 jobs, each of which is lost because our own citizens would rather buy an import car than an American-made car. That's 307,000 people out of work, on welfare, or working at places like McDonald's for about $12,000 per year rather than $40,000. They have less money to spend, which in turn puts more people out of work. That's what the trade deficit really means—all caused by short-sighted American management.

If we apply this 40% personnel cost to a year's trade deficit of 100 billion dollars, it equals more than 615,000 jobs lost, and that's just the first line jobs. When those folks stop spending, hundreds of thousands of others who provide them with goods and services end up out of work. The result is an ever expanding circle of sorrow and despair that moves through our economy like a plague.

Table 1-3 shows the type of money (in billions of dollars) that the Japanese have been able to invest in the United States over just the last 3 years as a result of their success in selling products to the world (most of it to the United States). Japanese investments in the United States have become so large that they are causing disturbances in traditional patterns of economic growth, interest rates, and stock prices. The Japanese don't own us yet, but it's getting to the point where their investments are having significant effects on our entire monetary system—all because they are more competitive than the United States in almost every industry.

Table 1-3.
Japanese investment in the United States, 1987–1989.

Type of Investment in the United States	1987	1988	1989
Bonds	72.9	85.8	99.7
Stocks	16.9	3.0	16.5
Direct investment (real estate, companies)	19.9	34.2	41.9
Total	109.6	123.0	158.1

The top six heavy truck manufacturers (heavy trucks being the types of trucks that trucking companies use) in the world are Japanese. You haven't seen many of their trucks in this country yet because it is a low profit, slow growth industry. In effect the Japanese have decided that moving into the heavy truck business in this country is beneath them. They're going to leave the crumbs of industry for us, one of which is heavy trucking.

The automotive industry is a sterling example of how not to respond to a crisis. Cars used to be the prototypical American industry—cold, hard American steel, smokestacks, produced in the industrial belt of America, an American industry if ever there was one. So what happened in 1989? For the first time, the top selling car in the United States was the Honda Accord rather than an American designed and built car. During the same year that sales for the former best selling Ford Escort fell 13%, 362,707 Accords were purchased in the United States, making it the top seller. Many of them were even built in our own country, often using the same U.S. workers that General Motors, Ford, and Chrysler blame for poor American productivity.

The sorry, whining, whipped dog attitude of the automotive industry and of much of American business as a whole is epitomized by a statement made by Ford spokesman Jon Roberts: "We're not too happy about it (losing the number one spot), but at least we still have numbers two and three."* Great. Thousands more people are out on the street and Ford "at least" has numbers

---

Los Angeles Times, January 5, 1990.

two and three. For how long? The Escort and the Taurus (the number three) faded because they didn't change as customer requirements changed over the last few years. That's Detroit's typical attitude (and that of American business as a whole)—get a winner and then sit back and relax, hoping that it will continue for another 10 years. That attitude has never worked very well, and now it invites disaster. Disaster never turns down an invitation. When will we learn to stop sending out invitations?

Table 1-4 shows the percent changes for the overall annual daily sales rates of various car makers in 1989 compared to 1988. At the same time that American manufacturers were losing market share and total volume, most Japanese manufacturers were selling more than the previous year. The situation in 1990 will be even worse if past history is any indication.

Table 1-4.
Annual daily car sales, 1989 compared to 1988.

Manufacturer	Sales	Percent change (1989–1988)
General Motors	3,276,941	− 9.4
Ford	2,099,773	− 4.2
Chrysler	917,506	− 13.1
Honda U.S.	389,472	+ 4.4
Mazda U.S.	41,584	+ 33.6
Nissan U.S.	103,134	− 7.4
Toyota U.S.	212,388	+ 195.5

Still doubting? You're going to have to learn to deal with reality if you want to get anywhere. Table 1-5 shows what has happened to the world market share of U.S. companies in basic industries between 1970 and 1987.

Table 1-5.
Changes in basic industry share, 1970–1987.*

Industrial category	Share of world market held by U.S. companies		Loss
	1970	1987	
Black and white televisions	65%	3%	62%
Color televisions	90%	10%	80%
Phonographs	90%	1%	89%
Ball bearings	87%	70%	17%
Machining centers	95%	35%	60%
Semiconductors	90%	64%	26%
VCR	10%	1%	9%
Audio tape recorders	40%	1%	39%
Telephone sets	97%	25%	72%

*U.S. Department of Commerce data.

The VCR situation is the best of the list, with a loss of only 9%. Of course, we only had 10% to start with. It just goes to show that one way to avoid being beaten badly is never to show up for the fight in the first place! As you can see, the situation in the automotive industry isn't unique; it's all too typical. American business has been beaten to the barroom floor of the world economy and is now being kicked into unconsciousness. Is there time to fight back and get up before a fatal blow is struck? Who can say? But we had better do something fast, both as individual American Samurai and as an economy as a whole, or we're finished as an industrial power of any consequence.

Things are looking even darker in the areas of advanced technology. The Japanese are poised to do the same thing to the computer industry that they're doing to the automotive industry. Japan already has the lead in such critical computer-related technologies as flat-panel displays, color flat-panel displays, CD-ROM (compact disk–read only memories) drives, erasable optical disk drives, key laser printer components, and tape-automated bonding.

A key element in manufacturing computer semiconductor chips, which is the basis of the entire industry, is stepping aligner equipment. The United States manufactured more than 90% of this equipment in 1979, compared with about 5% for the Japanese. The U.S. share had fallen to about 20% in 1988, whereas the Japanese share increased to more than 70%. More layoffs and plant closings, anyone?

During the same period, the American lead in DRAM (dynamic random access memory) chips has fallen dramatically. Guess who is now the number one manufacturer? Right, Japan. They now supply 70% of the worldwide market compared to the U.S. share of about 17% (down from 55% in 1980).

Prior to 1988 or so, the Japanese concentrated (on purpose) on developing their dominance of computer components. They are now, in the words of Sanford L. Kane, a former IBM Vice President of Technology and President of the now disintegrating U.S. Memories Corporation (a consortium set up to battle the Japanese, which is now failing because they haven't learned to work together), "Now, it's their intention to move up the technology food chain."* They started in laptop computers and had 43% of the U.S. market in 1989. Their share of all PCs (personal computers) has risen from 5.8% in 1985 to 13% in 1989.

The handwriting is on the wall. They are doing exactly the same thing in computers that they've already done in cars. They are producing quality goods at competitive prices and getting new products out faster and better than anyone. They are moving in slowly and carefully, according to a well-defined plan. A strategic business plan is an organized set of analyses that lays out well-defined future actions for the next 5 years that will attain desired objectives. It is not what most American businesses produce when they

---

Business Week, October 23, 1989.

plan—a 1-week exercise done 2 months into the year that is mostly graphics artistry, which is later ignored by all personnel (well, not *all* personnel can ignore a typical company's plan, because most of them aren't allowed to see it). We'll talk about plans in some detail in Chapter 15.

There are some who contend that the Japanese threat to computers is a mirage. They say that the Japanese aren't any good at software and at designing the more expensive computers. They used to say the same thing about Japanese cars and electronics. If I wasn't working 12 to 14 hours a day trying to turn this situation around in America, I'd bet every penny I have on the Japanese. They haven't lost many, and you never bet against a steady winner unless you have inside information. The inside information I have makes me even more positive that the Japanese (and other competitors) will win. American managers are ignorant of the techniques they should be using and are still (for the most part) denying the urgency of the situation.

It's often argued that much of this situation is caused by differences in tax laws, tax rates, government assistance to Japan's industries, and yen-dollar fluctuations (these contentions are ample evidence that keeping one's head in the sand too long can cause all sorts of cognitive problems). These excuses are a typical defense mechanism. As James E. Sierk, a Xerox vice president, said about his company's awakening to the real quality problem, "We tried to convince ourselves that the numbers were wrong or that it was a currency glitch or that the Japanese must be cheating somehow. Finally we realized that they were just managing better than we were."* Xerox turned itself around by doing many of the things we'll be talking about later, to the point where they won one of only two Malcolm Baldrige National Quality Awards presented in 1989. The plain, sad fact of the matter is that American products just aren't as good as many foreign products, especially Japanese products, and that American workers aren't as productive. This is not the workers' fault—workers don't run the system.

We'll see in later chapters that improved quality always leads to lower costs and higher productivity. An emphasis on quality first is at the heart of the Japanese business system. The Japanese edge in quality in almost all products is large and increasing. Let's just look at the automotive industry as one example (it's hard to compare quality in electronics anymore, because we make so few commerical electronics products in the United Sates). Figure 1-1 shows defects per 100 vehicles, often called "things gone wrong" in the automotive trade (it should be called "business as usual" for American car makers). The data was compiled by J.D. Power and Associates, the largest car quality research company. The chart converts Japanese quality levels to a constant level of 100, even though Japanese quality is getting better every year. You'll note that the distance between U.S. automakers' quality (domestic) and that of the Japanese increased in 1989. From 1985 to 1988,

---

Electronic Business, October 16, 1989.

General Motors, Ford, and Chrysler actually narrowed the huge gap, but they are now reverting to form and falling behind.

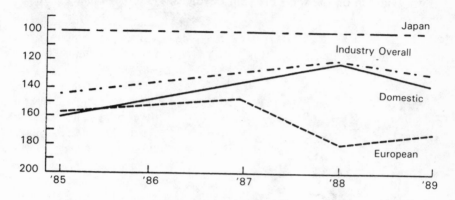

Figure 1-1.   Quality levels of Japanese, American, and European car makers. Index charts problems per 100 vehicles. Figures are weighted to give Japanese autos, whose quality other makers strive to match, a constant level of 100. While the line appears flat, there is actually a constant upward trend in Japanese initial product quality. (Source: J.D. Power & Associates).

BOTTOM LINE, BACK AGAINST THE WALL TIME

So, there you have it. Depressing, eh? Well, that's the plain, stark truth. We have to deal with it, one way or another. I'll be honest with you: the situation, no matter what you do, or what I do, or what the country does, will get much, much worse before it gets better (*if* it gets better, which is not exactaly a sure thing). If we each do what must be done, now, rather than later, we can minimize how far we fall. It's up to each of us to do what we can to stem the losses.

It's Alamo, Little Big Horn, and Roarke's Drift time. Each of these was a hopeless battle caused by management stupidity, but only two were slaughters of the outnumbered defenders. Let's just hope that the last stand of the American economy is a Roarke's Drift rather than another Custer's Last Stand.

We are in much the same situation as an army that has been thoroughly defeated in a series of battles because of generals using an outdated battle plan. We need to change generals, of course. But those of us in the trenches have to learn to fight more effectively, even as the stupid generals remain in charge back at the chateau, sipping champagne, while we're dying in the mud. Maybe, just maybe, we can hold the line with our lives and careers until the old generals die off and new leadership, chosen from the ranks, leads us to victory again.

It's not much, but it's all we have. It's all we've been left with by American management. Pass it on down the line: American Samurai never give up. Everybody up on the wall. Fix your bayonets. Here they come again.

2

The Myth of American Superiority as the Root of our Bad Management Practices

Nothing remains constant over time. Everything changes. The weather changes, cars wear out (some quicker than others; are you listening, American industry?), seasons come and go, we grow old and die, continents move across the face of the earth, stars are born and die, and even galaxies with their billions of stars eventually burn out. Nothing stays the same over time. Some changes take hundreds of billions of years and some take only seconds, but everything in the physical universe changes all the time. Nothing is constant but change itself.

The essence of existence at every level involves change and adaptations to change. Yet American business practices appear to be exceptions to this law: in the face of the stomp job we've been getting in the international marketplace, you'd think our business practices and strategies would be rapidly changing to keep pace. Wrong. Sure, we've got computers, we've got facsimile machines, and so on, but we've also got the same old management techniques and the same old, erroneous "theories" that we used in 1950. This chapter will explore why American management has been so criminally slow to change in the face of foreign threats.

One of the basic underlying problems is the myth of American business superiority. Most executives get apoplectic when I mention it, but it's true: American business superiority is a myth. It is a myth born from the seductiveness of a snapshot of a time long past. The myth of American business superiority (as well as the myths of economic and social superiority) is built upon an ingrained remembrance of a past era of American youth and vitality that is no longer valid. As Chapter One demonstrated beyond any doubt, we are clearly no longer number one in anything but size and name. The facts speak for themselves.

It's important to understand the evolution of the current American business

11

dilemma. You'll see that the current situation was unavoidable; we were destined to be heavily challenged for the number one spot of world business leadership. Nothing we could have done would have stopped the challenges. And nothing we could have done would have prevented us from losing some of our market share. However, if we would have reacted quickly and with some intelligence (but then, we're dealing with the typical American executive, so you can just about forget about quick decisions), we could have forestalled some of the horrific industrial losses we've suffered. Unless American business leaders wake up and start taking the appropriate actions now, we will suffer additional significant trade and business defeats in the next 2 decades that will make our current situation look attractive.

In this chapter we'll review historical events that have shaped the current business and political environment and the world view of American managers. This isn't a history book, but a full appreciation of the problem requires that its background be understood. Besides, if you're going to be an American Samurai, you'll have to be able to talk the talk as well as walk the walk when you're out there educating the masses and teaching your apprentices.

We'll also examine why American business leaders have been so slow to respond to the virtual gutting of American industrial leadership. Although it's difficult for me to be very sympathetic to any serious failings in the judgment of CEOs and company presidents who are pulling down salaries of 1 to 10 million dollars a year (or more), you'll see that some small part of their dimwitted reaction is almost understandable, given the environment in which they learned business. Yet, let's not waste too much compassion: sitting around moaning about unwilling workers, the lack of sufficient trade barriers (to force the American public to buy overpriced, poor quality products), and government interference, while doing nothing of substance, is a pretty serious failing. Just call me silly and idealistic, but I expect people who are making millions per year to be able to do their jobs and provide some leadership! Once you understand how American business leadership came to establish its world-class (able to compete with the best in the world) benchmark (a standard of performance) for "head in the sand" management cultures, you'll understand the problems we're going to have in changing how businesses operate.

Finally, we'll look at what the future will likely bring if we don't reverse our business slide. You'll see that the Pollyanna, best-of-all-possible-worlds future views from guys like John Naisbitt (and spouse Patricia Aburdene) are simply megabull.

THE SEEDS OF OUR ARROGANCE

The seeds of the current problems with American business competitiveness were planted long ago. It's possible to explain the situation by merely going back to the end of World War II and describing events from that point. To a large extent, the worldwide economic and industrial conditions created by World War II set us up for the mess we're in now, no doubt about it. However, if business (and government) leaders had known what to look for and had been inclined to take significant steps as late as the early 1970s, we still would have had difficulty in making the correct moves quickly enough; a slow and resistant response to the collapse of our market dominance in many areas was all but guaranteed by events that occurred long before World War II.

The trouble started as far back as the original settlement of the American continent. From the start, the notion was planted in everyone's mind that America was a place where new beginnings were sought, where possibilities for the future were unbounded and exciting (at least in theory). Much of the continent was unexplored. There was always some other place to go— endless expanses of adventure and new horizons, at least in fantasy, if not in reality. From the beginning, this idea was becoming part of a cultural consciousness that America and its people were different.

The Revolutionary War further heightened the perception that America was special. Here was an upstart possession throwing off the yoke of the preeminent world power. Who else could do it but Americans? And then the British Empire was forced to sign a treaty in the War of 1812 (of course, Britain was also engaged in a small tiff with the French Empire and Napoleon at the time, but there's no need to mention irrelevant details; we kicked their butt, right?). We were on a roll, developing a confident, cocky attitude about our capabilities and future—developing a belief that Americans are special and that they always win.

This first dose of self-confidence was followed by an event that provided the basic foundation for becoming a major commercial power. The American Civil War provided the spark that forced the United States to establish a consistent, centralized system of laws and commerce and a solid industrial base. These two characteristics are essential to a modern industrialized power. Prior to the Civil War, the individual states operated more or less independently of the federal government and maintained and established their own monetary, trade, tax, and tariff policies. In fact, until the war was well underway, states provided troops to the federal government on a voluntary basis. The Civil War provided the impetus for a single, consistent national government. This in turn freed the states from parochial concerns and enabled them to focus more energy on commerce and industry.

The Civil War also provided something much more important. There had been a certain innocence in the confidence of United States prior to the Civil War. The United States had been founded on an ideal of freedom. The promotion and protection of that ideal had been held high and used as either a motivation (the Revolutionary War and the War of 1812) or an excuse (the war with Mexico and the Indian wars). Prior to the Civil War, we had been a small country of quasi-independent states, a rural country. We weren't a center of art and culture as Europe was, but we were new, young, full of life, and fired by idealism. The Civil War changed all that. We were forced to grow up quickly. Suddenly, we were embroiled in a massive, horrible war in which hundreds of thousands died and in which the entire economy of the nation was devoted to supporting death and destruction.

This baptism of barbarity did two things to the American consciousness. First of all, it tempered our idealism. We had been bloodied in a war whose savagery completely overwhelmed sentiments about slavery and states' rights; nothing could justify the slaughter, suffering, and years of rebuilding. We had demonstrated that we could organize and operate industries and killing machinery as efficiently as the biggest European power, perhaps better. We had arrived on the world scene. And, perhaps even more importantly, we had done something that few others have done: we had fought one of history's most massive and destructive civil wars and emerged from the experience with a revitalized, stronger nation, primed to take on the world. Who else but the United States could do it? The self-delusions and myths continued to grow.

The pre–Civil War American image of itself as "winner" was revitalized during the settlement of the American West. The exploitation of the frontier and the edification of "pioneer spirit" provided the final, and ultimately most powerful, self-image: limitless, tough, vital, growing, unstoppable, and moving from growth to victory to expansion to growth. Where else in the civilized (meaning white and European) world could a claim be staked on untitled land and a life carved out in the wilderness? Where else was there a massive frontier full of fertile land ready for grazing and the plow, open to those tough enough to stake out their piece of happiness? Only in America, of course.

The images of cattle drives, Indian wars, sod busters versus land barons, Custer's Last Stand, wagon trains, bank robbers, gunslingers versus the marshal, the Texas Rangers, and so on, established themselves as American icons bigger than life and more permanent. The persona of the American West became part of the American cultural heritage, passed from generation to generation, incorporated into the very heart and soul of American mythology through movies, books, toys, and tales. Whether it was ever true or not, everyone believed that all Americans rode unlimited ranges and that one's destiny was limited only by individual capacity and courage. At the fundamental core of the icon was the central truth: we were number one and we never lost.

The American victory in the Spanish American War of 1898 and America's role in World War I only served to heighten images of America's invulnerability. Now, America really was a world power.

The Roaring Twenties further ingrained America's perception of itself as special by updating and reinvigorating the Wild West images via the exploits of tough talking gangsters, "Feds," bootlegging, and so on. The Depression wasn't exactly a positive ego boost, but it was worldwide, so who could blame us? (It probably was largely our fault, but details, details . . .)

World War II brought American self-image and achievements to their penultimate. The reality of our contributions was somewhat less impressive than our actual accomplishments. After all, most Americans learn history from American textbooks, not exactly an impartial source, when publishing companies are trying not to offend school boards, particularly during the cold war. The generally held American view is that the United States won World War II practically single-handedly. Nothing could be further from the truth.

The main military threat in World War II was Germany. Japan wasn't getting anywhere in China after initial gains and most certainly could not have maintained an invasion of North America. For most of the war, about 85% of the German army was fighting in Russia, where the largest land battle in the history of the world took place. Even if the United States hadn't entered the war, it is almost a certainty that Russia would have eventually worn down the Germans and would have been able to take as much of Europe as they wanted. A big deal is made out of American lend-lease aid to Russia, but it only amounted to 5% of their material at the height of the effort. No, the fact is that our role in World War II, while significant, was not that of the savior combatant.

Reality aside, however, the United States viewed itself as the sheriff who walked in when all appeared lost, guns blazing, and saved the day. This mistaken notion, by itself, wasn't any more damaging than any of the previous self-delusions about manifest destiny and superiority. The problem is that this particular dose of grandeur came at the worst possible time, when it would do the most damage to American business practices in the coming decades.

AMERICAN SAMURAI INSIGHT

Our own perceptions of our role in World War II, coupled with the economic situation created by the war, set us up for decades of misguided business practices.

After World War II, most of the prewar industrial powers lay in ruins. Before the war, Germany, France, and Britain had been the big three in terms of industrial and commerical power. When peace was finally won, their economies were either in ashes or had been bled white to support the war effort. The only major economy left intact was that of the United States. The world had come out of the Depression, the war was over, and Europe and Asia were ready to rebuild. There was a massive demand for commercial and industrial material, and there was only one place to get it—America.

The war had provided the impetus for a massive industrialization effort in the United States. When the war ended, this capacity, the world's biggest, was intact and ready to churn out products of all types in any volume. The United States became the number one peacetime industrial power overnight. There was no competition for many years. For 2 decades after the war, rebuilding countries didn't have the sales volume to support large-scale research and development efforts, not to mention the fact that they were rebuilding homes, factories, railroads, ports, and families. No nation could seriously challenge the United States because no nation had the resources to match our existing industrial capacity and growing economy.

Japan and Europe could make inroads here and there, but they were far, far behind the power curve in terms of market share and would have to work hard over a period of decades to erase their initial disadvantage. The jump that the United States got on everyone else due to the war lasted well into the 1970s. American dominance was so complete that it was common to read business articles in the early 1960s in which the American management system was described as being so powerful that other countries were being smothered and didn't have a chance to develop.

AMERICAN SAMURAI INSIGHT

It was easy to make the flattering assumption that the inherent brains, character, and efficiency of the United States was the fundamental cause. Easy, but incorrect.

This faulty view resulted from looking at a few years of American dominance and assuming that it was caused by the then current American management style. The cowboy, can-do-easy, arrogant superiority of our national psyche made such conclusions almost automatic. As we now know, this was wrong. Any management style, blessed with massive capacity, a huge market, and no competition, would have been successful. Even Don, Lee, and Roger (the Chairmen of the big three during the 1980s) could have been successful selling cars in that type of market (in fact, that's the only type of market in which they now do well, as we saw in Chapter One).

The accouterments of American business practices evolved rapidly during the 30 years after the war. The basic underlying assumptions didn't change, but tools and techniques proliferated. Management by Objective (MBO), compensation systems with their annual performance appraisals, labor and paygrades, job descriptions, the specialization of functions, the creation of the professional manager (a young snob with an MBA and no practical experience), and a variety of uniquely American practices came into the limelight. We'll see later that these practices are all counterproductive to successive competition in today's world (and were counterproductive then as well, but who could notice?). Over time, these phenomena came to define

American management. They were given credence and held up as ideals for all the business world to emulate because they were being used by the number one, all-time business powerhouse in the history of the world. Who could argue that they didn't work?

BAD LESSONS LEARNED

The demand-driven marketplace of the late 1940s, the 1950s, and the 1960s taught American management (and American society as a whole) a number of very bad lessons. American managers believed that everything that they were doing was good and that their system worked better than anything else. As a result, a number of practices that are killing us these days became the normal business methodology, taught in schools and on the job to everybody in business. Over time, they became as ingrained in the American business consciousness as firmly as the myth of American cultural superiority is drilled into every citizen from the first day of school.

We'll look in detail at the values this system has perpetuated in Chapter Four. Our current horrible competitive position is a direct result of following these hurtful practices for the last 45 years. They are so firmly entrenched that, even when executives agree that such practices should be stopped, they can't be changed; the inertia (the tendency to keep moving in the same direction) is just too strong to overcome.

AMERICAN SAMURAI INSIGHT

The myth of America the winner and the tradition of America the business expert blind us. Most people don't question America the winner because they've never known anything else.

As Marshall McLuhan has observed, "I don't know who discovered water, but it wasn't a fish." To most people, it seems as if the term "American business" is synonymous with being number one; it's hard for them to conceive of anything different. Television shows, newspaper and magazine articles, movies, and political campaigns have all trumpeted and reinforced everyone's perception of American business as number one.

Just think of the icons of modern America: technology, space travel, medicine, media stars, movies, shopping malls, suburbia, the two-car family. Everything that defines modern life in the "have it" nations came from the United States. Where else would it come from, you might ask. After all, we are where it's at. Right? How could a land full of Gary Coopers, John Waynes, and Rocky Balboas not be a winner? To even begin to admit that America is not number one would be contrary to almost every perception, belief, habit, and value that has been brainwashed into the American psyche. Nobody questions our management practices because everyone has been programmed to believe that our way is the only way. How could it be wrong? American Samurai, you shall be counting the ways.

THE PSYCHOLOGICAL BASIS FOR
RESISTANCE TO CHANGE

The psychological basis for this resistance to change is fairly straightforward. People fall back on the familiar and look for comforting patterns when disturbing events occur. They do this in order to find order and structure. When conflicts in our perceptions occur, we seek to reconcile the conflicts. We resolve the conflict in one of two ways: (1) we reject the new information and remain true to our old beliefs, or (2) we incorporate the new information into our existing thinking and thus change our basic view of the situation, arriving at a position that reconciles our old beliefs and the new information.

If the threat is great and personal security is at stake, people often do exactly the opposite of what logic demands. Instead of changing their perceptions and taking action to deal with the threat, they often become resistant to new ideas and refuse to modify their tactics. In effect, their refusal to change their thinking is an attempt to deny the threat. The greater the threat, the greater the tendency for denial.

Actually, this mechanism isn't totally useless. After all, a great deal of what happens in any one day is much the same as in the day before. We usually drive to work the same way, get our clothes from the same drawers, keep our toiletries in the same spot, and so on. It's easier to deal with the chaos of everyday events if we possess a world view that puts everything in perspective and allows us to quickly assess and react to key events without having to constantly monitor every detail. Much of what happens is simply processed without thought.

That's why, for example, you might find yourself driving through a new stop sign on the way to work every morning for 3 or 4 days before you "notice" it. You long ago had your trip programmed and weren't paying attention to details in the same way that you would if you were driving a rental car in a strange city.

The same mechanism works in the business world, both for small daily routines and for our larger cognitive maps of how the world operates. The largest part of what we do or experience is piled into the category of "already known and experienced." As a result, we don't actively attend to many situations. Just look at routine meetings. Most people sit there and doodle, catch up on mail, or do other work. They don't pay attention until they're "on" or until a topic that interests them comes up. They ignore what they see as same old material because it holds no interest for them. This is a great mechanism for saving energy if the topics in question are low priority, don't require team input, and will be handled by others.

A REALISTIC APPRAISAL OF THE FUTURE

Let's take a quick look at what a realistic appraisal of the future looks like in terms of U.S. business and the quality of home/work life. First of all, consider the international marketplace and the simple laws of supply and demand. As we've already seen, after World War II there was essentially only one industrial power, to pump out commercial goods for the world: the United States. There are now many. The absolute size of markets for almost all products has grown, of course, but not as fast as the number of key players who want to cash in on them.

The United States used to provide a large part of the world's industrial know-how, a majority of the tooling, and the biggest portion of the end products themselves. Now many countries (at least twenty) can afford to participate to some extent, and many can buy whatever technology they need. These countries have become not only consumers but also basic industrial producers and competitors.

AMERICAN SAMURAI INSIGHT

The preeminent position enjoyed by the United States throughout the 1960s is gone forever and will never, ever return.

This is a hard fact for many American "supremists" to handle. America is going to be a less moneyed, a less powerful, and a much less influential force in the world. In fact, our favored position started to erode as soon as Japan, the Far East, and Europe started to rebuild after World War II. We didn't notice that we were taking the hits for over 20 years because we were so far ahead.

Now, instead of being the only game in town, we have many capable and hungry competitors, each primed and ready to fight for more of the existing market. Many head-in-the-sanders and armchair academics (those people who haven't been out in the real world, seeing Americans lose their jobs and homes) contend that the spread of modern "civilization" and materialism to all corners of the world will provide the continual growth in demand that will keep all industrial economies booming. This is new and improved, all purpose, super concentrated bull.

It's true that, barring a total collapse of the world economy, there will be growth in demand for all products. It's too much to hope that rampant consumerism will be reined in before we fatally poison the planet (if we can't control the rape of the environment through the unbridled production of material goods here in the United States, with all the resources and disposable income we've been privileged to enjoy, how can we expect a starving third-world country or an up-and-coming second-world country to make more of a sacrifice?).

AMERICAN SAMURAI INSIGHT

The "continual growth" theory neglects the fact that every single country that raises its standard of living above the starvation line jumps into the manufacturing and technology game with all its hopes and resources.

As soon as a developing country gets a taste of the "good life" (which increasingly seems to include crime, drugs, landfills, pollution, high taxes, huge government bureaucracies, etc.—we sure have it great, eh?), they want to be able to afford more of the same, which means factories to generate goods to pay for more stuff.

As a result of this natural longing for a piece of the action, the list of established industrial competitors continues to grow. Korea, Singapore, and Taiwan are coming on strong. A host of other players are cinching up their gun belts for the fight. The European Economic Community will become a reality in 1992. Mexico, Brazil, India, and a number of other countries are showing signs of moving into the world market in significant, if not overwhelming, style. They're all going to get a piece of the action.

As if this wasn't bad enough regarding the prospect of increasing our own market share, the U.S.S.R. and Eastern Europe, for so long out in the cold as major players in the world markets, will be jumping into the fight now that they appear to be moving toward more open economies. Initially they'll be consumers of goods produced by other countries (insofar as they can afford it, which won't be much at first). However, they'll eventually establish enough industrial capacity to generate a surplus. Then they'll begin selling to everyone else in order to make foreign exchange. Every little bit will reduce the potential market share available to the other players.

The democratization of Eastern Europe and the progress being made by formerly impoverished nations is great in a "love of man," philosophical sense. But it's terrible news for any country such as the United States that has been enjoying an unnatural advantage and doesn't know how to compete. Every time another country fires up a new factory and puts in a long-distance line to take orders, we will lose more. If we're smart and make the changes that must be made, we'll limit our losses. If we're not smart, meaning that we continue to manage as we always have, we will lose more business, more exports, more jobs, and much more of our quality of life (as measured by materialist standards; those Americans who are into hair shirts and unheated homes will enjoy the new America that inaction will bring).

Of course, it's not only the United States that stands to lose. Every country that has enjoyed a large share of the market because of little or no competition will lose. Even Japan, doing many of the right things, has seen its share of the world steel market eroded by Korea. And that's only the beginning. The Korean and Yugoslavian forays into the automotive industry have so far been almost laughable. But they did get a few sales (showing that even a bad product from the competition hurts a little). The next time, they'll be a little better and hurt us a little more.

This type of challenge to the dominant shareholders in every industry is a natural artifact of a competitive market. You not only cannot relax when you're on top, but you have to work twice as hard to stay there. Once you prove there's a market, everybody else jumps in with lower investment and research costs and tries to take away some of what you started. We were on top, we didn't work hard at all, and now we're not on top in many fields. Can we work twice as hard to get back on top? Many say we can't.

OUR TECHNOLOGY EDGE IS ERODING

For a long time, our primary advantages were being way ahead on the power curve of manufacturing capacity and having an overwhelming lead in technology that was financed by our industry. Our manufacturing edge has already been lost, and we're in the process of losing our lead in frontier technologies.

AMERICAN SAMURAI INSIGHT

Over 80% of graduate science and engineering students in our major universities are foreign nationals who will be taking their knowledge home with them.

Entrepreneurs, trendy restaurants, pizza and chicken places, flashy suspenders, and TV shows are not going to save us. Our entire emphasis as a culture is not oriented toward business and technology. Japan produces dozens of engineers for every lawyer. In the United States, it's exactly the opposite. Don't get me wrong, I like smug, arrogant, condescending professionals as well as the next guy. It's just that lawyers and other nonvalued added workers don't build any capital; they don't make anything. All they do is drain off the existing productivity and hurt the system. We have a culture that encourages that type of damaging activity rather than fostering innovation, manufacturing technology, and industrial competitiveness.

OUR EDUCATIONAL SYSTEMS ARE A FAILURE

Unless this pattern changes, we're going to fall further and further behind in the race that we're already losing. Another nail in our coffin is our educational system. At the same time that technology is becoming more important, our educational system if falling apart. Not only can't our high school and college students read very well, do higher order math, or write a letter, many of them are just plain ignorant about the world itself. Every year, at least two or three surveys show that a frightening proportion (30% to 50%) of high school seniors can't even name the states bordering their own.

As you'll see later in this book, the number one resource that will determine the ultimate status of our nation as an economic power will be our people. The management challenge of the next 20 years lies in harnessing our people resources. Yet, this is the resource that receives the least attention from society from childhood to retirement. The educational system is simply one very important part of the problem.

PEOPLE ARE NOT INHERENTLY VALUED

The way in which day care is viewed, both by the nation and by businesses, is symptomatic of the lack of value that we place on workers and on people in general. Most mothers are working. They get by as best they can. Most often, the situation is not doing the kids any good. Our children need the best day-to-day love and attention they can get. Otherwise, they're not going to be able to realize their potential as workers or as citizens. But do we do anything about this obvious need? Of course not. We've got parents coming apart at the seams, running themselves ragged between baby sitters, missing work when the sitter or the children get sick, all because of no day care. Businesses don't provide day care because, quite frankly, they don't give a damn about their employees.

They say they do, but talk is cheap. They don't really believe that helping employees means helping themselves. They do what they must to meet the minimum requirements of local laws (a few communities require day-care centers for new, large office complexes) and the competitive market for attracting employees, but that's it. If businesses believed in people as their number one resource, they would provide day care regardless of the cost because they would know that it would pay for itself in future cost savings and productivity gains. And if it netted out as a loss, well, they'd do it anyway and figure out how to pay for it. But they don't even consider day care because people are just cannon fodder to most businesses; you don't invest in cannon fodder, you just use it up.

THROWAWAY WORKERS

Day care isn't the only gross display of evidence that employers consider employees to be little more than meat-based office equipment. ("Jenkins, tell personnel to hire another five pieces of meat equipment this week.") The increasing use of temporary workers is further proof that American business has developed a short sighted, throw away view of people. Rather than carefully planning their work so that the permanent work force can handle bulges in demand, many industries are increasingly turning to "temporary" employees. These temps, as they're called, are part-time workers provided by third-party businesses.

The majority of temporary workers used to consist of two types. The first were day laborers hired to do menial labor, such as unloading trucks or digging ditches. They were needed by small employers with an occasional, extraordinary requirement for additional personnel. The second type was secretarial help, most often used to fill in for vacationing, permanent workers or during special events such as inventory.

But no more. Now, even Fortune 500 corporations routinely use temps as a planned, ongoing portion of their work force. Why? Because they're cheaper and they can be gotten rid of easier. It's just another form of the two-tiered approach to compensation in which newer workers earn lower pay and benefits than workers with more tenure for the same jobs.

Most temps don't get paid very much (there are a very few highly paid, professional and technical temps who earn large salaries, but they are the exception) and have only the benefits that the temporary agency provides. This means no retirement, poor medical coverage, if any, and few other benefits such as educational assistance. The temporary agencies argue that these benefits are available, but it's a lie. In order to quality for decent benefits, a temp would have to work almost full-time for years, something that almost never happens, given fluctuations in demand and the agencies' deliberate manipulation of assignments so that temps won't attain the necessary seniority and thus drive costs up.

The companies using temps argue that they need the flexibility. Sure, why not? It's only at the expense of a human being, and it's easier than planning. Temporary employees have no job security, no chance at a better life, and almost no opportunity to move up the career ladder (everybody has a story about hiring a great temp who eventually became a permanent employee and worked his or her way up to president of the company, but these are folk tales). We are creating a vast underclass of people who are deliberately denied entrance to the mainstream of life.

Worst of all, companies really don't benefit from temps, but they're too stupid to see it. Temps have no real loyalty to the company and aren't usually on board long enough to learn the system and be a part of long-term improvements. They have an understandably short-term, "Where will I be working tomorrow?" outlook that can't do anything but hurt their effectiveness. But the company doesn't miss this contribution because it never considers that a piece of meat can make a contribution—just another example of throwaway workers.

COLLAPSING INFRASTRUCTURE

Another looming problem that requires vast resources that must come from somewhere is the infrastructure of this country: the roads, bridges, sewers, waterlines, power lines, buildings, and so on. The bulk of these assets were constructed during the boom years of 1945 to 1979. In a sense, modern America was built upon the battered economies of post–World War II. The money poured in, and we built suburbia. Now, the money is going out faster than it's coming in. We not only can't continue to increase our standard of living and quality of life, we can't afford to maintain what we've got. As a result, we're going to see an accelerating erosion of our cities, highways, airports, ports, educational systems, water treatment and sewage systems, and so on, unless something changes. This will require more money that we don't, and won't, have unless we can strengthen our industrial base.

AMERICAN SAMURAI INSIGHT

The only change that will save us will be a change that will provide the resources to improve the situation over the long haul.

INDUSTRIAL REBIRTH IS THE ONLY ANSWER

Increased taxes alone aren't the answer. Neither is simply "fixing" the school systems (whatever that means—many more fixes put in place by our educational professionals and government overseers and we'll be totally ruined). We must rebuild our ability to compete so that we can maintain our standard of living. That can come from only one place: increased sales of goods and services to the rest of the world. Unless we can sell more than we buy, we are going to see a continual erosion of everything we have.

A NATION OF "HAVES" AND "HAVE-NOTS"

We are rapidly becoming a nation split down the middle into haves and have-nots. The have-nots can't afford decent housing, education, and medical services. Millions of children are growing up in homes without adequate love, food, and prospects for the future. All of the entrepreneurs and home computers won't mean anything if this problem is allowed to continue. One way or another, we're going to have to pay to deal with the rapidly growing millions of have-nots. We can either pay now to educate and develop them (and benefit from their best efforts) or we can pay much, much more in 20 years to keep them under control and/or in jail.

Even for the middle class, the situation is deteriorating. Each year, fewer young people can afford to buy a house. There go their hopes and dreams. We can't build a world-class industrial society if our employees are listless and uneducated and have no hope for the future. But that's what we're allowing to happen.

THE FOLLY OF THE "WORK AT HOME WITH A COMPUTER" FUTURE

These problems are growing rapidly, but the futurists would have you believe that the problem will be solved by people staying at home to work on personal computers rather than driving to work. Most "futures" ignore basic realities of business and life in general. The image that the "home computerists" are selling is that great hordes of workers will stay home and do their work on computers. This is supposed to allow us to flourish as a country because everybody can work on computers in the comfort of their homes while the kids quietly play nearby. No more dirty factories or crowded freeways. Give me a break. What are all these people going to be working on?

The object of work is to make a product or service that can be sold. If everybody is home working on computers, what's the product? I mean, just how many insurance and credit card bills need to be typed? The problem with doing service typing at home is that volume work of this type is already being sent out of the United States, where it can be done at slave wages. In places such as Puerto Rico, there are already dozens of outfits where hundreds of poorly educated employees (mostly women—with no day care, of course) sit at lines of computer stations and crank out invoices by the thousands under close control and rigid production standards. That's the "future" world of computers if we don't change our view of work and workers; mindlessly inputting data as every keystroke is counted and supervisors continually prod for more volume.

Even if it could be done at home, how many Americans today are willing to sit at home and type out credit card bills for $4.00 an hour? Not many. And when we get to the point where Americans are willing to work for $4.00 an hour, we will have already gone into the toilet as an industrial power.

Sure, all sorts of other people could stay home and work right now if their current jobs consist mainly of typing, word processing, writing software, or typing mailing labels. We'll assume, for the moment, that these "homers" need little face to face contact with other personnel, require little direction and supervision, need very little skill development, and are self-motivated. Then there's the problem of buying all the equipment they'll need to maintain separate work places, the phone or hardwiring costs to connect them, supplies, liability insurance, tax laws concerning working at home, getting the work to them in the first place (bulk computer input in most companies is generated by someone reading printed material received in the mail and then typing it into a computer), etc. But I'll give them these points. The issue comes down to products and the type of jobs required to produce them.

Most computer-input jobs are either direct-service functions (preparing bills) or service elements of existing companies. Without basic industry to spin off these jobs, most of them wouldn't exist. For example, the accounts payable people at a car plant could probably get something done at home with the right setup. But they won't be working at all, anywhere, if nobody is building cars back at the factory. Basic, make-a-product industries generate the bulk of all other jobs, including typing and computer service jobs.

But that's not the half of it. You can't operate a hamburger franchise, a shopping mall, a car dealership, a gas station, a video store, a drugstore, a hospital, and so on, with employees who work at home. After all, how can you run a fast food business with a lot of home workers? I can see it now: "Thank you for your order, sir. You can pick up your fries at 19 Oak Street, your filet at 2010 Forsythia Drive, and your double thick shake at 34433 Main Street. Extra napkins and the straws are at 14 Shannon Drive. Thanks for dining at Journey Burger."

So forget the "home computer" future. For everybody but a handful of people, working at home will be a fantasy for the foreseeable future. The hope for a better future lies in revitalizing the basic business and industrial base of the United States so that it can compete at an advantage in the international market. That's the only way we can avoid a precipitous slide in our standard of living.

IT'S A FUNDAMENTAL PROBLEM THAT ONLY THE BASICS WILL FIX

The only way to do this is to change the foundations upon which our modern system of management is built. We must change the way in which we run our businesses. We must all become American Samurai, working a new way to restore American competitiveness and maintain our way of life. It's not going to be easy. But then, the way of the warrior is never easy. And it doesn't matter how tough it will be, whether or not you like it, or whether or not you feel up to it. You have no choice. The alternative to taking action is a whole lot worse. It's up to you, my fellow American Samurai.

4

The Management Theory and Practice That's Destroying American Business

American business is being eaten alive from within. A malignant cancer is steadily draining the energy and competitiveness from all areas of American enterprise. This cancer is the outdated theory of management and people that's been used by Western businesss since the Industrial Revolution. But this theory won't be found written down in places in which most American managers would find it. In fact, it's not written down in applied terms anywhere; all that's out there are academic derivations that don't look anything like the real world. In fact, most people, including business executives, don't even know that existing management practices are based on a theory at all. But the theory is out there, and it's being used every day.

AMERICAN SAMURAI INSIGHT

American management generally assumes that business practices and traditions are the way they are simply because that's the way it was meant to be; as if the current system is somehow mandated or preordained by the fundamental order of the universe. Nothing could be further from the truth.

Business operates the way it does because the people who set up policies and practices believe that they have a clear understanding of how things work. They establish conditions to take advantage of the cause and effect relationships they "see." This type of "understanding" is a theory. For example, almost every company with more than 20 people has a formal performance appraisal system. These systems are used because executives and personnel types believe that grading and ranking people fosters better performance and protects them from legal problems. Even if they don't consciously think about this logic, they usually install an appraisal system because everybody else has one.

As will be discussed in Chapter Nineteen, this particular belief is totally and completely false. The types of performance appraisal systems used in most businesses are damaging and harmful beyond belief. These hurtful systems continue to be used because everyone either believes or assumes that they work and therefore has never tried anything else. They don't even see the problems these systems create because the difficulties (if perceived) are accepted as part of the background noise and costs of doing business.

This situation exists across the entire panorama of American business: policies and systems practiced for so long that they've become calcified, locked in for all time without discussion and/or objective assessment of their effectiveness. After a while, nobody questions why; everyone just accepts them because "it's always been that way."

AMERICAN SAMURAI INSIGHT

Most practices of traditional American business are perpetuated much like the practice of wearing neckties; on any objective basis, it makes no sense, but it's been part of the business world for so long that it's expected without question.

Naysayers are forced to go along or else. If you doubt it, try showing up at your office job without a tie and arguing the issue; you'll find out that they'll allow all sorts of incompetents and troublemakers to stay on the job for decades but that they'll fire you in about a month or so for not wearing a tie. They'll simply say, "That's just the way it is, don't you understand?"

The basic assumptions about work (that is, the theory) that generate most accepted management practices are not as visible as necktie practices. And since the mere concept of any theory for business behavior seems irrelevant and academic to many executives, few people will even bring up the subject, much less question the theoretical basis for a particular business practice. The result is that business executives continue to practice, support, and defend existing theories of business behavior even though they may never think about what they're doing or even be aware that what they do is driven by a theory. The result it that things simply continue on as they have always been, squeezing the creativity and productivity out of everyone in the system.

If we're going to change things for the better in American business, this old theory must go. The first step is to take a look at it and examine the system of belief that's been generating the life style, rules, and regulations of American business for over 50 years. Let's lift the lid from this garbage pail and see what's been making noise down in the dark for all these years. Hold your nose.

I'll present the theory in two parts. The first section presents the Values upon which the entire theory is based. The second section details the Guiding

Principles (GPs) of the theory. These GPs are the operational practices (rules of behavior) that translate the Values into day-to-day behaviors.

UNDERLYING (BUT UNSPOKEN) VALUES OF THE TRADITIONAL BUSINESS THEORY

Value Number 1: React Quickly to Every Situation

We don't waste a lot of time standing around. Action is what we want. When things happen, we move fast, doing things, and making decisions. Tough guys don't sit around and agonize about every little decision. We take fast action when problems come up, and we react quickly to moves made by the competition.

It's part of the American psyche to take action. The problem is that the actions are almost always taken before we fully understand what's going on. Dr. Deming, about whom we'll talk later, calls this "tampering." Sort of like adding salt to a recipe before tasting it. Figure 4.1 presents one consequence of taking action too quickly. The chart shows engineering design changes for both a typical American company using the old theory of management and a company using a more intelligent management approach. Engineering design changes are made when a problem is discovered. As you can see, everyone makes a lot of mistakes up front as design ideas are translated into products. That's to be expected and even encouraged; lots of mistakes (changes in decisions) up front result in bold, new designs.

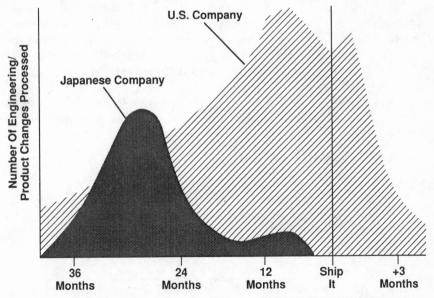

Figure 4-1. Engineering changes for Japanese and American manufacturers.

The problem is that American companies make increasingly numerous design changes as their designs get into the prototype phase and move closer to production. These late changes are expensive and time-consuming. They are caused not by poor engineering skills but by a management theory that does not allow the right people to work together early in the design stage. American companies that are changing their management theory, such as Xerox and Motorola, have changed their profiles to more closely match those of the Japanese companies. They do this by employing a set of practices known as *concurrent engineering* (see Chapter Twenty-two).

The Japanese call this drive for fast action, "Fast Gun, Slow Bullet." They say that Americans love to draw fast (make decisions quickly) but that the bullet (the results) takes a long time to get the job done because the gun was poorly aimed. We move fast and then must take lots of time to fix problems that were generated by hasty decisions. As we'll see later, if we take a little more time up front to work out future problems, the total time from start to finish is dramatically reduced. That's a "Slightly Less Fast Gun, Very Fast Bullet."

Value Number 2: Everybody Loves a Winner

Good results are all that count. Don't tell me what you did, just get it done. Our heroes are those who tackle the tough problems and get the job done, no matter what it takes. We reward our heroes by giving them larger portions of the organization to manage in the same way.

We have a fascination with results in this country that borders on the in-sane. Until you have read later chapters in this book, you will probably think that results *are* all that count. Wrong. American management reacts to problems in a fire-fighting mode. The biggest crises get the most attention first, as well as emergency "fix it" resources ripped from other functions or areas that don't appear to have any problems. The difficulty is that all of the little crises that will sooner or later become big crises never get any attention until they also become disasters. Pretty soon, there are too many disasters to handle.

Value Number 3: Go for the Fast Payoffs

If you're smart, you can keep the goods rolling out and the profits rolling in. Success is determined by sales and production volume and quarterly (or better yet, monthly) profits or ROI (return on investment). Keep your eye on the bottom line at all times and make it look good no matter what it takes or what trade offs you have to make.

This is American business at its most typical: keep the money pouring in for the brass and the stockholders. Sounds great, but it's all wrong. The problem is that this short-term mentality fuels all sorts of harmful practices that work against long–term business health. For example, it's easy to save money on training costs by simply not training employees. All sorts of businesses actually take people off the street and place them in semi-skilled jobs without any training. The workers are supposed to learn OJT (on-the-job). Worker training worker: one of the fastest ways ever devised to go out of business.

When I tell these so-called profit-oriented managers that they should train their workers first, they say that they can't afford it and that it would hurt their costs. Yet, the mistakes and rework (not to mention production delays and customer problems when the defects get out the door) cost a thousand times more per year per employee than the up-front training would cost. The problem with selling this supremely logical and profit-focused strategy to the typical American manager is that the costs of the mistakes and poor quality are already buried in the system. Everyone assumes that the problems are "just the way it is" and will always be there. Because the up-front training is seen as a new cost, it is rejected because it will hurt profits, wrong it would help long-term profits.

Value Number 4: Individual Achievement is How We Do Things

Advancements in business, as in every other field of endeavor, depend upon exceptional individuals who get the job done. The ones who get results are those who are tough or smart or tenacious enough to make things work in spite of organizational inefficiency and bureaucracy. Anybody can make it if they want it bad enough; most people just don't want it bad enough.

We talk a lot about teamwork in this country, but we don't really use it. Sure, we see a lot of it on sports teams, but they are an anomaly. We run our businesses as cutthroat, survival of the fittest contests in which the survivors are the ones who are tough enough to overcome their colleagues, other departments, and the huge, crushing inertia of the bureaucracy. We force our employees to kill themselves fighting against insurmountable odds in order to do great work.

Most people, who are not driven by raging internal fires, won't keep slugging it out after they've been slammed back a few times. They simply give up the fight and get by as best they can, accepting the loss of effectiveness and humiliation. The result is that the majority of people are being forced by the system to give only a portion of what they could give, and what they want to give.

If everyone was genetically altered to want to fight the system forever, we'd be in even worse shape. There simply aren't enough rewards in any organization to allow everyone to succeed in the prototypical get rich, make tons of money, have a corner office way. If everyone really fought as hard as possible to get on top all the time, no company would ever get a product out the door. Everyone would be doing whatever would get them the most, instead of focusing on what would best serve the long-term success of the business. The company would be torn apart.

Value Number 5: Employees Are a Pain in the Ass

People are nice in general, but it's different at work. Employees in general, especially those at lower organizational levels than yours (except for the people you like) are basically lazy, don't like to work, and don't take pride in what they do. Therefore, they must be continually watched and closely supervised. Until they are all replaced with machines, we'll have to use them, but we don't want to invest too heavily in "extras" for them because they'll only turn on us.

Many executives get upset when I contend that they run their organizations according to this Value. Their ignorance of what's really going on is understandable; they should talk to a few of their lower-level employees once in a while. Most of them have been spouting annual report and charity drive verbiage about "valuable employees" and "the dignity of man" for so long that they automatically assume that their businesses are run in that mode. Those of us who have worked in the ranks know that the "valuable employee" spiel is bull, plain and simple.

Why does the typical American company lay off workers as the first step when business downturns rather than cutting executive bonuses or across-the-board pay for all employees? Simple, because employees are a pain and it's better to simply get rid of them.

Value Number 6: Customers Are a Pain in the Ass

It's enough to make you sick—all this whining about customers and customer satisfaction. Customers don't know anything about how the business operates; if they did, they'd be happy with what they get. The best way to deal with customers is to tell them what they want to hear and then give them what you already know they want. Customer service is the lowest job in the company, for good reason.

Just look at what happens when somebody says, "There's a customer on the phone/out front." The customer might be another employee who needs something from your area, or it might be the person who buys your stuff. Everybody rolls their eyes and assumes that it's "problem time"; another whiner. Of course, it usually is "problem time" because the customer is most likely angry or upset at not getting what he or she needs. And since there's no mechanism set up in most businesses to make any fundamental changes in the systems that are upsetting the customers in the first place, there's no point in even going through the motions of listening. American business executives don't believe that they can learn anything from customers. As a result, employees considered by the organization to be losers or expendables are usually placed in customer-interface positions. Who else would tolerate the abuse?

Did you ever go into a department store and run into the store manager at the return desk? Of course not. Did you ever run into the owner of an automotive dealership at the service desk? Of course not, he's got an office near the sales floor. Work in the servive area would be unpleasant to an owner because of all the complaints. And besides, everybody "knows" that there will always be difficulties. Management has more important things to do than listen to a bunch of crybaby customers.

THE GUIDING PRINCIPLES OF THE TRADITIONAL BUSINESS THEORY

The following Guiding Principles (GPs) are the rules of behavior and operational policies that put the preceding Values into action in the typical company.

GP 1: Set Objectives and Manage to Them

The main problem with most managers and businesses is a lack of clearly defined objectives. The key point is to specify exactly what you want done so that even the most stupid, lazy employee will know precisely what to do without having to think about it. Then, manage to these objectives by insisting on frequent, detailed reports from everyone so that you'll know exactly what's going on.

Just clearly define what employees must do (they can't think for themselves, we all know it) and then make sure they do it, that's the way to manage. This approach is generally known as MBO (management by objectives). To an American Samurai, MBO is a killer toxin. The rationale is that by setting narrow goals, it is easy for a manager to determine if the work is getting done simply by cracking the whip and insisting on frequent reports. Just set the goals and watch the reports. Wrong—dead wrong.

An objective is meaningless by itself. Just think about it for a moment; what does setting an objective do? Consider the typical company that sets an objective of 10% improvement in profits for the next year. If you ask the managers how they plan to get that extra 10%, the answer usually boils down to something along the lines of "work harder." Sure, there are always a few briefings and sometimes even a so-called plan, but there's almost never a detailed set of step-by-step actions whose completion will attain the objective. If you ask lower-level workers, they usually know nothing about the objective or the plan other than a few rah-rah words they've heard in a speech or seen on a poster. So, on a day-to-day basis, they continue to work just as they always have, doing their best as they know it. That's what 99.9% of workers in all organizations do—just what they did yesterday, which is what they think will keep them out of trouble with their bosses. In short, there is no plan, only a little-known objective that will be attained only by chance. When it doesn't work out, it's the employees' fault—the blame is shifted elsewhere. When it works, the executives take the credit for putting together a great plan.

GP 2: Manage by Fear

The only thing that most employees respect is fear. If they're worried about what will happen to them, they'll do good work. Be tough and let them know who is in charge.

This is the prototypical carrot and stick approach to motivation, with the most valued carrot being stick avoidance. The emphasis on supervision in most companies is on ensuring compliance to authority and procedures—making sure that everybody does what they're told and that no rules are broken. The way this is done is through fear. Just look at the typical reaction of an employee to a visit by a manager or executive to his or her work area: fear—what have I done, what will happen to me now?

Fear runs rampant in every organization. If you don't believe it, you're one of the people generating it. The following are just a few of the fears that are tearing away at the self-esteem, confidence, commitment, and enthusiasm of employees in all companies:

Fear of being fired.
Fear of being laid off.
Fear of making a mistake.
Fear of not producing enough to stay out of trouble.
Fear of not getting a good performance review.
Fear of not getting a merit increase.
Fear of making an improvement suggestion because it will be viewed as a criticism of the old way.
Fear of getting in trouble for pointing out a mistake.
Fear of getting in trouble for admitting that you don't know something.
Fear of getting in trouble for working with another department or area.
Fear of not knowing how your job really works.
Fear of what will happen to your job and the company in the future.
Fear of looking bad by asking for help.
Fear of making a contribution to a team and having someone else get the recognition or reward.

Fear of not getting a promotion.

Fear of getting in trouble for asking questions about policies, procedures, and/or the work.

Fear of irritating the boss.

Fear of not improving your prospects for a better life.

Fear of customers buying another company's products or services.

Fear of getting in trouble if anyone finds out what's really going
on in your area and blames you.

You know that you experience many of these fears yourself on a daily
basis. These fears immobilize employees, leading them to take the lowest risk
posture if there's any risk at all (or causing them to freeze up with anxiety
and take no action when action is required). The result is that problems are
hidden, potential solutions are stillborn, and employees spend their time
managing fear, rather than managing their jobs.

Unless we change our way of doing business so that employees can direct
their efforts toward doing better work, rather than staying out of trouble,
we're dead. Fear doesn't work, never did, never will; it prevents work.

GP 3: Have an Answer to Every Question

The main function of managers is to stay up to date on exactly
what's happening on every item in every part of their organization. They must be able to instantly answer any questions from
above about what's going on down below. They must have an
answer ready for every question.

We've all been hit by this one—endless progress reports that eat up time
and effort and do absolutely nothing. A study conducted several years ago
at a major defense contractor found that of the 13 levels between the cold,
concrete, shop floor and the plush carpeting in the executive suite, six levels
did no value-added work; they only processed and massaged information
and passed it along. Think of the impact of all those extra people on costs
(and on effectiveness).

You can never know everything that's going on; no report can contain
enough information. You shouldn't even want to, because you've got other
things to worry about. The problem is that most bosses think that management's function is to "keep a finger on the pulse" of the business. Wrong.
Just measuring pulses is not meaningful. You have to be able to do something
when you get a bad pulse. The problem is that management doesn't know
enough about the activities that generate the pulses to do anything specifically
helpful. More often than not, management's input is misguided meddling.
And think about the fear—all sorts of problems that nobody dares to report
honestly. Even slightly negative news is "massaged" so that management
won't be angry.

Just look at what this approach has created. Endless meetings, briefings, burnt-out photocopying machines, and resultant retributions and busywork. And still the disasters keep happening—all the reporting hasn't helped and has actually made it worse.

GP 4: Don't Take Chances

Nobody likes a lot of mistakes. They make your boss, your area, and you, look like losers. The quickest way to make a lot of mistakes is to take a lot of chances by trying a lot of new things. Remember, results are all that count, and no trouble is the best result of all.

You already know that everybody is scared to death to make a mistake or look bad. You've felt it yourself. And we all know that the easiest way to make a mistake is to try something new. It's simple; if you want to avoid mistakes, don't try anything new. Nobody will get mad if you keep doing it the old way and it doesn't work out.

We don't succeed at anything by avoiding mistakes. We succeed by making mistakes and learning from them. Thomas Edison is reported to have attempted more than 2000 experiments before finding a light bulb filament that would work. Vulcanized rubber was discovered when someone at Firestone spilled rubber on a stove. 3M's Post-It Notes were developed as a result of a failed adhesive that wouldn't stick permanently. By making honest, tried-it-but-it-didn't-work mistakes a punishable offense, we absolutely assure that we'll never discover most of the better ways to do things, particularly in terms of input from lower-level employees.

GP 5: Volume Takes Care of Everything

Everybody knows that volume cures all ills. After all, it spreads your fixed costs over more items, making each less costly. So, no matter what you do, aim for selling and/or pumping out as many goods and services as possible.

"How do we do it? Volume!" is almost the anthem of American business. We talked about how the volume syndrome arose after World War II. Over the last 45 years, it's been burned into the American business mentality as a bedrock truth. We believe, as a nation, that volume means more of everything good, including profit. Bedrock wrong. Focusing on volume hides losses, much like an overweight person wearing baggy clothes. The fat's still there, but it isn't as readily visible, even as it is compromising our health and our ability to move fast.

Volume doesn't increase profitability, it hides costs. Sure, there's no doubt that it makes sense to build thousands of cars at a car plant instead of one, but that's not the issue. Most manufacturing facilities are already built and production rates are not directly driven by a need to pay off fixed costs in a short time frame. Volume breeds loose and sloppy management practices whose impacts are hidden. If you can't produce an acceptable per-piece profit on a low-volume run, you can't do it on a high-volume run.

GP 6: Do Not Deliver Bad News

Only crybabies run around pointing out problems. Instead of complaining and getting everybody upset, keep quiet and fix it on your own, like an adult. There's no need to let a lot of people know that you blew it or that you discovered that someone else in your area did (of course, this doesn't apply if another area makes a mistake; see GP 7). Besides, if you report bad news, you're implicitly criticizing the system and the people who manage it. You don't want to get them upset, right?

If you see a problem, ask yourself: is this the first time it's ever happened? If the answer is no (and for any problem in any industry, the answer is always no), don't go getting everybody upset by spreading the alarm. It only makes everyone look bad. And remember, managers only pay attention to things when there are problems. As long as a system is working OK, it gets little or no management attention. Paying attention is work for them and will mean work for you. If you report problems, you aren't fixing things, you're creating more work for people who already have a dozen *real* problems that are going to hell. And you caused more worry by reporting little problems? Ah, that's a nice career you used to have.

We've all seen this type of situation, and most of us have been forced to do it ourselves. And we wonder why the problems keep coming? There's no way they can stop.

GP 7: Mistakes by Others Are a Chance to Look Good

When another group or area makes a mistake, jump right on it and spread the gory details (exaggerated and amplified, of course) to all who will listen. If pursued successfully, this strategy will make even the worst mistakes in your area seem like wise decisions.

The principal focus of the traditional business approach is on mistakes. We don't do anything until there is a problem or disaster. Then, everybody is mobilized. This fascination with problems (after they happen) has created an environment in which management reacts to problems by doing the only thing that makes sense after you've allowed something to fall apart and you don't want to be blamed: you work to assign the blame to someone else— anyone else. We've all seen it.

There's a disaster, and everybody is pointing fingers instead of fixing the problem. And since nobody is working to prevent problems from happening (see GP 12), there are always a thousand problems. The trick to succeeding in American management is to make sure that the mistakes that happen in your own area of responsibility don't get the attention they deserve from vengeful executives. The best way to do that is to make sure that executives are too busy (and exhausted) from reacting to earlier mistakes made by other areas. Thus it's essential to make others' mistakes look as bad as possible.

GP 8: The Department or Work Area Comes First

The first loyalty of every employee is to be a team player in his or her department. Do not embarrass your area by discussing internal problems with personnel from other areas.

Loyalty to the work group is an entirely natural consequence of normal group dynamics. Humans have a natural propensity to feel more attracted to, and comfortable with, individuals with whom they have the most in common. One of the most important characteristics is physical proximity. It's largely for this reason that people support professional sports teams in their hometown, even if they've just recently moved there. Since people in a department usually work physically close to one another, they begin to identify more with their close associates than with other people in the company. Over time, the group's practices and policies, the behavior of the boss, (how he/she likes to be kissed up) and the social interaction customs of the group begin to differ from those of the organization as a whole. Pretty soon, it's "us" (a department or area) versus "them" (everybody else). This is why work groups will gleefully shaft each other even when the entire organization is hurt by the conflict.

Those who act in the best interests of the company as a whole put themselves at risk within their own work group. Everyone is taught that the cardinal sin is to make the boss or the area look bad. This mechanism creates suboptimization. *Suboptimization* is the phenomenon that occurs when each department or work area pursues unique sets of objectives that are in conflict with, or do not support, company-wide objectives. The result is that a great many areas and work groups look great although the overall organization may be dying. That's what happens when work groups begin to view themselves as "different" from the rest of the company.

Suboptimization has another, more subtle dimension. When groups begin to isolate themselves, all work activities quite naturally become allocated on a functional basis; finance works with forecasts and budgets, production builds things, engineering designs them, and so on. Each work group stakes out its territory and aggressively guards its turf. This functional view of work activities is damaging in and of itself, apart from the effects of suboptimization. Almost no work activities are the sole province of a single work group. Products engineered solely by engineers will have problems in manufacturing and sales. Finance reports generated without input from other departments are typically used little and understood less by other departments. Departmental divisions of activities simply compound the problems. Activities must be worked on by all of the people who are part of the process, not just the "owning" department (processes will be discussed in Chapter 23).

If companies wish to transform themselves, they must begin to take steps to combat these quite natural, but destructive, tendencies. This is part of the American Samurai challenge.

GP 9: Build Up a Network to Get Things Done

If you're going to be a winner, it is essential to set up an informal system of "connections" so that you can "end run" the system when you need something done fast.

We all know that when you send something through normal channels in most companies nothing much happens very quickly. Because businesses are organized to stop every possible mistake from occurring (which doesn't work, considering what happens in most companies everyday), every action must pass through a multitude of filters. This is compounded by the functional orientation, which adds work steps. If you want to get anything done in time to look good, it's essential to end run the system. This causes even more work for other persons, but that's their problem, right?

The key element in end running the system is to make all sorts of friends (acquaintances of convenience, actually) who will help you sleaze things through the system by bending the rules or pulling rank for you. That's why the company president can get his or her overheads done in 4 hours when it takes a regular employee 4 weeks. Why can't we have a system that works without the sleaze and the informal connections?

GP 10: Decisions Are Made at the Top

The role of management is to make decisions. Managers are the most knowledgeable and experienced people in the company and are most capable of making every decision they have time to review. Therefore, if there is any doubt, pass it upstairs for management analysis and review.

Then, if something happens, it's their fault. True, but management never takes the blame. Even if they screw it up, they'll blame the employees, the government, the Japanese, or the weather. Traditional managers see their job as one of making decisions. It doesn't matter what the decision is, they think it's their job to make it (they won't make it fast, or well, in many cases, but they want to be the ones to do it when they get around to it). As we'll see in Chapter 13. Part of management's roll actually is to make decisions—in some cases. Most of the time, however, management's role is to help others make the decisions. Since most managers don't know this, they jealously guard their prerogative to make any and all decisions that come up.

When they don't get a chance to make a decision, managers react as if someone has stolen their car—outraged and cheated. This belief system has created a situation in which management forces all information and decision making to the top. Employees who don't comply are dealt with severely.

GP 11: You Can't Change City Hall

Systems and procedures are there for a reason. They have been carefully developed and organized over many years, after long and careful analysis. Sometimes they may seem like a bother, but there is always going to be some sort of system and it can't make everyone happy all the time. That's just the way it is. Relax, it's that way for a reason.

Because our entire management system is unknowingly built upon these ingrained Values and GPs, there is little impetus, short of the threat of destruction, for change (and often, changes made in a disaster mode make the situation even worse). The problems we have, the defeats we suffer, the frustrations we endure, are viewed as natural artifacts of work itself. Very seldom are the underlying mechanisms even examined, much less questioned. The result is an American icon: an overweight, belly-over-the-belt older man, hitching up his pants and scowling, "Ah bin heah 20 !*#$$@! years and we always dun it this way. And now you want to change it. It won't work. If it was supposed to be different, it would be." I've seen it a hundred times. And it'll happen another 10,000 times a day until we begin to question the underlying mechanisms that drive our business decisions. We must constantly fight city hall for its own good.

GP 12: If It Ain't Broke, Don't Fix It

We have enough problems to work on everyday without worrying about minor adjustments in things that aren't causing any major trouble. Besides, why take a chance on changing something that's working good enough? Things are never going to work perfectly, anyway. Mature people learn to live with minor irritations.

We've all seen what happens when a minor improvement is suggested for something that hasn't totally fallen apart. The reply is invariably something along the lines of, "If it ain't broke, don't fix it" or its modern counterpart, "Why bother? Things aren't that bad." This sort of reply is caused by several mechanisms. The first is that many people understand, whether they consciously admit it or not, that management isn't really committed to fixing the underlying problems. They've seen all sorts of efforts come and go with no appreciable results. So they know that it's almost useless to try to campaign for significant improvements in anything that's not a disaster; fighting has too small a payback for the grief and abuse.

The second mechanism that perpetuates this Guiding Principle is related to management's fire-fighting syndrome. Since all decisions are made at the top, and management attends mainly to the usual plethora of emergencies and disasters, any suggestions for improvement are seen by management as suggesting that they do more work. Since they are already burdened with all sorts of large and small decisions and reams of reports to review, they feel stretched to the limit and don't want more. Therefore, nobody wants to hear about small problems; it's too much work, and, besides, who's got the time?

GP 13: Maintain the Caste System at All Times

We see the caste system in where people live, in what they drive, and in where they go to school. Some people just aren't as good as others, not as smart, not as intelligent, and not as worthy as others. Why should it be any different at work? It's not. There is a caste system and it must be maintained, or else management will lose its power and authority.

I call this the Egg Sucking Pig Canon of Business. American businesses generally operate under the assumption that there are various social castes, or categories of people, at work. You don't think so? If not, why are there different levels of benefits for hourly and salaried personnel? And various levels of goodies within salaried ranks, which get better as you go up the ladder? Why are there bells and whistles for hourly workers for breaks and lunch and none for salaried workers? Why is the emphasis in supervision at all levels on control, discipline, and enforcing procedures? Why do hourly employees often have time clocks when salaried people don't? Why are there different lunchrooms in many organizations for different levels of employees, with the better quality food (and usually lower prices) going to the higher-ups? Why are there different types of parking, with closer and more secure parking for higher-ups? Why are hourly employees penalized severely when they are occasionally late for work whereas salaried employees can usually come and go unsupervised?

In some companies, if hourly persons are late only 10 minutes, they get a "point." If they get 10 to 20 points in a year, they're terminated. If they call in because they're sick, they get a point. If their kid is sick and they have to stay home or come in late, they get a point. Why isn't it the same for salaried personnel and management? (It's interesting to note that this policy actually encourages absenteeism: If employees know that they will be late enough to get a point, they often simply take the whole morning or day off rather than coming in a little late.) Why, why, why?

The answer is simple: employees at lower levels are simply not "as good" or "as nice" or "as valuable." I'll always remember a visit to a Ford facility by then Ford Motor Company CEO Donald Peterson. The facility, a large assembly plant, had a full-time physician and two full-time nurses on duty every day. Yet, when Don was visiting, a special medical team was on stand-by with a helicopter outside the plant in case he or one of his entourage—

higher-level (more valuable) person—had a medical problem. Nobody even questions this sort of thing, but we can all see the cause: some employees are considered better than others.

Lower-level employees, as viewed by upper-level management, are considered necessary evils and are treated as such. Yet who builds your product or delivers your service? Not the folks in the offices, that's for sure. Let's look at the various levels of employees in the typical caste system and some of the key identifying characteristics. You'll recognize them in your organization.

Gods

These are the folks at the top of the heap. In most organizations, they are the corporate officers and the top operational person in an operating division or subsidiary. They are the people who come and go as they please, can start or stop programs at a whim, can hire anyone they want, can set up conferences at exotic places without anyone questioning the expense, and whose every whim (and perceived whim) is instantly attended by hordes of minions. The previously cited instance of Don Peterson and the special medical helicopter is one typical example. These are the folks who cause huge reports to be generated at a mere glance. I've seen entire programs canceled by a scared manager because he or she saw a slight grimace flash across a god's face when a program's name was mentioned. (Can you imagine how many good programs have been scuttled because of gas pains? Think of it, it's frightening.)

Gods are the people whose offices are larger and better decorated than the living rooms of most of the people who work for them. Ask yourself or anyone else why. The answer is always, "Because that's the way it is," or "They need it to work." Right. They get what they want, when they want it, and everybody works to assure that they are not bothered by a lot of irritations. Gods don't dial their own phones ("Mary, get Ed on the phone for me") and hardly ever write anything down—everything is taken in shorthand. Their privacy and accessibility is zealously guarded by the protectors of the inner sanctum; the Human Beings and Proto-Humans who serve them. The result, of course, is that the gods hardly ever hear anything that's not processed and homogenized to the point where it's innocuous and devoid of any real value or data. Gods are immune from almost all consequences, even if they run a company into bankruptcy.

Human Beings

This group is aptly named; they are treated at work like most people would like to be treated. The Human Beings are given pleasant, private, and comfortable offices and have plenty of support services. They do some real work but spend most of their time worrying about how to keep the gods from getting upset. In most companies, the Human Beings are the second-level executives, usually Vice-Presidents, of operating divisions and subsidiaries and senior staffers. They get a little supervision (they still have to go through the stupidity of the performance appraisal ritual, but they don't get any grief—they are assumed to have total skills). They can pretty much come and go as they please but they don't because they live in fear like everyone else (although their fears are of a less primal kind than those of lower-level employees).

Human Beings are the most static as a group; most of them have "topped out" career-wise and know they will not get to be gods. Thus, they can relax and enjoy their jobs. They spend most of their days in meetings with the Proto-Humans (see below) who serve them, figuring out how to avoid getting in trouble with the god they report to. A sure sign of whether or not an executive is a Human Being is if he or she gets invited either to meetings at corporate headquarters or to a god's home for a Christmas party or dinner.

Human Beings can hire and fire as they wish as long as they have planned ahead. Their god may insist on "checking out" the decision but will hardly ever overrule what the Human Being has decided to do. As long as they keep their god happy, they can do just about whatever they want. A Human Being has to screw up badly over a long period of time to get in trouble.

Proto-Humans (see also Pseudo-Proto-Human on p. 47)

Now we're getting to the folks who do some work. These are the upper-to mid-level managers and senior technician (engineers and the like) types. You can tell they do work because they get less support and facilities. This is the first caste whose members may occasionally be found in the "open office."

Proto-Humans aren't treated too badly because the gods and Human Beings realize that someday, somehow, a select few of the Proto-Humans will become Human Beings. Proto-Humans often get special parking and may even be allowed to eat in an executive dining room (unless the corporate office is in the same building, in which case only gods and Human Beings are allowed to use it; no level feels comfortable with levels more than one level lower). However, Proto-Humans are excluded from the really cushy perks provided to Human Beings and are subjected to micromanagement of their business decisions. Except on rare occasions, Proto-Humans aren't invited to corporate presentations and rarely get invited to "closed access" parties and social events.

Their travel requests are carefully scrutinized, they are constantly second-guessed by both the formal bureaucracy (personnel and the like) and their bosses, they may be spoken to if they come in a few minutes later, and they are continuously pumping out tons of busywork to assuage the appetites of the organization and their boss. If a Proto-Human's performance slips severely, most organizations will simply reassign him or her to a different area, hoping that the Proto-Human will get the message and quit (they never do).

Proto-Humans enjoy a natural protection provided by Human Beings, who are aware that today's Proto-Human could be tomorrow's colleague. Also, Human Beings like to fondly recollect their own Proto-Human days when they used to do real work; thus, it disturbs their peace of mind to do anything harsh to a Proto-Human.

Sub-Humans

Sub-Humans are the great mass of low middle to low-level managers, supervisors, secretaries, clerks, and technical/support types that crank out the sea of paper and products on which business floats.

These are the folks who do most of the office work, production management, and technical work. They are held to rigid performance expectations and are summarily dismissed if they don't perform (well, as summarily as any action is taken in American business, which is glacially slow). They must adhere carefully to all policies and procedures and must justify every action in advance. They are not allowed to make independent decisions. They are given few support resources. Their office environments can be recognized easily: file boxes stacked high; piles of paper; jammed in, close packed offices; and lots of noise. The furniture is usually old and battered and little cleaning is done.

There are three main types of Sub-Humans: Tiger-Sub-Humans, Slug-Sub-Humans, and See Through–Sub-Humans.

Tiger-Sub-Humans

These are young fire-eaters who think they are on the way up and will do almost anything to get there. It is their energy and boundless enthusiasm for the future that keeps most businesses going. They provide the fire from within that fuels the face the company presents. They make things happen, overcoming bureaucracy by brute force and effort. Without their efforts, many organizations would simply collapse inward under the oppressive weight of mismanagement by Gods, Human Beings, and Proto-Humans. The enthusiasm of Tiger-Sub-Humans is fondly observed by Proto-Humans and younger Human Beings because it reminds them of their own Tiger-Sub days. This breeds a certain amount of tolerance for the many inevitable minor Tiger-Sub violations of policy and procedure. Tiger-Sub-Humans comprise about 15% of all Sub-Humans in a lucky company.

Slug Sub-Humans

We've all seen them: the tired, burned-out hulks of what could have been productive workers (many were never productive, of course, having been brought into the organization brain dead, enthusiasm dead, or both). These are people who have given up trying to swim to the shore of Proto island (if they ever wanted to) and are merely treading water, trying to stay afloat, hoping they will be picked up by retirement before they go under. Slug-Sub-

Humans comprise at least 15% of most organization's Sub-Humans and may account for as many as 40% in poorly run organizations.

See Through–Sub-Humans

In any company these are the bulk of the Sub-Human work force. They do not have much potential to reach Proto-Human status and probably won't deteriorate into Slug-Sub-Humans (although some may). These are the people who show up and do the best they can, given the realities of the situation. With the right leadership, most could easily develop to the point where they would be able to do the job of any Proto-Human. However, they are not allowed to develop: They are simply left alone to do what they're told. They are "see through" Sub-Humans because management looks right through them most of the time, not even acknowledging their presence.

There is an additional category of Sub-Human: The Pseudo-Proto-Human. These are a very elite group of Sub-Humans who, by virtue of their close support role to either gods or Human Beings, are treated much like Proto-Humans. Far and way the most common variety of Pseudo-Proto-Human is a secretary to a god or Human Being. Pseudo-Proto-Humans always gets outstanding performance reviews, are invited to all the "brass only" parties and are permitted to bend the rules about attendance and the like. The secretaries of Proto-Humans are never, ever accorded the status of Pseudo-Proto-Humans.

Egg Sucking Pigs

Finally we get to the worker who is both the backbone and the majority of the American work force—the Egg Sucking Pig. Egg Sucking Pigs are, almost by definition, blue collar workers. Egg Sucking Pigs are known by numerous other names such as Production Pigs, Plant Pigs, Factory Pukes, Slugs, and so on. The caste is so clearly obvious that you'll often hear the managers of Egg Sucking Pigs proudly refer to themselves as Egg Sucking Pigs, as in "Well, what do you expect, we're only factory pukes," when another demeaning order comes down from on high (being Sub-Humans, the supervisors of Egg Sucking Pigs are not Egg Sucking Pigs, of course, but it's a touching gesture of solidarity).

In some industries such as insurance, the lowest level of office workers are actually Egg Sucking Pigs rather than Sub-Humans. Egg Sucking Pigs are rigidly managed and held accountable to the absolute letter of the organizational law. One false step and they're nailed. They almost always have time cards and time clocks, even when the rest of the organization doesn't, and they almost always have fewer and worse benefits. Their cafeterias are usually dirty, the food less appealing (and often more expensive than that provided in the executive dining room), their parking far away and poorly secured, and their work areas far less attractive and comfortable than those of the Sub-Humans.

Egg Sucking Pigs are viewed as less than nothing. At the first sign of a slip in business, they're laid off. Their jobs aren't even considered as being careers, so it's no sweat if they're out of work for 3 to 4 months per year. Nobody stops to think about how they're supposed to raise their families, buy homes, maintain their dignity, and so on. After all, they're only Egg Sucking Pigs, right?

Worms

Worms are even lower than Egg Sucking Pigs. Worms are stuck in the mud of business. They have no rights, no say, no involvement. Management treats them worse than used cat box liners; they aren't included in any communications, aren't put in employee development programs, and aren't permitted to participate in the educational and recreational programs of the organization to which they're assigned. However, they're expected to work just as hard as regular employees. Sure. These are generally temporary workers ("temps") who work for an outside employment service or are summer help.

SUMMARY

Now you see what we're up against. You've known it all along and you've probably recognized the symptoms of a dying, inefficient theory of business many times. Now, you know why—you see the failed theory behind it. The failed theory just outlined must be changed and it must be changed fast or we're all in much more trouble than we have now. The remainder of this book outlines a new approach, proven in numerous organizations, that will reverse the precipitous slide of American business. However, a new theory alone will not save us; it will take action by thousands of dedicated American Samurai, each doing his or her best to drive change into the calcified structure of modern American business.

5

The Code of the American Samurai

The Code of the American Samurai outlines the way in which business must be run if American industry is to once again achieve success. The Code of the American Samurai is comprised of twenty Coda. Each Coda states a specific belief or practice that is not negotiable: either you accept them all and practice them all without question (to the best of your ability; we'll discuss that in a moment) or you compromise your principles and practice an easier (and therefore ineffective) system of management.

If you're thinking that this sounds a lot like a religion, you're right. This is a religion—of business and, to a certain extent, of life. We are talking about something no less than a complete transformation of the basic principles of American business. The transformation will be a move from the typical values we discussed in Chapter Four to a more effective, more productive, and more personally rewarding system of beliefs. Insofar as such changes deal with the manner in which people are valued and treated, adoption of The Code would necessarily require changes in broader aspects of society such as education and medical care. After all, you can't profess, as does Coda 4, that: "Employees are every organization's most valuable resource; when they do not do a good job, it is almost always management's fault" and then limit the application of the belief to only work situations. For example, since it's management's fault if workers don't do a good job (as you'll see in Chapter Eight) then students, who have far less control over their situations than do managers and workers, can't be held responsible if they don't learn at school. Students don't run the schools, they just show up. As you'll come to see as we discuss each of the twenty Coda in Chapters Six through Twenty-five, The Code outlines an entirely new order of behavior, which applies to all aspects of life. This book is concerned principally with business applications, but it is my hope that adoption of The Code by businesses will eventually influence some degree of similar improvements in the broader scope of human affairs.

The energy to fight for such changes, both in business and in life as a whole, will require religious-like dedication and fervor from each American Samurai. It will take faith, hard work, and sacrifice to restore American competitiveness. Many will suffer. People will get fired for pushing too hard, many workers will lose their jobs due to productivity improvements, and all of those who attempt to live by and implement the Code of The American Samurai will experience frustration, rejection, and resentment as they deal with the dinosaurs of the old way.

The promulgation of The Code will also require another aspect of religious-like faith. American Samurai will have to fight for The Code in advance of absolute, unassailable proof that they are right. This is much like the situation in which religious missionaries find themselves. There are hundreds of millions of devote, faithful practitioners of myriad faiths throughout the world. Few, if any, have ever seen their god or have witnessed the after-life in which they believe. Yet, their faith is strong and countless missionaries aggressively proselytize among the "unbelievers" (anyone not of their faith).

The promotion of The Code will require a similar faith on the part of each and every American Samurai. Now, don't get me wrong; I'm not asking you to blindly accept The Code. There is proof that each of the twenty Coda works. I'll show it to you. In that respect, The Code is not similar to a religion: I deal in facts and logic, The Code is based on fact and logic, and I would expect you to demand no less.

The problem is that to the unbelievers, to the traditionally minded business people who comprise 99.9% of all management, any proof will be shrugged off. They have eyes but they cannot see. The scales will fall only when they are struck by a meaningful personal insight into the nature of work, motivation, and competitiveness. It is my hope that this book will provide the means for some small number of them to see the light. But many, even if they are privileged to observe in their organization overwhelming evidence that The Code works, will never achieve this insight, and there is nothing that can be done about this. Such is the nature of fear and resistance to change. If you and I can show a new way to a sufficient number of people, that may be enough to turn the tide of competitiveness back in our favor. If so, we will have served The Code well. That is all we, and our country, can ask of each other.

WHERE DID "THE CODE" COME FROM?

Every aspect of human life today is built upon the discoveries and work of countless people who came before us. The Code is no different. Elements of The Code can be found in many places over the last 60 years. Douglas McGregor's Theory X–Theory Y concepts correlate with many elements of the underlying philosophy behind much of The Code. The classic work of Coch and French at the Harwood Manufacturing Company in the late 1940s uncovered fundamental knowledge about productivity and quality that most companies are still not using and that is central to The Code.

Whereas these and many other contributions were important, no one has had more influence on The Code than Dr. W. Edwards Deming. Dr. Deming is the man who is most often associated with the transformation of Japanese industry from bombed-out wreckage to economic powerhouse. Born in 1900 (and still lecturing as of this writing), Dr. Deming received a Ph.D. in physics from Yale and went to work for the Department of Agriculture. He studied statistics with Walter Shewhart, the creator of statistical process control charts (we'll see how these operate when we discuss Coda 1 in Chapter Six) and eventually took a job working with the Census Bureau. During World War II, Dr. Deming spent a great deal of time teaching industries how to use statistical process control (SPC) techniques to improve quality and productivity.

After the war ended, there was little interest in either SPC or Dr. Deming's teachings. As we've seen in earlier chapters, American business attended only to volume, to meeting a huge, pent-up demand for consumer products. As Deming is quoted in Mary Walton's book, *The Deming Management Method*, in 1949, "there was nothing [left of SPC in American business], not even smoke. Meanwhile, Japan was down and out. Immediately after the war, the American plan was to keep the Japanese down, as punishment for their aggression (the real motivation was racist; we didn't try to starve out Germany, but, then again, they're European). When the cold war began to heat up, the United States realized that it would be wise to have a strong buffer country (if not an ally, at least cannon fodder) between the Soviets and our Pacific interests. A revitalized Japanese industry became a key strategic goal.

General Douglas MacArthur then began to bring in American industrial experts to help get Japan back on its economic feet. Deming was one of the first. In 1950 he began to give a series of lectures to Japanese management. He began speaking with middle management but quickly saw that only top management could effect industry-wide change. Within a year, he had spoken to thousands of Japan's industrial leaders. And they listened. They rebuilt their industries on the basis of Dr. Deming's teachings (and those of many others). The Japanese Union of Scientists and Engineers (J.U.S.E.) expressed their respect for Dr. Deming and their gratitude for his help by establishing the Deming Prize in 1951. This award is presented each year to companies and to individuals who best apply Dr. Deming's teachings.

THE JAPANESE INFLUENCE

The Japanese have not been content to simply apply the teachings of Dr. Deming and others. In the last 20 years, they have expanded and built upon the concepts they learned in the 1950s. As a result, they have developed a number of new management approaches to planning and operations such as Quality Function Deployment (QFD), Hoshin Kanri, Poka-yoke, and many others. Individuals such as Shigeo Shingo, the late Kaori Ishikawa, and Genichi Taguchi have, by developing these additional tools, created the framework for an entirely new, and more advanced, philosophy of management. The irony is that experts from the United States taught the Japanese how to focus on quality and now the Japanese not only practice it better than we do (much better), they have extended our teachings to an entirely new level, one that very few American companies practice.

The Code incorporates these new tools to the extent that they are practical to American business needs for the next 20 years. The Code does not present a complete, "ideal" outline for every aspect of business and management. American industry couldn't handle that much at this point. The problem is that the Japanese have been practicing the "fundamentals" since the 1950s. They have a solid foundation upon which to place their second-generation competitiveness tools. In this country, we have not even established a solid practice of the basics as a tradition.

Even if we had the desire, as a nation, to begin immediate, industry-wide implementation of something such as Hoshin Kanri, it would fail. Not having practiced the basics, we could not effectively implement the extremely detailed and exhaustive planning system that Hoshin Kanri (which means "gleaming metal" in Japanese) requires; it would collapse under the weight of our traditional values and guiding principles. For this reason, The Code does not stipulate the detailed practice of these advanced tools. The Code is a doctrine for our present time and situation. It will, and should, evolve as this situation improves.

THE CODE

The twenty Coda are at the same time independent and mutually supportive. They are independent in that each deals with a specific aspect of business life and practice. For example, Coda 14 states,

> **The traditional systems of job descriptions, performance appraisals, merit pay, and pay for performance are useless, damaging, and wasteful; they must be abandoned and replaced with a system that encourages and rewards teamwork and group effort.**

There are specific reasons why traditional performance appraisals are damaging to productivity and competitiveness. It is important to isolate these reasons, discuss them, and offer alternatives. Yet, this Coda does not stand in isolation. As will be discussed in Chapter Nineteen, if you were in a position to mandate the implementation of this Coda, and then extend its philosophy and resultant influence to all aspects of business work life, you'd end up with policies, practices, procedures, and behaviors that would approximate the spirit of the remaining nineteen Coda. In the same way, each of the Coda deals with a single aspect of what must be a comprehensive, new order of business. Each Coda is also an integral part of a greater whole, mutually supportive and complementary of all other Coda.

Let's take a look at the fundamental tenets of this new order of business life. The twenty Coda of The Code of the American Samurai are:

Coda 1. **Management's obsession with outcomes must be abandoned and replaced by process improvement activities.**

Coda 2. **Out-of-process defect inspection must be eliminated and replaced with defect prevention strategies and/or 100% in-process inspection (Poka-yoke).**

Coda 3. **Process-related decisions must be based upon objective, statistical analyses of micro-process inputs, events, and outputs, not subjective reactions to macro-process results. Policy-related decisions must be based upon The Code of The American Samurai.**

Coda 4. **Employees are every organization's most valuable resource; when they do not do a good job, it is almost always management's fault.**

Coda 5: **Quality of product and service, not volume, sales, or profits, must come before all other considerations.**

Coda 6. **Suboptimization and "management by fire control" must be abandoned and replaced by the implementation of an organized plan for the continuous improvement of key processes with the goal of maximizing customer satisfaction.**

Coda 7. **Excellence in all critical process outputs must be identified through the use of comparative benchmarks.**

Coda 8. **The role of management is to set policy that establishes and sustains this Code, conduct long-term planning, pursue bold new innovations that generate order of magnitude increases in quality and profitability, and lead through coaching and teaching.**

Coda 9. **The role of employees is to continuously improve their work processes (Standardize, Do, Check, Act) as if the processes they work were their own businesses.**

Coda 10. **Business plans must be action documents that provide every member of the organization with sufficient detail to clearly understand what they must do in order to help the organization attain its objectives.**

Coda 11.   All employees must receive extensive skills and knowledge training about their jobs, the company, and the tools of process improvement. Training is a long-term investment in profits, not an expense.

Coda 12.   The concept of performance to specification decreases quality and hides costs. It must be abandoned and replaced with an awareness that any variance from the ideal increases costs.

Coda 13.   Suppliers are critical team members who must be educated, valued, and treated as equals in the quest for quality. Selection of suppliers based upon price must be abandoned and replaced with selection based upon total life-cycle cost.

Coda 14.   The traditional systems of job descriptions, performance appraisals, merit pay, and pay for performance are useless, damaging, and wasteful; they must be abandoned and replaced with a system that encourages and rewards teamwork and group effort.

Coda 15.   Organizations and their policies and procedures must be redesigned to optimize cross-functionality, "flatter" reporting structures, streamlined communications, and accelerated decision making.

Coda 16.   Low- cost, low- technology process improvements must be pursued before technological solutions are implemented.

Coda 17.   Concurrent (or simultaneous) engineering must be implemented on all new products and product modifications (which is simply a process orientation to product development but sufficiently important and specialized to merit individual attention).

Coda 18.   All decision making must be reached by consensus decision making on the part of appropriate groups of hands-on process workers.

Coda 19.   All nonsalary management perquisites (special dining rooms and parking lots, club memberships, more lenient attendance policies, etc.) must be terminated immediately. No worker is a more inherently valuable human being than any other.

Coda 20.   The time for talk is over. It is time for each and every American Samurai to stand tall and be counted, to put this Code into practice today, so that American business and life will be better tomorrow.

Now, relax a bit. Don't try to digest, understand, resist, or design implementation plans in your mind for the entire Code all at once, right now.

I know how you're probably feeling. Most people who have just read the entire Code for the first time have one (or more) of several reactions:

1. They immediately focus on a particular Coda they don't like and begin to enumerate the reasons why it doesn't and could never work. You might say they are ignoring the forest because of one particularly galvanizing tree they don't like.
2. They are overwhelmed with the seeming complexity and breadth of The Code's content and don't know where to start in getting their thoughts organized. These folks aren't afraid to enter the forest and they aren't afraid of it; they just don't see a path and don't know whether to look for one or to simply pick a spot and plunge through the bush.
3. The Code appeals to them because it speaks to many of the concerns they've had as employees and/or managers. These people like the woods because they've occasionally found comfort under a big tree. They don't know what lies in store for them in the deepest recesses of the forest, but they know they'll like it. These people typically key on one or two Coda and start planning how they will get started on them tomorrow at work.
4. They are angered and upset at the overall flavor of The Code and have completely made up their minds that they don't like it. The Code's dismissal of many of the trappings of traditional business and its "power to the people" flavor are threatening to many traditionalists. Those who have this reaction are plains-dwellers; the cool, dark forest is somewhere they've never been. They can't understand why they would ever want to sit under a tree, much less visit (or, God forbid, live in) the deep woods.

Whoa! All of you are trying to do too much, too soon. In effect, each of these reactions is a classic example of traditional business' obsession with instant results. We're going to practice Coda 1 and do this one step at a time, paying careful attention to the *process* of developing your understanding. Each of the twenty Coda will be discussed individually in Chapters Six through Twenty-five, respectively. The Code is organized so that the discussion of each individual Coda provides an additional portion of a foundation that permits successive Coda to be more easily discussed and explored. You'll find that you'll begin to make connections and achieve insights of your own somewhere around Coda 10.

Complete insight, of course, will never come. Each time I lecture on these topics or present my 2-day seminar, I achieve new insights. Each time I read an article or reread a book by one of the giants of modern business such as Deming, Ishikawa, or Shigeo, I make new connections and deepen my understanding. The purpose of this book is not tell you everything there is to know. No one can do that. The purpose of this book is to get you started on a path of personal commitment to a new way of working—to turn you into an American Samurai. Now, let's get to it.

6

Management's Obsession with Outcomes must be Abandoned

Coda 1.   Management's obsession with outcomes must be abandoned and replaced by process improvement activities.

What you read about or hear about business every day is what happened rather than why it happened: profits fell by 10%, training expenses were 25% over plan, ROI ("return on investment") went up 4%, sales increased 240%, 10,000 automotive workers were laid off, a plant closed, another 20,000 jobs were lost to foreign competition, market share rose 13%, etc.—all results.

As you'll come to see, this emphasis on results, on outcomes, with little or no attention paid to *how* the results were obtained, is a subtle but all encompassing and damaging force in American business. This emphasis on results is driven by the existing management philosophy's dictates of "Everybody loves a winner," "Go for the fast payoffs," and "Mistakes by others are a chance to look good." American business is driven by its culture to results as birds are driven by instinct to migrate. This obsession with after-the-fact results must be replaced with something that works.

RESULTS ARE TOO LITTLE, TOO LATE

Results are almost always visible too late for action to be taken. What parents of a teenage ax murderer wouldn't have raised their child differently if they had known ahead of time about the crime? By the time the police show up at the door, it's years too late to do anything but point fingers and feel guilty, even if it's not clear what might have been done differently. The same scenario operates at work (minus the axes, generally). Consider the almost required quarterly, monthly, or weekly staff meetings that most managers feel compelled to hold: the entire focus is on results, things that have already happened. It's too late to do anything but a post-mortem. What waste the time?

THE SEARCH FOR THE GUILTY AND THE
PUNISHMENT OF THE INNOCENT

If a result is bad, it's automatically assumed that somebody screwed up. The discussion is usually kept on the topic by the boss until a guilty party is identified (the almost automatic, default choice is one or more Egg Sucking Pigs or Sub-Humans). We've all seen it: the gleeful, feeding frenzy as the mob closes in to make themselves look good by making every minor error appear to be a disaster ("Mistakes by others . . .") and the slow twisting in the wind of the person on the spot who has no idea of what happened. After all, last month (week, year, etc.) things turned out fine.

ANYBODY SEE THE GUILTY ONE? NO?
OK, YOU'RE IT!

There are several problems with the search for individual responsibility. First of all, in most companies, other than a lot of complaining, finger pointing, and a few threats, not much is done to the guilty party unless the problem was a total disaster. How many management people have you known who have been fired for serious but nonfatal mistakes? Not as many as tough talking American business would have us think. Hardly any, actually. I once worked in a car plant where somebody forgot to place an order for white paint (the most popular color) and a 3000-person plant had to shut down for 6 hours. The loss was in the hundreds of thousands of dollars, but the paint buyer is still working there. I'm not suggesting that the paint buyer should have been fired (far from it), but you'd think that some tough talking executive would have fired the guy on the spot.

So, since we're not going to do anything significant to the guilty party, why waste the time trying to find him or her? And that's if you can find the person! If employees do something that they are afraid they will be blamed for, they have advance warning and a head start in covering their tracks. When the search for the guilty starts, anyone directly responsible is usually miles away about the time some poor, innocent, unsuspecting employee gets hit with the blame.

THE BOTTOM LINE IS: INDIVIDUALS IN A SYSTEM
AREN'T RESPONSIBLE FOR MOST OF THE PROBLEMS

An even more basic problem with assigning blame is that an individual usually isn't personally and singly responsible for a specific problem. Sure, you can track down the name of the file clerk who misfiled the Jenkins report if you don't have anything better to do, but why bother? As Michael C. Keel, Vice-President and Division General Manager of General Dynamics Corporation says, "I don't think any employees get up in the morning, look themselves in the mirror and say, 'I'm going to go into work today and lose a couple of reports' (or miswire a chip, or make a typo on a letter).''

The fact is that most mistakes happen because the system in which the work is done allows or even mandates that the errors will occur at some rate. Experts contend that from 85% to 95% of all defects and mistakes in any situation occur because of the overall system in which the work was done, not because of the individual in the system. In most situations, you could change all the people and replace them with similarly educated and trained personnel, and the same things would happen.

EVIL, THY NAME IS IMMEDIATE SOLUTIONS

Whereas the preceding issues are important, the fundamental problem with managing by results is that results scream out for immediate solutions by everyone who views them ("Go for the fast payoffs"). Profits down by 10%? The almost immediate response is, "We want improvement now!" Everybody has a fast answer because they know that's what is expected ("Strap on those guns and step out in the street, pardner, it's time to be a hero.") The problem is that few people really understand the system that caused the results. In the typical business environment, even fewer care; all they want to do is to come up with an answer, any answer, to get the boss off their backs.

The key point is that whatever generates a particular result, good or bad, occurs far in advance of the result itself. In fact, by the time the result is visible, it's too late to stop more of the same from happening because it's "already in the pipeline." Specific factors cause results; it is those causes, not the results themselves, that must be addressed in order to improve the results.

PROCESSES: HOW THINGS HAPPEN, NOT WHAT

The alternative to this focus on results is a *process* orientation. A process is simply an input(s), a subsequent event(s), and the resultant output(s), as in:

INPUT	EVENT	OUTPUT
- - - - - - - - →	- - - - - - - - →	- - - - - - - - →

A process can be simple, such as filling in a form:

INPUT	EVENT	OUTPUT
- - - - - - - - →	- - - - - - - - →	- - - - - - - - →
(Form, pen, worker)	(Person fills out the form)	(Changed form)

This type of simple process is called a *micro-process*. A micro-process is a process that has clearly defined inputs and events, with one easily recognized principal output or result. Other examples of micro-processes are welding, soldering, typing a letter, making change, and inspecting a part.

The other general type of process is a *macro-process*. Macro-processes are processes comprised of a number of micro-processes. They can be relatively simple or bewilderingly complex, comprised of many thousands of subsidiary micro-processes. A very simple macro-process might look like the following:

```
INPUT – – →EVENT – – →OUTPUT
              becomes
         INPUT – – →EVENT – – →OUTPUT
                       becomes
              INPUT – – →EVENT – – →OUTPUT – – →
```

Each output becomes an input to the next process. It's easy to see this at work when a piece of paperwork, product, or data is routed through the system. When each person/machine completes its action, an output is created that then becomes an input to the next event. Complex macro-processes may not be simply linear. In the preceding example, there might be other chains of micro-processes overlayed and/or criss-crossing this process path.

The process of preparing and processing a purchase order in the typical bureaucracy is a classic macro-process:

INPUT	EVENT	OUTPUT
– – – – – – – –→	– – – – – – – –→	– – – – – – – –→
(Decision to purchase something	(3 months of paperwork and approvals)	(You might get what you ordered 6 months later)

This macro-process is made up of dozens (at least) of micro-processes that are used to manually complete a form, get it typed, put it in a computer, obtain signatures, route the paperwork, obtain estimates, confirm costs, place the order, confirm the order, and so on.

If the preceding macro-process had been defined as the "materials acquisition process," it would be more complex and would also include such micro-processes as receiving the goods, delivering the goods to the purchaser, notifying finance of the receipt, cutting the check for the supplier, etc. Some of these so-called micro-processes are actually smaller macro-processes that are themselves comprised of a great many micro-processes.

The preceding examples make it clear that there is no single, "right" way to define a process or set limits to it. How a particular process, macro or micro, is defined depends upon what you're trying to accomplish.

WHAT'S IN A PROCESS

Inputs to a process are people, information, materials, machines, computers (also machines), energy, policies and procedures, and so on. *Events* can be people doing something, machines doing something, time passing, en-

vironmental changes (such as when temperature changes affect the spray painting of cars), social changes (higher employment rates may make it more difficult to hire the right workers in a recruitment process), and so on. *Outputs*
are manufactured products, other material such as scrap, changed people
(graduating students are supposedly changed), modified systems, information, forms (a type of information, actually), and so on.

INPUT	EVENT	OUTPUT
- - - - - - - - -→	- - - - - - - - -→	- - - - - - - - -→
People	People do something	Material
Information	Machines do something	Changed people
Materials	Social changes	System changes
Machines	Environmental changes	Scrap
Computers		Information
Energy		Materials
Policy		Machines
Procedures		Computers
Forms		Energy
Environmental factors		Policy
Corporate culture		Procedures
		Forms
		Environmental factors
		Corporate culture

For every single thing that happens at work (or anywhere), there is at least
one micro-process with inputs, events, and an output. For most of the things
that happen, such as the macro-process of building an HMA (Hybrid Micro-
assembly; a complex "computer" chip) or generating a new engineering
design, there are thousands of micro-processes involving tens of thousands
of inputs, events, and outputs. We have arrived at a key point in your developing understanding of The Code. You are about to develop an insight that
is fundamental to everything that follows in this book.

AMERICAN SAMURAI INSIGHT

**You cannot "fix" an output. In order to change an output, you
must identify and then change the relevant inputs and/or events
of the involved micro-processes that influence the output.**

Think about this for a moment. How often have you heard things such
as, "I want this shipping problem fixed and I want it fixed today!"? Or how
many times have you witnessed some manager (perhaps yourself) look at a
report, see an output that he or she doesn't like and bark out an order that's
supposed to "fix it"? Aside from pure luck, almost all of these decisions
are based on a "fast gun" appraisal of macro-process outputs, with no real
understanding of the inputs and events.

Dr. Deming has labeled this meddling *tampering*. He defines tampering as taking action without *profound knowledge.* If you have profound knowledge of a process, you understand the inputs, events, and outputs and how they influence one another.

Another key point is to realize that you cannot "fix" macro-processes. Their outputs can be measured, but the causes are hidden deep within a maze of micro-processes. An off-the-cuff action to "fix" a macro-process has almost no chance of succeeding. In order to "fix" a macro-process output, all of the inputs, events, and outputs of the constituent micro-processes must be identified and understood.

In the typical company, management spends almost all of its time reviewing macro-process outputs and taking actions to fix them. Typically, every person in supervision does this at least three to four times a day. Some do it dozens of times a day. As our bad luck would have it, the ones who do it most tend to be high-level executives and/or those who are considered the "doers" ("React quickly in every situation"), the ones who get things done. As you now know, what they're doing is tampering. No wonder things never seem to get any better.

AMERICAN SAMURAI INSIGHT

The only people who are in a position to provide accurate information about micro-processes are the workers who do them.

The only people who really understand the hands-on operation of a micro-process (inputs, events, and outputs) are the ones who perform the process every day. They are usually the only ones *not* involved in coming up with solutions. We'll talk more about the implications of this insight in Chapters Twelve, Thirteen, and Fourteen.

IF NOT OUTCOMES, WHAT DO WE TRACK AND HOW DO WE TRACK IT?

At this point, you understand why examining macro-process results (after-the-fact results) is a waste of time and dangerous. Micro-processes, not macro-process results, must be monitored and controlled. This leads to the obvious question, "How do we measure micro-processes and what do we measure them with?" Well, strange as it may seem, we're still going to be measuring results! Not macro-process results, but micro-process results or, as they're often called, in-process results. Micro-process results are extremely useful because they're "close" to a problem; if something goes wrong, we can see it right away, we can quickly identify changes in a critical cause of the problem, and we can "fix" it immediately, before more process output is ruined.

In Chapter Seven, as we examine Coda 2, we'll see just how micro-process measurement should be conducted; you're going to learn how to handle one of the primary weapons of an American Samurai.

7

Out-Of-Process Defect Inspection Must Be Eliminated

Coda 2. **Out-of-process defect inspection must be eliminated and replaced with defect prevention strategies and/or 100% in-process inspection (Poka-yoke).**

This Coda is the antithesis of the quality control philosophy almost universally held in American industry. The abandonment of the current approaches and the application of this Coda alone, without any other actions, would dramatically improve the cost and quality competitiveness of every American company.

Since the beginning of the Industrial Revolution, defect detection strategies have been the primary quality assurance technique for manufacturers and service organizations. *Defect detection* refers to inspections that are conducted after a process, or product, has been completed. Defect detection usually involves inspection of macro-process results. This is a flawed technique when used as the primary quality control tactic, but it's been used to such an extent that companies actually brag about how much they use it. Lands' End, a leading direct mail merchant, boasts in their catalog of the dozens of times they inspect each of their products.

As you know after reading Chapter Six, counting loose threads around a collar after the shirt is made is an example of a macro-process (making the shirt) result. The typical catalog reader (and the typical American business person) believes that this is an indication of a superior quality control system. Wrong. Even if it catches most of the bad stuff (if you're lucky), it's costly and self-defeating.

It is more accurate to describe this traditional mode of macro-process results inspection as *out-of-process defect inspection*. Shigeo Shingo, a leading Japanese quality expert, calls this type of inspection *judgment inspection*. "Out-of-process" is the key phrase in identifying poor quality control tactics. "Good" quality systems, as we'll see later in this chapter, use in-process data collection. In-process data collection involves the examination of micro-process results immediately after, or during, the micro-process. This approach is central to successful implementation of Coda 2.

As you'll see, classic defect detection, or out-of-process inspection, doesn't prevent mistakes. Instead it drives up costs and perpetuates all sorts of bad management practices. A short story will demonstrate the difference between out-of-process defect detection and in-process, or defect, prevention strategies.

THE CLARA JOHNSON STORY

An interesting lawn mower commercial ran on TV a couple of years ago. It was intriguing not because of the product but because of the manner in which it described quality control efforts at the lawn mower plant. Since then, I've used something I call "The Clara Johnson Story" to illustrate a number of points about the merits of measuring micro-process outputs compared to measuring macro-process outputs. I always present this story in my 2 day seminar because it demonstrates so many important points about the right and the wrong way to improve quality and lower costs. We'll expand our analysis of this story again in Chapter Eight when we talk about statistical process control.

The commercial showed an attractive woman, called Clara Johnson, who was standing near a fully assembled, shiny, new lawn mower. Unlike most assembly plants I've worked in, this one had attractive lighting, polished, mirrored surfaces, and all sorts of accouterments obviously designed by an advertising type who had never been in a real plant. The voice-over said that before each lawn mower was shipped it got the Clara Johnson test. At this point, Clara bent over, fetchingly tightening her custom-fitted coveralls in all the right places, and pulled the starter cord. The lawn mower started (of course) and Clara looked over her shoulder and shouted, "Ship it."

This procedure was intended to reassure the lawn mower–buying public that the quality of each lawn mower was good because it passed the "Clara Johnson" test. However, the fact that this flawed approach to quality could reassure the American public demonstrates the appalling lack of quality awareness in this country. We American Samurai have a long battle ahead of us.

THE PROBLEMS WITH A CLARA JOHNSON APPROACH TO QUALITY CONTROL

There are several serious problems with any defect detection, "Clara Johnson" method of controlling quality. Each drives up costs, guarantees lower quality, and degrades customer satisfaction by allowing poor products to get out the door.

"Clara Johnsons" Are After the Fact

Now that you have a process orientation, you realize that a lawn mower "start" or "no-start" (as such things are called in businesses in which motors are involved) is the result of the macro-process of building a lawn mower. This macro-process is comprised of at least hundreds of micro-processes. A bad outcome from any one of these micro-processes (such as the micro-processes of putting in a spark plug or adding enough gas for the start test) could cause a no-start.

By the time a lawn mower fails a Clara Johnson test, most of the assembly mistakes that could have been made have been made. It's a fact of manufacturing life with traditional quality control systems that problems run in batches. For example, if a mower doesn't start because a bad spark plug was used, there's a good chance that other mowers have also had defective spark plugs installed because all or part of a box of plugs was bad. Or, if a substitute operator is performing some element of the plug installation micro-process incorrectly, he or she will most likely contribute a number of successive failures. By the time the first no-start gets to the test, many more no-starts have already been "hard-wired" into the system.

You see this in all manufacturing plants. By the time a problem shows up at the end of the line, there are usually another 5 to 1000 similarly compromised products behind it with the same problem, too late to stop. Each of these defects must be repaired.

Repairs Cost More Than the Original Work

It is usually much more expensive in labor costs to repair a defective unit than it is to make it in the first place. Also, any repair cost is an additional expense to the original manufacturing or assembly cost. In the lawn mower example, a no-start must go through the following steps (we'll assume that a bad spark plug is the root cause of the no-start):

1. Take the mower to the repair shop (or have the repair person come to it).
2. Test and determine the cause of the no-start.
3. Take out the old plug. (This disassembly is easy with a spark plug; with a car engine or a computer drive, disassembly may require the removal of many parts.)
4. Obtain a replacement plug and put it in. (This means that either the plugs and installation tools must be stocked in two places, on the line and in the shop, or somebody must get them from the supply area that serves the assembly line.)
5. Process the old plugs. (Collect them somewhere and then process paperwork to get money back from the supplier and/or have them replaced.)
6. Test the new installation by pushing it over to Clara again.

Think of how much money is wasted when this happens to ten mowers in a row. The costs for a lawn mower repair would be relatively small compared to repair costs for cars, airplane components, or high tech products. I've seen car plants with over 300 vehicles waiting out in the "shop" (a euphemism for an outside parking lot) for the same repair.

Costs of the preceding process are not the whole story. Every repair increases direct labor costs, parts costs, inventory levels (which increase receiving and material handling costs, purchasing costs, storage space requirements, and thus inventory and land taxes), and even Worker's Compensation costs and health care costs (some of the repair people will invariably get hurt or have medical problems). In addition, repairs necessitate additional handling of the goods, which always increases the risks of "system" damage (scratches, drops, repair mistakes such as ruining an entire electronic chip while attempting to repair a loose wire), which must then be repaired.

In typical American heavy manufacturing and consumer products companies, these impacts can account for as much as 40% of total product costs. In some industries, one of every four jobs is created by quality problems, repair, and rework (including front office and engineering support).

Damage to Customer Satisfaction and Loyalty

"OK, OK," you might be thinking, "so defect detection strategies drive up costs. At least they make sure that no bad products get out the door. Right?" Wrong, out-of-process breath! Reliance on defect detection actually guarantees that some bad products will get to customers. Warranty and returns are only a small part of the story. And remember, a happy customer tells seven to ten people about the experience, whereas an unhappy customer tells 15 to 20 every *month*. You might say that, "Bad products just keep on giving." We'll be talking about the entire panorama of customer satisfaction issues in Chapter Eleven.

Let's look at the ways in which end of the line inspection can't protect your customers:

1. After-the-fact inspection, as a technique, just plain doesn't work

After-the-fact inspection doesn't catch all the mistakes. Although at first glance, it would seem that any reasonably motivated, trained person could spot a defect, this isn't true. Human beings just don't do inspection work very well, even under the best of circumstances. Human attention and perception weren't made for monotonous, boring, repetitive jobs. The more detailed the work, the worse the results. That's why the military changes radar screen monitors every 15 to 20 minutes in critical situations. After about 15 minutes of watching a screen closely, even highly trained, motivated operators don't see clearly visible "bogies" and do see things that aren't there. When an inspector is checking hundreds of units each day, over and over, in a much less threatening environment, bored and uninvolved, things always slip through. That's just the way it is.

Adding another level of inspection (to check the first inspection) still doesn't catch all the defects. For example, if a first inspector would catch 90% of all defects, and a second inspector would catch 90% of the remaining defects, these two inspectors would, theoretically, reduce the defects that got by both of them to 1% (10% of 10%). A third inspector would reduce the final defects of 0.1%, or only one in 1000. (This may seem like a good level of quality, but it isn't, for reasons that will be discussed in Chapter Seventeen).

Unfortunately, even if you were able to pay a fortune in inspection costs and still stay in business, things don't work that way in practice. If you put five inspectors on a job, each doing a successive, independent check of the product, lots of defects still get through. It's not just that defects slip through the inspections because of momentary lapses in attention and/or perception difficulties. It turns out that each inspector has a tendency to let up a little when he or she knows that other people are providing a safety net. There's a tendency to slack off and "let the system handle it." It's not because they don't care—it's human nature.

2. Inspection takes you "away" from your processes; you don't always know what's most important to inspect

This is a more subtle, but much more important, limitation to out-of-process inspection. Out-of-process inspection creates a management mindset and work approach that directs everyone's attention away from the critical micro-processes that generate the defects in the first place. With a defect detection orientation in operation, management tends to perceive of "the work" (all of the micro-processes that produce the product) as a single "black box." If management is not aware of the importance of specific micro-processes, it seems logical to catch defects as they come out of the black box. And, without a process orientation, a cursory look into the maze of micro-processes in any business is frightening and frustrating to the traditional manager. Not having a philosophy and methodology with which to fix the micro-processes, it's easier to do what everybody else is doing: macro-process inspection, inspection, inspection, followed by costly repairs.

This "hands off the processes" style effectively eliminates any possibility that the hands-on process workers will be able to develop a comprehensive understanding of their processes. They won't be given the support, training, or time to do anything substantive (or be provided with an awareness that they are supposed to change things for the better). Without an understanding of the relationships between inputs, events, and outputs, process outcomes will vary in ways that nobody can predict. The result will be defects that will pass right under the noses of the inspectors because they won't be attuned to a "new" problem; they'll only be inspecting by the book.

For example, let's suppose that we're concerned about a wire bonding procedure (wire bonds attach components to circuit boards and make electrical connections). In a traditionally run company, the folks who do the bonds just do what they are told. They have very little knowledge of what happens to the board before they get it and of what's done to it after they're finished with it. The workers don't understand the inputs and outputs and have only a marginal understanding of how the technology of the event (their process) really works; they just do it. After they do their work, an inspector checks the bonds that were just done, not other things that were already inspected earlier in the process.

As it turns out, because of the design of the board, the process of making the bonds occasionally damages a nearby wire that was previously attached and already inspected. This damaged wire occasionally causes the product to fail when it gets to final test. Then, the entire product must go through the same steps that a no-start lawn mower goes through (diagnosis, tear down, repair, retest, etc.). Very expensive. Worse, some of the damaged wires work for a while, just long enough to pass inspection and test before they get to the customers and fail. Now, there is an angry customer in addition to all of the repair costs.

Yet everyone was doing their job just as well as they could. The problem is that the very narrow perspective of inspection by "the numbers" inhibits the type of understanding of micro-processes that would develop if the workers who were doing the wire bonds had more data and training about the entire macro-process. If they were able to talk with the inspectors, see quality data, and participate in a group problem solving effort directed at the damaged wire, they would be able to modify their procedures to eliminate the defect. In an inspection after-the-fact environment, this type of insight and participation is not only absent, it's actively discouraged.

THE ALTERNATIVES

Now you know why after-the-fact defect detection doesn't work to improve quality and lower costs. Never did, never will. Even though the preceding material may seem so simple that it's painfully obvious, don't expect that management will appreciate the insight without extensive training and selling. They don't think like you do, they're not American Samurai. They are part of the old way, and they don't have the slightest idea why the old way isn't working.

The alternative to defect detection is defect prevention. *Defect prevention* is a body of approaches that focuses on eliminating the primary causes of micro-process defects. There are many ways to approach defect prevention, some better than others, some more well known than others, but they all have one thing in common: they focus on preventing defects at the micro-process level. As we discuss the various approaches, we'll integrate them into our hypothetical lawn mower plant and discuss how they might work. (You'll find these types of "story" examples very useful in your efforts to explain these concepts to the uninitiated. It's easier for people to keep an open mind about a hypothetical lawn mower plant than it is for them to consider that their own operation is doing something wrong.)

Mistakes are made, and defects are produced, at the micro-process level. Every manufacturing defect (and every paper/data process defect) can be traced to a specific action or set of conditions. If these conditions are changed, the defect will not occur.

AMERICAN SAMURAI INSIGHT

The key to "good" quality control systems is to push inspections as close to the defect-producing event as possible.

This would obviously require extensive micro-process analysis and quite a bit of effort, not to mention a complete change in the way in which an organization's approach to quality is operated. That's the reason for The Code of the American Samurai.

In our lawn mower plant, this approach would require that inspections be conducted and data collected at the end of or, better yet, during the specific micro-processes that create no-starts. For example, instead of finding out in the repair shop that no-starts are caused by bad spark plugs, we would be far better off to collect data about the spark plugs right in the spark plug area. Let's say that we had decided that spark plug gap was a root cause (a *root cause* is a primary cause of a micro-process output) of no-starts. If the gap is too large or too small, the mower will not start. The following paragraphs describe the two principal ways in which the inspections are conducted.

The Typical Strategy

A common approach is to have an inspector check the spark plug gap sometime after the plugs are put in. This approach differs from a Clara Johnson only in that it's an inspection of a result closer to the process than in a Clara Johnson. The logic is that if a box of bad plugs appears, not too many will be put on before the inspector starts finding them and reporting the problem. The trouble with this approach is twofold: (1) the defective plug must still be pulled and replaced (with all of the attendant costs), and (2) in many organizations, quality control data is reported, at best, only daily. As a result, this approach often does hardly anything to reduce defects and lower costs. (This is a common reason for the failure of so many quality efforts that are based upon statistical process control, which will be discussed in Chapter Eight.)

This type of approach is often called *informative inspection*, because the data is used to focus on key areas that require corrective action.

Operator Process Control

Inspection done by the worker who installs the plugs is *operator process control* (OPC). As the name implies, the operator "controls" the process by being trained to take action to correct problems. Clearly, it makes more sense to have the operator check the plug before he or she puts it on rather than after. Except for the odd oversight or two, this approach completely eliminates the need to remove and replace defective plugs because of spark plug gap problems (or many other problems with spark plugs, such as non-conductivity, that could have an impact on performance of the mower). This type of system leads to tremendous improvements in quality and overall costs, but it doesn't happen on its own. Operators must be trained and provided with the resources and support to do things they've not been allowed to do before, such as think and make decisions.

If we wanted to implement OPC in the lawn mower plant, the workers in the spark plug area would be taught about spark plugs, how they work, the complete dimensions of the no-start problem, how to test the gaps, what to do when a gap isn't right, and perhaps SPC methods (depending upon how the data was to be collected). They would then be in a position to "control" the spark plug process.

Successive Checks

One of the problems with OPC approaches is a fear that an operator will sometimes get sloppy about checking his or her own work. A *successive check* system, in which each successive operator in a process checks key aspects of the work performed by the immediately previous operator, greatly reduces critical defects. When a defect is discovered by an operator, he or she immediately returns the work to the previous operator. This rapid feedback and correction stops errors from moving on, or piling up, down the line. It also facilitates a great deal of worker communications within the process group. Successive checks are most effective when the number of items inspected by each worker is kept small, no more than three, and each of the items is 100% inspected.

In our mower plant, a successive check system would require that the person who worked on the mower after the spark plug installation test the gap and immediately report the problem to the spark plug installer/gap setter. The situation would then be corrected by the installer/gap setter. As you can see, there are several problems with this approach: (1) the errors are allowed to occur before they are checked, and (2) if the workers are far apart, it is difficult to communicate quickly.

SOURCE INSPECTION AND POKA-YOKE

Source inspection and Poka-yoke (pronounced POH-kah YOH-kay) take the inspection of the micro-process to the source of errors, that is, to the very causes that lead to the error. All of the methods previously examined (except in an OPC system, in which the spark plug gap is inspected prior to installation) involve catching problems after they occur (although they would in some cases be caught very quickly after the error). These two techniques catch them before they occur or stop them in progress.

Shigeo Shingo is one of the towering giants of quality control done the right way. He invented SMED (single minute exchange of die; a powerful method of cutting the time and cost of retooling) and conceptualized and named the Poka-yoke and source inspection tactics. The latter two techniques have been used here and there in the past without formal names; Mr. Shingo is the one who has turned them into an overall quality improvement strategy.

Source Inspection

Source Inspection is the inspection and correction of conditions that lead to errors before they have occurred. In our spark plug plant, source inspection would involve finding out what was causing the spark plug gaps to be incorrectly set in the first place. Unless the lawn mower plant manufactures its own plugs, this would require taking action on something that's being done at the spark plug manufacturing plant.

AMERICAN SAMURAI INSIGHT

Process improvement methods must not be limited by the artificial barriers between OEM (original equipment manufacturers) and manufacturers. The entire macro-process, from raw materials to field service, must be viewed as one, with the "doers" of every micro-process pursuing every process improvement technique possible.

When you consider that most manufacturers buy at least 60% of their parts and simply put them together, the role of suppliers is key. If the plugs in our example are made by someone else, there's no way that gap defects can be eliminated unless the supplier takes action. We'll be looking at the best way to involve suppliers in Chapter Eighteen.

Let's say that the supplier has a machine that automatically bends the spark plug head to set the gap and that occasionally the machine goes out of adjustment. Source inspection involves making the determination that this is the problem and then setting up conditions that prevent the machine from going out of adjustment or stopping it and alerting the operator when it does. For example, a photocell might be hooked up to set off an alarm and stop the machine if the clearances on the bending arms started to "drift" from the ideal. This would *prevent* any defective spark plugs from being produced. As long as the machine and photocell were maintained, a defective gap would never be produced.

Note that if the supplier doesn't use this type of method (or Poka-yoke), it doesn't matter if the supplier provides perfect parts. If they're shipping perfect parts only because they're inspecting "out" the bad ones, the spark plug buyer is paying for the extra cost of the scrap, rework, repair, and inspections, one way or another. Better (and much less costly) for everyone to simply have it done right the first time at the supplier's factory.

Poka-yoke

Poka-yoke means "mistake proofing" (to avoid [yokeru] inadvertent errors [poka]). The essence of Poka-yoke is to set up conditions that automatically conduct 100% in-process inspections of operator actions and/or processes. The intent of Poka-yoke is to avoid, or immediately detect, errors caused by lapses of operator attention and vigilance by building safeguards into the system.

One example of Poka-yoke that many people are familiar with is wrapping a band of tape or fastening a jig around a drill bit so that it won't go too far into a surface. If you're drilling a hole to hang something on the back of a door and you don't want to drill through the door, you place the jig to "tell you" when you're in far enough but not too far to come out the other side. This is a simple Poka-yoke.

A more "industrial" example involves drilling holes in a metal plate. Occasionally, an operator will pull the drill out before it goes all the way in. When assembly is later attempted, the part has to be redrilled. A useful Poka-yoke consists of two limit switches and an alarm. Once the drill bit starts down and trips the first switch, an alarm is set off if the second switch (the one tripped when the drill bit reaches its desired depth) is not tripped before the first one is again set off. This warns the operator that the last hole was not fully drilled.

In our lawn mower plant, a simple Poka-yoke might involve the operator simply pressing the spark plug down on a feeler gauge fixture to test the gap as he or she gets ready to install it. Of course, the best approach in this case would be source inspection at the spark plug plant so that no tests of any kind would be necessary. If there was also a problem with the torque applied to screw in the spark plug, the Poka-yoke might consist of a torque wrench that would sound an alarm (or at least provide a readout) if proper torque was not applied as the plug was installed.

Some techniques that can be used as Poka-yoke are:

1. Guide pins (to identify omitted holes in parts and/or to assure proper mating of parts)
2. Limit switches (to monitor proper placements and orientations)
3. Photocells (to indicate proper location, existence of holes and attachments, and presence/absence of parts)
4. Checklists (to assure operator attention to procedure)
5. Alarms (to alert operators to error conditions)

6. Shut-off switches (to stop equipment when an error condition is sensed)
7. Leftover parts baskets (to hold sets of components that are to be added to an assembly so that none are forgotten)
8. Scales (to weigh assemblies and compare against ideal to determine if all parts are present)
9. Counters (to determine if all parts/actions have been used/completed)
10. Templates of shape/size (to determine part matches with ideal)

As you can see, these Poka-yoke applications are not independent; they can be used in any combination or sequence.

This is Going to Work in American Business?
You're Joking, Right?

I have the same reaction myself. You can see that the entire approach of Coda 2 is to realize that the system, not the people in it, is the cause of mistakes. If you want to eliminate the mistakes, you have to control all of the micro-processes in the system so that mistakes will not occur. A realization that this is, indeed, the way it is, does not set well with American executives in general. The way they see it, if you can't blame somebody for a mistake, what are you left with? What would they do all day? The sad fact is that most managers are not willing to do the hard work that's required to fix the system. They would rather just sit back and blame the workers.

Almost none of them understand the processes they "manage" (most aren't aware of processes as operating systems in the first place), and few would know how to fix a process even if they were willing.

The more fundamental problem is that a realization that processes are king requires a manager to view his or her employees as resources, rather than problems. This is a transition in philosophy that many managers fight with all their will. Instead of thinking of employees as Sub-Humans and Egg Sucking Pigs, a manager has to start thinking of employees as the only ones who can really make any processes work better over the long term. Creating this change in management perceptions and world view is the greatest challenge faced by American Samurai.

8

Lies, Damned Lies, and Statistics

Coda 3. **Process-related decisions must be based upon objective, statistical analyses of micro-process inputs, events, and outputs, not subjective reactions to macro-process results. Policy-related decisions must be based upon The Code of The American Samurai.**

Benjamin Disraeli, Earl of Beaconsfield (1804–1881) and a British Prime Minister, once said, "There are three kinds of lies: lies, damned lies, and statistics." However, Lord William Thomson Kelvin (1824–1907), the developer of the Kelvin scale and once president of the Royal Society (at its time, the foremost scientific body in the world), stated a seemingly opposite view concerning the value of statistics:

> "When you can measure what you are speaking about, and express it in numbers, you know something about it; but when you cannot measure it, when you cannot express it in numbers, your knowledge is of a meager and unsatisfactory kind; it may be the beginning of knowledge, but you have scarcely, in your thoughts, advanced to the stage of science."

People who don't understand and/or aren't comfortable with statistics and numbers often take refuge in Disraeli's position. Those who are comfortable with statistics side with Lord Kelvin. In reality, there's no conflict between the two positions. Properly used, statistics provide a powerful mechanism for making objective decisions. However, like anything else, statistics can easily be misapplied. This is particularly true in business. The point Disraeli was making is that you can make statistics say almost anything you want if you apply them selectively or if you are using them before a naive audience.

For example, if children were trying to convince their parents that it was safe to swim unsupervised in a certain stream, they might report that the average depth of the water was only 10 inches (don't ask me how a child would know that, this is only an example). This may be true, although the water depth may vary from 1 inch to 10 feet. A parent who did not want the children to swim in the stream might dwell on the fact that one spot in the creek was 10 feet deep. The parent might also use the argument that every year, dozens of children drown. Who's right? They both are, in terms of absolute fact. The problem is that the quoted "statistics" avoid the real issue.

The issue is not how deep the water is, but whether it's safe for the children to swim there. You see, the entire situation of safe swimming can be described as a process. The output the parents want is safe and happily tired children who will go to bed early and leave them in peace. The output the children want is fun and a little freedom to do something they think is exciting. The inputs include the stream (depth, pollution, speed of current), hazards in the area (evil strangers, broken glass, and so on), the number, ages, experience, and skills of children who will be swimming, how far the stream is from help, how long they'll be gone, and so on.

Concentrating only on the depth of the water is pointless (after all, almost every municipal swimming pool has an average depth of at least 4 feet with diving areas more than 10 feet deep). In order to rationally evaluate a process, you have to assess all inputs and events. In fact, the outcomes that the children and the parents want may be possible to obtain without any swimming at all (for example, by taking them to the movies).

In business, statistics and numbers that are analogous to the water depth or child drowning data are tossed around with impunity. There's lots of data, all right. All that is ever seen in business are numbers, numbers, and more numbers. Look at the business section of the paper—pages of numbers. Look at any company's annual plan or quarterly review documents—nothing but pages of graphs, charts, and numbers. Almost *all* of these numbers are irrelevant to the millions of underlying micro-process events and inputs that determine business success or failure. Paying attention to numerical results to the exclusion of the more important background data concerning microprocesses is stupid and shortsighted.

It's surprising (and sickening to an American Samurai) if you think about it, but traditional business, for all its numerical trappings, makes most of its decisions on the basis of subjective opinions and "seat of the pants" guesstimates. In fact, most decisions in business are based on management data directly analogous to basing the "to swim or not to swim" decision (for any pool, stream, or even playing in the sprinkler) on only the stream depth or national child drowning data.

THERE ARE TWO KINDS OF DECISIONS IN BUSINESS

Two distinct types of decisions determine what goes on in any business. Decisions are made about processes and decisions are made about policy. The two are very different and require different sets of data, different techniques, and different people to make them.

Policy Decisions

Policy decisions are one-time events that are not part of an on-going input, event, output sequence in any but the most global manner. For example, let's suppose that a company CEO decides to implement a nonsmoking work environment in the company. This is a policy decision. Whereas there are inputs, events, and outputs, this decision isn't going to be made everyday. It's a point event that stands alone. The fact that these events are singular and nonrepeating makes it almost impossible to analyze their effectiveness statistically. Nonsmoking policies can be debated until the cows (nonsmoking) come home, but it's difficult to determine what to measure and how to measure to assess whether the policy decision was "right."

Other examples of policy decisions are adding or deleting a holiday, changing over to flex time, deciding to add a new product, changing a marketing strategy, deciding to move a facility, deciding what awards to give to employees, and so on. Reaching each of these decisions is a macro-process, but the objective is so global that it's often difficult to evaluate whether the decision is correct or not, based upon short-term observations of the decision's impact. It is typically impossible to isolate the consequences of a policy decision from the simultaneous impact of all of the other events that are occurring at the same time.

For example, some companies have switched to flex time. Was this a good decision? Hard for some of them to say. Some employees seem happier, some don't, sometimes absenteeism goes down, sometimes it doesn't. There is usually no clear-cut answer as to whether a policy decision is right or wrong. So what do you do instead of analyzing the results and modifying the decision (inputs and events), as you would do for a process?

Simply put, all policy decisions must be made on the basis of The Code of The American Samurai. This is where following The Code is a lot like a religion; you have to believe and act according to the Coda in advance of proof—you must have faith, my fellow warriors. Policy decisions are the culture drivers for an organization. They are made by management, and they set the tone for the types of behaviors that are expected and accepted.

Either an organization is going to function according to The Code or it is not. If it is, then all policy decisions must be made in accordance with all of the Coda. It's difficult, in some cases, to know if you're doing the right thing. That's OK, as long as you try to do the right thing. Over time, it will work out. For instance, take management decisions about disciplinary policy. In a traditional business environment, any problem is associated with employees. If a particular employee can be isolated with regard to a defect or problem, the immediate response is to come down hard. It's routine in American industry to suspend workers (generally only Egg Sucking Pigs and Sub-Humans) without pay for errors. Most of the time, the process was to blame, but the traditional manager doesn't know about processes, so he or she nails an employee.

In an enlightened business that would like to survive the 1990s, management knows that punishing employees is counterproductive. So what do they do with a problem employee? First they try to understand the process, then they train the employee, fix equipment, correct tooling, or change the process, and then they watch the next set of outputs to see if the employee can now do the job. If not, they try to find another job for the employee. Suppose nothing works. When have they done enough to warrant getting rid of the employee? Who knows? For every enlightened company, there will be a different answer, just as every devout religious person does things slightly differently when faced with daily temptations. As long as an organization lives by The Code, it will make many more good decisions than bad ones. That's all anyone can hope for, and it's orders of magnitude better than anything the traditional management system has been able to deliver.

Process Decisions

Remember that a process is a set of inputs, events, and outputs. Whereas anything that happens in the universe can be defined as a process, it helps to think of business processes as those processes that have continuous output on a daily basis—the things that produce and keep a business going from day to day. The output may be chips coming off a line, bills being processed, tomatoes being shipped, etc. Business processes such as these must be kept going for the business to survive. For any of these processes, the inputs can be adjusted and the events modified in order to modify the outputs. But, no matter what, the output must be kept coming, day after day.

Process decisions must be made on the basis of objective analyses of statistical data. When possible, the data should deal with micro-process inputs, events, and outputs because only micro-process data is "close" enough to the source of the critical events and conditions that must be improved. And, as we'll see throughout this book, the most appropriate process decision makers are the operators of the micro-processes themselves—the people who do the jobs. Much of this chapter will deal with explaining how this statistical data must be handled.

MANAGING WITH STATISTICS

Let's go back to the lawn mower plant. Suppose that the place is being run by Mr. Traditional, who just took over as the new plant manager. He knows that business runs on numbers, so Mr. Traditional wants to see some reports. The first one he sees shows the data presented in Table 8-1.

Mr Traditional goes nuts when he sees this report. An average of 13% no-starts!?! Not in his plant! He calls in the production manager and tells him, "Just look how things have gotten worse over the last 3 days. From 8% to 10% to 17% no-starts! Do something and do it now!" The production manager says he'll handle it. Note that the plant manager has no idea what's going on. How could he? You know, but he doesn't, that whether mowers start or not is about as macro a process result as you'll ever see in a lawn mower plant. There's no sense in even worrying about it at the end of the line.

Table 8-1.
No-start report for days 1 through 6.

Day	Mowers tested	Number of no-starts	Percent of no-starts
1	120	14	12
2	110	13	12
3	105	17	16
4	102	8	8
5	132	13	10
6	129	22	17
Totals	688	87	13

Upon leaving the plant manager's office, the production manager goes out and talks to a few supervisors, who do whatever they usually do to various employees when there's executive pressure. Some of them yell at employees, others crack down on minor problems (such as trash on the floor), and some of them go to their people and have a joint bitch session about management. The head test person goes over to Clara and tells her to try harder to get the mowers to start. He tells her, "Maybe you're not pulling hard enough on the starter." As he walks away, she mutters under her breath, "I've got your starter, bucko, swingin'." Ah, American management and Egg Sucking Pig relations at their best.

Over the next 2 days, the plant manager keeps a close eye on no-starts. Now that he's "on" the problem and taking action, he's sure he'll see some improvement. For the next 2 days, he observes the data shown in Table 8-2.

Table 8-2.
No-start data for days 7 and 8.

Day	Mowers tested	Number of no starts	Percent of no-starts
7	87	2	2
8	117	5	4
Totals	204	7	3

"Ah, that's better," he tells himself, "An average of only 3% no-starts. It just took a little management action, that's all." He tells the production manager, as they're eating lunch in the Human Beings–only executive dining room, "Every now and then, all you've got to do is crack down a little. Take action, yessir, that's the key."

The production manager agrees, "Right on. I think I've got 'em straightened out." He has no idea why things got better, but he's willing to take the credit for it. An interesting point involves the plant manager's positive reaction to 3% no-starts. Why does he think that 3% is acceptable? Why doesn't he think that's bad, too? He couldn't tell you, other than to say that it "seemed right." It might be that 3% is slowly putting them out of business. This is the subjective approach to using statistics.

Convinced that "the problem" with no-starts is over, the plant manager turns his attention to more pressing problems, such as the upcoming charity drive, his article for the company paper, plant housekeeping, and planning for his trip to corporate headquarters for the quarterly review. Four days later, he happens to see another no-start report. He is shocked to see the data shown in Table 8-3.

Table 8-3.
No-start report for days 9 through 12.

Day	Mowers tested	Number of no-starts	Percent of no-starts
9	101	18	18
10	115	12	10
11	116	14	12
12	145	25	17
Totals	477	69	14

"I turn my back for an instant and look what happens! We go from 3% no-starts to 14%," he rages to the production manager. He demands to know what's going on. The production manager says he can't understand what happened, he already took care of it. He promises to check it out. The plant manager's wrath spreads down the chain of authority like a load of goose manure poured down an up escalator during the holiday rush. Nobody escapes and everybody gets it.

Everybody promises to try harder. The problem is, nobody knows what to try harder at; they're all doing the best they can. Clara pulls harder on the lawn mowers for a few hours but snaps off three starter cords (that then have to be repaired). She stops pulling as hard when the repair people yell at her. She goes back to pulling the cords the same way she always has.

For the next 3 days, the plant manager makes sure that the no-start report from the prior day is his first priority each morning as he sits in his second floor office overlooking the front lawn (where few work processes are conducted). Over the next 3 days, he observes the results shown in Table 8-4.

Table 8-4.
No-start report for days 13 through 15.

Day	Mowers tested	Number of no-starts	Percent of no-starts
13	129	5	4
14	120	10	8
15	87	3	3
Totals	336	18	5

"Well," he crows to the production manager, "We finally got that shaped up. It just shows that you can't let up on the pressure for a minute. From now on, I want to see that no-start report first thing every morning and I want it posted in all break areas and on all bulletin boards every day." Great, now everybody has more administrative work to do. And for nothing. Nobody really did anything to impact no-starts (except Clara, who caused another $100.00 worth of damage in trying her best to reduce no-starts). It looked as though the output changed, but nothing *in the process* changed. Let's take a look at why we say this with certainty, even though the plant manager thinks he "handled" it.

Common and Special Causes of Variability

Regardless of how good or bad the lawn mower plant is run, the number of no-starts will vary from day to day. Even if there is an average of one no-start per day, on some days there will be three or four, on other days there will be either a lot or even none, and most days there will be none or one. The same type of variability is present in any process, for example, golf. Even the most consistent, careful golfer doesn't get the same score every game or round. A steady golfer who shoots an average of 85 will sometimes shoot a 75 and sometimes a 95, although most of the scores will be somewhere around 85. Even an occasional 72 or a 97 would not be totally unexpected. Such variability in all things is a fact of life.

For any process, whether it's bowling, golf, or lawn mower no-starts, the factors, all of the inputs and events, that cause this normal variability in outputs are called *common causes of variability*. Common causes of variability are all of the influences typically present in a situation. The common causes of score variability in golf are factors such as differences between one ball and another (even of the same brand), small unnoticed changes in grip and swing, changes in wind, temperature, concentration, attitude, motivation (whether bets are on), familiarity with the course, general physical condition and attitude of the golfer, and so on.

In any given round, these common causes (and many others) will more or less balance out, and the outcome of the process will be a score that's most often somewhere around the golfer's average. If, say, the golfer was up a little late and the course is a little wetter than he or she is used to, the final score may be a little on the high side of the average if all of the other common causes of variability balance out.

Special causes of variability are either causes that are not normally present or common causes that are dramatically different, thereby becoming special causes. When special causes are present in a process, the output would be expected to change dramatically. For example, if a golfer were to use a brand new set of clubs or had not had much sleep for the past 2 nights, you'd expect that the score might be significantly higher. Of course, it might not be; you'd have to look at the score. This is a key point.

AMERICAN SAMURAI INSIGHT

The presence or absence of a common or special cause of variability cannot be determined by definition; it can only be determined by analysis of the process output.

For example, many sports enthusiasts will swear by a new piece of equipment, such as a ball, glove, new type of bicycle wheel, and so on. They honestly believe that "it" really makes a difference. They are claiming that it is a "special cause" of variability in their performance, that it will have some effect on the process outcome (just as the plant manager believes that his actions changed the no-start situation). People who make these claims are sincere, but they often make them without any real understanding of the nature of random variability. Let's take a look at the lawn mower no-start data in a way that will permit us to graphically observe the variability of the process and determine whether any special causes of variability were present during the 15 days for which we had data.

STATISTICAL PROCESS CONTROL CHARTS

A statistical process control (SPC) chart is one that displays data over time and determines whether conditions are changing with respect to the way they are expected to occur. We'll develop one type of control chart, a P (proportion) chart, for the no-start data. The data for the entire 15 days is shown in Table 8-5.

If the daily proportion of no-starts for each of the 15 days is plotted, the result is the graph shown in Figure 8-1. Tradition favors the use of proportions, rather than percentages on this chart. We'll show proportions on the charts to be "pure," but we'll speak of the data in terms of percentages. There are several features of this P chart that are different from a typical frequency polygon.

Note the center line, marked CL, passing through the middle of the P chart. The center line shows the average percent of no-starts for the entire 15 days. The average is 10.6% (10.55% to be exact) no-starts for all 15 days.

From the preceding discussions (and your own intuition), you realize that there's no reason to expect that each day's no-starts will be exactly 10.6%. Some fluctuation about the overall average would be expected, even if nothing extraordinary occurred. And that's just what the P chart shows. On day 9, no-starts were at their highest, whereas on day 7, they were at their lowest. On only 2 days (days 5 and 10) did the number of no-starts come close to the average of 10.6%.

Table 8-5.
No-start data for days 1 through 15.

Day	Mowers tested	Number of no-starts	Percent of no-starts
1	120	14	12
2	110	13	12
3	105	17	16
4	102	8	8
5	132	13	10
6	129	22	17
7	87	2	2
8	117	5	4
9	101	18	18
10	115	12	10
11	116	14	12
12	145	25	17
13	129	5	4
14	120	10	8
15	87	3	3
Totals	1715	181	10.6

But how much variability is to be expected, and when is the variability too much, or sufficiently strange, to signal that something unusual might be influencing process output? The two dashed lines, the upper control limit (UCL) and the lower control limit (LCL), provide part of the answer. They delineate the upper and lower limits of the variability that can be expected if only common, everyday sources of variation affect the process output; that is, if nothing unusual is happening. When a process output is outside the control limits, it is said to be "out of control."

Control limits on any type of SPC chart are equidistant from each side of the mean (unless one of them "bottoms out" on zero) and encompass the values between which 99.73% of the outputs can be expected to fall under normal circumstances (when only common causes of variability are present). The selection of 99.73% as the proper amount is based on statistical considerations and tradition. For those of you who are interested, the formula for the control limits is: $P \pm 3\sqrt{((P)(1-P))/N}$, where P is the average proportion of no-starts over all the days and N is the average number of mowers tested each day for all the days. For the sake of simplicity, several complications that are involved in the calculation of control limits have been ignored for the purposes of this example.

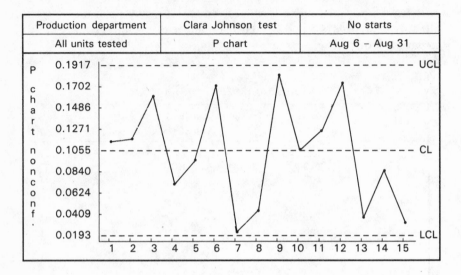

Production department	Clara Johnson test	No starts
All units tested	P chart	Aug 6 – Aug 31

Figure 8-1. P chart of no-starts with mean of 0.1055.

The UCL for proportion of no-starts of 0.1917. Thus, it would take more than 19.17% no-starts on a given day to fall "out of control" on the high side. The LCL is 0.0193. This requires that no-starts be less than 1.93% to fall "out of control," or below, the LCL.

As you can see from the P chart, none of the no-start proportions falls beyond, or outside, the control limits. There are other conditions, not involving points outside the control limits, such as a "run" of seven or more points all above or below the center line, which also indicates that a process is out of control. This, or any type of non-random pattern, indicates that something different (or "special") is preventing normal oscillation about the mean. Thus, for the macro-process of no-starts, the P chart demonstrates that the only sources of variation that are working appear to be the usual everyday things that generate normal variability; that is, only common causes appear to be at work. The conclusion that must be drawn is that the lawn mower no-start process did not fundamentally change over the 15 days.

The plant manager thought he was having an effect, but he did not. The small dips that coincided with his tirades were probably only chance events. If these dips continued for any length of time and/or were more pronounced, they might begin to represent a non-random pattern and you might be able to conclude that Mr. Traditional was having an effect on no-starts.

HOW TO USE SPC THE RIGHT WAY

You know from Chapter Seven that lawn mower no-starts are about as extreme a "Clara Johnson" as you can get (after all, that's the definition!). Let's see how we might apply SPC the right way to the lawn mower no-start situation. The first thing we would do is try to discover what the root causes of no-starts are. We check out the root causes by having the repair crew keep track of their failure diagnoses for all no-starts. After 15 days, we might get back a pareto chart like the one shown in Figure 8-2. Keep in mind that we wouldn't get back any decent data unless the people in the repair area trust management, are trained to collect data, and believe that they're not going to get in trouble. Once again, you see how the entire Code hangs together.

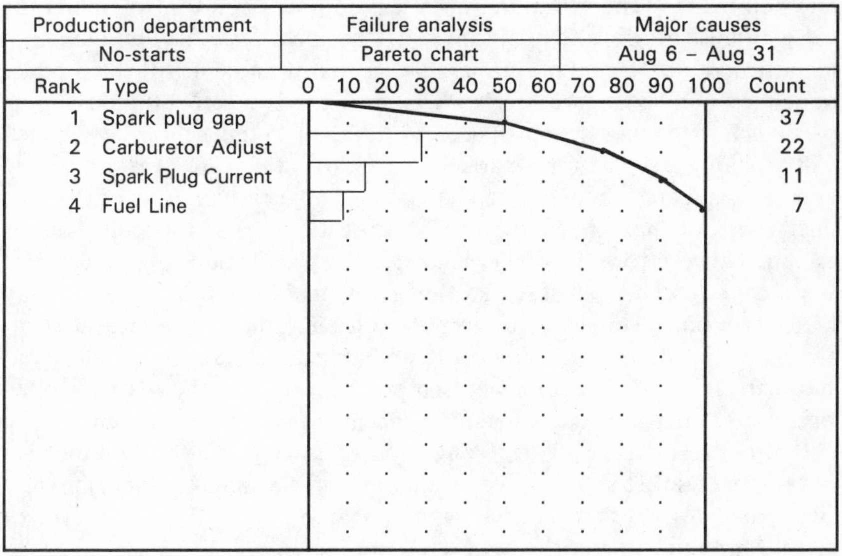

Production department	Failure analysis											Major causes	
No-starts	Pareto chart											Aug 6 – Aug 31	
Rank Type	0	10	20	30	40	50	60	70	80	90	100		Count
1 Spark plug gap													37
2 Carburetor Adjust													22
3 Spark Plug Current													11
4 Fuel Line													7

Figure 8-2 Pareto chart of causes of no-starts.

A pareto chart rank orders, from most to at least frequent, in graphic form, the assigned causes for a specific output. We see that spark plug gap was the biggest hitter in causing no-starts, with 37, which was about 48% of the total number of no-starts. Carburetor adjustments, spark plug current, and fuel line problems accounted for 22, 11, and seven no-starts, respectively. The pareto chart makes it clear that the first place to look in order to fix the no-start problem is the spark plug gap process.

The next step would be to go to the spark plug installation area and study the process by which the spark plug gap is set and the plugs are installed. All of the inputs, events and outcomes of the operations related to spark plug gap would have to be analyzed, which must involve the participation of the workers in the area. People who do not work on a process day-to-day do not understand it well enough to fix it. And if you want the honest help of the people in the area, they must believe that management is not looking for someone to blame for the problems. You can see that this involves a lot more things than just putting up a few SPC charts.

Let's say that you get the cooperation of the people and determine that the problem is the shockingly bad gaps that are already set when the plugs arrive. To this point, the operators had not been setting the gaps or even measuring them. After all, they were ordered with the correct gaps, so why should they be checked? After reading Chapter Seven, you know that the best approach to fixing this problem would be to require the manufacturer to change its process so that the plugs would be perfect without any inspection.

Let's suppose that you call the vendor and he or she promises to do better. You tell the vendor that the specification limits (not control limits) for the gap must be 45 to 55 thousandths of an inch. *Specification limits* are identified values for important parameters that must be met if the product or service is to function correctly. The ideal gap is exactly 50 thousandths of an inch. Anything greater than 55 or less than 45 thousandths of an inch will probably result in a no-start. These specifications are generally set by engineers and are supposed to be based upon objective analyses of the product's performance. In reality, many specifications are simply pulled out of the air. However, we'll assume that our gap specifications are acceptable.

Of course, you're not sure that things will get better immediately or stay better over time. You decide to keep an SPC chart on the gap measurement right in the work area. It's best if the workers can be trained to understand the chart, take the measurements, and put them right on the chart. If someone else has to collect the data and/or update the charts, it's expensive and and often creates a feeling of " 'Big Brother' is watching you" on the part of the workers. Let's say that you train the workers and have them measure five spark plug gaps per hour at random (say one every 12 minutes or so) as they are pulled from the box.

Please note that this approach is much different from the Poka-yoke approach, in which 100% inspection is used to prevent all defects. With SPC charts, there is always some danger of defects getting through. But, if you're starting out from scratch in trying to fix problems, SPC is often the logical first step as you try to locate your biggest problems. As you begin to focus on a problem, source inspection and Poka-yoke techniques should be implemented as soon as root causes are identified.

X Bar and R Charts

After 15 hours of collecting and charting five spark plug gaps per hour, we might have a chart such as the one shown in Figure 8-3. This chart is an

X bar and R chart. "X bar" is a statistical term that stands for average or mean, and "R" stands for range. This SPC chart is a different variety than the P chart we used earlier. It is one of several SPC charts that is a variable chart, or one that measures variable type data. A *variable chart* is used to measure dimensions, weight, pressures, clearances, and anything that has a theoretical true zero and at least equal intervals between numbers.

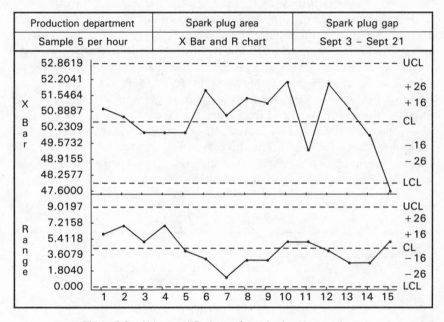

Figure 8-3. X-bar and R chart of spark plug gap settings.

The P chart we looked at earlier is one of several attribute charts. *Attribute charts* assess the presence or absence of characterisics, most often defective versus nondefective, pass versus fail, scratched versus not scratched, etc. Variable charts are more powerful because they tend to be closer to the key micro-processes that cause problems. Attribute charts are useful for assessing general situations, but they generally don't help in identifying root causes.

You can see that the X bar and R chart has two graphs: the top one for the averages or means (X bars), and the bottom one for the ranges. The center line (CL) for each chart represents the average for each statistic, just as it did in the P chart. The center line in the top chart is the overall average (often called the grand mean) for all of the spark plug gaps covered by the 15 hours. The center line in the bottom, or range, chart is the overall average of all ranges. Both charts have upper (UCL) and lower (LCL) control limits.

The upper and lower control limits for the X bar section of the chart are 52.8619 and 47.9381 thousandths of an inch, respectively. The upper and lower control limits for the range section of the chart are 9.0197 thousandths of an inch and zero, respectively. The control limits on these charts are calculated with different formulas, but they do the same thing that the control limits of the P chart did. They delineate the values between which you expect to find 99.73% of all outputs generated by common cause sources of variability.

You can see that the mean for the first five is 51 thousandths of an inch. This mean was obtained by taking the five measurements for the first hour, adding them up, and dividing by five, as shown in Table 8-6. You can see that this hourly mean is slightly above the overall average (or grand mean) of 50.4 thousandths of an inch, but within the control limits.

Ranges are calculated by taking the absolute value (no plus or minus signs) of the highest score in one sample and subtracting the lowest score. A *sample* is whatever set of measurements are used to generate each point on the chart; in this case it's the five measurements taken each hour. For the first hour, the largest gap was 54 thousandths of an inch and the smallest was 49 thousandths of an inch. The difference was 6 thousandths of an inch. As the lower graph on the chart (the range) shows, this range was below the upper control limit of 9.0197 thousandths of an inch.

Table 8-6.
Calculation of statistics for X bar and R chart.

Measurement	Hour one	
1	53	Mean = $\dfrac{\text{Total}}{5}$ = $\dfrac{255}{5}$ = 51.0
2	48	
3	54	
4	51	Range = highest − lowest = 54 − 48 = 6.0
5	49	
Total	255	

As Figure 8-3 shows, the process remains in control for both the range and the mean until hour 15. In this type of chart, it is important that both the sample averages and ranges stay within their respective control limits. Everything looks fine on this chart (even though it's two charts, it's still called "a chart") until hour 15, when the spark plug gap means falls "out of control" to 47.6 thousandths of an inch, below the lower control limit of 47.9381 thousandths of an inch. This indicates that something has caused the sample mean to deviate more than it would be expected to change if only common causes of variability were influencing spark plug gap. Thus, something special has occurred (it doesn't matter if you know what happened or not; the data is telling you that something happened). You can see that the mean is out of control whereas the range is not. The process is out of control for a specific period when either the mean or the range for that period is out of control; both are equally significant.

The power of this type of chart, when used properly, is that as soon as the out of control condition is detected, the worker can take action to correct the situation and/or notify the proper personnel. This prevents additional defective output from being produced. As control charts get "closer" to the root causes of problems, and as the sampling period approaches real time, SPC techniques begin to look a lot like the Poka-yoke that set off alarms—bad output is immediately halted.

It's important to realize that the out of control condition on hour 15 simply means that something is changing; it is sort of like an alarm. You can see that even when it's out of control on hour 15, the mean of the sample is well within the specifications of 45 to 55 thousandths of an inch. The process is still producing "good" output (the five scores for the hour were 50, 45, 46, 47, and 50 thousandths of an inch), but something changed. The danger is that the process will continue to change if the special cause is not identified.

The out of control condition doesn't have any relationship to "good" or "bad"; it simply signifies change. In fact, if a process has been producing continuous and consistently bad output (meaning that it's in control), it's possible (and desirable) to have an out of control condition occur so that things suddenly improve. Then, the appropriate action should be to quickly analyze the situation in order to identify the special cause that created the good results so that the special cause can be made into a common cause.

Using SPC Effectively

There are other types of control charts, but they all do the same thing—they monitor processes and signal when the process has changed. There are several keys to effective use of SPC:

1. The charts must be used to monitor the key inputs and events of micro-processes. This is hardly ever done. If you look around in most companies that claim to have an "SPC program," you'll find a lot of charts being kept on "Clara Johnsons," macro-process outputs such as final test pass-fails. An easy way to spot an epidemic of Clara Johnsonism is to note what type of charts are in the majority. If there are a lot of attribute-type charts, such as P, NP, C, and U charts, then you can be sure you're in macro-process measurement land. These are all charts that have one graph on the chart. All of the attribute charts simply monitor numbers or proportions of good versus bad or number of defects. They are thus end of the line graphs, used where final outcomes are assessed.

   Many companies get stuck on the attribute chart phase of an SPC effort because attribute charts fit in with the old philosophy of finding fault ("Mistakes by others are a chance to look good," "Employees are a pain in the ass") and managing by results. Attribute charts, if used alone, are simply an updated way of the same old management by macro-process results.

2. The charts must be kept close to the process they are measuring. Too many organizations keep these charts in a notebook on the bottom shelf of some manager's office and update them once a week. Worse than worthless, these are a waste of time and labor. Keeping control charts anywhere but at the process they're tracking is like having a fire alarm for your house sound in another house 5 miles away. By the time they finally get the message to you, your house has burned down.

3. The workers who perform the process must be the same ones who record the data on the charts. It is not necessary for them to calculate control limits, but they should do their own sampling and update the charts.

4. The workers who perform the process must be instructed in proper responses to out of control conditions. What do they do with the material? Whom do they call? How can they make the adjustments (if possible)? All of this must be written down and explained clearly. Any necessary training must be provided.

STATISTICS IS ONLY A TOOL

A lot of people, especially new converts, get carried away by SPC. They believe that SPC charts will transform industry. Wrong. SPC is only a tool, much like a hammer. Hammers are important when you're building a house, but a house could be built without one. It would be difficult and costly, most likely, but it could be done. An organization can be transformed without SPC techniques, but it's not easy.

At the same time, it's easy to use SPC incorrectly. We've already seen it in our example. Just having a hammer alone (whether you can use it properly or not) doesn't turn you into a carpenter, an architect, or a building contractor. A hammer won't even cut a board (very neatly, anyway).

SPC is one of many tools, such as Poka-yoke and a number of others we'll be looking at in later chapters, that must be applied under the rubric of The Code of the American Samurai. As an American Samurai, you have many weapons. The largest part of your mission is to have the courage to apply them and the wisdom to select the most appropriate weapon for each challenge. You already have the courage, and shortly you'll have the wisdom.

9

Employees are the Number One Natural Resource

Coda 4. Employees are every organization's most valuable resource; when they do not do a good job, it is almost always management's fault.

This Coda takes us to the crux of the issue; right down where The Code lives. If this Coda is not adopted as a fundamental tenet of management, an organization will not be able to achieve maximum competitiveness, regardless of how well the other Coda are implemented. (If this Coda were to be aggressively implemented, the spirit of most of the other nontechnical Coda would appear.) More than any other, this Coda provides a solid foundation upon which the others operate. Yet, it is this Coda that is most actively and emotionally resisted by the traditional manager.

You can almost hear millions of American supervisors in our decaying, noncompetitive plants reading this Coda and exclaiming, "It just ain't right!" You can almost see (close your eyes and check it out) their bellies stretching their shirtfronts to the limits of polyester's bursting strength while they shake their heads and scowl. Whereas it's disturbing for many traditional business people to have to accept new concepts and tools such as SPC, poka-yoke, and so on, the smart ones will eventually come around. They'll have to, if they want to survive. The last one on the block to start practicing The Code may very well be the first one out of business.

But even as American management begins to apply some of the new tools, they'll resist the adoption of this Coda with the tenacity of a middle manager defending his or her reserved parking spot. "Consider all those Egg Sucking Pigs, Sub-Humans, and Proto-Humans as the most valuable resource? You have *got* to be kidding me! We've been to college, we live in better neighborhoods, we drive Beemers and Volvos, we stay late at the office, we've been with the company 20 #$%@!*&?# years, and it's *OUR* fault when workers don't do a good job?!? Now just a minute!" they'll whine, "We're the ones who run this place! The employees just work here," they'll contend. Ah, my fellow American Samurai, as you can see, we're in for a long struggle.

THE BASIC ISSUES

The basic issues are simple to state but difficult for many to accept. All employees, not just the brass and not just the hourly workers, are the most important resource of any organization. All levels of employees are equally important *if* they're doing their jobs as The Code specifies. When employees don't do a good job (or, more accurately, when process outputs are not satisfactory), it's almost never the employees' fault.

We'll look at *why* this is true strictly from a logical, objective basis. But since most of the resistance to this Coda is emotional, we'll also take a look at the organizational, psychological, and behavioral influences that perpetuate management's negative view of employees (and vice versa). The long-term consequence of these negative perceptions is the caste system discussed in Chapter Four. As long as this caste system remains a force in American business, this Coda will not be widely practiced and American business will not be competitive with those who have seen the light.

Part of the issue is that managers in traditional organizations think that they are better than other types of employees. Nobody who has seen the difference between an executive dining room and the employee cafeterias of a large corporation can argue that point. But an equally important, more subtle issue is the one that values machines, automation, computers, and capital more than employees of any kind.

THE OBJECTIVE FACTS—WHO DOES MOST OF THE WORK?

When Management's Away . . . The Mice Bust Their Tails

Have you ever been working in an organization when almost all of the management went off-site to a conference, training session, or meeting? Ever notice what happens back at the ranch when there are only a few gods or Human Beings left on executive row? Business as usual. In fact, more work generally gets done because the employees are happy that management is finally off their backs for a few hours. Just think about it; all of the brass can stay away for weeks at a time. The carpeted splendor of mahogany (teak, walnut, etc.) row can be silent except for the sound of disproportionate numbers of idle support staff doing their nails and sipping coffee. The executive parking spots can stand empty, swept only by the cold stares of employees trekking in from the satellite lots in the next state. And yet, all is not silent!

Leave the deserted, paneled luxury of executive row and descend into the warrens of the plant or office. There, even in the absence of second-to-second supervision by upper (or any) management, hordes of Sub-Humans and Egg Sucking Pigs toil amidst the cracked linoleum floors, cold concrete, bent up old steel desks, grimy bathrooms, too few computers, and no support staff.

Everything is still working—people coming and going on time, material being received, phones being answered, orders being taken, paper work moving through the system, and customer problems being handled.

Lest you think it's a charade, walk around to the back of the plant and check it out. What do you see? Trucks pulling up and product being loaded. Miracle of miracles—the business operates without management being there to point out that somebody got back 5 minutes late from lunch or that one of the workers left for an unauthorized bathroom break.

And Yet, When a Few Mice Are Away

Now, contrast this to what happens in a large plant when hunting season starts, when there's a flu epidemic, or when a snowstorm hits. All of a sudden there are not enough Egg Sucking Pigs and Sub-Humans. You've got management types running all over the place looking worried and tampering as they sputter and moan, but you can't get the product out the door. In car, truck, steel, electronics, and shoe plants, there have been thousands of times when, for the lack of a mere 10 to 15 Egg Sucking Pigs, whole departments or plants have had to shut down for the day or the week. And employees are *not* the most valuable resource? Come on, wake up and smell the coffee. (By the way, out in the plant, you have to pay for it; it's gratis on executive row, and somebody else, generally an opposite sex support staffer, will be sent to fetch it for you.)

Look at It from a Micro-Process Viewpoint

The preceding is predictable when you look at business from a process perspective. We can talk about macro-process outputs such as profits, units shipped, ROI, and so on, but the work that generates these results gets done at a micro-process level. And if you simply count up the number of discrete, hands-on micro-processes that are performed by various levels of personnel, you quickly find that lower-level employees do almost all of the work on micro-processes.

AMERICAN SAMURAI INSIGHT

The micro-processes that make a business run are largely performed by lower-level employees. Management's role in these processes should be one of assisting the workers to do a better job, not tampering in the process itself.

We'll talk more about the specific roles of management and employees when we discuss Coda 7 and 8 in Chapters Twelve and Thirteen, respectively. Once you look at micro-processes, it's clear that management's denigration of employees' relative value is ridiculous.

The traditional manager just can't deal with this concept. He or she has been thoroughly brainwashed by the traditions of the business world that says that management people are different and better than workers. Workers *are* different, but only because of the way the system treats them and the way in which they're forced to react.

BASIC PSYCHOLOGICAL CONCEPTS

Dr. Deming, bless his heart, says that one of the most important requirements for the transformation of American business is a profound knowledge and understanding of psychology. I'll vote for that! Let's take a quick look (this isn't a psychology textbook) at some of the fundamental concepts of human and organizational behavior that determine how people and systems behave so that we can understand why workers usually come up short in a priority ranking of business assets.

The Basic Nature of People

If you ask the executives of an organization how they would describe their bask work characteristics, you'd get a list like the following:

> Creative
> Flexible
> Honest
> Seek a sense of achievement in their accomplishments
> Open to new ways of doing things (Sure, we've all seen this atti-
>   tude in management a lot, right?)
> Take pride in their work
> Enjoy meaningful work
> Need little supervision
> Like to know what's going on
> Seek responsibility
> Like to feel "in" on things or involved

Very flattering and very positive. And probably true (from their perspective). And if you were to ask the rank and file to characterize themselves, you'd get much the same sort of thing. Everybody feels this way about themselves. And, for most people, that's the way they are, or try to be. I've never met anyone who contended that they were inflexible, not creative, dishonest, etc.; you get the point.

Yet, in organizations, most people aren't permitted to act according to their natural inclinations and demonstrate these characteristics. For example, how many workers on an assembly line are ever given the opportunity to "need little supervision"? Not many. They get tons of supervision every day, whether they need it or not. And how many clerical personnel in an insurance company are given opportunities to be creative and flexible in how they do their jobs? For most of them, any deviation from the rigid standards, even if it's in the name of customer satisfaction, means immediate trouble. Almost everybody in every company likes to know what's going on and to feel "in" on things. Yet, how many organizations provide the rank and file employees with even the most basic operating information about costs, scrap, rework, or future business prospects? Almost none.

Few Sub-Humans and Egg Sucking Pigs (and not all that many Proto-Humans) are included in the distribution of data such as cost per sale, total cost per labor hour (loaded with all costs), scrap costs, etc. Why? The common refrain is, "They wouldn't understand," "They aren't interested," or "They don't care." Wrong. Of course, some don't understand, some aren't interested, and some don't care, but then, neither do some vice-presidents.

Yet, when management asks employees to work harder to reduce costs, everybody wonders why the lower-level employees often don't take it seriously. How could they? They have no basis on which to make any type of an assessment. Then, when these employees respond sarcastically to entreaties to work harder or when output doesn't get better (how could it if no processes change?), management throws up its hands and says, "Well, what do you expect from Egg Sucking Pigs, anyway? That's just the way they are!" This reinforces management's inclination not to share information, and it perpetuates the "they aren't as good as us" attitude, which leads to more cynicism on the part of the Egg Sucking Pigs, and so on, in a vicious circle— the death spiral of American business.

SELF-FULFILLING PROPHECIES
PERPETUATE THE CASTE SYSTEM

The statement in the preceding paragraph is part of the continuous, repeating cycle of a *self-fulfilling prophecy*. A self-fulfilling prophecy occurs when person A's expectations influence person B's behavior such that person A's expectations are fulfilled. Traditional managers scoff at this concept because they claim that such "psychological" nonsense doesn't influence them. Wrong.

The evidence is overwhelming as to the effect that self-fulfilling prophecies have on behavior. Almost any time a person or group is led to believe that they are winners, they'll win more often than they'll lose. Almost any time a person or group is led to believe that they are losers, sure enough, they'll lose. If a teacher is led to believe (as part of a research study) that a group of average students is very smart, not only will the teacher rate them higher at the end of the school year, but the students will do better on standardized tests than a control group of similar students who were portrayed as "normal" students.

This "good" self-fulfilling prophecy happens because the teachers sends verbal and nonverbal signals of encouragement and confidence to the students that he or she believes are smart. It's a fact that simply giving a student a few seconds to think after calling on him or her will dramatically increase the probability of a correct response. Some people just need the time to get focused. If the teacher thinks the student is smart, the extra time will gladly be given. There are all sorts of similar, subtle, small behaviors, such as smiles and compliments for trying, that are given to perceived "winners" that generate consequent positive improvements in performance.

Groups of sales people who are told that they are superior and special and who are led by a manager who reinforces this perception will be outstanding achievers. At the same time, if members of a group of sales people are told that they are substandard, they will meet this expectation. How might this work? When a person feels like a failure, he or she will attempt to avoid more humiliation. For a salesperson, this might mean not making as many sales calls (and thus avoiding rejection) or not "pushing too hard" in a sales call for the same reason. Persons with high self-esteem, on the other hand, will boldly plow ahead and take the risk. If they succeed, their confidence will be enhanced. If it doesn't work, the failure is blamed on something besides themselves, and the salesperson moves on to the next challenge.

As Eliza Doolittle, in George Bernard Shaw's *Pygmalion*, said:

> "You see, really and truly, apart from the things anyone can pick up (the dressing, and proper way of speaking, and so on), the difference between a lady and a flower girl is not how she behaves, but how she's treated. I shall always be a flower girl to Professor Higgins, because he always treats me as a flower girl, and always will; but I know I can be a lady to you, because you always treat me as a lady, and always will."

There's no doubt about it—to a large extent, you get what you expect from workers. So, what do most traditional managers expect from their employees? Nothing but trouble, most often. Few will say it openly, however, because they know that executive management would be angry if anyone did not spout the company line about "beloved" employees and the "dignity of man."

However, you can get down to the truth about what an organization thinks about its people simply by observing how it treats them. If you consider the punitive and demeaning practices that are behind the caste system, you quickly arrive at the following list of management perceptions about employees:

Don't like work and will avoid it
Are doers rather than thinkers
Aren't creative
Don't enjoy meaningful work
Avoid responsibility
Seek security above all else

Must be closely supervised
Don't take pride in a job well done

Just think for a minute: if all of the thousands of micro-processes in an organization were being done by workers with these characteristics, how could any organization stay in business?

CONTROL MECHANISMS ARE DEMEANING

Yet, if you look at the policies and procedures that are used to manage the work lives of most employees, it's clear that the preceding negative characteristics are operational. For example, in most companies, Egg Sucking Pigs get fewer sick days than Proto-Humans and Human Beings. The argument for this is that if you allow Egg Sucking Pigs to have more sick days, they're so lazy they'll use them to avoid work. Yet, we all know managers and executives who seem to be out sick at least a day or two every month without anyone saying a word.

Take time cards (please). In most organizations, only the Egg Sucking Pigs have time cards and/or buzzers to tell them when to take a break or eat lunch. Why? Well, we all know what happens when "they" are not closely supervised. Yet, the suspicion that people in general can't be trusted results in many organizations having time cards for all employees, up to and including the Human Beings. Even though most personnel at the Proto-Human and above level don't have to punch a clock, the cards are still there, just to let everyone know that they're being "watched." This sort of passive reminder is not only demeaning and insulting, but expensive. Organizations that use time cards spend thousands, sometimes tens of thousands, of dollars per month to tally and check time cards. It's all pure profit lost. An exception system (employees submit paper work only if they are not at work for some reason) would save the largest part of that loss. Yet, organizations still insist on keeping the cards because they don't want to lose the control.

It's interesting (in a nauseating sort of way) to note that even in those organizations in which time cards are a tradition for all personnel in operating units, including division presidents, you'll usually find that they don't have them at corporate headquarters, not even for support staff. If you ask why, you usually get an answer along the lines of, "Well (arrogant sniff), *we* don't need them here. We are (arrogant sniff) professionals." Right.

The irony is that good employees are turned bad by a system that treats them as if they were lazy bums. Management tightens up on the controls, and the employees resent it and express their displeasure in "safe" ways. Management sees the resistance and claims it as justification for its original behavior, and off you go—a self-fulfilling prophecy that eats up profits and productivity.

I'VE GOT YOUR LAZY . . . SWINGING

When I was working for Ford, I happened to bump into an hourly employee I knew one day when the lines were shut down for lunch. I knew he was assigned to a job toward the end of the line, but he was carrying a bunch of parts for windshield wiper motors, something that's put on earlier in the assembly process. I walked along with him and asked what he was doing.

He told me that he had once worked in the area that put the windshield wiper motors on the fire walls of the trucks. He said that he had taken great pride in the way his area had done their jobs but that he wasn't happy now. New people were doing it and doing it wrong. He stopped by a truck and pointed at a wiper motor. "See that? Wrong brackets. For a different motor. Forces a crimp in the hose and then the wiper won't work. You catch a few of them in test, although we don't test 'em all. I can't see it happening to a customer. We get few enough orders as it is." He explained that he had mentioned the problem to the workers who did it, but they kept changing jobs so often it didn't do any good. He said that he had also tried to tell a process engineer and several supervisors about it, but nothing ever happened (nothing ever does in a traditional work environment).

So, he explained, during lunch, he would walk over to the bracket area, get a handful of brackets, and then walk the line during lunch, fixing as many as he could. When I told him that what he was doing was great and that I'd like to spread the word, possibly in the company paper, he was aghast. "Don't do that! I'll be a cast out around here if anybody thinks I'm suckin' up to management. I'm just trying to build a good truck. My job is riding on it." Some Egg Sucking Pig, eh? You can see that this guy should have been more closely supervised during lunch, to keep him in his area so that he wouldn't be out making trouble. Who created this environment in which a worker has to hide the fact that he's making an extra effort to turn out a quality product? Not the employees.

AMERICAN SAMURAI INSIGHT

> **Businesses run in spite of typically short-sighted and abusive management because the lower-level workers, the Sub-Humans and Egg Sucking Pigs, shoulder their outrage and humiliation and still try to do the best job they can.**

Whose Fault Is It, Anyway?

A key part of this Coda states that when an employee doesn't do a good job, it's management's fault. Fault is an important concept in American business, so let's deal with it right now. As we discovered in our discussion of Coda 1 in Chapter Six, most managers, when there's an unfavorable macro-process output, automatically seek a repository for the blame that is roaring down the management hierarchy like a ton of manure down a loading chute. Because of the caste system, the most common recipient for this blame is the Egg Sucking Pig closest to the spot at which the problem was discovered (which may be nowhere near the micro-process that generated the problem). This is the mechanism by which the time-honored tradition of "killing the messenger" arose; you've got to blame somebody, so why waste time looking? Just save time and grab whoever is handy. Handy, but stupid and damaging, as you now realize.

Let's do two things here. First, let's see if blaming someone does any good. Then, let's see who's really at fault for work-related problems. What's the purpose in blaming someone for a mistake? It should be a desire to reduce the probability that the mistake will occur again. We'll assume that most people are not trying to make mistakes and that most mistakes happen for a variety of reasons ranging from forgetfulness to poor training to carelessness. If someone does not know they have made a mistake, such as putting a part on backwards because they didn't realize which end was the "front," they need to know the right way so that they won't continue to produce bad output. Simply pointing out the error isn't blaming, it's information. If statements such as, "Why did you do that?," "What's the matter with you, anyway?," "That was a pretty stupid thing to do," or "If you do it again, you're in trouble" are attached to the information, then it's a blame. What's the point?

A blame is a deliberate attempt to use embarrassment or humiliation to punish an employee for a mistake. As we saw earlier in this chapter, this will only serve to lower the employee's self-esteem and perpetuate the employee's perception of management as a bunch of arbitrary clowns (how many middle managers can you get in a Nash?).

AMERICAN SAMURAI INSIGHT

Fixing blame serves no purpose other than to allow supervisors to release pent-up frustration and anxiety on defenseless employees. Supervisors should never be allowed to use the phrase, "It's your fault," for any purpose.

Let's assume that the employee gets a good old-fashioned, screaming, ranting and raving, ripping the phones off the wall blaming (if you haven't worked in a car or truck plant, you haven't seen anything near world–class management tantrums). Assuming that the employee didn't make the mistake on purpose, how does dropping a load of blame change the micro-process inputs and events that led to the mistake in the first place? Only for the worse. If the employee was doing the best job he or she could, blaming him or her doesn't improve any of the inputs or events that influence the micro-process output. All that will be changed will be the employee's morale and self-esteem, both for the worse, possibly resulting in less attentiveness and enthusiasm. This will most likely lead to other problems such as increased absenteeism, more sick time, and additional inadvertent errors. All because management decided to kick the dog instead of doing something constructive.

If we look at micro-process inputs and events, we'll find that management, not employees, has control. If there is a problem with an input or event, it's management's fault in a traditional work environment (in an American Samurai type environment, nobody would waste time finding fault). In fact, management controls practically everything (in terms of initiating change and/or setting establishing conditions) in a traditional work environment. Table 9-1 presents various inputs and events and describes management's role in each.

Table 9-1.
Typical inputs and events and
management's role in them.

Input/event	Who controls/determines/selects
People	Management selects, hires, supervises and trains
Materials	Management selects
Machines	Management selects/dictates resources, maintenance, allocations
Energy	Management driven or a given
Procedures	Management designs and enforces
Environmental factors	Management driven or a given
Computers	Management selects/dictates resources, maintenance, allocations
Policy	Management sets, enforces
Forms	Management selects
Corporate culture	Resullt of all the above—management driven
People do something	Management determines training, level of skills required, assistance given
Machines do something	Management selects and dictates use
Social changes	Result of above or extraneous forces
Environmental changes	Extraneous forces if not management set (such as air conditioning, etc.)

Given the information in Table 9-1, how can anyone in their right mind contend that employees are responsible for most inadvertent errors in process outputs? Employees *wish* they had that much input and control!

AMERICAN SAMURAI INSIGHT

Seventy percent to 95% of micro-process outputs are determined by the overall system in which the process operates. As long as the system is not changed, the outputs will remain relatively constant regardless of the people working the process.

Whereas extraordinary individuals can sometimes change the system (for better or for worse), the plain fact is that the systems in which we work put tremendous limits on what we can do. In most companies, if you removed all the people and replaced them with another group with similar experience and training, system outputs would probably stay about the same (after things settled down). If an employee is making errors on a job, a new, similarly skilled employee, given the same amount of training, will generally make the same types of errors.

So don't even think about blame; it's a waste of energy and time, and it only makes the situation worse. When mistakes occur, a search should be launched for a root cause.

He Ain't Heavy (Equipment); He's Your Egg Sucking Pig

Let's suppose that somebody offered the chief executives of the big three car makers a machine that would improve the efficiency and the quality of every process in all of their operations by 20%. This machine would simply be placed in the middle of any plant or office complex, plugged in, and every process within 500 yards would be miraculously improved by 20%. Even if each machine cost 10 million dollars, it's a fair bet that even automotive executives would be smart enough (OK, OK, *some* would be smart enough) to realize that each machine would pay for itself in a year.

This machine would sell because it would appeal to the traditional manager's fondness for easy, technology-based solutions. Machines are easy to deal with, people aren't. Since most managers have been taught to arrange numbers, engineer things, do case studies, buy equipment and so on, that's how they attempt to fix things. We'll talk more about this tendency to go for the technology when we get to Coda 16 in Chapter Twenty-one. On the other hand, people seem complex, unpredictable, and ornery. It's hard to deal with them (given how they're treated, what else could we expect?), so everybody avoids it.

The problem is that no machine will ever be able to simultaneously improve all the micro-processes in an organization. Processes are worked at the micro-process level. Lower-level employees carry out most of the micro-processes. Therefore, if you want to fix, or improve, any or all of your micro-processes, you have to do it through the people who do the processes. There's no other way. Even if the rank and file employees and Proto-Humans in your organization really were stupid, vile, clumsy, brutish oafs, they'd be *your* stupid, vile, clumsy, brutish oafs, and you'd have to work through them to make any changes. Even if they were the worst there are, they're the most important resource you've got because they affect every micro-process. And since every business is really nothing more than a bunch of micro-processes, the folks who run them are the most vital asset of any business.

It's time for American business to wake up to this basic, simple fact before it's too late. Take the message to them, my fellow American Samurai.

10

Quality Isn't Number One—
It's The Only One!

Coda 5. **Quality of product and service, not volume, sales, or profits, must come before all other considerations.**

Quality is a big topic in American business these days. Every other executive is loudly proclaiming that they are "for" quality and that nothing is more important than quality in their company. Some of them are lying outright, of course, but most of them mean well. The problem is that they have no concept of what quality really is and even less understanding of what it would take to attain it in their organizations. In fact, most of them would be happy if the whole quality frenzy would just go away so that they could "get back to business" (assuming that their domestic and foreign competitors leave anything for them to go back to).

Why are all of these gods and Human Beings talking about quality? Because everybody else is. They'd like to have it, whatever it is, but most of them are only after it because they can't very well be against it and still make a good impression on consumers and stockholders. In today's world of 30–second "news" stories and 10–second "sound bites," everybody in business jumps on whatever bandwagon is passing through in order to be fashionable. Quality is the latest bandwagon. Meanwhile, while they talk about quality, they continue to do business the old way, the way that's not working.

LET'S GET ONE THING STRAIGHT

Quality is the number one determinant of business success. Real quality, that is, not end-of-the-line, inspect it to death, try to find enough product to ship quality. Businesses that have attained world-class quality (their products can compete anywhere) don't do it to be fashionable; they do it to make money. The bottom line is that attending to quality first, in every process, pays off on the bottom line.

This concept of quality is largely misunderstood in the traditional management environment. Quality is usually thought of in terms of the final product—a macro-process output view of quality. If the final product is good, quality is good. Now that you understand the difference between a Clara Johnson (defect detection) and defect prevention, you know that the battle is over by the time the "name goes on"; all of the costs are already "cooked into" the product (not to mention the fact that inspection will invariably miss some defects, which will reach the customers).

QUALITY DOESN'T MEAN JUST FIXING MISTAKES OR PREVENTING THEM

There's another cost to this failed view of quality that's not so apparent. Over and above the profit losses created by rework and repair, there are other, larger losses incurred by the traditional approach to quality. If a plant is working well and turning out good quality products, there is little incentive to examine processes to improve them. The guiding principles of "Don't take chances," "Volume takes care of everything," "Do not deliver bad news," "Decisions are made at the top," "Mistakes by others are a chance to look good," "You can't change City Hall," and "If it ain't broke, don't fix it" operate to keep everybody focused on pumping out the goods and attending only to disastrous problems. As a result, opportunities for tremendous improvements in efficiency and profitability are never explored unless they happen to manifest themselves with a great many defects. A comprehensive, enlightened, American Samurai approach to quality focuses on all possible improvements, not just large defect reduction opportunities.

THE MALCOLM BALDRIGE NATIONAL QUALITY AWARD

One blueprint for such a comprehensive approach to quality is outlined by the judging criteria of The Malcolm Baldrige National Quality Award. This award was established in August 1987 by the U.S. Congress to foster a quality-oriented philosophy in American business. The Baldrige, as it's commonly called, was named in honor of the late Secretary of Commerce, Malcolm Baldrige, who was killed in a rodeo accident (he was an amateur cowboy) as Congress was debating the award legislation.

The Baldrige is analogous to Japan's Deming Award, in that the award represents the embodiment of world-class quality. It's tough to win one. The usual glossy, filled with cream puffs, corporate snow job of documentation doesn't impress the Baldrige examiners. The first step for applicants is to prepare a written application. Larger companies must pay $2500 and submit a 75-page package of data. Smaller companies pay $1000 and submit a 50-page package. Some companies that have won have had to spend hundreds of thousands of dollars and put together teams of ten to 20 people to gather data and compile the report.

The written data is reviewed by a rotating panel of industry experts who rate each response in over 100 areas of quality operations. The theoretical top score is 1000 points. Companies that earn more than 601 points are visited by a team of four to six raters. During the on-site visit, the raters talk with employees, review data and processes, and generally verify that the written claims are being practiced. The raters then submit their ratings and their subjective impressions and evaluations to a panel of nine judges. The judges review all of the recommendations and then pass their recommendations for award to the Secretary of Commerce, who makes the final selection.

In 1988, there were 66 written applications submitted and 13 site visits made. Three companies—Motorola, Globe Metallurgical, and the Commercial Nuclear Fuel Division of Westinghouse—won the award in 1988. In 1989, only 40 companies applied. Word was beginning to get around that the Baldrige was no cakewalk. Ten of them earned on-site vists, and awards were made to two—the Business Products and Systems Division of Xerox and Milliken and Company.

The criteria that are used to judge the award pretty much sum up what a company must do to attain world-class quality. The seven categories (with the total possible point value) are:

1. *Leadership* (120 points). The extent to which senior management has been successful in creating and sustaining a quality culture.
2. *Information and Analysis* (60 points). The effectiveness of the organization's efforts to collect and analyze information for quality improvement and planning.
3. *Strategic Planning* (80 points). The extent to which quality requirements are integrated into the organization's business plans.
4. *Human Resources Utilization* (150 points). The success of the organization's efforts to utilize the full potential of all of its employees for quality.
5. *Quality Assurance of Products and Services* (140 points). The extent to which the organization's systems are effective in maintaining quality control of all operations.
6. *Quality Assurance Results* (150 points). The degree of the organization's success, determined by quantitative measures, in improving quality.
7. *Customer Satisfaction* (300 points). The effectiveness of the organization in determining and meeting requirements for customer satisfaction.

As you can see, competing for the Baldrige requires much more than simply defect elimination. It requires a complete transformation of the total organization. All of the sources of inefficiency in the traditional management environment—not just defects—must be eliminated.

The application guidelines for the Baldrige can be obtained by writing or calling the United States Department of Commerce, National Institute of Standards and Technology, Gaithersburg, MD 20899, (301) 975-2036, FAX (301) 948-3716.

THE SEVEN DEADLY SINS

Taichi Ohno, a quality and productivity expert from Toyota, lists the following seven sins, which are routinely committed by traditional manufacturing operations:

1. The waste of making too many units
2. The waste of waiting time at a machine
3. The waste of transporting units
4. The waste of processing waste
5. The waste of inventory
6. The waste of motion
7. The waste of making defective units

The elimination of these seven deadly sins is the true goal of an enlightened quality program. As you can see, only number seven deals specifically with defects, and not in the same way as a defect detection system. The other sins deal with issues that traditional "test the hell out of it" quality methods don't even examine. You could have parts stacked high at each machine (number one), employees standing around waiting for material (number two), forklifts running all over the place (number three), and so on, but a traditional quality program would only focus on finding defects through screening. Even in the face of all this waste, if defect levels were acceptable, the quality program would be deemed successful and no action would be taken to eliminate the root causes of the first six sins.

The waste of making the defects (number seven), that is, the profits lost in making the units themselves, isn't an issue in a traditional quality program. That cost is assumed to be part of the inevitable overhead of the business, such as landscaping and lights. Such an attitude is stupid. Not only can the cost of making defective units be eliminated, the costs incurred by every one of these sins can be dramatically reduced by putting real micro-process–oriented quality before all other considerations. Each and every one of these sins is a critical quality issue. Attacking the micro-process inputs and events that drive these sins always yields incredible cost and quality benefits.

AMERICAN SAMURAI INSIGHT

The "quality" goal of a world-class business is not to eliminate defects. It is to increase profits, win market share, and improve

operations through process improvement efforts of every sort at
the micro-process level. An inevitable side benefit of these efforts
is a decrease in defects.

JUST WHAT IS QUALITY?

Quality definitions run the gamut from complex to homespun. Some definitions focus on specifications (a problem that will be discussed in Chapter
Seventeen, Coda 12), whereas others focus on defect levels. Once you become a fully practicing American Samurai, you won't seek such definitions
because you'll realize there's no point. Quality is a condition, not a thing.
Quality is a result obtained when a process output meets the requirements
of the customers of that process. Since the requirements of customers change
from day to day (or minute to minute), you can't define quality as a set
number of defects per million or as a predetermined percentage of units passing inspection. Quality is a system that can quickly respond to changing
needs. Quality is having made the sacrifices to establish a system that enables
quality processes and products as a result of quality in thousands of micro-
processes. In short, quality *is* managing with The Code of the American
Samurai.

I hope you are beginning to see how all of the Coda hang together. Processes can only be fixed at the micro-process level; that's where quality
"lives." The workers who perform the micro-processes are the only ones
who truly understand what's going on in those processes. Thus, true quality
depends upon the efforts of employees to improve their processes and their
customers' satisfaction.

HOW DOES WORLD-CLASS QUALITY PAY OFF?

Companies that have put quality first have reaped tremendous benefits.
World-class companies (and no company becomes world class without putting quality first) have achieved the following levels of performance in addition to the elimination of defects:

50% to 100%	finished good inventory reduction
70% to 90%	work in process reduction
40% to 70%	space reduction
30% to 50%	capacity increase
70% to 90%	shorter lead times
25% to 60%	overhead reductions
25% to 60%	cost reduction

All of this is achieved through an approach to quality that works at the
micro-process level. The Business Products and Systems Division of Xerox,

a winner of the Baldrige in 1989, claims the following gains from 1984 to 1988 as a result of their push for quality:

Labor overhead	50% decrease
Materials overhead	40% decrease
Days of supply on hand	66% decrease
Invoice adjustments	70% decrease
Retrofit costs	53% decrease

You don't get these benefits by focusing on defects. You get them by focusing on micro-processes and doing whatever is necessary to improve the customer satisfaction of the people the process serves.

Milliken and Company, a carpeting and textile manufacturer, the other 1989 winner of the Baldrige, attained dramatic improvements by putting quality first. From the early 1980s to 1989, they decreased carpet delivery time from 12 weeks to 7 days, increased their product offerings from 300 to 1600, and decreased the minimum order requirement from 100 square yards to 5 square yards. They claim to have missed only one delivery date in all of 1988.

Motorola, a 1988 winner of the Baldrige, was getting only 92% defect-free parts from suppliers in 1982. By the time it won the award, the quality of suppliers was at 99.73%. At the same time, Xerox cut the number of its suppliers from about 4500 to about 450, to whom it awarded all of its business. Several of those 450 have not shipped a single defective part in 3 years. The traditional management approach is to have as many suppliers as possible in order to hold down costs. The enlightened management style is to cut costs by having very few suppliers, each of which is required to pursue American Samurai techniques. We'll discuss supplier issues in detail in Chapter Eighteen (Coda 13).

It's not necessary to win the Baldrige or even compete for it in order to reap the benefits of a comprehensive quality effort. Modern of Marshfield, Inc., is a small (100-employee) custom sofa and sleeper manufacturer. They started down the road to a total quality environment in September 1988. In a little more than a year, with virtually no increase in total sales, they realized the following benefits for fiscal 1989 compared to fiscal 1988:

- 232% increase in cash
- Receivables decreased by 40%
- Long-term liabilities decreased by 25%
- Total liabilities reduced by more than 40%
- Debt-to-equity ratio decreased from 1.8 to 1.0, in an industry in which the median is 1.5
- Increased inventory turnover from about three per year to six

This type of improvement speaks volumes for the benefits of a comprehensive quality effort. Quality first pays off big.

WORLD CLASS IS BETTER QUALITY THAN YOU THINK: CHECK THE NUMBERS!

Whereas a comprehensive quality effort reaps many benefits, often the most visible aspect of performance is defect reduction. Therefore, we must spend a moment discussing defect reduction as an outcome. In the traditional business world, quality is often defined in terms of Acceptable Quality Levels, or AQLs. AQLs essentially specify how bad you can be and still be considered "good," that is, how many defects you can produce and still be considered a good supplier. Typical AQLs are 99% and 99.9%. But even 99.9% isn't as good as it seems. Consider what 99.9% quality would mean in everyday life:

Twenty domestic airlines' planes would crash every day
500 incorrect operations would be performed every week
Almost 4000 prescriptions would be incorrectly filled each week
2.4 billion dollars per week would be credited to the wrong accounts by banks
In a family of four drivers, there would be about five car wrecks per year (with teenagers, this estimate may be way too low)
18,000 pieces of mail would be lost by the Postal Service every hour

So, even though 99.9% "quality" looks good, it wouldn't be good enough for our personal lives. It's even worse in business. What looks like great quality for a single part or process is often shockingly poor when it is part of a complex process. Final throughput yields demonstrate this phenomenon. *Throughput yield* is the percentage of a part or product that is good output. Thus, each process has a throughput yield, which is simply the percentage of process outputs that is OK. *Final throughput yield* is the yield obtained after a number of processes, or after a specific stage of processing.

Table 10-1 presents an example. Suppose we have four tests that a unit has to pass in sequential order in order to be acceptable. Let's say that each test has a 90% success rate (10% fail each test) and that we're going to run 100 units through the test. Table 10-1 is a diagram of the testing process, showing the percent of the unit that passes and fails in each successive test.

Table 10-1.
Throughput yields for four tests.

Yield	Test 1 In	Test 1 90% Pass	Test 2 In	Test 2 90% Pass	Test 3 In	Test 3 90% Pass	Test 4 In	Test 4 90% Pass	Final throughput yield
Units	100	90	90	81	81	73	73	66	66%
Failures		10		9		8		7	

Since we started with 100 units, the numbers of units passing and failing each test, as well as the final throughput yield, are expressed as percentages. Note that 100 units, our starting sample, enter test 1 and that 90 units (90%) pass and 10 (10%) fail. These 90 successful units then enter test 2 and 90% pass (81 units). Thus, only successful units continue down the test sequence. As you can see in the "Final throughput yield" column, even though the "quality" of each test was 90%, the final throughput yield across the four tests was only 66%.

There are several key points here. The first is that it doesn't matter if the "tests" are actually tests, such as resistance tests or paint inspections. It works the same no matter what the process is, parts or tests. The four "tests," or throughput yields, could have simply been four parts, each one coming from a lot that had 10% defectives (90% good), they could have been a mixture of parts and tests, or they could have been all process outcomes (as in administrative processes). If we had an assembly with four parts that was tested three times, there would be seven outputs in the calculation of the final throughput yield if we wished to evaluate the cumulative effects of part quality and testing quality. Seldom, if ever, are yields across processes equal; the equal yields in Table 10-1 were used for demonstration purposes.

The second key point is to notice that the number of repairs is much more than 10% that might be implied by a 90% quality level. Simply after one pass through all four tests, 34% (the total of all of the failures) of the units have to be repaired or reworked. And that's not the end of it. Some of the 34 units will fail subsequent tests when they are retested. And the repairs themselves may cause more defects that aren't even covered by the preceding tests.

This problem becomes severe when the number of parts/processes is very large. There are approximately 2000 parts and processes involved in assembling and testing a TV set. If every part/test has a 99.9% pass rate (1000 defects per million), the final throughput yield of perfect TVs would be only 13.25%! If the quality levels are improved to 99.99% (only 100 defects per million), the final throughput yield would increase to 90%. You can see that individual part and/or test quality has to be extremely high in order to assure that the product is almost perfect (and repair/rework costs remain low). Table 10-2 presents percent throughput yields for various quality levels and the number of parts and processes involved.

As Table 10-2 clearly demonstrates, at least 99.9999% good must be attained at each part and process to assure virtually perfect quality. Even with only one bad part/process in a million (99.9999% good), final throughput yield for 2000 parts/process is only 99.8%. I say only, because although 99.8% sounds great, that's still two defective units in every thousand. With something like TV sets, two bad ones out of a thousand can kill you with customers. Of course, not all defects are make or break the product situations. Many may be defects that affect only fit and finish or defects that the customer will never see (slightly bad solder connections, etc.). The problem is that you can't always distinguish a permissible defect from a killer defect. You have to work to eliminate them all.

Table 10-2.
Final throughput levels for various
part counts and quality levels.

Percent defects each part/ process	Defects per million	Total number of parts and processes in the process					
		10	50	100	500	2000	10,000
95	50,000	60	8	0	0	0	0
99	10,000	91	61	37	< 1	0	0
99.9	1,000	99	95	90	61	37	< 1
99.99	100	99.9	99.5	99	95	90	37
99.9937	63	99.9	99.7	99.4	96.9	88.2	53
99.9999	1	100	100	99.9	99.9	99.8	99
99.9999998	0.002	100	100	100	100	100	100

The quality level throughput shown on the bottom line of Table 10-2 represents something called "six sigma" quality, or a situation in which the $C_{pk} = 2$. This is a situation in which one side of the entire distribution of a process output will fit between the mean of the process and the closest specification limit two times. This level of quality has become the golden chalice of many world-class companies. As you can see, it assures virtually perfect quality.

AMERICAN SAMURAI INSIGHT

At the level of 100 bad parts/processes per million or better (99.9% good), it's virtually impossible to detect bad parts or processes by means of sampling. The only way to achieve this level of quality is to design out defects within the processes by using source inspection, concurrent engineering, and Poka-yoke.

WHAT DOES PUTTING QUALITY FIRST REQUIRE?

Putting quality first means just what it says: nothing must come before quality. Think about what this would mean in the typical business. Everything you see in business operations, plans, and daily paper work concentrates on schedules, volume, units produced, sales, profits, and so on. Quality is an afterthought most of the time. This must change. As you can tell from this chapter, a quality program that is world class is much more than a defect removal system; it is a comprehensive approach to the total working environment.

Curt Reimann, director of the Baldrige Award program at the Department of Commerce, cites the following eight criteria that examiners look for:

1. A detailed plan for continuous improvement of all processes
2. Metrics and a system for monitoring these improvements
3. A strategic plan based on benchmarks that compares the company's performance to the best in the world
4. Supplier partnerships that focus on continuous improvement and lowest total life-cycle costs, not price
5. A proactive and profound understanding of customers that anticipates their needs
6. A lifetime relationship with customers that covers the entire product life
7. A defect-prevention approach
8. A commitment to improve quality that starts at the executive suite and is maintained by all employees

The practice of this management style requires a lot more than a few "work harder" posters and "Quality is Job One" banners hung in the plant. For the typical American business, it will take a complete turnaround of every policy, procedure, and management action. Dr. Deming is fond of saying that, out of the more than 600 persons who attend his 4-day seminar, not more than a handful will ever do anything about what they hear. It's just too much trouble and too hard.

It *is* hard, but the alternative for all too many businesses is obliteration by the competition. It's up to American Samurai to do what we can to make sure that we've done all that can be done to save our own organizations, to wake them up before it's too late.

11

It's Never "Soup Yet" in the World of Process Improvement

Coda 6. **Suboptimization and "management by fire control" must be abandoned and replaced by the implementation of an organized plan for the continuous improvement of key processes with the goal of maximizing customer satisfaction.**

This Coda deals with the manner in which an organization prioritizes the issues to which it attends on a day-to-day basis. We'll talk about suboptimization and management by fire control as evils that degrade quality and drain precious resources. We'll then discuss the important concept of customer satisfaction as the universal process improvement goal. Finally, we'll present the Plan, Do, Check, Act (PDCA) cycle—a process improvement methodology that can be applied to the continuous improvement of all processes.

MANAGEMENT BY FIRE CONTROL

In a typical company, nothing gets attention unless it's a problem for somebody. For example, a lawn mower plant could run at 5% no-starts for decades without anyone saying a word. However, if a new plant manager has a thing about no-starts, all of a sudden it's a problem, even if 5% was, far and away, the best no-start rate in the industry (such a horrible rate couldn't be the best—it's only an example). The no-starts were "a problem" and got attention in our demonstration because the plant manager said they were a problem. If a plant manager with a different "sore" spot had shown up, the 5% no-starts might never have been mentioned. This strategy for allocating attention to issues is nothing more than management by fire control; you wait until a fire breaks out and then you take action, *if* it's sufficiently irritating.

A major drawback of this approach, aside from issues of tampering, is that only a handful of an organization's thousands of processes get any attention. After all, there's a limited amount of management time available—far too little to do more than find and react (by tampering) to a mere handful of problems. Worse yet, the allocation of attention is highly subjective, since it's based solely on the personal reactions of a small number of managers.

Finally, and perhaps most damning, management by fire control permits thousands of processes to operate at low levels of quality and cost-efficiency. If an organization wants to be world class, it can't allow such waste to continue. And that's not all: the massive losses generated by thousands of unattended (in terms of making them better) processes is multiplied by the effects of unrestrained suboptimization.

AMERICAN SAMURAI INSIGHT

Even when everything appears OK in the traditionally run organization, the strong forces of suboptimization and management by fire control are working to degrade the performance of existing processes.

SUBOPTIMIZATION—IF YOU CAN'T BE WORLD CLASS, YOU MIGHT AS WELL HAVE FUN FIGHTING

We mentioned suboptimization in Chapter Four when we were discussing the traditional guiding principle of "The department of work area comes first." You'll recall that suboptimization occurs when departments or areas attempt to maximize their own performance without concern for impacts on other areas or the overall organization's goals. You could say that suboptimization is tampering motivated by a narrow self-interest. Suboptimization is a cancer run wild in the typical organization. Every department or area is out for itself, each trying to look better than the other while the performance of the organization as a whole deteriorates.

People from other departments will gleefully screw you over ten different ways, all the while claiming to be "doing it for the company." What they're really doing is making themselves look good. The finance department in almost any company is a prime example. Just think about it: finance doesn't make anything, they're a pure overhead operation whose purpose is to tally up the numbers and keep operating management informed of financial macro-process results. Yet, in most companies, they have become a law unto themselves, operating solely to improve the appearance of their own macro-process outputs, regardless of the effects their actions have on the overall system.

I've sat in many meetings where finance people manage to veto equipment purchases sought by production, not because of the merits of the equipment relative to processes, but because the finance people held the "opinion" that the equipment wasn't needed. Based on a 5% understanding of manufacturing issue at hand, they're making a decision about what equiment will be operating in the plant for the next 10 years? Could anything be more insane? It happens all the time because finance functions have suboptimized their objectives to the point where many CEOs actually believe that satisfying the finance department is their primary concern. Wrong. Managing by financial results is the best way to drive a company into the ground.

Finance controls one macro-input—money—which influences all the processes of other departments. They attempt to influence other departments' macro-process outputs by varying their one input as they watch last month's macro-outputs. It's much like someone trying to drive a car down a crowded street by manipulating only the gas pedal while watching a replay of what the fuel gauge, not the window, showed 24 hours earlier. Micro-processes cannot be managed or improved from the end of a huge macro-process.

The difficulty is that, given normal variability, it often looks as if "managing by the numbers" works, especially if it's expected to (another self-fulfilling prophecy). Meanwhile, operating units are dying for want of critical funds (or, maybe wasting funds because they really don't need all they were allocated but would never, ever admit it because they'd get their budget chopped even more the next year). Suboptimization strikes again: finance looks great, others suffer.

Of course, all departments are guilty of suboptimization in one way or another. Engineering often earns praise for getting their designs completed early, under budget, or right on time (OK, OK, so it could never happen in real life; it's only an example). Only then does production find that all the design shortcuts make it impossible to build the design with the equipment they have (try telling that to finance!). Suboptimization strikes again. Or, personnel makes itself look great with the brass and the community by launching an internship program for street gang members. While personnel is going to recognition dinners and basking in the glow of "its" new program, manufacturing and maintenance are in deep trouble: they have to eat the added labor hours, added training costs, and other costs incurred by personnel's "great idea." They get beat up at every staff meeting by finance for going "over budget," and the whole operation suffers due to lowered productivity. But personnel looks great; suboptimization strikes again.

How Suboptimization Gets Started

Loyalty to the work group is an entirely natural consequence of normal group dynamics. People have a natural propensity to feel more attracted to, and comfortable with, individuals with whom they have the most in common. One of the most important characteristics is physical proximity. It's largely for this reason that people support professional sports teams in their city, even if they've just recently moved there. Since people in a work area are usually closer to each other than to people from another group, they begin to identify more with their close associates than with people from other areas.

Over time, the group's work practices and policies, the behavior of the boss, and the social customs of the group all begin to differ from those of the organization as a whole. Pretty soon, it's "us" (a department or area) versus "them" (everybody else). This is why work groups will gleefully shaft each other to gain a little, even though it may hurt the overall organization a lot. Of course, because suboptimization has been accepted for so long as the natural order of things, very few managers recognize that the practice is hurting everyone. After all, the business keeps on running even as they battle. True enough in the old days when the customer could be made to eat the losses and take whatever product dropped from such an inefficient system, but not anymore.

Suboptimization has a more critical, but subtle, dimension. When groups begin to isolate themselves, all work activities quite naturally become allocated on a functional basis—finance works with forecasts and budgets, production builds things, engineering designs them, and so on. Each work group stakes out its territory and aggressively guards its turf. This functional view of work activities is damaging in and of itself, apart from the effects of suboptimization. Almost no work activities are the sole province of a single work group. Products engineered solely by engineers will have problems in manufacturing and sales. Finance reports generated without input from other departments are typically used little and understood less. Pretty soon, each department is generating policies and procedures intended to make its job easier and to make itself appear to be in control and successful.

Yet, each of these tamperings impacts decisions and work procedures in other departments in ways that aren't even known. For example, let's say finance requires production to add another line on a weekly report to show direct charging new employee training hours as a percentage of total production work hours (ever notice how finance always orders other departments around, especially "plant" departments?). Production discovers that they don't have a record of the total hours because most of the training at issue takes place when the new hires are still under the supervision of personnel. Production goes to personnel to get the data, but they don't keep a total of all hours, since they track each employee individually.

So, in order to satisfy an out-of-the-blue, tampering-generated, data requirement from somebody in finance who "wants to take a look at the numbers," personnel has to spend 15 minutes each week tallying up the total training hours and then production has to get the data, calculate the percentage, and put it on the report. Not a big deal, but another 30 minutes of time wasted for no point. Worse yet, if the percentage changes in a subjective way that finance doesn't like (as it is bound to do even in a stable system), finance and upper management will demand an explanation ("Mistakes by others are a chance to look good"), thereby generating hours of additional work. Suboptimization strikes again.

This type of thing goes on every hour in every company that's stuck in the traditional management mode. If organizations wish to become more competitive, they must begin to take steps to combat the quite natural, but destructive, tendency to suboptimize. This is part of the American Samurai challenge. It can be only met by pursuing process improvements that are based on customer satisfaction criteria.

CUSTOMER SATISFACTION

Suboptimization can be dramatically reduced (it will never completely disappear in any large company—group dynamics will always keep it on life support) by focusing employees' efforts on customer satisfaction. Most people think of customers in the context of retail stores; if you purchase goods or services, you're a customer and the supplier is the store. Within an organization, employees think of customers as the end users of the products their company makes. They generally think of the entire organization as the supplier. If the company makes cars, car buyers are the customers. If the company makes camping equipment, the customers are the folks who buy the equipment so they can feed the mosquitoes with their bodies on weekends.

Supplier-Customer Links within Processes

This is a very limited view of the supplier-customer relationship. There's much more to it. In Chapter Six, we discussed the diagram of a simple chain of processes, which is repeated in Table 11-1.

Table 11-1.
A simple chain of micro-processes.

INPUT – – →EVENT – – →OUTPUT
                    becomes
          INPUT – – →EVENT – – →OUTPUT
                              becomes
                    INPUT – – →EVENT – – →OUTPUT – – →

Instead of thinking of processes solely as input, event, and output links, it's helpful to conceive of them as the chain of supplier-customer links shown in Table 11-2.

Table 11-2.
Chain of supplier-customer links.

    SUPPLIER – – →CUSTOMER
              becomes
          SUPPLIER – – →CUSTOMER
                    becomes
              SUPPLIER – – →CUSTOMER
                        SUPPLIER – – →CUSTOMER

What's really happening is shown in detail in Table 11-3. An employee, supplier A, receives inputs and performs an event. The output is then provided to the next employee in the chain, customer A. Customer A takes the inputs, performs an event, and becomes supplier B as the output is passed on to Customer B, and so on. Every employee functions as both a supplier and a customer, sometimes with dozens of different processes and many different customers and suppliers. Of course, not all suppliers and customers are employees. Machines and computers are often parts of the micro-process chain.

Table 11-3.
Supplier-customer relationships in a chain of micro-processes.

```
SUPPLIER A          CUSTOMER A
uses       performs receives
INPUT – – →EVENT – – →OUTPUT


                    CUSTOMER A
                    becomes
                    SUPPLIER B                CUSTOMER B
                        uses      performs    receives
                        INPUT – – →EVENT – – →OUTPUT
```

Every macro-process in every company contains anywhere from several to thousands of these supplier-customer links. The process cannot be optimally successful if all customers aren't receiving exactly what they need, when they need it.

This view of work is radically different from the suboptimizing philosophy of the traditional work environment. In a traditional organization, employees are ordered to keep their noses to the grindstone and "just do the work." A customer orientation demands that employees talk to customers and suppliers on a continuous basis so that they can provide each other with better products and services. Simply the communications dimension of such contact is a powerful force for change, since it works to reduce suboptimization and reinforce a unifying set of objectives.

AMERICAN SAMURAI INSIGHT

Improving the quality of micro-process supplier-customer links not only breaks down departmental barriers: it fosters a commitment for responsible support between individuals, exposes long-hidden problems, and fosters support for the common goals of the organization.

What Is "Customer Satisfaction," Anyway?

The requirements for the satisfaction of internal customers aren't much different from those of external customers who end up with the macro-process output. Table 11-4 presents a generic list of the customer satisfaction criteria for both internal and external customers.

Table 11-4.
Generic internal and external customer satisfaction parameters.

Internal customer requirements	External customer requirements
Easy to handle	Easy to use
There when you need it	Available when you want it
Not complicated	Easy to learn to use it
Defect free	Defect free
No surplus stock taking up space	Reasonable cost
Requires little time to work on it	Good service
Minimal handling	
Fast response time for problems	

These requirements boil down to this: customers want it faster, easier, and cheaper. Sounds easy, but there's more here than meets the eye!

The Customer May Not Always Be Right!

The old saw goes that a merchant had a sign in his store, which he showed to all employees on their first day. It read:

> When dealing with customers, there are two rules.
> Rule 1.   The customer is always right.
> Rule 2.   When the customer is wrong, refer to Rule 1.

This little saying appeals to many people because it seems so clear and so simple. Good old Yankee values. Alas, it is wrong, but not for the reason you think. The customer always has the *right* to customer satisfaction. However, the customer may not always be right in specifying exactly what it will take to satisfy his or her requirements. This is particularly true with internal customers. Internal customers often have a limited perspective of their process, because they may see only a part of it. If they were to get exactly what they asked for, they might be in big trouble, as the following short story illustrates.

The Story of the Red Shoes

Once upon a time, there was a man, let's call him Norbert, who had been active for many years at the Proto-Human level of an archly conservative political party. Once day, Norbert received an invitation to attend a nomination dinner for membership to the inner circle (Human Beings and gods) of the party. The dinner was being given at the palatial estate of the guru of the party. Rumor had it that if one conducted oneself with taste and decorum at this dinner, membership to the inner circle was a sure thing. Since this meant a lot to Norbert, he planned to do everything right.

The invitation said, "White tie and tails." Norbert had never worn a tuxedo, so he asked his neighbor what this meant. The neighbor not only explained but offered to lend Norbert his tuxedo, since they were similar in size. Norbert gratefully took the tux and got it cleaned. Two days before the dinner, Norbert tripped over a shoe in his house and thought, "What kind of shoes do I wear with the tux?" The neighbor was out of town, and Norbert was at a loss. As he was worrying about it that night, he was flipping through TV channels with his remote control and happened to see an MTV video featuring the lead singer from the rock group, Creatures from Hell, who was wearing a tux. Norbert watched attentively until the camera panned back. "Voila!", he exclaimed. The star, who Norbert had read was worth millions, was wearing red plastic running shoes. "My problem is solved," he thought. "Those people are always going to big shot parties. They ought to know what to wear."

The next day, Norbert went to Rodeo Drive in Beverly Hills so that he could get the very best red shoes possible. He went to a classy looking store and walked in. Three beautiful saleswomen converged on him, pushing a huge, velvet, padded chair on wheels. One said, "Welcome to our store, sir. Please sit down and make yourself comfortable." Norbert sat down. The second salesperson said, "While you are shopping, please let us serve you a complimentary refreshment. What would you like?" Nobert had a Virgin Mary (he wanted to be sharp for bowling later that night). Meanwhile, the third salesperson was removing Norbert's shoes and socks. She said, "Please permit us to give you a complimentary foot massage, foot bath, pedicure, and complimentary socks while you are considering our merchandise."

So, feet being massaged with warm, scented oils, drink in hand, he told them he was interested in red plastic running shoes. Promptly, they wheeled him to their extensive red plastic running shoe gallery. There were thousands of red plastic shoes. They found just the pair for him after a few more drinks and a complimentary neck rub and haircut. As they were ringing up his sale and validating his parking, they discovered that Norbert was the ten-thousandth customer of the store. Not only was his purchase free, he would be featured in their next magazine ad, for which he would be paid. They pulled his car up to the front of the store, and Norbert left, having paid nothing for a $1229.95 pair of shiny red, designer, signature running shoes, foot massage, haircut, pedicure, drinks, and a possible career in advertising.

At this point, Norbert sounds like a happy customer if there ever was one. Wrong. Norbert wore the red shoes to the dinner, was the butt of jokes all night (behind his back) and didn't get nominated. Worse, the loyal party hack who nominated Norbert also ruined his own chances of moving higher in the party. Everybody suffered, although Norbert got *exactly* what he wanted, and much more, on time, and at a great price. The problem was that Norbert got what he wanted, not what he needed.

Now, contrast this with a Luckier Norbert. Luckier Norbert decided to go to K-Mart for his shoes. He drove to the store, parked in the paper strewn lot, and pushed his way through the throng of beggars, charity solicitors, and screaming children that always gather outside K-Mart doors. Luckier Norbert headed for the huge "SHOES" sign and began to look for red shoes. He couldn't find any.

Savvy to the way of K-Mart, Luckier Norbert listened carefully. There, he heard it—the sound of gum being popped by an adolescent mouth; a salesperson was nearby! Luckier Norbert triangulated on the repetitive sound and located a young man talking on the phone to his girl friend, arranging a date that night. "Like, yeah (snap), like I'll pick you up at, like 8 (pop), yeah, rad, like tickets to the Creatures from Hell, like. . . ." Norbert tapped him on the shoulder and asked for help in finding red shoes. The teenager turned to Luckier Norbert with a disgusted look and said, "Hey, dude (pop), like I'm talkin' here, man. The red shoes are like over there, man. I'll be over in like a minute, dude." The youth turned back to his phone call.

Forty-five minutes later, Luckier Norbert was still trying to find a match for a single size 8½ left foot red plastic shoe he had found in a huge pile of marked down junk. The teenager finally came by on his way to break and said, "Got what you need, Pop?"

Luckier Norbert answered, "No. I can't find another one of these."

The teenager replied, "Well, like that's a tennis shoe, dude. Like I thought you said 'running shoe.' Like what are you gonna use 'em for, man? Like we got running shoes, tennis shoes, golf shoes, basketball shoes, aerobics shoes. Like you just can't wear any shoe for anything, dude (snap)!"

Luckier Norbert replied, "Oh, no. I don't need them for sports. I need them so I can wear them with my tuxedo tomorrow night."

The youth's face lit up. "Hey, like great, dude! My main man, Screaming Pigsbreath, lead singer of the Creatures from Hell, always wears, like red shoes with his tux, too. Totally rad, dude, like I didn't know you were so, like rad (snap)."

Luckier Norbert's eyes narrowed to slits as an alarm went off in his head. He asked the youth, "Doesn't everybody wear red shoes with tuxedos?"

The teenager snapped his gum loudly, took it out of his mouth, threw it into a bin of furry, pink slippers, and smirked, "Like no way, man. Only totally rad dudes do that. The slimers like my dad, like he's an attorney, they only wear black shoes with a tux."

Luckier Norbert dropped the red shoe as if it were on fire and picked out a pair of shiny, black plastic dress shoes. He took them to the register up front and then had to wait for 30 minutes as the clerk made repeated attempts to get a "price check" because nothing in a K-Mart ever has a price tag on it. Finally, after 2 hours and 10 minutes, Luckier Norbert made it home, having paid $49.97 for $29.97 shoes that had been incorrectly tagged.

Few people would say that Luckier Norbert got treated better than our first Norbert. Yet, Luckier Norbert got better customer satisfaction. He didn't get what he wanted, but he got, sort of by blind luck, what he needed. He wore the black shoes to the dinner and made a big hit by being obsequious and quiet. He got the formal nomination.

The moral of this story is that, although customers aren't always right in what they say they want, they are always right in demanding to be given what they need.

AMERICAN SAMURAI INSIGHT

It's up to suppliers to work hard to make sure that customers get what they need, not just what they say they want.

We'll discuss supplier-customer relationships further in Chapter Eighteen, when we examine Coda 13.

QUALITY IMPROVEMENT AND CUSTOMER SATISFACTION

The challenge in meeting customer satisfaction requirements is to set up a process improvement approach that assures that both suppliers and customers completely understand the process in question and jointly agree upon the customer requirements for the process. In order for this to happen, customers and suppliers must be able to talk with each other and study the process together. This sort of thing cannot be done by management working alone in their offices. The people who run the processes are the only ones who understand how the processes work in the day-to-day environment. They must be included in all efforts to improve customer satisfaction. Once again, you can see how the individual Coda all work together.

THE PLAN, DO, CHECK, ACT (PDCA) CYCLE AS A PROCESS IMPROVEMENT METHODOLOGY

Just hoping that internal suppliers and customers will work together isn't enough to assure that effective process improvements will be implemented. Few organizations have a tradition of logical, consistent process improvement. They haven't trained people to identify problems correctly, employees don't understand how to determine customer requirements, and few employees accept the fact that they should even try to improve things. Therefore, it's absolutely essential to institute a consistent, formalized methodology for pursuing process improvements. A single, consistent approach to process improvement means that the organization will begin to develop a uniform process improvement vocabulary, practice, and tradition.

One well-known approach to process improvement is the Plan, Do, Check, Act (PDCA) cycle. It is a conceptual formalized technique for referring to the continuous process of studying a process and testing new ways of making it work better. Many people refer to it as the "Deming cycle," whereas Deming and others refer to it as the Shewhart cycle, in honor of Walter Shewhart. It's the same thing. As Figure 11-1 shows, the Deming cycle is an ongoing pursuit of the planning, testing, and evaluating of process improvements. The 12-step process improvement methodology is a more detailed representation of the PDCA cycle.

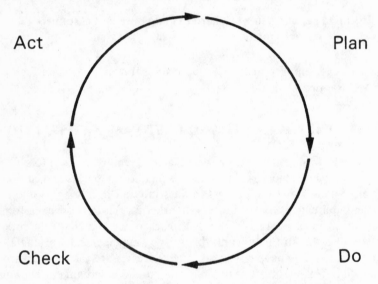

Figure 11-1. The Plan, Do, Check, Act (PDCA) cycle.

A Process Improvement Methodology

Whereas the PDCA cycle is a valuable conceptual tool, it is not sufficiently detailed to provide detailed guidance. For example, to some people, "check" means to ask the boss if he or she likes something. Therefore, a more detailed road map for process improvement efforts is required. The following process improvement approach covers all of the fundamental actions that must be conducted in order to assure that process improvement efforts don't miss something important. It doesn't matter if the approach used has four steps or 20, as long as it does the same things. Figure 11-2 presents a schematic representation of the 12-step process improvement methodology I recommend. Any good process improvement approach "does" the same things as this approach. As you can see, this 12-step approach is nothing more than a detailed breakout of the PDCA cycle.

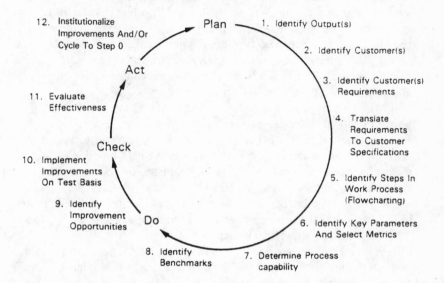

Figure 11-2.   The 12-step process improvement technique.

The following sections explain (where necessary) salient points about each of the 12 steps.

1. *Identify output(s).*
2. *Identify customer(s).* There is more than one type of customer, and they must all be considered. The three basic varieties of customers are Owner Customers, Evaluator Customers, and Implementor Customers. Owner Customers are generally higher-level executives who are mainly concerned with macro-process performance. Evaluator Customers are generally inspectors and technical types who pass judgments as to the acceptability of the process output as it compares to established standards. Implementor Customers are those people who will have to work on, or with, the output.

   Customers must be identifiable as warm bodies, not organizations. For example, the "audit department" is not a good customer definition; it's too vague. Sally Smith, senior auditor, *is* a good customer identification because Sally can be interviewed and can participate in the process improvement team.
3. *Identify customer's requirements.* Each of the preceding customers must be interviewed, face to face. Guesses about what they want will not cut it.

4. *Translate requirements to customer specifications.* Specifications will be discussed in detail in Chapter Seventeen. Essentially, specifications translate desirable satisfaction parameters, such as "small," to observable values that can be measured, such as "no bigger than 10 inches by 5 inches." If someone says that they need a report "early in the week," they must be made to specify exactly when "early" is.

5. *Identify all of the micro-process inputs, events, and outputs by flowcharting the process.* This is esentially a diagram showing each input, event, and output in the order in which it occurs.

6. *Identify key control points and develop metrics.* Control points are important spots in the micro-process chain. Metrics are outputs in quantifiable, observable form, such as spark plug gap, no-starts, and so on.

7. *Determine process capability.* This involves taking a baseline measurement of process functioning before any changes are made, so that the effectiveness of future changes can be accurately determined.

8. *Identify benchmarks.* Benchmarks are the best performances that can be identified for similar process outputs in similar situations. We'll discuss these at length in Chapter Twelve.

9. *Determine candidate process improvement actions.* These are the solutions to the problem. They must be developed by a team that includes hands-on process doers. There are two kinds of solutions: short-term and long-term. Often, it is necessary to take quick action to stop the flow of poor output from a process. This may even be tampering if it must be taken quickly. That's OK, as long as the short-term fix is recognized as an interim step. All too often, short-term, tampering solutions are the last step in process improvement in traditional work environments because management attention is soon diverted to the next fire. The key solutions are the long-term solutions: the "fixes" that will make the process better permanently.

10. *Test each candidate process improvement action.* It's not enough to come up with solutions and simply jam them into the system. What looks good on paper may not work, for a host of reasons. Each candidate solution must be tested and evaluated on a limited basis (if possible). This takes patience and seems like a waste of time to a traditional ("fast gun, slow bullet") manager. It is the only way to make sure that a "fix" doesn't make more trouble than it eliminates.

11. *Evaluate effectiveness.* The results of the tests of the solutions must be jointly evaluated by the process improvement team and by the customers and suppliers involved, before changes are institutionalized.

12. *Institutionalize effective improvements (or try going back to step nine).* The institutionalization of process improvements requires more than just tossing out a solution. Employees must be trained in new procedures, the changes must be documented so that personnel changes don't "wipe out" everyone with knowledge of how to do it the new way, and a system

must be set up to make sure that new employees and other departments understand and perform the process in the new manner. This takes a lot of time, patience, and hard work. If this is not done, all of the other steps are wasted.

The Process Improvement Cycle Must Be Never Ending

Processes don't stand still. Neither should process improvement activities. Just because a process is "fixed" and is now operating 25% better than before doesn't mean that there's nothing more to be gained. American management is infatuated with big hits in productivity improvements. When improvements start to come in on the order of 1%, 2%, or 0.5%, management tends to lose interest and assume that there are bigger fish to fry somewhere else. Wrong.

AMERICAN SAMURAI INSIGHT

The single, most significant advantage of so-called "Japanese management" is an almost fanatic dedication to obtaining continuous process improvement in very small increments. The Japanese call this Kaizen, which means continuing improvement.

Anyone can get a big improvement out of a process that's obviously in rough shape. That's been the way we've been making heroes and company presidents in the traditional management environment for 200 years. That's the easy way, alright, but it won't do the job in a highly competitive situation in which everyone has roughly the same technology and skills. Once a process has been reasonably developed, studied, and improved, the competitive edge goes to the organization that gets an additional 5% to 10% improvement, not all at once, and not through one action, but through 100 to 10,000 small improvements over a period of years. Those companies that implement The Code of the American Samurai will get these additional improvements. All of the others will fall behind, missing the little improvements that are always there while they search for nonexistent "heavy hitters" that dominate American business fantasies. There are no easy answers: do not waste time searching for them.

EVERYBODY INVOLVED, ALL THE TIME

Of course, management doesn't have the time to pay attention to any more than a handful of processes. That's why, when a process falls apart unexpectedly, you often hear, "I can't watch everyone and everything!" They're right, and they shouldn't even be trying. All employees must be trained, coached, and empowered to continuously seek out and test improvements in their processes by applying the process improvement methodology just reviewed. With everyone involved in pursuing process improvements, management's role as a fire-fighting force is large eliminated. Processes are "fixed" (improved), even when they're not broken. It's no longer necessary to wait until a fire breaks out; the employees are out there searching for the first signs of potential fires, even before there's smoke.

GOOD MISTAKES ARE ABSOLUTELY NECESSARY

Traditional management generally has no trouble buying into the concept of continuous improvement. However, when it comes to implementation, they balk at the fact that work groups will be making all sorts of decisions and trying all manner of process improvements, many of which will not work. Management sees these mistakes as bad. Wrong.

AMERICAN SAMURAI INSIGHT

Good mistakes, those made with careful preparation and understanding of the process in question, are valuable improvement tools. Good mistakes should be encouraged and rewarded as often and as thoroughly as possible.

Thomas Edison tested more than 2000 types of filaments before he found one that would work satisfactorily for the first electric bulb. The only way to do that was to continuously Plan, Do, Check, and Act, each time learning something, each time getting a little closer to the answer. The same principle applies to processes. Every process can be improved. However, if failed improvement attempts are punished, the number of suggestions will quickly drop to near zero.

TRADITIONAL SUGGESTION SYSTEMS ARE WORTHLESS

That's why traditional suggestion systems are worthless. Management says they want suggestions, but they punish employees for making them. How, you ask? Just look at how much trouble an employee has to go through in a typical company to submit a suggestion: forms, signatures, multiple copies, etc. Then, there is a wait of 6 months to 2 years for an answer. Of course, if the suggestion even hints of remotely implied criticism of the way in which something is currently being done, the employee is forced to defend the suggestion from all sorts of vicious, suboptimizing attacks.

After all that, the suggestion is usually turned down by someone in personnel who doesn't understand anything about the technical or fiscal issues involved. And we wonder why suggestion programs fail? If we offered to push thumbtacks into employees' foreheads, we'd get few takers. Yet, the suggestion submittal and review procedure in most companies is only marginally less painful than a thumbtack in the head.

In companies that successfully establish a process improvement methodology as a standard work process, each worker makes two to four suggestions per week, 100 to 200 per year, 90% of which are examined within the work group within 5 days. These aren't the big hitters in most cases, but small, 0.25% type improvements. And, best of all, at least half of them don't work! Why "best of all?" Because if the employees were afraid of failure (or of the suggestion process itself), they wouldn't be busy thinking up the other half of the suggestions that *do* work.

Problem Solving and Process Improvement: A Little Difference

There is a small difference between process improvement and problem solving that sometimes creates conceptual difficulties among novice users of these techniques. The 12-step methodology of process improvements assumes that you are seeking to improve the performance of an existing process. You're seeking to make the process faster, better, and less costly, even though it may currently be acceptable.

In a problem-solving situation, the starting point is often not a clearly defined process. Instead, you're starting with a symptom, which is "the problem." The lawn mower no-starts in Chapter Eight were a symptom; they could have been caused by any number of processes. When the problem first manifests itself, the responsible process is often not obvious.

Therefore, one additional step—defining the problem—must be taken before the process improvement steps can be launched. Coming up with an accurate definition of a problem is not as easy as it sounds. This is often the most conceptually difficult step. This is primarily because waiting to define a problem seems almost un-American to managers who want to go out and "do" something.

For example, suppose a secretary delivers a letter to his or her boss and the boss thinks that there are too many typographical errors in it. The problem, in the boss' view, may be that, "He or she made too many careless typing mistakes because of inattention." This is a classically bad problem definition (and the usual, knee-jerk, "blame the employee" reaction). The errors could be due to the boss' poor handwriting, sloppy dictation, too many rush jobs, a typewriter that is difficult to use, a substitute typist helping out, and so on. Acting on the bad, "blaming" problem definition would result in problem solutions that would focus on the attention/motivation level of the secretary and ignore other causes. The consequence of implementing the wrong solution, aside from a waste of time, might include offending the secretary, causing him or her to quit sooner than otherwise might have occurred (higher turnover), or substandard work in the future (self-fulfilling prophecy). All these added problems are created, and the real root cause of the problem might never be addressed.

A good problem definition does not include blame or likely causes. For this example, a good definition might be: "There were five typos on the letter, more than twice as many as any other letter I've gotten back this week." Without any blame being assigned, the boss and the secretary could then investigate the problem (by using the 12 steps outlined in the preceding section) without having prejudged the causes.

It's Not As Easy As It Sounds
(But You're Tougher Than You Look)

As you have just seen, there's a lot more to improving processes than simply bellowing out, "I want to see a 10% improvement—fast!" Real, ongoing, lasting process improvements require a trained and properly led work force, a process focus, involved employees, and the patience to do it right. You have to carry the message to American business.

12

Drive a Stake into the Ground, Not into your Foot: Benchmarks Instead of Objectives

Coda 7. **Excellence in all critical process outputs must be identified through the use of comparative benchmarks.**

The traditional management approach places great value on objectives. The intent of an objective is presumably to drive a stake into the ground so that the employees will know where they have to go. After the brass sets the objectives, the troops are exhorted to strive toward the objectives. Everybody nods off during the same old speeches and returns to work to continue to do whatever they think they should be doing, which is generally what they've been doing for years. Not only does the traditional manner of setting objectives not function as a "stake in the ground," it almost guarantees that nothing will change. It's more like a stake in the foot, something that stops any movement except flailing about and circling in one spot.

WHY OBJECTIVES DON'T WORK

Objectives by themselves are pointless because they have no perceived relevance to the processes that a particular employee performs. Workers don't know what they're supposed to do differently in order to attain the objectives. In fact, neither does management, which is why they set macro-level objectives, rather than making planned changes to the micro-processes that generate macro-process results. It sometimes seems that management must be assuming that employees will magically intuit the necessary behaviors and process changes that are required simply because of the mere existence of objectives set on paper somewhere in the organization. Wrong.

For example, an objective for the coming year might be to increase profits by 5%. Why 5%? Why not 4%, 10%, or 20%? Where did 5% come from? Generally, the answer (in those rare instances in which someone will talk) is something along the lines of, "It seemed right," or "It's what we needed to make the numbers look right.'' Everyone who hears about the objective (which will be hardly any of the Egg Sucking Pigs) will go back to work and do whatever they think is appropriate. Some will complain, some will try to do something to help and will screw things up royally, some will forget almost immediately, and some will ignore the entire exercise and keep on doing what they've always done. A few will actually do something, by pure chance, that actually helps move the macro-output in the proper direction.

All in all, not much happens when most objectives are set. We've all worked in organizations in which the objectives of the annual plan are missed by a mile and nobody says a word. Everybody knows the story; objectives are nice if they are met, but if they are not, the subject is not brought up. If someone is impolite enough to insist on excuses, management simply falls back on the standard, CEO, annual report whine—it was (pick one or all): the government, the unions, the Japanese, fickle consumers, trade barriers, or (best of all, most common, and my favorite) "Oh, that. Heh, heh. Well, it's not really the problem it appears to be. It's just a schedule slip. We'll get it next year.''

Since most objectives are developed from no more than a ''seat of the pants'' intuition or a ''gut feeling'' on the part of management, it's probably no big deal that they're not hotly pursued. However, autonomous objectives have a negative effect outside of the productivity that's lost because the organization isn't focused; they demonstrate to employees that management is totally out of touch with day-to-day work processes. Management is seen as a bunch of public relations speech makers who don't know what they're doing.

More critically, if management thinks that setting objectives means that the organization is moving ahead and becoming more competitive, they're in for a shock. They'll be making their 1% to 3% increases each quarter and then, WHAM, they'll get blindsided by an unexpected competitive challenge. Or, they'll find out that the 1% to 3% was ''pencil whipped'' into reports to avoid retribution for nonperformance. Insular objectives, coughed up from a self-centered, introspective executive committee, can't possibly be reponsive to the increasingly volatile changes that are becoming commonplace in today's business arena.

The Substitute For Objectives

What is needed is an alternative process that not only points out the destination but also shows how to get there—something that will not only specify ''how much'' is needed but will also provide information and insights as to the nature of the processes that are necessary to attain the ''how much.'' This alternative to disconnected (from reality) objectives is called benchmarking. *Benchmarking* is the process of comparing processes and products against the best that can be found.

Anything can be benchmarked, whether it's a product, a process, or a service. Benchmarking, if done properly, provides more than just an objective, or goal; benchmarking provides a *means* by which to reach the goal. Rather than wondering what to do about a disjointed objective, employees can, with benchmarking, seize upon some real meat as to how to make things work better.

There are two dimensions to benchmarking: (1) the benchmark itself, which is typically a statement of a specific level of an output, and (2) process information about how the benchmark was attained. As an example, let's look at a process that employees in almost all large organizations hate: the purchasing system. This is the process that eats up 1 to 6 months (or more) between the time a purchase order is submitted for something (such as a bookcase) and the merchandise is delivered (or perhaps only ordered). If you were to benchmark this process (and we'll talk about how to do that in a moment), you might discover that the world's best purchasing system does the job in 2 weeks. Great. Now you *really* hate your purchasing department. The benchmark itself is interesting, but, other than confirming your personal opinions about the competency of the purchasing staff, you're out in left field as to what to do in order to improve things.

The process of benchmarking, to be cost-effective for the effort involved, must also provide information about the nature of the processes that were used to get orders filled in 2 weeks. The type of buying systems, the type and extent of automation, the types of training given to buyers, data on how many orders are completed by each buyer each day, the types of approval limits and signatures required, and so on, could be critical. Depending upon the "fit" between your company and the "benchmarkee," any or all of the preceding might indicate exactly where to begin fixing the ordering process.

There are other benefits to benchmarking. The first involves staying in touch with the realities of the marketplace and the competition. Very often, organizations tend to become introspective over time, looking within, rather than without, for innovations and change. This is a severe, but often unrecognized, problem in comparatively "closed" industries, in which there is very little influx of experience from outside industries. Industries such as aerospace/defense, automotive, public utilities, the military, and nuclear power are prime examples, although there are many others. Given the nature of the work, few people with non-industry specific experience are viewed as qualified. Over time, organizations in "closed" industries barely question any of their practices because no one knows a better way and no one questions standard procedures. Benchmarking is an outstanding way for these industries to get a "breath of fresh air" concerning their processes and performance.

Even for industries in which "outsiders" are frequent, there's still a strong tendency for an organization to pursue the idiosyncratic interests of the current management team. For example, business is slowly coming to understand that maintaining large inventories of material is costly for all sorts of reasons: you have to pay for the stuff before you use it, it takes up costly space, and you've got to pay to move it around at least two more times (stock it and then pick it later) before you use it. More and more companies are trying to move as close to Just in Time (JIT) systems as they can.

Yet, I still see organizations that are spending millions on high-bay, automatic-retrieval systems because somebody in management, without any research on their industries' (or any other industries') best practices, decided that it would be sexy to have something to show visitors. Benchmarking can provide additional hard data about what the leaders are doing. That may be enough to stop some of the more costly pet projects from being pursued by executives of inbred, "closed" industries.

Equally important, continuous benchmarking provides a strong measure of insurance against being blindsided by unexpected stretch moves on the part of the competition.

THE STEPS OF BENCHMARKING

Benchmarking is a process much like the process improvement methodology presented in Chapter Eleven. There are many ways in which to organize tasks, but if it is done correctly, all of them contain the same basic procedures. The following approach is simply one way to make sure that all the bases are covered completely.

1. IDENTIFY MACRO-PROCESSES THAT ARE KEY TO COMPETITIVENESS

You've got to start in the right place by identifying the "make or break" macro-processes that are key to survival and success in your industry. Every process is important in terms of its bottom line impacts, of course, but some drive competitiveness more than others. In the commercial electronics industry, for instance, time-to-market span (from concept to product introduction) is critical; 1 month late and the market can be lost. In the automotive industry, inventory levels and labor hours per build (car) are vital.

When benchmarking is first begun in an organization, there is almost a tendency to want to "benchmark the world." Unless your organization is well along the way to world-class quality, forget it. First of all, it's a time-consuming and resource-intensive effort to be the benchmarking and implement changes. Start off with a few key macro-processes, and you'll have more than enough to handle.

The macro-processes and their outputs, as such, are worthless for designating appropriate places to seek benchmarks. After all, if you were an automotive manufacturer with a 14-hour per build can and you found out that the benchmark in the world for a similar vehicle was 8 hours, you would not be able to do much except feel bad. You need to get inside the macro-processes in order to reach a level of detail that will tell you something.

2. ANALYZE KEY MACRO-PROCESSES TO DETERMINE CONSTITUENT MICRO-PROCESSES

Each key macro-process will be comprised of many, if not hundreds, of micro-processes. Of course, micro-processes exist within micro-processes. Where do you stop in your analysis? You must take the analysis of micro-processes to a level of detail where, if you were told the nature of the inputs, events, and outputs of the process, you'd understand exactly how to do it. For example, suppose you were going to benchmark the macro-process of writing a general interest, trade, nonfiction, business book such as the one you're now reading. At the macro-level, the benchmarks could be total unit sales, total dollar sales, hours to write it, total time from idea to publication, and so on. Any or all of these macro-benchmarks might be of interest but would do you little good at the "I want to write a book like this" level. Who cares if someone wrote a book like this that sold 2 million copies or wrote one in 5 days? (No, it wasn't this one!)

These findings are too general, too macro, to be useful. So let's narrow our search and take the processes down to a level of detail where we can get some insight into the processes. Suppose you're interested in the time required to write such a book. You might find that the time to write each chapter varies from 1 hour to 1 day. Still not very useful. Now, suppose that you go down to a lower level of micro-process that involves steps in the writing of each chapter. Then, as you were doing the benchmarking, you might find out that it took the writer 1 hour to outline each chapter and that he or she used a personal computer with outlining software to do the outlining. Now, you're starting to get somewhere; you're at a level where you're getting some data that *may* be useful. Knowing about the software provides you with a possible process improvement opportunity that you may be able to incorporate into your own book writing processes.

3. IDENTIFY KEY MICRO-PROCESSES

Once you decide the appropriate level of micro-processes, it's important to limit the number of micro-processes to a reasonable amount. You're going to have to do research on each one, and there's a limit to the amount of time and money you'll be able to allocate. There's also the not inconsiderable amount of time you're going to be asking folks from other organizations to devote to the effort. So make sure that you only go after the key micro-processes.

4. IDENTIFY KEY METRIC(S) FOR EACH MICRO-PROCESS

It's critical that you define exactly the metrics that are used for each of your key micro-processes. If you don't know how to measure it in your own processes, you may end up with the wrong kind of data. For example, if you were benchmarking a world–class croissant making operation, you'd be extremely interested in the length of time it takes a world-class operation to mix the dough, how long it takes to roll out and fold the patons, the maximum temperature the dough reaches in each stage, and so on. If you were a novice and went out to collect benchmarking data, you might end up with data on what went in the dough (everybody knows already), the type of machinery they use (most likely already known as a result of machinery salespeople), and so on.

AMERICAN SAMURAI INSIGHT

If you haven't conducted a number of intensive process improvement efforts involving the micro-processes you're trying to improve, you're probably not ready to do any benchmarking. You won't get the right answers unless you've struggled with the questions yourself for a while.

5. IDENTIFY POTENTIAL SOURCES OF INFORMATION

There are many potential sources of benchmarking data. The most convenient source of data, if you're part of a large, multidivision organization, may be your own corporation. At the same time, you may be surprised at the amount of parochialism and guarded suspicion that exists between sister divisions. It's a legacy of the traditional management style (loyalty to the group and suboptimization working again).

The next most obvious source of benchmarking data is the competitors that are threatening your organization or the companies that are already recognized as pace setters in your industry. After all, the best place to start is with the ones who are already doing the processes well.

But don't be short-sighted; you can learn a lot from industries that are totally unrelated to yours. I've always been a proponent of extensive industry cross-pollination in hiring for this very reason. Even though I have never worked in a construction company, I have no doubt that there are industry-specific practices that, if studied and modified, would provide benefits to non-construction business. Don't forget, every business does things such as ordering, sales, administration, shipping, and so on. There may be bold new ways of doing things that nobody in your industry knows about. And vice versa. The only way to find them is to look under strange new rocks rather than under only those on the garden path.

Two great sources of leads about companies that should be investigated are consultants and equipment vendors. These people get out to a lot of companies and see a lot of processes up close, especially when a customer of theirs is trying something bold that requires dramatic modifications of existing systems. You're not asking them to spy for you or give you restricted data, you're only asking for potential sources.

It's also a good idea to do an extensive literature search in the appropriate industry/functional areas. Not only will you discover many leads, you'll learn a lot that will make it easier to efficiently ask questions. Reference librarians of major libraries can direct you to numerous industry- and function-specific databases and reports.

6. DETERMINE HOW THE BENCHMARKS WILL BE COLLECTED

The preceding efforts may actually yield some usable benchmarking data themselves, although most data from the literature and industry reports is often homogenized and averaged to the point at which specific practices are not obvious. If you can't get the data you need directly from consultants, equipment suppliers, or written/electronic databases, magazines, and/or reports, you'll have to go out and collect it directly from other companies. This is the last option to consider because it is the most time consuming and expensive. However, eventually everyone who does benchmarking has to go out and "press the flesh" to get some data.

Direct collection techniques range from person-to-person phone conversations with appropriate technical personnel within target organizations to mass surveys sent out by mail. Often, it is necessary to conduct on-site visits to the companies in the target group. Some companies combine methods, such as sending out surveys and then following up with phone calls and trying to get invited to an on-site visit.

7. COLLECT THE DATA

A key consideration in any benchmarking effort is arranging for the cooperation of the target companies. If I were an industry leader, I might be less than enthusiastic about sharing data with competitors who will threaten me more if they improve their operation. That's one reason why you're apt to get better cooperation from companies outside of your industry; they don't see your gains as a potential loss to them, and they are more willing to cooperate in the spirit of making all businesses more competitive (except their competitors). This is one of the reasons why third-party consultants are often hired to perform benchmarking studies. Generally, the consultants guarantee anonymity to all parties and promise them that any company that contributes data will get a copy of the findings. I don't think that the consultant approach is worth the tremendous expense involved. Such a study can cost 200 to 400 thousand dollars and end up being a bunch of general macro-process outputs, which are worthless. A related problem is that companies that hire consultants to do their benchmarking generally haven't taken the time to study their own processes; as a result, they don't know what to ask for or how to use what they get. Do it yourself.

8. ANALYZE THE DATA

Once you've got the data in-house, you're ready to break it down. There are several aspects of the data that are important. If you've studied your own processes extensively prior to the benchmarking effort, you'll know exactly what to look for. First of all, you'll be looking at the absolute level of performance of the macro- and larger micro-processes you're benchmarking, such as number of sales calls made in a week, wire bond defect rates per million bonds, time to process a purchase order, inventory turns per year, and so on.

This data, when compared to your organization's performances, will give you some indication of where you stand. You will know where their stake is in the ground relative to your organization's stake. The next step is to determine what the terrain is like. You'll need to examine as much of their "how they did it" data as you can get, that is, the inputs and events that led to the benchmark outputs. This should be expressed as a flowchart of process inputs, events, and outputs, to the appropriate level of detail.

Once you have the process flowcharted, you're ready to compare what they've got with what you're doing. The obvious applications and incompatibilities should jump right off the page at your process experts. It will be clear almost immediately why the benchmarked company is doing as well as it is.

9. ESTABLISHING IMPROVEMENT GOALS AND DEVELOPING ACTION PLANS

Now, finally, you're ready to actually set some meaningful improvement goals. This is done by looking at the types of changes that must be made in your systems in order to match those of the best organizations. The extent to which your organization can improve in the next 3 months or over the next year will depend upon how much has to be done. The changes may require entirely new approaches or involve minor modifications to what's already being done. If hardware and software are involved, there will be resource limitations and time constraints.

The plans to implement the improvements must be drafted with the participation of all the process owners involved. Particular attention must be given to maintaining levels of customer satisfaction as the changes are implemented. It should be clear to you at this point that it would be extremely difficult to orchestrate smooth changes in the involved processes if you didn't have an in-depth understanding of both the old and the new processes. Never attempt benchmarking until you intuitively understand every dimension of the existing system you're trying to change.

A key caution at this point involves setting objectives. If the objectives to improve performance are set as a result of a detailed plan and participation of all involved process doers, there's no problem. The danger is that once traditional managers get their "fast gun, slow bullet" hands on the benchmarks, they want to mandate performance objectives on a week-to-week, month-to-month basis. If this happens, all of the benchmarking data collection effort was wasted. You can't pistol whip employees to reach objectives, whether they're arbitrary objectives or those derived from benchmarks.

10. DOING, CHECKING, AND ACTING ON THE PROCESS CHANGES

From this point on, process changes will be implemented, verified, and acted upon exactly like all other process changes. The metrics of the various micro-processes must be monitored on a real-time basis and fed back to the process owners.

11. INCORPORATING BENCHMARKING INTO PLANNING

Proper planning techniques using benchmarks will be discussed in Chapter Fifteen, when we discuss Coda 10. As you can see, the use of benchmarks provides a plan with reality based, market-driven objectives, in place of subjective, unconnected goals.

12. SUCCESS: LOOKING OVER YOUR SHOULDER

Even if your organization makes it to the top and becomes the leader in its industry (well, we can hope, can't we?), benchmarking never stops. You may get to the point where you have, for example, the best micro-assembly manufacturing operation in the world. That doesn't mean that each and every one of the individual, constituent micro-processes is the best. You'll still have much to learn. That's why the successful Japanese companies continue to scout industries the world over—they're hoping to find better ways to perform specific micro-processes. They want to make sure they stay on top.

THE BURDEN OF THE AMERICAN SAMURAI: A NINJA BY ANOTHER NAME

This is the first of several Coda that a brave and resourceful American Samurai can't do something about on his or her own. Up to this point, any of the Coda could be performed on a limited basis "in secret" within a section or department without causing trouble. Even a despot isn't going to care all that much if you've put a few control charts up (Coda 3). And, as long as you keep production up to reasonable levels, you're not going to get in a lot of trouble even if you practice Coda 5 (quality first), as long as you don't try to sell the philosophy from a soapbox at a staff meeting.

However, benchmarking is a little different. You can't very well take on the entire organization's planning function and insist that benchmarking be the starting point for all plan objectives, working from macro-processes to micro-processes. You can do some limited benchmarking in your work area (if you've got the time), but that's about it. Unless you're a big shot (really big, with clout, not just a senior manager type), nobody is going to allow you to run off and interact with other companies and share data.

So, in regard to this and many other Coda, you'll have to cover up your disgust and work quietly within the system to move their stagnant thinking toward the light. For the first time, you'll have to act more like a Ninja than a Samurai. The Samurai proudly wears his swords and publicly displays his beliefs and honor for all to see and admire, but not when it's dangerous to his or her continued survival and ability to wage the long struggle. A Ninja hides from overwhelming enemies and does his or her work in the dark, springing from ambush only when he or she is assured of victory (or at least of not losing) so that the fight can be carried to another day.

It's a rough life, but then, the way of the warrior has never been easy. Saving American business is just another dirty job, and you just volunteered. You are an American Samurai, and you are hardened to the ordeal. Read on, fellow warrior.

13

"Real" Managers Aren't Bosses

Coda 8. **The role of management is to set policy that establishes and sustains this Code, conduct long-term planning, pursue bold new innovations that generate order of magnitude increases in quality and profitability, and lead through coaching and teaching.**

Ask employees in almost any organization which adjectives they associate with "management" and the responses invariably include descriptions such as inflexible, unapproachable, authoritarian, bureaucratic, snobbish, and rigid. "Management" is viewed as a psychologically distant group of aristocratic rule makers.

If you ask employees to identify adjectives that describe "boss," the responses are psychologically closer but more negative, such as mean, irritable, petty, unfair, pushy, uncaring, and stupid. While I'm the first to agree that there's no shortage of bosses (or people in general) with these characteristics, all bosses can't possibly be inherently that bad, any more than all employees are fundamentally lazy.

Even when management and bosses are "good" people, they usually generate many of the preceding negative reactions from employees. They don't plan it that way. In fact, they don't plan it any way; they're just "being" managers. The problem is that, in a traditionally managed organization, management does its job the way it's been trained, by circumstances and experience. The traditional philosophy of work teaches managers to be bad managers and supervisors.

AMERICAN SAMURAI INSIGHT

Most managers have never been trained to manage the correct way. They don't know how to be a leader rather than a jailer.

Just look at how a typical college graduate becomes a manager. He or she joins the company in a lower-level job. If they're unlucky and end up in manufacturing (looked down upon because of the way in which the people who work in it are treated by the rest of the organization), they may be asssigned as a supervisor of hourly employees in order to get a little "seasoning." This is a euphemism for, "We'll put him (or her on some rare occasions) with those animals for a few months to see if he can take it." That's great, isn't it? A wet behind the ears, green college graduate is put in charge of employees with 10 to 30 years of experience who produce the company's product. It's as if nobody cares what happens, as if it were a big experiment. Not only doesn't the new "supervisor" know anything about people in general, he doesn't know anything about supervision. He knows even less about the work. Yet he's supposed to supervise the workers. How? Impossible.

After a few months, the "seasoned" supervisor is moved to another area, to "supervise" more processes he or she doesn't know how to do, managing another crew of 10- to 30-year veterans. And all the while, the rookie is watching and learning from the existing supervisors who manage according to the way they were taught. This goes on every day, at every level, in thousands of organizations.

People learn to manage by watching other people manage. And what they learn is a set of behaviors that hasn't fundamentally changed since the beginning of the Industrial Revolution. The Values and Guiding Principles of the traditional management theory that were examined in Chapter Four are burned into them.

Let's match these Guiding Principles with a variety of the typical behaviors they generate. You'll see that these behaviors comprise the majority of any supervisor's/manager's day. I think you'll see that almost all management behaviors in the traditional work environment are based upon the negative view of workers espoused in the Traditional Guiding Principles.

The Guiding Principles of The Traditional Management Theory	*Resultant Behaviors and Practices*
Set Objectives And Manage to Them	1. Insist on frequent reporting
	2. Punish shortcomings quickly
	3. Don't accept excuses
	4. Don't modify plans because of employee input and whining
	5. Require lengthy activity reports
	6. Break big objectives into small increments and closely manage each employee's work on each one
Manage by Fear	1. Get tough occasionally to show power
	2. Act tough on details
	3. Watch them closely

	4. Make surprise visits to catch them and keep them guessing
Have an Answer to Every Question	1. Demand to know every detail of employees' actions 2. Make them ask for approval for every detail
Don't Take Chances	1. Don't let employees take any actions on their own 2. Tell them as little as possible 3. Don't share information 4. Spend a lot of time gathering data on "political" issues
Volume Takes Care of Everything	1. Push for production all the time 2. Hold employees to rigid performance standards 3. Maintain detailed productivity records on each employee 4. Punish below-average performers
Do Not Deliver Bad News	1. Don't listen to whining from employees 2. Massage or hide "bad" data about the area in lengthy reports 3. Do not let employees talk to employees in any other areas; punish those who do
Mistakes By Others Are a Chance to Look Good	1. Attend to gossip and listen for problems 2. Spread around bad news
The Department or Work Area Comes First	1. Keep problems quiet 2. Make sure employees cooperate minimally with other areas; punish those who openly talk about the area's shortcomings
Build Up a Network to Get Things Done	1. Spend a lot of time schmoozing and socializing 2. Order employees to break the rules for "special" people
Decisions Are Made at the Top	1. Use upper management as an excuse not to do things for employees 2. If there is any doubt, either don't do it or write a lengthy report to ask permission
You Can't Change City Hall	1. Let problems go by unless they irritate you personally 2. Don't fight the system on behalf of employees; that's just the way it is

If It Ain't Broke, Don't Fix It	1. Make sure employees mind their own business; you'll decide when a problem is a problem
	2. Punish employees who change things without asking
	3. Insist on rigid adherence to policies and procedures
Maintain the Caste System at All Times	1. Don't be friendly with employees
	2. Don't eat with employees
	3. Act arrogant and condescending with employees
	4. Punish employees who attempt to interact with higher levels of management

Do you feel a little disgusted with this list after the additional insights you've developed over the last twelve chapters? I hope so. It might have been funny before, but it shouldn't be funny now.

Just think about it for a minute. What does the typical manager do in a day? He or she holds meetings to find out what the Sub-Humans and Egg Sucking Pigs are doing, reads reports about what they're doing, reads and approves routine housekeeping paperwork that must be signed to make sure that the employees aren't doing anything wrong, attends numerous meetings with other managers to discuss cross-functional problems created by stupid employees, reports to his or her boss in meetings and reports, takes care of disciplinary problems that can't be dodged any longer, and responds to urgent problems that pop up. Once a year, he or she generates material for some sort of cursory plan and writes up and conducts performance appraisals on his or her people. Throw in a few trips to meetings or conferences and some outside customer contacts (which vary according to the job), and you've got the routine of about 95% of all managers pretty well outlined by the Guiding Principles of the traditionally run business. No wonder we're in trouble.

There's not a word in that list about processes, teaching, coaching, statistical process control, pursuing bold new ways of doing things (quite the contrary), and leadership.

AMERICAN SAMURAI INSIGHT

It's ironic, but the first challenge of an aspiring, transformed manager is to stop doing almost everything that he or she has been doing in the past.

The Traditional System Doesn't Teach Useful Management Skills

The typical manager's activities discussed in the preceding paragraphs are limiting and damaging, more suitable to draft animals than people. Almost all of them are related to tight control and direction of subordinates' activities—keeping a lid on things, making sure that the employees don't do anything too wrong. None of these activities has anything to do with fostering an understanding of a process orientation toward work, the use of statistical techniques, or the importance of supplier-customer linkages within the organization. As you review the remaining Coda, you'll see that the traditional management approach not only doesn't encourage any of these "good" concerns, it actually works to thwart any spontaneous ignitions of an enlightened approach to work from employees.

Under the traditional system, as long as employees stay within the limits of performance that the organization has established, they are left alone. The processes they operate are assumed to be fine as long as there is no trouble. The skills and knowledge levels of managers and employees are assumed to be acceptable as long as there are no obvious problems. As far as the traditional style of management is concerned, no news is good news; a manager doesn't really have to do much if no problems pop up. He or she is presumed to be running a tight ship as long as things are quiet.

Wrong. We can no longer afford to have management simply function as the jailers of a minimum security, day-care center. In order to maximize productivity, organizations must have everything their people can give them. This means that employees of the successful organizations of the 1990s are going to require managers who can lead and teach their employees; managers who proactively provide their employees with the coaching and support they'll need to meet future challenges.

THE NEW ROLE OF MANAGEMENT

The American Samurai manager does almost none of the things that consume the time of the traditional manager. He or she focuses on teaching and coaching employees to control their processes and satisfy their customers. This frees up the management time and resources that are essential for developing long-range, customer-driven plans that involve all employees. The time that used to be spent responding to crises by tampering and micro-management can then be devoted to studying, thinking, and learning about bold, new innovations. The enlightened manager provides a solid leadership example by living The Code every minute and developing policy that encourages its practice. Let's take a look at each one of these new management roles in detail.

Management Function One: Leadership

Leadership is not "being in charge." Being in charge or having a title means nothing in terms of leadership. That's why employees laugh at CEO exhortations in company newspapers; they know the difference between being "boss" and running things. CEOs are in charge, but very few of them have anything but the most remote impact on day-to-day work activities. Sure, a CEO can close a plant and put several thousand families into poverty, but there's nothing that the typical CEO can do to change the behaviors of men and women on the plant floor. That takes leadership, not position.

Leadership is the use of earned respect and approval to motivate and guide a group to achieve a predetermined objective. The American Samurai manager earns the respect of his or her people by treating them all as decent, intelligent people who are winners. When employees are treated with respect and dignity, when they are expected to perform, are trained to perform, and believe they can perform, they will perform (a self-fulfilling prophecy). The American Samurai leader demonstrates his or her commitment by actively modeling The Code and serving as the symbol of its living application. You can't do that by sitting in an office and sending out memos. You've got to be a people leader, someone who's out there doing it and teaching others to do it, hour after hour, day after day.

Too many managers believe that leadership is a logical and fact-based exercise. It's not. It's a warm, interpersonal identification of the employee with the leader and his or her values. A leader must be out in front of the employees, living what he or she expects them to live, demonstrating a consistent pattern of support and concern through all avenues of behavior and policy. That's leadership. Few managers today even know what it means.

Management Function Two:
Teaching and Coaching

A common lament of managers at every level is, "I don't believe it, it happened again! This problem never goes away. Every time I turn around, it happens." It doesn't matter what the problem is, because they *all* keep happening over and over. The fact is, problems continue to happen because nobody teaches employees how to take control and master their processes. Every disaster is followed by a flurry of tampering and new rules and regulations that absolutely guarantee that the old problem (and lots of new ones) will happen again. It has to, because the root causes have not been removed.

Managers must forget about controlling and directing; they must begin to teach and coach. Employees don't know how to solve problems and improve processes. Where would they have learned? They don't understand variability. They don't understand supplier-customer links and processes. It's up to their bosses to teach them. Sure, employees can learn the basic facts in a training class, but training alone, without active involvement by management on a day-to-day basis, won't cut it. When was the last time an employee thought, upon seeing the boss coming, "Oh, good. It's time for more training and coaching"? This has never happened in most American companies.

Managers must begin to coach and guide their employees on a real-time basis so that the employee always knows how he or she is doing and the areas in which to improve in order to more fully satisfy his or her customers. This means that the boss will have to teach them how to identify customers. More critically, the boss (and all management) must, on a moment-to-moment basis, demonstrate that quality and customer satisfaction come before all else, all the time. Any discrepancy between words and actions will quickly kill employee commitment and enthusiasm.

Management Function Three: Leading Innovation

It's amazing how little time the typical manager has for thinking, reading, and reflecting on new ways of doing things. In the traditionally run company, management is so busy putting out fires that there's no time to learn about new things; any time spent thinking will mean that another problem doesn't get tampered with. Have you ever noticed how guilty most managers feel when you catch them reading a business book or maybe just sitting at their desks with their feet up? It's as if sitting still was a crime. If we aren't in constant motion, we feel guilty. As a result, almost all decisions are made on the run, in seconds. We're afraid to take the time to think for a moment before acting.

This style would seem to presume that every manager has total and complete understanding of every situation and total recall of every piece of knowledge about every problem. Of course, that's nonsense. But that doesn't stop the snap decisions (or the dire results of such tampering). We must abandon this devotion to the "fast gun." Managers must take the time to think about new ways of working, take the time to read books like this (and hopefully, many others in the Bibliography), take the time to visit other companies, and take the time to read business magazines to get hints of how other organizations are competing. Management must take the time to think and learn so that they can lead innovations. They can never lead innovations if they never have a chance to look for them.

There's a parable, probably apocryphal, about Henry Ford, the founder of the Ford Motor Company. As the story goes, a consultant told Ford that he ought to fire a particular man because, the consultant said, "Every time I pass the guy's office down there, he's sitting with his feet up, looking out the window." Henry Ford is said to have replied, "Last year, that guy came up with an idea that saved me millions. I'm hoping that if we leave him alone, he'll come up with another one."

Making the necessary time to discover and lead innovation is a critical part of management's responsibility. Innovation is a new way of doing something, a tactic or a strategy that boosts performance up to an entirely new level. For example, empowered and properly led employees could continuously improve the work flow of an invoice-processing operation. Over time, they might use the process improvement methodology described in Chapter Eleven to dramatically reduce the throughput time of an invoice. From their perspective, these employees would be doing all they could. Yet, for all their efforts, they are cutting a faster and better path through a large jungle from their perspective at ground level. They're doing a great job, but they do not have the "above the treetops" opportunity to view the organization and the industry, which might show them an entirely new way. There might already be cleared, grassy meadows just to their right or left.

Management has the advantage, if it can take the time, to go above the trees and gain a broader perspective of the process, to hover above the trees and see more of the landscape. Management might find that "grassy meadow" or a flagstone-paved garden path only feet away in another industry. If the management of the invoice area were to visit other companies, do some research, gather some benchmarks, or perhaps brainstorm new concepts, they might discover a way to eliminate 90% of the invoices in the first place. Instead of chopping through the trees an inch at a time, it might be possible to get the same result with no chopping. That's something the employees, at ground level, couldn't know, and will never know. They don't have the time and the mandate to explore other organizations.

That's why it's absolutely essential for management to make the time to pursue innovations. And the only way to make the time reliably over the long haul is to teach the employees to take over their own processes. Too many American companies force their management to be right in there chopping along with the employees in order to get the path cleared a little farther and a little faster. This approach always misses the big hitters (and it establishes an environment in which the employees aren't free to go after all of the little hits they'd find if they weren't being micro-managed every second). In this type of organization, there are always a lot of people sweating and chopping, pushing the path along; however, the path never seems to go anywhere that anyone likes.

Management Function Four:
Understanding the Variability of Key Processes

It's the manager's responsibility to understand the factors that contribute to the variability of the key processes under his or her span of control. It's also the manager's job to make sure that employees are analyzing and improving these processes in a systemic manner. That's the only way a manager can reliably hope to improve the long-term performance of his or her area. The ultimate measure of a manager's effectiveness in a fully enlightened, living by The Code organization is the variability observed in the long-term performance of key macro-process outputs. If the processes are understood and being properly maintained by employees, there should be very little variability (assuming that inputs from other areas are also under control).

For example, a CEO might be judged upon the value of stock, profit margins, and so on. The CEO, as part of his or her implementation of The Code, would pay particular attention to the key inputs that drive the stock price and profits. Key inputs to these outputs at that organizational level would include such "smaller" macro-process outputs as individual divisions' net profit margins and ROI (return on investment). There would be many others, of course. As the CEO coaches and teaches his or her direct reports (and the organization as a whole), it's critical that he or she lead and encourage efforts to precisely understand the mechanisms by which the lower-level macro-processes increase or decrease the larger macro-process outputs. Of course, at the CEO level, the macro-processes are driven by everything and CEO coaching can be only strategic, not tactical.

At a plant manager level, one key macro-process output that influences the CEO's concerns would be total scrap and rework costs. The plant manager, to be effective, would have to foster in his or her people an understanding of the variability of all of the factors that drive scrap and rework. This would require a great deal of teaching and coaching on the part of the plant manager, as well as the other members of the management team. If the root causes of scrap and rework were truly understood, scrap and rework metrics would demonstrate a very low absolute level and little variability. And when variability would occur, it could be quickly attributed to a known cause.

Management Function Five:
Setting Policy and Procedure

In Chapter Eight, we discussed the difference between policy and process. *Processes* are ongoing systems of inputs and events that produce outputs. *Policies* are discrete decision events; they happen once and are static until the decision is reversed. They influence processes but don't have an output of their own (except in the most general sense). The way in which policies are handled is a make or break issue in terms of organizational effectiveness.

Very often, companies will decide to implement something like The Code (perhaps Dr. Deming's "14 Points") but will not aggressively pursue policy changes that support the transformation. This is a killer mistake.

AMERICAN SAMURAI INSIGHT

An organization's policies and procedures are more than words, they are the blueprint for its thinking, its culture, and its valuation of people.

Policies and procedures may not always be followed and everyone may not know them, but they set the tone for how the human resources are valued and utilized. Every day, the policies of an organization affect each employee much like a religion's holy book affects all the believers; every follower doesn't have to read it every day (or at all) to be influenced by it, because it controls the entire faith in thousands of little ways. Policies and procedures have the same effect in a business.

For example, every company has policies that dictate attendance. Most management types who do not supervise Egg Sucking Pig level employees never think about such policies. Management people don't get penalized when they come in late, and they can easily take a "sick day" if they need a day for personal business or to kick back and relax. However, such policies have a major impact on lower-level employees, who have more problems with transportation (their cars are older and in worse repair) and child care (they can't afford the best). As a result, Egg Sucking Pigs and Sub-Humans tend to be victimized by attendance policies that heavily penalize a missed day or late arrival here and there. The mere existence of such a policy works insidiously to foster the caste system and the myriad of evils it breeds.

Many companies claim to be working on a transformation but never even consider changes in these types of abusive policies. Many companies even have a different level of reimbursement for personal car mileage and meal expenses on travel for Proto-Humans and above, compared to that allowed for Egg Sucking Pigs. There's no way to justify these types of punitive policies, except as instruments of caste reinforcement. It is management's duty to systematically remove these policies and substitute policy that maintains the spirit of The Code.

Management Function Six: Planning

We'll examine the detailed planning responsibilities of the American Samurai manager when we discuss Coda 10 in Chapter Fifteen. However, it's important to place planning in the proper perspective in this chapter. Planning is not an isolated, once a year event that involves a few briefings, lots of paper, and the usual excuses about why last year's plan didn't work, although that's what passes for planning in most companies. That's not planning—it's bull. A plan, done properly, is a detailed set of actions that will attain specifically identified goals. As you can imagine from the preceding discussions, it's impossible to put together a good plan unless the variability of key processes in understood and a work force is present that's skilled in controlling their processes. If an organization doesn't have a process approach, no plan can work because there won't be any comprehensive understanding of how things work.

It's a manager's responsibility to make the time to set the stage for proper planning. Then, the plan must be a living document that sets the stage for all process improvement activities throughout the organization. In other words, the plan is the blueprint for running the business for the plan period. As any of you who have participated in so-called planning in traditionally run companies know, the plan is usually forgotten shortly after it is presented. It's no wonder we aren't competitive.

MANAGEMENT ISN'T A JOB DUTY
AS MUCH AS A TASK ELEMENT—
EVERBODY MUST BE A BIT OF A MANAGER

"Management is almost always thought of in terms of status or position. Managers get offices, workers don't. Management means ties, "workers" means no tie. Managers call the shots, everybody else listens. That's a very short-sighted and limited view of management.

AMERICAN SAMURAI INSIGHT

In reality, every employee has elements of management in his or her job. We must have all employees, to the level that's appropriate to their duties, teaching and coaching associates, seeking innovations in their work, planning for better processes, and seeking to understand and reduce variability.

As you ascend the management ladder, the "management" component constitutes a bigger part of the job, but it's there a little even at the entry level. It's essential that every manager adopt this view. We must begin to think of all employees as "owner-managers" of their processes. What better way than to put them in charge of managing (to the extent appropriate to their experience and skills) their own jobs. That's the only way we're going to get full-blown, all out efforts from all of our people. That's the only way we can save American business from its sadly deserved fate.

14

"Real" Employees Do It Their Way!

Coda 9. The role of employees is to continuously improve their work processes (Standardize, Do, Check, Act) as if the processes they work were their own businesses.

THE SECRET OF JAPANESE PRODUCTIVITY

Many people think the secret of Japanese success in business is due to a culture that enhances selflessness—people willing to sacrifice for the group. Others think the secret is the willingness of Japanese workers to kill themselves for the company—working harder and faster than the employees of any other nation. Others attribute the Japanese "miracle" to high technology. They're all wrong. The secret of Japanese success has almost nothing to do with all the "cultural" factors. The success of the world–class Japanese companies (and the few American companies that have embraced a new way of working) is based upon a management style that empowers employees to take control of their work processes and continuously improve them. They do this without having to be told to do so by the boss and without having to ask permission. The workers own their processes, and they continually strive to improve the quantity and quality of their work. Let's take a look at how this works.

PROCESSES DETERIORATE OVER TIME

Just think of it. In a typical company, there are thousands of processes operating every day. In a traditionally managed organization, processes can be categorized in two ways: either (1) they're getting attention from management, or (2) they're operating on autopilot and getting no attention, other than being performed by employees. The only processes that get attention from management are those few processes that are "on fire," those that are having major problems.

148

Most of the attention given the fires, as we have discussed, will be in the form of management tampering that will make the situation worse. Those processes that are not actively being compromised by management are only marginally better off; they're also deteriorating. That's because customer requirements continually change and process outputs must change with them in order to maintain the required level of performance. Line A in Figure 14-1 graphically demonstrates what invariably happens to every process over time, either because the inputs and events deteriorate, customer requirements change, or both.

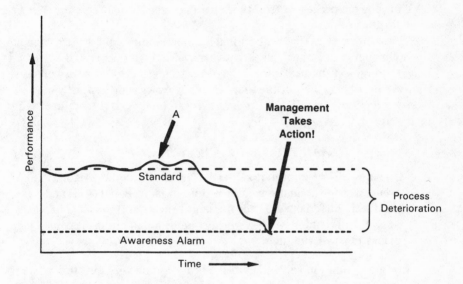

Figure 14-1. The deterioration of a work process and the subjective alarm threshhold (SAT).

Traditional managers don't appreciate this. They have a view of process performance that approximates Figure 14-1. Just turn the process on, and it runs along at the preset level. Wrong.

For every process, there's a point at which performance decreases sufficiently to attract attention. This point is different for every process and is not constant over time or people.

AMERICAN SAMURAI INSIGHT

In a traditionally run organization, the criteria for attending to processes is subjective, unique to each individual, time sensitive, and not predictable. The result is that processes are attended to, and tampered with, on a haphazard basis. The consequence is chaos.

The point at which a process attracts attention is the *"subjective alarm threshold"* (SAT). Figure 14-1 displays the relationship between expected performance levels and the SAT. The problem is that each manager's SAT for a given process varies according to the sensitivities of the person and his or her circumstances on a given day. You've all known a manager or boss who went nuts at the least little overspending on budget, in effect moving the SAT very close to the expected performance standard. Other managers, at the same time, for the same process, may be more forgiving, in effect having a personal SAT for budget variances that's much lower than the expected standard. Depending upon circumstances, a manager may move his or her SAT for a given process several times per day, depending upon how things are going.

For example, after three subordinates come in and request extra money for equipment or personnel, an executive may eventually "have had enough" and get tough on the next supplicant. In effect, the SAT for that process is raised after being low for the first three employees. This type of variability makes it extremely difficult for employees to predict, and therefore plan, their actions.

AMERICAN SAMURAI INSIGHT

The most severe impact of subjective alarm threshold variability occurs when the management of various organizational levels and areas have different SATs for the same process at the same time. This is, unfortunately, the typical state of affairs in most companies most of the time.

How many times have you heard the brass of your organization push a new "important thrust" such as "Quality Is Job One," "Productivity Plus," "Management Excellence," or any one of dozens of tired, old phrases that most experienced employees immediately recognize as another "bohica" (bend over, here it comes again) program from management? More than you can bear to recall, I'm sure. Yet, there are always a few who decide to trust management one more time and try to work in the spirit of the latest exhortations.

If the executive push is on for "quality" instead of volume, the employees are led to believe that the SAT for quality is right up against the expected performance line. This implies that no deviation from outstanding quality will be tolerated and that every employee must attend to quality every second so that quality performance does not deteriorate even a bit. So what happens almost immediately when a conscientious employee cuts back on production a little in order to turn out a top quality product? Or someone questions the wisdom of passing along a defective or questionable part?

You guessed it: they run smack into some dork in middle management who has a different agenda. The dork's SAT is miles below the expected performance line for quality: he or she wants to hear nothing about quality. This manager knows that what the top brass says has nothing to do with what goes on on a daily basis down in the bowels of the organization; the orders don't reach that far. The employee gets nailed because he or she was responding to a stated SAT level for quality that had nothing to do with the dorkmeister's actual SAT for quality.

EXECUTIVES SET SUBJECTIVE ALARM THRESHOLDS—BUT, SURPRISE, NOBODY PAYS ATTENTION!

I'm always amused to listen to CEOs and company presidents hold forth on subjects like quality, safety, and the like. I think they actually believe that people listen to them and that their orders are implemented. Employees below the level of Human Beings know that's total bull. Down in the ranks, nobody cares what the gods and Human Beings say because the words of the executives are never, ever translated to measurable actions all the way down the management ladder to the Egg Sucking Pigs in the trenches.

I've heard CEOs talk on closed circuit, company-wide TV about how an absolute dedication to quality was the single most important concern of every employee from that point on. Then, later that day, I've seen hourly employees told to "keep their mouth shut" and pass along a defective part, unless they wanted to be "sent to Labor Relations" (which would mean a day or 3 off without pay) by managers who had heard the same speech.

Meanwhile, back in fantasy land (corporate headquarters), the top brass think that everything is going along fine on their push for total quality. Just think about what happens. The CEO buzzes one of his private secretaries and asks her to put a call into one of his direct reports in the next office. So, we have a guy making 3 to 10 million a year, asking a guy who is struggling to pay for two homes, five cars, and four private school tuitions on a mere 1 to 2 million per year, "How's the quality program going?"

Now, suppose you're that guy. You say to yourself either (1) "How could it be doing anything; nobody in the ranks listens to the bull that we pump out up here," or (2) "How the hell would I know?" It's unlikely that you'd give the first response since your recollections of what it's like as a real worker would have been so long ago (or never have happened) that you wouldn't remember how everyone reacted to corporate blabbering. So, your reaction is the second, but, because of the homes, tuitions, etc., you can't ever tell the truth any more. So you answer, "Great, Boss, just great. Your speech was just what they needed to hear and they're really jumping right on it. Great, just great."

The CEO would thank you, hang up, and have his secretary put in a call to the company's consultant quality guru. The CEO would tell the guru how great things are going. The guru would then mention how great the company is doing to lots of people. How could either one of them know the truth?

When you hang up, you say to yourself, "Maybe I better check this out, just in the one in 10 million chance that the truth could somehow get to the CEO and turn out to be different from the lie I told him." So you get on the horn and put in a call to one of the guys who works for you who makes 500 to 800 K. Now, this guy knows that there are all sorts of problems out in the plant, but he doesn't know too much about them because it's just a rat's nest and nothing ever seems to get better. He knows that the push to cut costs and head count and to simultaneously maintain production is probably getting most of the attention and that nobody is doing "quality." But he also knows that, with falling sales, he'll never get another job making 500 to 800 K, so he tells you, "Great, just great. It will take some work, but they'll really get it done now." When he hangs up, he calls one of his regional managers, who goes through the same dance and who then calls one of his plant managers, who also lies and says the quality push is going well.

The plant manager calls his Production Manager and his Human Resources Manager, both of whom are making 90 to 150 K, and asks how the quality speech was received. The HR guys in any company know that such programs are all bull (takes one to know one), but they also know that they aren't living in great big houses with beautiful, ex-secretary young wives (this is almost a given with older HR executives for some reason; check it out) because they've been in the habit of telling the truth over the last 30 years. So the HR guy lies and then calls up one of his Sub-Humans and orders him or her to put together a report showing how great things are going on quality. This report will then be sent up the pipe, reassuring all those who wanted to know.

The Production Manager also lies and then works to back up his story by going one further. He will provide real proof. Every day for the next few weeks after the speech, he makes sure that each department puts on extra people to fix defects before they are inspected. This drives down the defect rate at formal inspection points and "proves" that the quality program is working. If you don't believe this (which hurts, I have to admit), you need only ask any person who has ever worked in an assembly plant of an American automotive manufacturer. He or she will tell you stories about pencil whipping quality numbers that would make a Honda or Toyota executive beam with competitive joy.

Suppose that the question finally got all the way down to an Egg Sucking

Pig, who answered, "Quality? Nobody gives a rat's ass about quality around here. All we do is push production, and God help anyone who tries to do quality first. Quality, my ass!" Just how much of a chance do you think this reply has of getting more than one level past the supervisor who hears it? If you answered "absolutely zero," you are correct. No bad news is *ever* passed up the line in a typical company, unless it's so obvious and horrible that even huge lies and pencil whipping can't hide it.

So, even if the truth starts out at the bottom of an organization and attempts to journey to the top, it has a short, nasty, and brutish life. I stumbled across a great, unattributed poem (of sorts) that crudely, but accurately, depicts the semantic and operational aspects of the "back up the organizational structure" reporting of how great things are going in the trenches. My apologies to the anonymous author(s) for not being able to credit him or her for perceptive wit and insight into management processes.

IN THE BEGINNING WAS THE PLAN

And then came the Assumptions
And the Assumptions were without Form
And the Plan was completely without Substance
And the darkness was upon the faces of the Workers
And they spoke amongst themselves, saying:
"It is a Crock of Shit, and it Stinketh."
And the Workers went to their supervisors, and sayeth:
"It is a pile of dung, and none may abide the Odour thereof."
And the supervisors went to their managers,
And sayeth unto them:
"It is a container of Excrement, and it is very Strong
such that none may Abide it."
And the managers went to their directors,
and sayeth unto them:
"It is a Vessel of Fertilizer,
and none may abide its Strength."
And the directors went to their VPs, and sayeth unto them:
"It contains that which aids plant growth,
and it is very powerful."
And the VP went unto the President and Sayeth unto him:
"This powerful new plan will actively promote the growth
and efficiency of the department,
and of this area in particular."
And the President looked upon the Plan, and saw that it was good.
AND THE PLAN BECAME POLICY.

That's why the folks on top think they know what's going on. They never do, in a traditionally run company, because they never hear the truth and all they see is distorted and pencil whipped macro-process outputs.

If we're going to be successful in eliminating this situation and totally involve employees, we must seek a different way. This new way is a key part of the Japanese approach to work.

THE ANSWER

The secret of Japanese success rests largely on *Kaizen*, pronounced "Ki (as in 'eye')-zen," which means improvement. Kaizen is not a specific technique, but an overall approach. The foundation of Kaizen is both a process orientation such as we have already discussed and a philosophy of work life that in general parallels the participatory mandates of The Code.

Perceptions of Job Functions

A key element of Kaizen rests on the differences between American, or Western, and Japanese perceptions of job functions. In the West, employees are generally seen as having two types of duties:

1. *Maintenance*—keeping things running and doing the work.
2. *Innovation*—coming up with bold new ways of doing things, such as new technology, new systems and so on.

Figure 14-2 displays these two job functions across the employee supervisory hierarchy.

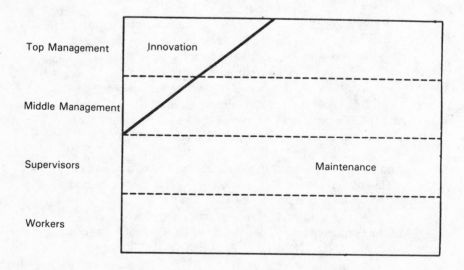

Figure 14-2. Traditional management's view of job responsibilities.

The bulk of workers, up through the Sub-Human level, spend all of their time on maintenance duties, pumping through the paper and the products, in rote, dig-a-ditch fashion. Some small part of each job might involve participation in improvements, but the "we don't want them slacking off while there's work to do" attitude of management stops most tentative employee efforts to improve processes. As you reach Proto-Human and Human Being levels, the amount of time spent on Maintenance, actually doing grind work, decreases and there's some time that's expected to be devoted to new ways of doing things. In essence, workers work and higher levels of mangement are supposed to come up with new systems. Of course, we know this isn't the case, since management spends most of its time in the trenches fighting fires and tampering.

In technology-driven companies in which dramatic advances occur almost weekly (such as the PC industry in its youth), the pursuit of innovation occupies a larger part of every employees' time, since the entire fabric of the work is driven by continual changes in the underlying technology of the product. However, once the industry stabilizes, its job function profile invariably resembles the one in Figure 14-2.

The Japanese view of job functions is much different. They believe that employees also have two job functions; however, their two functions are different:

1. *Maintenance*—as in the West, this is doing the work.
2. *Improvement*—making the process better.

Lower-level workers naturally spend most of their time devoted to maintenance. As you move up the organization, every level of workers and management spends more time working on improvements, and less time simply pumping out the work. It's a whole new role for employees and management.

**Two Types Of Improvements:
Innovation And Kaizen**

The Japanese define two types of improvement activities: Kaizen and innovation. Figure 14-3 graphically displays the allocation of effort for each of these improvement types (and maintenance) across the hierarchy of job levels.

Figure 14-3 may not look earth-shaking, but it has profound significance in explaining why Japan is kicking in our industrial teeth. Every level of worker, including the hourly, entry-level employee, is seen as having a formally defined duty to improve his or her processes via the application of Kaizen. From the supervisory level up to the CEO, every employee is expected to be devoting an equal and large part of his or her day to Kaizen. Starting at the middle management and higher levels, a significant amount of time is specifically directed at innovation.

As you can see by comparing Figures 14-2 and 14-3, the principal difference between the Japanese and Western approaches is Kaizen, the on-going pursuit of improvements by every employee, every day. That, and only that, explains the majority of the Japanese competitive advantage up through the late-1970s (since then, other advantages have been coming on line as well; we'll talk about them in later chapters).

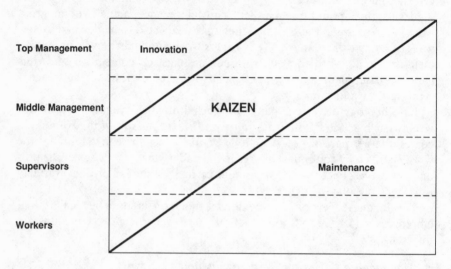

Figure 14-3. Job responsibilities in a world–class Japanese company.

Innovation and Kaizen Are Philosophies

Innovation is an approach to work (and life) that focuses on big, order of magnitude leaps ahead. Kaizen is an approach that favors small, gradual improvements. To a large degree, the typical Western company is innovation oriented in its philosophy of work and its strategy of product development. All world-class Japanese companies are Kaizen oriented. Let's compare some general characteristics of both approaches to get a feeling for the overall type of work environment each drives.

KAIZEN	*INNOVATION*
Low technology	High technology
Group efforts	Rugged individualism
Small improvements	Huge leaps
Emphasis on processes	Emphasis on profits
Everybody involved	A few heroes do it all (well, they get the credit)
Maximize use of conventional knowledge	Look for new technology

Use human resources first	Use machines first
Improve what you have	Start over with new stuff
Focus on adaptability	Focus on creativity
Attention to small details	Attention to big picture
Widely shared information	Information restricted to top management
Cross-functional approaches	Functional specialists who seldom cooperate
System is adapted to the people	People adapt to the system
Value people	Value systems/technology
Employees as partners	Employees as meat robots
Little cost to practice	Expensive to practice
Safety of workers is a top priority	Safety of workers is a secondary consideration
Difficult to practice: requires willpower and determination over years	Easy to practice: simply spend lots of money fast
Small, gradual changes	Huge, infrequent leaps
Management as coaches and thinkers	Management as jailers and mad scientists
Everyone is a key player	Participation requires status or special credentials
Squeezes the last drop of productivity from the system	Uses volume to spread costs of inefficiencies
Can always be profitable	Requires growth industry to make money
Management patient in pursuing changes and improvements	Management wants quick results

If you compare the two columns, you can see that every American company you've ever worked for was characterized by the right column (unless you've been very lucky and worked for a Baldrige winner or possible contender). Take safety, for example. When a safety improvement is suggested in an American plant, a prime consideration is whether or not the improvement will be cost-effective when comparing potential injury costs to the installation cost of the safety improvement. If you can't show big savings (a fast return-on-investment), forget the change. Of course, if the media is involved, as when somebody is killed, the change will go through immediately, for public relations reasons.

In a Kaizen-oriented company, employee safety is never compromised for reasons of cost. How could it be when the employees are considered the prime asset? When Japanese executives tour less than world–class American plants, they are appalled at the obvious safety hazards that would be immediately corrected in a Japanese plant, regardless of cost.

THE REQUIRED COMBINATION OF INNOVATION AND KAIZEN

There's a critical distinction between Kaizen and innovation that's often lost on first time acquaintances of Kaizen. It sometimes appears as if innovation itself is bad, something to be avoided in a world-class company. Nothing could be further from the truth. Remember, we are talking primarily about innovation and Kaizen as philosophies of management. Notice that Figure 14-4 shows that innovation is a critical component of the Kaizen approach, but as job duty, not as a management philosophy.

AMERICAN SAMURAI INSIGHT

Innovation as a management philosophy is self-limiting because it precludes the active process improvement of most employees. Innovation as a personal job duty is absolutely essential to organizational success.

Our problem in the United States is that we've taken the cowboy-like, rugged-individual mentality, which is absolutely required for absentminded professors and frontier-technology engineers working alone, and expanded it into a management approach that is the kiss of death when applied to group endeavors.

In essence, we've got to learn to manage our individual thinking and creativity with innovation values, and we've got to manage our team, group, department, and organizational efforts with Kaizen. Individual brainstorming and sudden flashes of insight by advanced thinkers are, by definition, solitary acts. They are often fueled by group input, but they rely most heavily on the gifted individual. That will never change. However, we've got to learn to use Kaizen from the very instant the idea is brought into the real world for action.

INNOVATION IS OUR STRENGTH, BUT WE'RE WEAKENING FAST

Surprise of surprises—we actually have an advantage over the Japanese (or anyone else), if we choose to augment it with Kaizen. That strength is our ability, as a nation, an economy, and individuals, to pursue innovations better than anyone else. The very personal and national characteristics that are ruining our competitive corporations are the ones that make us great scientists, engineers, and systems conceivers; nobody has been better at coming up with ideas and advancements out of whole cloth. The United States still wins the most Nobel prizes and still comes up with most of the new frontier, cutting-edge technology in most fields. We still run almost all of the leading graduate schools and research centers in the hard sciences. We're successful in these areas because they have, in the past, depended upon a few daring thinkers, operating by themselves, rather than on large teams.

If we could rein in this fascination with innovative personalities just enough to allow Kaizen to flourish as an organizational mechanism, *while still maintaining the values of innovation as a personal work ethic for our scientists and thinkers*, we would have the best of both worlds. We would be unbeatable. The problem is that time is running out.

We used to be the hands down technology leaders in every field. That's not the case anymore. Sheridan M. Tatsuno, in his outstanding (and scary, if you're an American business person) book, *Created in Japan: From Imitators to World-Class Innovators*, demonstrates that the Japanese are quickly moving to become the world's best innovators. He points out that three of the top four companies receiving U.S. patents in 1987 were Japanese: Canon, Hitachi, and Toshiba. In 1976, the top four were all American. Tatsuno also notes that at the 1987 International Solid State Circuits Conference, the "Olympics of semiconductor research," the American share of technical papers decreased to 43% from 61% in 1981. Over the same period, the Japanese share increased from 25% to 44%. We are losing our edge as the innovators of the world.

One of the reasons for this change in the balance of innovation power is that technology is increasingly becoming so complex that one person can no longer "get his or her arms around" enough knowledge to fully develop and/or implement the technology. More and more, successful innovations require large teams to bring together all of the essential components of a technology. We're bad at that and getting worse. The Japanese are great at it, and getting better. More and more often, they're getting the first hint of an advance from one of our efforts and then they're quickly bringing teams of Kaizen-oriented experts together to fully develop the technology. In very few cases can one person, however endowed, hope to compete with a cooperative team in developing a complex technology.

That's why the Japanese are eating us up in electronics. That's why they're ahead in high-density TV. An interesting case study of the Japanese success in applying Kaizen to innovation involves recent progress in magnetohydrodynamics (MHD). MHD is a technology that will permit propulsion systems with no moving parts for seagoing ships and submarines. Large, superconducting magnets are used to generate an electric field in seawater, which is given an electric charge. This creates a thrust that can quietly propel a ship or submarine. This technology was part of the plot in the Tom Clancy book and the movie *The Hunt for Red October*.

The United States tested MHD in the 1960s, but at that time magnets that were strong enough had not yet been developed. In the late 1980s, Japan launched a formal effort and is now working on a 100–foot test ship. The cooperating Japanese companies are Toshiba, Mitsubishi, and Mitsui. It's the same old story: some bold thinker in the United States comes up with an idea and then the Japanese assemble a team and develop the technology into a usable product. There's not much doubt as to who will have the first practical MHD vessel. We lose again.

And we'll continue to lose unless we begin to apply Kaizen principles to our organizations by living The Code. If we don't, we're going to be pushed out as the leaders in innovation as well as production and marketing.

THE STANDARDIZE, DO, CHECK, ACT (SDCA) CYCLE

If the spirit of Japanese success rests with Kaizen, the basic mechanism is the Standardize, Do, Check, Act (SDCA) cycle. This is the mode by which all of the Kaizen-related activities are realized. Figure 14-4 presents the SDCA cycle, which is simply the Plan, Do, Check, Act cycle applied to the Kaizen-related improvement activities of any process.

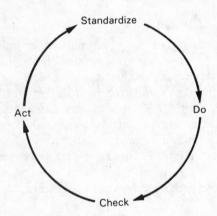

Figure 14-4.   The Standardize, Do, Check, Act (SDCA) cycle.

The point of interest in this representation is the "Standardize" element. In effect, performance standards are established for each process jointly by employees who work the process and by management. These standards are not objectives as such but are, in the thinking of Toyota, the optimum combination of employees, machines, and material. Standards are viewed as the only way to assure that quality, cost, and production requirements are met on time and safely. The employees then work the process (the maintenance aspect of their job function) while continually seeking ways to improve the process (Kaizen) and raise the standards.

The application of the SDCA cycle allows the employees to continuously explore avenues of process improvement while doing their jobs. They do this without having to be directed to do so by management and without management having to "notice" a problem first.

When a possible improvement is discovered, it is tried (Do), it is analyzed (Check), and then appropriate action (Act) is taken. If the change improves the process, it is incorporated into the standards (Standardize). If the change didn't help, or made things worse, it is dropped and other improvements are considered.

AMERICAN SAMURAI INSIGHT

It is critical to understand that most Kaizen-led improvements are small, not big hitters. However, it is the accumulation of thousands of such small improvements, year after year, that results in systems significantly better than anything that "pure" innovation can produce.

Just to demonstrate how "small" is small in terms of acceptable Kaizen improvements, consider Nissan. The smallest unit of time considered for Kaizen is 1/100th of a minute or 0.6 second. Any suggestion that will save at least that much is seriously considered by management. Can you imagine what would happen if you took an idea that would save only 0.6 second per operation to a typical American manager? You'd get thrown down the steps (and if you weren't near steps, he'd carry you to some). Yet, it's thousands of these small improvements, one after another, that yield 50% to 60% productivity advantages over several years.

This process is ongoing and is driven by the employees, not management. However, a key element is significant lower-level supervisory authority for implementing changes. In the typical Japanese plant, lower-level supervisors have significant authority and responsibility to quickly implement process improvements of a Kaizen nature. Suggestions are enthusiastically received and quickly tested. In the typical American company, lower-level supervisors have no authority and are caught between workers who dislike and distrust them and a management that disdains them. As we've already discussed in earlier chapters, suggestions are viewed by supervisors and upper management as annoyances and are actively (although clandestinely) discouraged, by means of burdensome documentation requirements, management attacks on the idea, and glacially slow feedback systems.

THE PLAN, INNOVATE,
CHECK, ACT (PICA) CYCLE

The innovation function of each job is reflected in the Plan, Innovate, Check, Act (PICA) cycle, which is the innovation analog to the SDCA cycle. The PICA cycle is shown in Figure 14-5. The PICA cycle demonstrates that innovations are planned (Plan), tried (Innovate), and analyzed (Check) and that actions are taken (Act). These are not Kaizen-type, step-wise, built on existing technology, "squeeze the last ounce out of what we've got" improvements. These are the bold, new systems advancements, totally new ways of doing things.

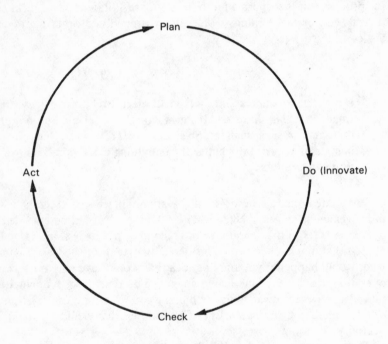

Figure 14-5. The Plan, Innovate (Do), Check, Act (PICA) cycle.

But, even though we're talking about bold, new innovations, the systems are first tried on a test basis to see if they work. Teamwork is used to coordinate the testing, evaluating, and implementation, rather than simply issuing higher order mandates. This is Kaizen even in innovation.

Figure 14-6 displays the profile of process improvement that can be expected when both Kaizen (SDCA) and innovation (PICA) are actively nurtured in an organization. Note that innovation fuels occasional, sudden, impressive bursts of improvement, whereas Kaizen (SDCA) fuels slow, constant process improvements. The beauty of this approach is twofold:

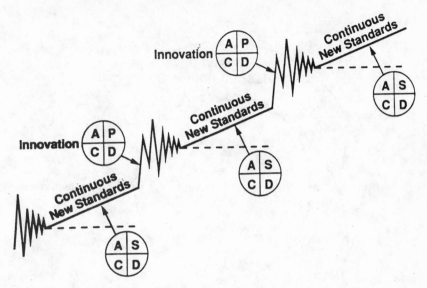

Figure 14-6. Process improvement patterns with the SDCA and PICA cycles.

1. Management is free to spend more time on innovations because it is not continually fighting day-to-day brushfires. Therefore, more and more carefully thought through innovations are obtained.
2. Processes are continuously improved by employees without management having to consciously direct attention to them.

An approach that relies on innovation alone can't hope to compete. That's us, folks.

Figure 14-7 displays the relationship between SDCA (Kaizen) and PICA (innovation) on a daily basis. Each person has such a circle for his or her own work. Each of us is working in the inner circle when we're doing the grind it out work and working on small improvements. We're on the outer circle when we're working on innovations. As you go higher up the organization in a Kaizen-oriented organization, the amount of time devoted to the SDCA cycle should remain constant (doing your own work a little better), while the amount of time devoted to the PICA cycle should increase.

If someone is not a process doer, he or she has no reason, or capability, to make SDCA decisions. Thus, it is not appropriate for a supervisor or manager to be making process decisions about his or her employees' inner SDCA cycles. That's Deming's tampering. A supervisor simply doesn't know enough about the processes. It would do typical American managers well to think about how they inappropriately spend time on the inner SDCA of their employees instead of attending to their own processes through Kaizen activities or innovation.

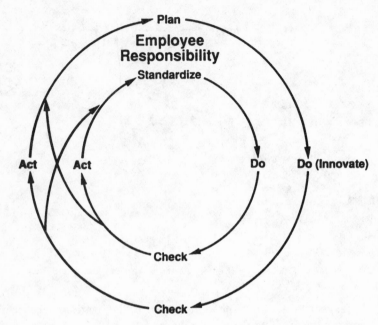

Figure 14-7. The interrelationship between the SDCA and PICA cycles.

Suggestions Systems

As you can see by now, Kaizen, innovation, SDCA, and PICA are not unitary techniques or specific actions. They are both the elements of, and, taken as a whole, a philosophy of work. As such, they are an essential part of the overall Code of the American Samurai. You can see that there is considerable overlap with a lot of what we have already discussed. It's hard to say where a philosophy starts and where it stops.

One of the most visible characteristics of Kaizen in a world-class organization is the suggestion program. These are not the pale imitations that we see in the United States, but systems that generate millions of suggestions (that are actually tried!) every year. It's interesting to note that we are the ones who took the concept of suggestion programs to Japan in the early 1950s. Once again, they've "Kaizened" our idea and made it work while we haven't. Some companies in Japan get millions of suggestions per year and take action on and/or answer every one, most within a couple of days.

The suggestion topics that are typically addressed in organizations with a Kaizen orientation include improvements in one's own work (SDCA), improvements in product quality, safety improvements, new products, improvements in office and administration procedures, reductions of work hours (labor), saving time, eliminating drudgery, and removing nuisances from the job.

THERE'S NO INNOVATION ANSWER TO IMPLEMENTING KAIZEN; IT'S GOING TO BE A LONG, SLOW SDCA EFFORT

One of the problems with trying to "sell" The Code is that American executives want an innovation answer; they want quick results and not a long, drawn out process. They are in for a shock. As you can see, the introduction of a Kaizen mentality into American business is going to be a long, tough battle. But, if each of us doesn't start now, it'll be all that much longer and we'll end up saving less of what's left.

15

Real Plans: Not 8½ × 11-Inch 10-Pound Doorstops

Coda 10. Business plans must be action documents that provide every member of the organization with sufficient detail to clearly understand what they must do in order to help the organization attain its objectives.

We've all seen it, and we've all been forced to play along. You know what I'm talking about—the annual, 2-week exercise of complete irrelevancy with outstanding graphics: the Annual Plan. The 8½ by 11-inch, 10-pound, perfectly produced, numbered-copy doorstop. Those people sufficiently privileged to get them (which isn't many in most companies) stick them on their bookshelves and forget them. Why do we punish ourselves?

Seems like every company has to have one, although nobody uses them. It's like neckties. Have you ever wondered why we pay 25 dollars for a stupid piece of stain-attracting, folded material with patterns so ugly that even our great-grandmothers wouldn't cover a couch with it, carefully fold it around our necks so that the ends match, and then wear it around all day, even in the hot summer, get it stuck in seat belts and desk drawers, dipped in coffee cups, and snagged between our bellies and the desk top? Why do we do it? Nothing but tradition.

And that's exactly why most companies have a plan, just tradition. I'd like to strangle the 16th-century fop who tied the first scarf around his neck and started the whole tie thing, almost as much as I'd like to find out who first started annual planning in its misguided form and fasten his or her lips together with a velo or spiral binding machine.

"Oh, sure," you're probably thinking, "Ford, General Motors, IBM, ITT, and other companies do annual plans only because of tradition. Right (snort). They're huge corporations, so they must do them for a good reason. They must use them . . . don't they?" Sadly, I must answer: no, Grasshopper, they don't use them. And I'm sad that you doubted me. You must learn to respect your teacher. I've worked for a number of Fortune 100 companies, and I've seen their planning processes. I know, It wasn't pretty—their plans were useless.

AMERICAN SAMURAI INSIGHT

Almost all companies' annual plans are a complete waste of time and resources. They don't do anything worthwhile and actually worsen the situations they were supposed to correct.

However, there are a very small number of American companies that are planning the right way. These companies learned a new way from—guess who?—the Japanese. This new approach (which truly is "Japanese management") is discussed below.

WHY HAVE A PLAN?

Let's start right at the beginning, logically and orderly. Let's look at why businesses might think they must have annual plans. This will allow us to examine the problems with the typical planning procedure and the characteristics of plans that might really do the job right.

What Plans Are Supposed to Do

Now, don't think about the plans you've all worked with in the past (unless you're one of the lucky few). Just think about what the perfect plan would do. What would you expect a plan to do if you were betting everything you and your entire family has on a new business?

The plan would have to provide detailed guidelines, objectives, and action items that would accomplish the following:

1. *Deliver a product or service that satisfies end-user customers.* This is, after all, the most critical, bottomline requirement. If you don't get and keep the customers, it's "live under the overpass time" for the family.

    This implicitly demands that customer needs be known and anticipated for at least the planning period (and more). This requires that the plan incorporate specific action items for determining what customers want, how they feel about current efforts/products (yours and those of other companies), and what they expect in terms of quality, service, and price.
2. *Be profitable.* Not only do you have to get and satisfy the customers, you've got to make enough money to take care of the business and your employees and their families.

    This means that the plan must detail the requirements and action items for assuring that all processes are brought up to the minimum standards (as in Standardize, Do, Check, Act) that will generate profits and quality.
3. *Be more efficient than the competition.* It's not enough to make money, you've got to do it better than the competition so that you'll have the resources to move quickly, seize new opportunities, and react to changes in the market and customers.

The plan must detail the means by which all key processes in the organization will be benchmarked and continuously improved. Nothing is ever good enough today to be good enough tomorrow, and the plan must incorporate the metrics, benchmarks, and action items that will allow for objective tracking of ongoing efforts to improve.

Doesn't sound much like your company's plan, does it? World-class Japanese companies and some American companies have such plans. That's why they're kicking their competitors' heads in.

The Problems with the Traditionally Designed and Applied Annual Plan

Typical plans don't do any of the preceding, which is the problem with them in a nutshell. Let's take a look at each of these problems as they appear in the business plans of traditionally run American companies. You'll appreciate the extensive changes in planning that must be adopted by American business.

1. *The plan is based on objectives.* Many plans are simply executive level "wish lists" of objectives. They have nothing to say about how things will be done (or who will do them) in order to reach objectives. A list of objectives is not a plan, it is worthless.
2. *The plan does not "tie in" to daily operations.* The plan doesn't have any impact on how day-to-day work is done. The work goes on much as it always has, with no consideration given to doing processes differently. You know you're dealing with this type of plan when the plan for a given year isn't even developed until the year is partially complete.
3. *The plan is a secret.* In many companies, plans are kept under wraps and hidden from the majority of middle management and all lower-level employees. Yet, somehow, executives expect the plan objectives to be met. Just showing someone the objectives won't do it, of course, but if people never even see them, you're absolutely guaranteeing that you won't attain them except through luck (and if you're going to rely on luck, why waste time on a plan?).
4. *The plan is a compilation of isolated department plans.* This is typical in many companies. The plan is created by having departments or areas send in their contributions. The result is a hodgepodge of conflicting, irrelevant, and redundant actions and objectives. That's OK, however, because the plan will be ignored anyway, and everybody will simply go on doing whatever they did before; in fact, that's what they input to the plan.
5. *The plan is developed "on high" and passed down.* This is what happens when some pencil neck Human Beings at "corporate" decide that they know what's best. So, knowing nothing about ongoing operations at particular divisions, they generate a detailed plan about what each operating unit should do for the next year. Since they know next to nothing about

the processes, they can't include any information about how to get to the objectives. This type of plan is always followed by requests for "updates" or reviews as to "actual versus plan" status throughout the year. It's all a waste of time and resources.

6. *The plan is not correlated with other conditions or situations.* Many plans don't tie in capital planning, head count requirements, and equipment purchase lead times. Objectives are blithely passed out, but then it's impossible to get money and people in order to reach objectives. Employees are told to "make do." That's why the objectives aren't met.

7. *Participation in the development of the plan is limited.* In most companies, it's common for the great majority of employees to have no input at all in the annual plan. This means that information about vital processes never reaches those who are actually running the processes that make the company go.

8. *The plan is not based on customers.* If the plan doesn't start with concern for customer requirements, it's off track in the first place.

9. *The plan can't measure progress.* Far too many plans have broad objectives for an operating unit (a macro-process generator) but no way in which to measure constituent micro-processes in order to assess ongoing progress. With the typical plan, progress can only be monitored in attaining the few macro-process outcomes. If things aren't going well, the problem is difficult to diagnose because micro-processes aren't included in the plan.

10. *The plan objectives are written to optimize returns from the compensation system.* This is the all-time, classic, double whammy: tying worthless planning to even more worthless pay for performance systems. Pay for performance and related insanities will be discussed in Chapter Nineteen (Coda 14), but they impact planning as well. Many organizations require managers (note that "hourly" employees are always excluded) to tie their plan objectives to their merit pay objectives. Therefore, they include only those objectives they are sure they can reach, so that they'll have the maximum probability of getting the best raise. Whether such objectives are good for customers or the company isn't considered, because the purpose of such objectives is to get a raise, not enhance quality and customer satisfaction.

You're probably wondering, after reading this list, why any companies do plans. Remember the necktie: it's a tradition. They don't think, they just do. Now let's take a look at what a plan must do to work properly. You can already appreciate that a proper plan requires a complete new system, not just a different way of organizing the 2 weeks of frenzied charting and graphing once a year. It requires that The Code of the American Samurai be operating.

What A Plan Must Have

If a business plan is going to do something besides employ printers and destroy our forests, it's going to have to be a lot different from anything we've got now. And it will require a lot more work than the system that has been called planning. In fact, the plan will serve as a blueprint for almost everything that happens in the organization over the plan period. Some of the characteristics of this new planning process are:

1. *Be based on a vision of the future.* If you don't know where the journey is supposed to end, it's hard to determine what action to take at any given point in time. As the old saying goes, "If you don't know where you're going, you may get there."
2. *Everybody must be involved and informed.* No source of valid information can be excluded from consideration in developing the plan. *Also*, every employee, in one way or another, must be involved in making the plan work. All employees must understand their part of the plan and what they must do to make it work.
3. *Be based on specific and measurable process outputs.* If a desired output is stated, it is essential for the plan to address the specific micro-processes that generate the output. These processes must have metrics, and the plan must outline how progress on these metrics will be monitored and updated so that corrective actions, if necessary, can be taken.
4. *Every objective at every level must support the overall plan goals and vision.* No objectives can be "loners" that are in the plan because somebody "thought they should be." Everything must support the fulfillment of the overall company goals.
5. *Specific responsibilities.* The plan must identify specific managers who are responsible for seeing that plan actions are implemented and monitored. These managers must inform, teach, and lead their employees in the implementation of the plan.
6. *Management at each level must integrate and correlate their goals so that suboptimization does not occur.* Once a manager decides on a set of objectives for his or her area that will support the vision and objectives passed down from higher levels, he or she must work with other managers to assure that one area's plans do not negatively impact those of another area.

JAPANESE PLANNING

World-class Japanese companies have a system that has the characteristics we just discussed. This is one of those areas in which so-called "Japanese management" really is Japanese; it's something they've developed and implemented all by themselves. The Japanese call their approach to planning "Hoshin Kanri." *Hoshin Kanri* literally means "gleaming or shining metal" or "pointing direction." A more common translation, in this context, is policy deployment. Hoshin Kanri is often called "management by policy." None of these names is very meaningful in descriptive terms. By any other name, it is a planning and management system/philosophy/approach that is part of a bigger whole—an overall, enlightened view of management.

Let's take a quick look at how Hoshin Kanri fits into the overall Japanese management approach. Bob King, the Director of GOAL/QPC, in Boston, Massachusetts, a major force for quality improvement in American industry, developed what he calls the Total Quality Control (TQC) Wheel. TQC is one of the many names that the Japanese have given to the complete management approach that emphasizes customer satisfaction, a process orientation, and never ending improvements. Other names that mean the same thing are CWQC (Company Wide Quality Control) and TQM (Total Quality Management). TQM is becoming the popular name for this overall approach in the United States (although many companies say that they "have" TQM, most are only playing games).

The TQC Wheel, shown in Figure 15-1, displays the relationship between the various elements of Japanese management. As you can see, at the center of the wheel is a *customer-driven master plan*, from which everything emanates. The three offshoots of the master plan, the things that realize the plan and make a business run, are daily control, cross-functional management working on issues related to quality, cost, delivery, and profit (QCDP), and Hoshin Kanri.

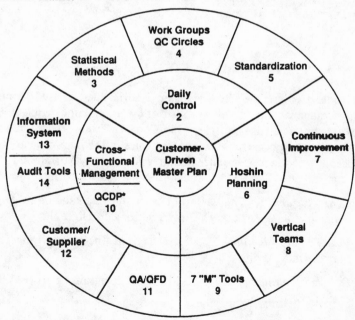

Figure 15-1. The Total Quality Control (TDQ) Wheel.

The daily control aspect involves process measurement and improvement activities. Standardization, which was discussed in Chapter Fourteen, is exactly the same thing here: how the work is done. The statistical methods discussed in Chapter Eight (Coda 3) are the ones involved here. Work groups and quality circles (QC) are exactly what they sound like: groups of employees working to improve processes and raise standards (SDCA).

Cross-functional management is the mechanism by which the entire management structure is focused on the requirements to simultaneously improve quality, cost, delivery, and profits (or products). This is done through audit systems, keeping track of key data, information systems, which pass the data to everyone who needs to know, mechanisms for involving suppliers and customers as part of the team (supplier relationships will be discussed in detail in Chapter Eighteen, Coda 13), and Quality Assurance/Quality Function Deployment. Quality Function Deployment (QFD) is a system for translating customer requirements to product and process features.

As you can well imagine, Hoshin Kanri is not simply a way to jam all sorts of bull and graphs into a binder that's passed around among upper management. It is a management tool that is the central driver for the complete operation of the business. Just to give you an idea of how different this approach is, let's take a look at some of the basic tools used to analyze data and obtain consensus among managers. You'll see that they're things that most self-respecting traditional managers would be embarrassed to be seen with. They'd be afraid that observers would think they were wasting time, rather than doing "productive work" (such as tampering or setting objectives).

THE SEVEN MANAGEMENT TOOLS

These tools aren't restricted to Hoshin Kanri. They're used throughout Japanese management for all sorts of applications and problem solving (related techniques will be discussed in Chapter Twenty-Three, Coda 18). However, they play central and repeated roles in the planning process and have been key to the process since their development by Yoshimobu Nyatani in the early 1980s. These seven tools are usually divided into three types:

General Planning: The Affinity Diagram (often called a KJ Digraph, from the Japanese) and the Interrelationship Digraph.

Intermediate Planning. The Tree Diagram, the Matrix Diagram, and Matrix Data Analysis.

Detailed Planning. The Process Decision Program Chart (PDPC) and the Arrow Diagram.

As you'll realize in our discussion of each tool, Nyatani didn't invent the tools. Each of them has been used extensively in various applications and industries for years. However, Nyatani is the one who developed the concept of applying them as a package to systematic planning.

Affinity Diagram (AD). An Affinity Diagram is constructed by grouping ideas around a central theme into "like" groups on the basis of whatever underlying themes seem logical. It's usually done on a large board with taped-on note cards or Post-It Notes. It works best when a complex idea, problem, or objective comes up and there is no standard way to handle it. As ideas or concepts come to mind, they are placed on the board. If two or more seem to fit together, they are placed next to each other. As groupings evolve, the team gives names to the groupings by placing header cards over each group. By voicing and then grouping all of the factors that come to mind, the team working on the problem can put things into perspective and bring out a great deal of related and critical information.

Interrelationship Digraph (ID). The Interrelationship Digraph is much like the AD in that it's used to place in perspective a large number of factors relating to a single issue. However, in the case of the ID, the interest is not in what factors group together, as in the AD, but in how the factors relate to each other; which ones most closely influence the others. The same technique of notes and a board is used. Once items are placed on the board, factors are connected to each other by lines if they appear to be related. Those items "pointed to" by the most factors are, by definition, the key factors in the situation.

Tree Diagram (TD). The Tree Diagram is used to map out a course of action for a given objective. The objective is put on one side of a board (with cards and tape or stick-on notes) and the question is asked, "What needs to happen to attain this objective?" The answers are put to one side of the objective in a column. The same question is asked of each of them. The cards from an Affinity Diagram or an Interrelationship Digraph (if these tools were also used) can be a great source of input and new ideas for a TD.

Matrix Diagram. There are many types of matrix diagrams. They all show relationships between two or more sets of data. For example, if you wished to relate the various design features of a portable radio with different customer requirements, you might have a matrix diagram like the one shown in Table 15-1.

Many different symbols can be used to categorize relationships between factors. In Table 15-1, the dash "-" denotes a negative relationship, in which the two factors are in conflict. For example, having powerful speakers will drive weight up, hence the dash. The "O" denotes no particular relationship (between battery power and durability, for example), and the " + " shows that there is a positive relationship between two factors (such as having powerful speakers and a more powerful battery). This type of matrix analysis, although in a much more complex format, is the basis for the mechanism of Quality Function Deployment (QFD).

Table 15-1.
Matrix diagram of radio features.

Desired customer feature	Design requirement		
	Light weight	Small size	Battery power
Durability	−	0	0
Speaker power	−	−	+
Easy to carry	+	+	−

Matrix Data Analysis (MDA). Matrix Data Analysis is used to place products or concepts on a two-dimensional grid in order to evaluate them. This technique has been used individually for many years in product development and advertising research. For example, let's say that we wished to characterize a number of automobiles on the two dimensions of sportiness and power. Figure 15-2 presents one possible MDA that such an analysis might develop.

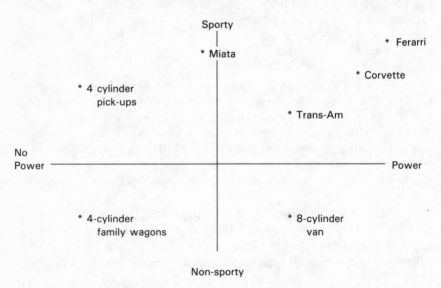

Figure 15-2. An example of Matrix Data Analysis.

This technique is very similar to what you might get by conducting factor-analytic studies of survey data (assuming that the people who do the matrix have insights into what the survey data might show).

Process Decision Program Chart (PDPC). This technique is simply a flow chart of all the possible things that can go wrong with a process or an idea. It is similar to a tree diagram in that it outlines an approach. It is different in that the tree diagram outlines what should be done; the PDPC outlines everything that could go wrong so that corrective or avoidance actions can be planned. As specific problems, paths or outcomes are suggested, they are put on cards (as in the other tools) and placed under the main problem. Countermeasures are then suggested and put off to the side of the main problem.

Arrow Diagram. Arrow diagrams are combinations of the famous "time line" Gantt charts of traditional business and flow charts. Arrow diagrams are used to show all of the relationships between process actions in terms of sequence, interrelationships, and time. An arrow diagram is a Gantt chart with a process orientation.

APPLYING THE SEVEN TOOLS TO HOSHIN KANRI

The Japanese generally divide Hoshin Kanri into the following stages:

1. Develop a 5-7 year vision (5 YR).
2. Develop a 1-7 year plan (1 YR).
3. Operationalize within departments (DPTS).
4. Implement the plan (DO).
5. Monthly audits (MO).
6. Annual review by president (PRES).

Table 15-2 relates each of these stages to the tools that are most often the key to them.

Table 15-2.
Hoshin Kanri planning tools and planning stages.

	Affinity diagram	Interre-lationship digraph	Tree diagram	Matrix diagram	Matrix data analysis	Process decision program chart	Arrow diagram
5 YR	X	X	X	X			
1 YR	X	X	X	X			
DPTS		X	X			X	X
DO		X	X			X	X
MO	Uses statistical tools and problem-solving approaches						
PRES		X	X	X			

PLANNING IS BUSINESS

As you can see, these management tools are not simply onetime grabbers that are used to generate fluff. Rather, they are critical thinking, creativity, analytical, and consensus building mechanisms that are an inherent part of the Hoshin Kanri process. This type of planning is the sort of planning that American industry must begin to embrace, or it will fall even further behind.

This transformation isn't going to come overnight. The problem is that anything even remotely like Hoshin Kanri can't work unless it is built on a firm foundation of process analysis, statistical data, wide-ranging participation, and open, honest management. If all of the other Coda are practiced, this one will eventually come by itself.

16

Training Makes Money The Old-Fashioned Way— It Earns It!

Coda 11. **All employees must receive extensive skills and knowledge training about their jobs, the company, and the tools of process improvement. Training is a long-term investment in profits, not an expense.**

Training is perhaps the biggest sinkhole of wasted resources, misguided problem solving, and management stupidity in all of business. Training that shouldn't be done is done all the time (to the wrong people), training that should be done is almost never done (not even to the wrong people), problems that have nothing to do with training are addressed with training, and problems that are directly related to poor or too little training are never even mentioned in the same breath with the word "training."

Training is a mess in American business, and, until it's straightened out, it's going to be difficult for the overall situation to get any better.

THEY TRAIN BABIES, DON'T THEY?

You'd think that training would be more intelligently used in business, given the way it's addressed in our private lives. As private citizens, we demonstrate a serious and long-term commitment to extensive training of all types. The problem is that we don't think about why we do it, we just do it (the neckties and tradition again). Consider the whole ordeal of raising children; it's nothing but one huge, expensive training exercise. We may not spend months developing materials and instructional systems, but we do the training.

Babies are born helpless. Then the training starts. Everything we want them to learn, we have to teach them. Want to talk to them? No problem, teach them to talk. It only takes 2 years to get up to a vocabulary containing a whopping 250 words. Want to stop changing diapers? Ok, wait a year and a half while you change them 10 times a day and then start 6 months to a year of toilet training. Want them to learn to support themselves and be responsible citizens? Fine, spend the next 20-plus years sending them to school, hiring tutors, advising them (they'll listen until they're about 10 years old, then forget about advising them for the next 15 years), and correcting their misjudgments. Want them to learn to wreck your car? (Some call it learning to drive.) No sweat. (That's not true!) It'll take 3 to 6 months of evening and weekend arguments.

Now, *that's* a training effort! The conduct of such a program shows patience for results, proper timing, extreme tolerance of large resource expenditures, and respect for the developmental needs of the child. All of these are classic requirements for a correct training effort. Yet, the very same manager who is going through all of this with 3 children at home will turn down a subordinate's request to go to a 2-day training session in "How to lead employees" with some lame excuse such as, "You don't need it," or "We can't afford it." Work-related training is seen as a bother, a cost, a perk, or a waste. This attitude is wrong, wrong, and wrong.

Learning Does Not Happen by Osmosis (Good Learning, That Is)

Business often acts as if employees learn new skills through osmosis—absorbing knowledge and skills from the atmosphere by merely being there. Consider the average first-line supervisor (a boss of Egg Sucking Pigs) in a traditionally run company. This supervisor is required to direct the activities of two to 30 employees as they cost-effectively produce a high-quality product (well, that's what the wish is). He or she has to mediate disputes, communicate upper management policy and data, teach procedures, monitor production, solve problems, do his or her technical work, and a dozen other critical tasks. Yet, how many front-line supervisors in the typical company have had training to do any of these things? Not many. The supervisor is somehow supposed to have management and people skills merely by being in the job. Most supervisors are either green college graduates or people promoted from the ranks. Neither background provides a shred of training in how to lead people effectively. And since most upper level managers come from this background, most of them never get any dedicated training in how to manage people.

Just think about it; first-line supervisors directly lead at least 50% of the work force in most organizations, but they get little or no training in how to do it. And we wonder why employees are angry, why there are quality problems, why turnover is high, and so on? There's nothing to wonder about. If you put an untrained 10-year-old behind the wheel of a car in a crowded parking lot, would you be surprised at a few smashed cars? Just being in the car won't teach driving any more than being a supervisor will teach supervision.

THE TRADITIONAL APPROACH TO TRAINING IS NOT TO DO ANY

Employees who hire into Nissan are required to take weeks of training during their first year on the job. The situation is similar in most other world-class companies, in which 2% to 4% of total operating budgets is spent on training. Every employee is given detailed training in the history and philosophy of the company, a process orientation, and an understanding of variability, SPC, and how to do their job. The "how to do the job" is not a once-over rehash given during a tour of the work area, but detailed instruction in the standards (SDCA) of the job and the techniques used by the work group to improve their processes.

Contrast this approach with what happens to most employees on their first day on the job in a traditionally run company. They are processed through personnel, perhaps sent to a few hours of general orientation, and then dropped off in their new work area. If they are doing a job that others also do, one of the other employees may be tasked to "show the new person the ropes." Within a day or so, sometimes within only an hour, the new employee is expected to be "doing the job." Everyone recognizes that there may be some mistakes and so on, but they're expected—for a short while. It's assumed that the employee will quickly master the new skills and knowledge required by the job. There's no way this can lead to outstanding performance, but that's the way American industry trains.

It's a perennial complaint in almost every company that purchasing takes too long to process orders. Yet, how many of the processors or buyers have been trained to do their jobs? Usually none. They learned the job from other employees, who learned from those before them, and so on. In subtle ways, each employee in the long line of "trainers" changed the job and the procedures a little. Over time, these changes resulted in ways of doing the work and setting priorities that are radically different from the originally intended procedures (not that the original procedures were probably any better, having been instituted without any kind of a process orientation) and certainly different from what's required to meet customer needs. Yet, when the system clogs up or there's a problem with throughput, nobody ever stops to wonder if the buyers and paper pushers really have all the skills and knowledge they need. Of course, given your evolving American Samurai insights, you now know that, in most companies, there's nobody who would even know what should be trained, since the processes that make up the work probably aren't even understood.

We Don't Do Skills Training

Every job or task seems simple if it is described in generalities; "To do a heart transplant, you take out the heart and put a new one in." Sounds great, let's try one! Things turn out to be more difficult when you actually study the process (meaning, when you know what you are talking about).

AMERICAN SAMURAI INSIGHT

Every single task or job in the universe has significant task

demands and complexities that are known only by the people who do the job or task.

Because management calls the shots about tasks, but doesn't understand the constituent processes (not having done them or closely studied them), everything looks easy and straightforward. Thus, the logic goes, there couldn't be any need for training—anyone could do it. Wrong.

This stupidity is particularly easy to see in regard to skills training. In American automobile companies, new Egg Sucking Pig employees (in those rare years in which business is good enough to hire new people—there won't be many of those in the next 10 years) are taken right to the job and given a little informal instruction, usually for an hour or 2. Then, they're on their own. Some managers contend, "So what? All they do is put on a few bolts. What's to train?" If there's nothing to train, why do things go wrong? What's the worker supposed to do when things don't fit right? Bang it into place? (That's what they do if they're not trained.) How is the worker supposed to get any better? And even if the job "only" involves tightening 6 bolts on a tire, in what order should they be tightened (it does make a difference) and to what torque? And how does the worker determine if the torque setting on the torque wrench (if there is one) is correct?

All of these things *must* be trained, or there is no reasonable way to expect the worker to be as effective as he or she must be to do a good job. As things now stand, it would be difficult to do this type of training in most automotive plants since process sheets (the step-by-step instructions on how to do things) are always out of date—ask someone if you doubt me). Not only that, some of the questions (e.g., "How do we work together to get better?") would not be understood by the management in most companies.

It's not just the automotive companies, it's everyone. I've consulted for companies in which employees doing wire bonds and soldering of very small connections on electronics equipment had been hired right off the street and put to work without any training at all. They were supposed to learn "from each other." And then we wonder why some new American-made electronics products have had first-time failure rates (they don't work when you first turn them on) of 2% to 50%. This is not just from mom and pop operations; in 1989, a new hard disk drive from a major PC company had failure rates of 70%. And we wonder why the Japanese, with their extensive hours of training for each new employee, are beginning to eat up the PC market.

Consider this: in some world-class Japanese companies, new machine shop trainees are given extensive instruction in how to properly use a hammer. Can you imagine that in an American plant? Management would have a heart attack over it. Yet, the Japanese want the employee to master the basics that are the foundation for everything that is done. No part of the process is too small to warrant excellence.

We Don't Do Management Skills and
Knowledge Training, Either

We've already discussed the lack of supervisory training (how to work with and lead people). The traditional management approach restricts most other types of management training as well. How many finance people in your organization have had 2 weeks of training in the last year in their specialty field? None, I'll bet. And don't try to tell me about college courses that the company pays for and that are taken by only a small number of employees; these have nothing to do with a specific company's processes. Also, 2- or 3-day conferences are almost totally worthless as training experiences. Some are marginally useful, but most aren't. How many times in the last year has your organization brought in outside experts to give an intensive 2-day specialty course to your engineers? Not once, I'll bet. "Too expensive," says management. Wrong.

It's the same everywhere. The entire business world is becoming more competitive every second. Almost all employees are expected to be more productive, but they're supposed to do this by magic. If you want people to do their work in the best way, they either have to invent it themselves or learn it from someone else. If an organization won't pay to let them learn it from someone else, it's not the type of organization that will provide the conditions (living by The Code of the American Samurai) that will permit them to develop it on their own. And if the competition is changing, no one can afford to reinvent the wheel for all advances. You need to learn the latest and then change it more. That requires continual cross-fertilization of ideas and approaches in all areas, which requires training.

We Don't Do Enough, Even When We Do It

Even when some worthwhile training is done in the traditionally run organization, it's almost always not enough. American business focuses on results and worships schedule. Training is approached in the same way. When a skill or knowledge requirement is identified (or forced to awareness by a disaster), the very first parameter put on the training is a time limit, as in the following: "Well, Johnson, that accidental fatality was a shame, yessir. Let's have some safety training. Put together a 1-hour program for the troops. That should do it. Yessir." After the 1-hour training program is completed (if it is completed; many training programs are called—few are completed), the problem is declared solved simply because somebody up top decided that a certain "dose" of training was appropriate.

This duration-based approach to training and learning is displayed in Figure 16-1 and is contrasted with the training approach used by world-class organizations and those who want to be world class.

The central issue in all training is not the length of the training but the learning curve shown in Figure 16-1. The vertical axis tracks amount of knowledge or skill possessed, and the horizontal axis tracks time in training (or training effort). The learning curve is a negatively accelerating one, meaning that the rate of increase in knowledge or skill slows down over time. Almost all learning of skills (and much task-based job knowledge) proceeds in this manner. Training (assuming that it's at least moderately successful) yields large initial gains in understanding and skill. As the training effort proceeds, the rate of learning begins to slow down. Eventually, a point is reached at which additional training doesn't yield big increases in skills.

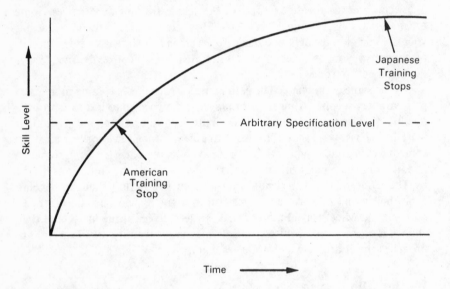

Figure 16-1. Learning curve and training "stop points" in traditional and Japanese companies.

It's easiest to see this in terms of a skill, such as soldering. When a rookie first enters a soldering training class, he or she learns quickly as the basics are mastered. If soldering skill is measured in terms of successful solder connections, we might find that the trainee quickly moves from 10% good solder connections after a few hours of instruction on day 1 to 80% on day 3. Invariably, the rate of improvement then slows. Further improvement requires that more difficult skills be learned and that more firmly ingrained bad habits or work motions be unlearned. At some point, an individual begins to approach his or her theoretical best performance, meaning that additional gains will be small and slow. Thus, 2 more days of training may increase performance only an additional 10%, resulting in a score of 90%. Additional training would no doubt yield further increases, but they would be smaller each day. Another 4 days of training might bring the performance level up to 95% to 98%.

There are two points worthy of special attention here. The first is that every person has a unique learning curve for every skill and knowledge. This is due to factors such as previous experiences, genetics, attention span, motivation, motor skills, and so on. If the amount of training to be done is determined by how long the training experience is, you have no idea how far up the learning curve an individual will be. After 16 hours of training, regardless of the topic, some employees will be far up the curve, whereas others, doing their best, will be only half as far along. A large part of this difference between individuals (assuming the trainers are skilled, which is not always true) is due to the preceding factors. You can't determine whether someone has mastered "enough" skill simply by specifying how much "time" to train.

The second point, even more fundamental, is that you can't specify how "much" skill is enough, regardless of time spent in training or skill levels attained after training, unless you intimately understand the process in question. The soldering situation provides a real-life example. Let's assume that we're talking about soldering performance on a U.S. government-procured contract to build electronics testing equipment. The government has very stringent performance specifications for defining what is an acceptable solder connection and what is not. Not only does the connection have to carry electricity, but it must be the right shape and it must be shiny (some of these requirements do nothing but drive up costs, but they're there and cause phenomena such as the proverbial $800 toilet seat).

On this type of work, the government requires that each solderer be certified. This almost always involves sending employees to a 40-hour, in-house soldering course. The government sets the training requirement at 40 hours and says that at the end of 40 hours the employee must be able to attain 80 points out of 100 on a soldering performance test. This 80 points is equivalent to achieving an 80% rate of acceptable solder connections. This situation is represented on Figure 16-1 as the point at which American industrial skills training typically stops; at an arbitrary point. Is this 80% good? No way in hell.

In fact, this performance level absolutely guarantees that the employee will produce at least 20% unacceptable solder connections on the job.

AMERICAN SAMURAI INSIGHT

We train our employees to produce poor quality by setting training success standards so low that on-the-job mistakes are guaranteed.

Just think about it: if an employee can only get 80% correct solder connections in a supportive training environment (in which the instructors want them to succeed so that the instructors will look good) with lots of detailed instructions and rapid feedback, how can they do any better when they get out on the job? They can't. On the job, they won't get feedback on their performance until an inspector checks the work, which could be hours or days later. That's like trying to hit a baseball while blindfolded and not being told how a particular swing worked until a day later. In addition, supervisors are on the employees' backs, pushing for production. And equipment usually isn't as good or as well maintained on the job (remember, the training people want the trainees to succeed, so they attempt to set up ideal conditions). As if these factors were not enough to create more errors, the work itself is typically more complex on the job. There's no way an employee can be better on the job than he or she was in training in this type of situation.

Yet, this is exactly the situation with soldering on almost all government contracts. And people wonder why there are problems and high costs of rework? There's no reason to wonder, we're building them into the system.

How Much Training Is Enough?

How much junk do you want? If you can live with 20% defects, either you're in an industry that's protected from competition or you've got stupid customers. Neither condition usually endures for long, because competitors soon teach customers what to demand (ask the American auto makers, they learned the hard way).

The only sensible way to determine the appropriate level of training is to understand enough about the processes in question to be able to determine at what point the knowledge or skills gains for an individual employee begin to level off. Then, that particular level of performance must be analyzed to determine whether it is acceptable in terms of overall quality. If the best that an employee can do is not good enough to assure good quality, the employee must be used on a different job.

Not All Problems Are Training Problems

American industry has a love-hate relationship with training: it hates to do any but loves to throw up training as the remedy of choice for problems (perhaps because management realizes that very little training will actually be done). No matter what happens, it's assumed that most problems are training problems. Is there an ethics problem in which some of your male supervisors are using their positions to have sex with their employees? The almost universal answer is to have yet another ethics training program.

This is hardly ever a training problem. Training is an answer when the root cause of the problem is lack of skill or knowledge. In this case, the supervisors know it's wrong (they don't tell their wives and girl friends about it, do they?). The problem isn't training, it's lack of management guts to enforce established procedures and mores. More ethics training is a waste, unless management will enforce ethical conduct. I've been in companies in which management, when confronted with obvious and blatant ethics problems of this nature, made excuses, tried to explain away or belittle the evidence, and got angry at the message bearer, rather than take action. Yet, they almost always suggested training if problems continued to occur. This is not a training problem. Once employees and the predators among them see a lax response to violations, they know that ethics is a joke and that nothing will happen to violators. More training won't change that.

It's the same with many other situations. Safety problems, lax attendance or tardiness, and many quality problems are not training problems. In the case of many quality problems, the employees know what the problems are, but the system won't allow the problems to be dealt with. Training the employees by giving them a lot of talk about "Quality Is Job One" won't do anything.

Guilt-Spasm Training

Guilt-spasm training (GST) is given in most companies every 5 to 10 years or after a major problem surfaces. For example, nobody even thinks about safety training in most companies until a legal problem surfaces or somebody gets hurt (a typical example of management by fire control). Then, there's a flurry of safety training for a few months, after which everybody forgets about safety until the next accident (because other fires occur and grab the attention). The same sort of thing happens with management and supervisory training, although less often, because few problems are attributed to management skill deficits (most are blamed on employees).

If an organization conducts an honest survey of employee attitudes and discovers that employees hate both the organization and management, some small amount of training will be conducted (many companies conduct dishonest surveys and try to snow the employees into thinking that a bad situation is good; this never works, but companies keep trying). Most typically, an hour or so of training is given to supervisors to tell them how to run a short meeting with employees in order to "discuss and resolve the problems uncovered in the survey." Once a few meetings are held, everyone forgets the survey problems until the next crisis.

A PROCESS ORIENTATION LIGHTS THE WAY TO NECESSARY TRAINING

If an organization is run according to the mandates of The Code, necessary and required training will be self-evident. Once work processes are understood by management and the hands-on process workers, it's clear after some analysis whether a problem requires training or a system change in order to correct the root cause of the problem. Thus, unnecessary training is not done, and required training is obvious.

THE BOTTOMLINE BASIC TRAINING THAT
EVERYONE MUST HAVE

Any organization that is determined to be world class must provide a certain amount of basic training in order to create a consistent and uniform skill and knowledge base for all employees. The general type and content of this training, appropriate audience, and approximate training program lengths (assuming competent training personnel and fairly intensive training) are as follows (note that I am giving times, even though training time doesn't equate to learning curve progress; the actual learning of all of the following material will occur on the job. The classroom training is simply an introduction):

General orientation to the organization (all employees—2 days)

A detailed explanation of the purpose, operation, and mechanics of the business of the organization, including contact with high level management personnel, facility tours, demonstrations and/or examinations of actual products), lunch with a group of workers and executives, and in-depth discussions of the philosophy of the organization. Not more than 1 day, and not the first day, should be devoted to the usual safety films, health plans option selection, and so on.

General orientation to the new employee's work area (all employees—1 day)

The new employee should be shown around the entire department, given a detailed tour of the area, shown representative major functions, and introduced to area management. The tour must be conducted by a member of senior departmental management and must include lunch with a group of supervisors and employees. The new employee must be personally introduced to all of the employees in his or her work unit and shown what they do. The new employee must be introduced to his or her customers and suppliers.

The new philosophy of work (all employees—2 days)

This would be either a detailed presentation, with some group exercises or discussion, of The Code of the American Samurai or of Dr. Deming's 14 Points. Each Coda (or point) must be discussed in detail, with ample opportunity for discussion and questions. It is essential that this class be presented by an authoritative member of management who knows what he or she is talking about.

Statistical Process Control (all employees—2 days)

The nature of central tendency and variability. How to calculate, understand, and interpret means, ranges, standard deviations, C_{pk}, the normal curve, and z-scores. How to calculate and interpret X Bar and R, Individuals and Moving Range, and P and U charts (the other types of charts are really superfluous and merely complicate the teaching situation). The students must be required to calculate and construct examples for all concepts and charts.

It may be necessary to conduct a 1-day elementary refresher (or, sadly for our educational system, first-time) course for employees who do not understand how to use a calculator, how to reduce simple algebraic equations, and so on.

Problem Solving (all employees—2 days)

A detailed examination of the 12-step process improvement, problem solving methodology presented in Chapter Eleven (or an alternative such as Ford Motor Company's eight-step "Team Oriented Problem Solving"). The best approach is to briefly overview all of the steps and then have teams of employees in the class (assigned any way you want, it's better if they're with people they don't know and/or report to), solve a problem by working on it one step at a time, and then stopping to share their results with the class before moving on to the next step. In a properly orchestrated class, it is possible to do two problems this way.

Concurrent Engineering (all senior management, all engineers, all non-engineering department heads, and selected process workers in all departments; the identities of these people will be self-evident once senior management understands the concept—1 day)

Concurrent (or simultaneous) engineering will be discussed in detail in Chapter Twenty-Two (Coda 17). This class must describe what concurrent engineering is, how product design teams work, how the organization is using them (and it better be!), the fundamental points to consider for design for manufacturability (and everything else as well—all of the "ilities"), and some of the tools of concurrent engineering (such as Design for Assembly). The class must include simple product design challenges for randomly selected teams to tackle. In my concurrent engineering seminar, I require teams to design a mousetrap in the morning and an electrical control box in the afternoon. Teams use the presented tools to analyze before and after designs and present their designs to the class as a whole.

Design of experiments (selected engineers, staff personnel in various departments, and all senior management—2 days)

Design of experiments (DOE) will be discussed in Chapter Twenty-One (Coda 16). This is a critical tool that has important applications in most companies. It's important that engineers, as well as key management in production areas, understand how to use it. The seminar must include an experiment for the class to use as an example.

Management-style feedback/awareness (all supervision—3 to 5 days)

As has been discussed in several areas, American management doesn't learn how to manage people effectively. It's essential, if an organization is serious about transforming itself into a world-class contender, that it teach its supervision what management really means. A great deal of this education is provided by the preceding training experiences as a whole, but it's not enough. It's important for each supervisor (at every level) to have a clear picture of how he or she handles interpersonal relationships at work and of how he or she is perceived by subordinates and other employees. This type of training can take many forms.

I recommend that a packaged program be purchased and presented by in-house personnel. There's simply too much effort, expertise, and expense involved in developing a good program in-house. Since the program must include management-style questionnaires completed by both those attending and some of their subordinates, colleagues, and/or supervisors, it's doubtful that many internal departments could develop meaningful, valid instruments. One excellent program that I have used for many years is available from Teleometrics International, The Woodlands, Texas. The program materials have high face validity (they look great), and students enjoy the experiences. There are many other fine, packaged programs available, but Teleometrics is right up there with the best of them.

Most packages such as Teleometrics take 4 to 5 days but can be given effectively in 3. It's a good idea to follow up the packaged program with another 2 days of intensive training in how to interact with employees and groups: what to say, how to act, what not to say, what to do in order to take advantage of the insights obtained by the packaged program. These efforts are best developed in-house, since they must be tailored to organization specific situations.

Other Training

The preceding classes represent the very basic essentials. If you won't, or can't, do them, you're in big trouble. As we've seen (and will see in later chapters), few of these skills and knowledge are picked up informally. They must be learned through training. If you don't train employees in these skills, you won't get the skills.

But the preceding classes aren't the totality of what could be, or should be, done. As this training is cycled in over a 12- to 18-month period and provides a solid "base" of elementary skills, other training is essential. Management must learn about Hoshin Kanri, benchmarking, Poka-yoke, and Quality Function Deployment. Once your organization begins to get involved in the elementary training outlined on the preceding pages, key members of management will begin to come up with suggestions and insights as to how to pursue this next level of training. If they do not, your company is dead meat.

TRAINING IS AN INVESTMENT THAT *ALWAYS* PAYS OFF BIG

There are those of you, I know, who read these minimum training requirements and almost passed out. "My company do all of that training? You've got to be kidding me! That's more training than most of our 20-year employees have had in their entire careers." Probably true. And it's the reason why many American companies are following the leaders in their industry rather than leading. Repeat after me: Training is *not* a cost—Training is *not* a cost—Training is *not* a cost. Repeat it a hundred times until you no longer think about it, you no longer question it, you no longer try to reason it out. Training is *not* a cost—it is an investment that always pays off big.

AMERICAN SAMURAI INSIGHT

If an employee requests training, you can't afford not to provide it. The continued development of employees' skills, knowledge, and self-esteem is the single best investment a business can make. It will yield lifelong benefits to society, the business, and the employee.

If employees are the number one resources of every business (and they are), their development, even if it doesn't directly benefit one of your business processes immediately (as in upgrading a process skill that can be used tomorrow), will pay off. It may not pay off today or tomorrow, and it may not even pay off for the company that pays for it, but it *will* pay off.

Take the simplest example: company paid college courses. Consider a secretary who has been going to college at night for years, all paid for by the company. When this employee completes the degree, he or she will probably quit and move on to a better job. This will happen because, in a typical company, once a secretary, always a secretary. The cynical might say, "Why waste our money? After we pay for their school, they leave." Ignoring for a moment the fact that the company "drives" such people out by not providing meaningful opportunities, this response is stupid on other counts.

The cost of this training is returned time and time again to the company, even as the employee is still working as a secretary. On a purely "being there" level, he or she will be much less likely to quit and move on until school is finished, thereby reducing the considerable but invisible losses caused by turnover. He or she will be more optimistic and enthusiastic because there is hope for a better future. He or she will feel more powerful, confident, and "good" about himself or herself and will be bringing new skills and insights to the job in ways no one an see (self-fulfilling prophecy).

WE'RE ALL IN THIS TOGETHER

Of course, the greatest benefit is to the employee and his or her family. They are afforded an opportunity to improve their lot in life, upgrade their future standard of living, be more productive members of society, raise more informed children, pay more taxes, and build a stronger society. No company can divorce itself from this responsibility; every organization must do its rightful share. We're seeing right now the horrendous effects on business of not having a school system that turns out literate people who can work in a technological society. The buck for a better society stops at every company's door. Training employees to the hilt and encouraging them to develop themselves at company expense is the way in which organizations pay for the right to demand loyalty from employees. It's also part of the price they pay for the privilege of operating in a free country. It's time for every company to start paying its bills.

17

Conformance To Specification Costs You Money

Coda 12. **The concept of conformance to specifications decreases quality and hides costs. It must be abandoned and replaced with an awareness that any variance from the ideal increases costs.**

A *specification,* commonly called a "spec," is a predetermined value, or set of values, that circumscribes the limits of acceptability for a specific parameter of a product or service. The parameter in question, such as length, width, weight, or strength, is often called the *quality characteristic.* Each quality characteristic has a metric that permits objective measurement of the quality characteristic. Length might be measured in centimeters, weight in pounds, and strength in pounds required to break the product.

Specifications can be *unilateral* or *bilateral.* Unilateral specifications are a single value, which can be of two types: *bigger is best* and *smaller is best.* For example, when you buy rope, there is generally a unilateral specification as to the rope's strength, such as 500 pounds. This means that the rope is rated to hold at least 500 pounds, but may hold more. This is a "bigger is best" specification in which the quality characteristic is more acceptable as it gets larger. Whereas there is a minimum level of performance of the quality characteristic that must be attained to meet customer requirements, 500 pounds in this case, there is no practical limit on how large the quality characteristic could get. Presumably customers who wished to purchase a rope rated at 500 pounds would not be upset to get one that would hold 600 or 700 pounds. However, they might be upset to get one that would hold 1500 pounds, if they stopped to consider that they might be paying extra for strength that they did not need.

Clothing shrinkage is often a unilateral specification in which the shrinkage is generally stated as "not more than 2%, meaning that the quality characteristic "passes" if it has shrinkage of 2% or less. This is a "smaller is best" specification, in which customers would be happy to get little or no shrinkage but could live with 2% or less.

Bilateral specifications are those in which a band of acceptable perfor-

191

mance of the quality characteristic is stated. Resistors are given bilateral specifications for the quality characteristic of resistance. A resistor may be acceptable for its stated use if the resistance is between 15.5 and 16.5 milli-ohms. The smaller value of the metric is commonly called the *lower specification limit* (LSL), or lower spec. The higher value of the metric is typically referred to as the *upper specification limit* (USL), or upper spec. The exact midpoint between the LSL and the USL is generally referred to as the *nominal specification*. The nominal specification, 16.0 milli-ohms in this case, is where you'd like to have everything if possible.

Engineers often refer to specifications as *tolerances,* meaning that specs delineate how much deviation from the ideal, or nominal, you can "tolerate" and still have the product work. When a quality characteristic is between the LSL and the USL, or on the correct side of a unilateral spec, it is said to be *in spec, within spec,* or *in tolerance.*

You Can't Tolerate "In Tolerance"

This is the rub, as it were. Take the preceding resistance example. Suppose you had two identical circuits that each contained 20 resistors. In circuit A, let's say that all 20 of the resistors are exactly at 15.55 milli-ohms, every single one of them in spec, above the LSL. In circuit B, let's suppose that every one of the 20 is exactly in spec at 16.45 milli-ohms. Is there any chance that the two circuits will perform the same? Of course not.

If the circuit output is critically sensitive, neither circuit might produce an acceptable performance, even though every single one of the resistors is in spec. Every resistor would have passed an inspection, but still contributed to a failure. This is an example of *tolerance stack-up.* Whereas this example is extreme in that such a distorted distribution of resistances would occur infrequently, it is not unusual. Real-life examples abound. We'll discuss one of them in a moment.

WHERE DO YOU DRAWN THE LINE WITH SPECIFICATIONS?

The traditional view of specifications is that any measurement that falls between the LSL and the USL is acceptable. This is not true. For example, let's suppose that we are manufacturing light bulbs and that the specification limits for the diameter of the filaments are 50 mils (50 thousands of an inch) for the LSL and 60 mils for the USL. The nominal value, the ideal target for all filaments, is 55 mils. The situation is graphically displayed in Figure 17-1.

Hopefully, the specification limits were established by carefully studying the requirements of bulb operation, longevity, energy usage, and brightness (don't be too sure that this is the actual case with real products; all too often, specifications are pulled from the same spot that generates most of the world's organic, animal based fertilizer). We'll assume that these specs were established by a testing program that determined that bulbs with filaments thinner than 50 mils would burn out too soon, and/or break too often during manufacturing, shipping, and customer handling. And we'll assume that it was determined that filaments thicker than 60 mils tend to burn too unevenly, get too hot (leading to glass stress and possible cracks), and use too much energy.

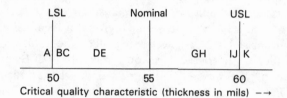

Figure 17-1. LSL, USL, and nominal values for hypothetical light bulb filament.

The problem is, any such specs, even if they're determined with research, are a compromise. Is there any real difference between a filament at point A in Figure 17-1 and one at B? Or between one at J and one at K? Of course not. There may be a very small increase in the probability of failure for a filament with a thickness at B compared to A, but the same might be said of the differences between B and C, both within spec. Yet, filament A would be rejected during inspection, whereas B would not. This is a *step function* view of quality. A loss is associated with a filament at point A, but not with a filament at point B; the loss increases from zero to complete, in a stepwise fashion, exactly at the specification limits. This does not reflect reality: any deviation from the nominal value increases the odds of failure and thus increases costs. Filaments at D and H fail more often than filaments at E and G. You can see where we're going with this, I hope.

AMERICAN SAMURAI INSIGHT

Specifications allow marginally acceptable outputs to be accepted as "good." This decreases customer satisfaction, drives up costs, and discourages efforts at process improvement.

After all, why should anyone go to the considerable trouble and expense of trying to fix a process if everything is in spec? Try it, and you run into the old, "If it ain't broke, don't fix it" Guiding Principle. Let's look at an example of how costs can be driven up by a product that's in spec.

Ford and Mazda Transmissions

Ford executives tell the following story repeatedly at quality conferences.

It is a classic example of the consequences of "tolerance stack-up." It seems that Ford and Mazda (partially owned by Ford; if you can't lick 'em, join 'em) were both producing an identical automatic transmission, with identical plans and machinery. Yet, it turned out that warranty costs for the Ford transmissions were many times higher than warranty costs for Mazda-made transmissions.

Ford decided to investigate by having a sample of brand new transmissions from each of the two plants sent in for testing. There, the transmissions were disassembled and every part painstakingly measured.

One of the technicians was measuring a group of identical gears from a Ford-built transmission with an electronic gauge. The result was a distribution of variability much like the one shown in Figure 17-2. Every gear (each represented by an "X") was well within spec, a marvel of excellent "QUALITY IS JOB ONE!" American-built quality, just like the engineers wanted.

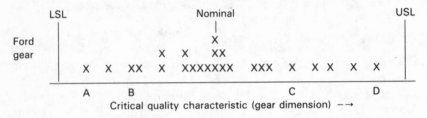

Figure 17-2. Ford pattern of variability

The technician then began measuring another group of the same gears, but from Mazda-made transmissions. Finding little or no variability, the technician called the supervisor over and announced that the gauge was broken. Sure enough, the gauge showed little or no variability—must be broken. Just to be sure, a few of the previously measured Ford gears were measured with the gauge. The variability returned—the gauge was fine! The difference was that there was little or no variability in the Mazda-made gears! They demonstrated a pattern of variability similar to that shown in Figure 17-3.

The key to the differences in warranty costs is clear when the two patterns of variability are examined. Consider what a transmission does: it transmits power by having gears of different sizes turn each other. In order to operate smoothly, the gears must fit together precisely. A less than perfect fit between the teeth of any pair of gears results in friction, heat, wear, and vibration. Eventually, the wear can get to the point at which the gears fit so badly that every transmission shift is an exercise in whiplash. When this happens, people take their cars in for warranty work.

Suppose that we have two identical gears meshing, one with a dimension at point A on Figure 17-2 and the other at point D. Both gears should ideally be at the nominal point so that they would generate very little vibration.

But they are far from it, although well between the specification limits. There will be considerably more vibration and wear generated by this set of gears compared to the vibration generated by gears with dimensions at points E and F on Figure 17-3. Gears with dimensions at points B and C on Figure 17-2 wouldn't be as bad as those taken from points A and D, but they still couldn't begin to operate as smoothly as the worst case Mazda gears from Figure 17-3.

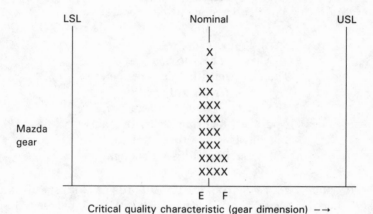

Figure 17-3. Mazda pattern of variability.

AMERICAN SAMURAI INSIGHT

Building to specification fosters variability and poor quality. "In spec" simply isn't good enough for world-class products.

Edgar A. Guest states this beautifully in a classic poem:

GOOD ENOUGH*

Edgar A. Guest

My son, beware of "good enough"
It isn't made of sterling stuff;
It's something any man can do,
It marks the many from the few,
It has no merit to the eye,
It's something any man can buy,
Its name is but a sham and bluff,
For it is never "good enough."

---

*From *Collected Verse of Edgar A. Guest,* The Reilly and Lee Co. Publishers, Chicago, 1934.

With "good enough" the shirkers stop
In every factory and shop;
With "good enough" the failures rest
And lose to men who give their best;
With "good enough" the car breaks down
And men fall short of high renown.
My son, remember and be wise,
In "good enough" disaster lies.

With "good enough" that's short
Of what you can do and you ought.
The flaw which may escape the eye
And temporarily get by,
Shall weaken underneath the strain
And wreck the ship or car or train,
For this is true of men and stuff—
Only the best is "good enough."

The key point here, aside from the general problem with specifications, is that, employing the same equipment and plans, the Japanese were producing transmission gears with almost no variability. How did they do it? You guessed it (I hope!)—they focused on never ending improvement of processes, constantly striving to remove variability. This can only be done by pursuing The Code of the American Samurai day by day.

YOU CAN'T IMPROVE QUALITY BY TIGHTENING SPECIFICATIONS

The typical strategy for dealing with the preceding situation in traditional American business has been to "tighten up the specs." The reasoning (if you can call it that) is that if you want less variability in delivered product, all you've got to do is tighten up the specs during inspection. There are two fundamental and crippling problems with this strategy: (1) it drives up costs unbelievably, and (2) it cannot guarantee that bad products will not get through to customers.

Let's consider the cost problem first, using the gear example. Shown in Figure 17-4 is the Ford gear distribution (originally shown in Figure 17-2), with the upper and lower limits of the actual variability of the Mazda gears from Figure 17-3 superimposed on it. If Ford wanted to make sure that all Ford-made gears were no more variable than the Mazda gears, the traditional approach would be to tighten up the specs. Rather than changing processes, the LSL and USL would simply be moved to new values, at points G and H, the extremes of the Mazda gear distribution.

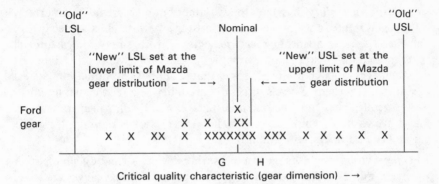

Figure 17-4.   Tightening up the specs on the Ford gears.

Using defect detection, after-the-fact inspections with the new specifications would result in the rejection of all gears with quality characteristic measurements at G or less and at H or more. In Figure 17-4, this means that 18 of 25 original Ford gears would be rejected. At that rate, in order to get 25 good gears, it would be necessary to produce 89.28 gears, assuming that the process isn't changed and that it still produces the variability originally shown in Figure 17-2. Every gear that's rejected must be reworked or scrapped. That's all added cost. And the costs don't stop there. The inspections also increase costs.

A manufacturer with an output distribution similar to that shown for the Mazda gears (Figure 17-3) would have a tremendous competitive advantage over a manufacturer who attempted to "inspect in" quality by tightening up the specifications. That's why the only sensible way to improve competitiveness is to focus on improving the process to eliminate variability.

The second problem with this approach is that it's virtually impossible to "inspect out" all the bad parts. Some always slip through. No matter how hard you try, some get through to a customer, causing loss of business and added costs. If you don't produce any defects, you don't have to pay to inspect for them, and none can get through to customers.

GAUGE CAPABILITY AND REPEATABILITY

There's an added complication that hardly anyone talks about when it comes to measuring whether or not a quality characteristic is in spec. The issue is this: is the measurement (inspection) procedure sufficiently precise to catch such small differences? Often, probably most often, this is not the case. There is frequently more error in the measuring process than there is variability between parts. This situation can have a profound impact on quality, but only a few people are aware of it.

There are all sorts of sources of variability. The one we've been discussing is *true variability,* in which the variability in measurements accurately reflects variability in the quality characteristics; the variability we see is real, and there is no error in our measurements. Unfortunately for customers, that's not the only source of variability. There are several other types of variability (not related to the processes that produce the product) that affect decisions about them. These sources of variability degrade the measurement process itself. They must be taken into account and controlled if measurements are to be accepted as valid. These sources of variability are gauge variability and operator variability.

1. *Gauge variability.* A gauge is a measuring device. It can be a simple ruler or a 10 million dollar piece of testing equipment. No two gauges are alike. In the case of rulers, the differences between them are small, constant, and generally noncritical, but they are there (not so with tape measures, which can stretch at different rates and to various final lengths). In the case of electronic or mechanical gauges, the differences between them are not constant and can be significant, particularly as gauges "drift" out of adjustment over time.

2. *Operator variability.* Different people use gauges differently. They hold them differently and read them differently. Even if three different people consecutively measure the same length of wood with a ruler, you'll hardly ever get the same measurement from all three.

Consider what happens when these two types of variability (as well as true variability) interact in an inspection situation. There may be only one inspector with one gauge. How do you know that the inspector is accurately detecting true variability? You don't. How do you know that the gauge is properly set? You don't. In both cases, it's assumed that both the gauge and the inspector are right on target, which is hardly ever the case. And what happens when there are many inspectors using many different gauges? Chaos. I've seen employees sent home without pay for days because their work wasn't in spec according to an inspector. But with a different gauge used by another inspector, measuring the same product, there was no problem.

The analysis of the impacts of these types of variability is called *gauge capability and repeatability.* Not one engineering school in a hundred even mentions the topic, and not one company in a thousand knows what it is. The typical guidelines used by those few traditional companies that assess gauge capability and repeatability say that the situation is good if total measurement errors account for "only" 10% of the distance between the LSL and the USL. If error takes between 10% and 40% of the distance, the situation is termed questionable and should be examined if cost-benefits permit. Over 40% is seen as requiring action. Seems a little loose to me.

AN ALTERNATIVE APPROACH

The alternative approach to specifications is to focus continually on reducing variability so that all output is as close to the nominal as possible. Genichi Taguchi, a leading Japanese statistician and quality guru, has proposed a technique that he calls the "Loss Function." It is often referred to as the Taguchi Loss Function. It is an attempt to estimate the cost, or loss, of any deviation of a product from the nominal, or ideal, value. We'll work through the light bulb example, from Figure 17-1, to illustrate its operation.

There are three general types of loss functions. They are analogous to the various types of specifications: bigger is best, smaller is best, and nominal is best (both a USL and an LSL). We'll look at the one for nominal is best (the concept behind the others is identical, but the formulas are different). The equation for the "nominal is best" loss function is:

$$L(y) = \frac{Ao}{(LD - 50)^2} (y - m)^2$$

This equation generates a line that looks the one shown in Figure 17-5. The least loss is generated at the nominal—when the quality characteristic is at the nominal, the loss generated by the quality characteristic is the least that it can be. As the quality characteristic deviates to either side of the nominal, the loss to society increases quickly.

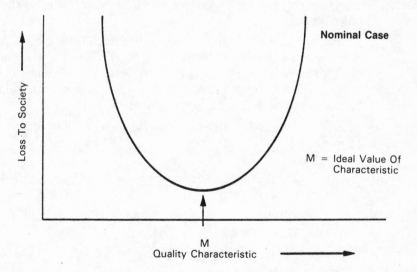

Figure 17-5. The Taguchi Loss Function.

This is a radically different and more realistic view to quality costs than the step function view discussed earlier. Let's define the terms of the Taguchi Loss Function equation and associate them with the values in our light bulb example.

L(y)   Loss to society in dollars (or any other currency). This is not just rework cost, repair cost, and warranty cost, but the total loss to everybody, everywhere, caused by the deviation of the quality characteristic from the nominal value. This is a much different concept of loss than the traditional one that's been used. In the case of our light bulb, we are talking about the total loss incurred when a light bulb burns out. This includes the cost the customer incurs by having to drive to the store to get another one, the risk of an accident if the bulb goes out over the basement steps, and so on.

Ao   This is the cost to repair or replace a defect in the quality characteristic we are measuring. Let's say that it costs 10 cents every time a filament must be thrown away at the plant because it cannot be used.

LD-50   This is the amount of deviation in the value of the quality characteristic from the nominal (ideal) that would cause 50% of light bulb customers to notice a difference in product performance. Let's say in this example that it's 3 mils. This means that 50% of a sample of typical light bulb users would notice a difference in the performance of the light bulb if the diameter of the filament changed by 3 mils or more from the nominal value of 55 mils.

y   This is the value of the quality characteristic that's being evaluated. For this example, let's assume that it's 51 mils. This is above our LSL of 50 mils (the USL was 60 mils). We'll be calculating the loss associated with a filament that is well within specification and that would be used in a traditional environment.

m   This is the nominal, or ideal, value for the light bulb filament thickness, 55 mils, halfway between the LSL and the USL.

Substituting our values into the equation gives us:

$$L(y) = \frac{Ao}{LD-50)^2} (Y - m)^2 = \frac{\$0.10}{(3.0)^2} (51-55)^2$$

$$L(y) = \$0.177$$

Thus, there is a total loss to society of 17.7 cents every time a filament is produced that has a thickness of 51 mils, *even though it passes inspection and is shipped to a customer.* This is the key point: quality characteristics that do not exactly correspond to the nominal cause a loss somewhere. It may not always be easy to find, but it's out there. Somebody pays for the deviation from the ideal in every case.

As you can see, this sort of approach has nothing to do with specification limits. All that counts is deviation from the nominal. This puts the emphasis on reducing variability and moving the mean of a process output as close to the ideal (m) as possible. And to do that, the focus must be on processes and their continual improvement, not specifications.

CAN THIS IDEA BE SOLD?

Surprisingly, it's easier to sell this concept than most others in this book. Alas, it's for the wrong reason. In a suboptimizing environment in which everybody is always fighting it out for resources with other departments, the Taguchi Loss Function can generate some very helpful data. In a traditional environment, when you want money to make an improvement in a process, you usually have to show that the investment will return itself in 2 to 3 years. This is a short-sighted, ignorant view, but what else do you expect? The typical sources of pay-back are reduced rework, less scrap, less returned paperwork, etc. Much lying and inflation of data goes on, but it's often hard to pump up the estimated returns enough to make a pet project look good (so that you can look good).

The Taguchi Loss Function makes it easier to "sell" projects because the estimated losses are always much higher than simple scrap and rework costs. Just look at our light bulb example. A bad filament, caught at the plant and tossed, costs 10 cents. The estimated loss to society from every good filament at 51 mils is 77% greater, or 17.1 cents. You can imagine what a resourceful proposal writer can do with this sort of thing. While working for Ford, I was able to successfully support a proposal for a 1 million dollar per year investment in quality improvements because I was able to show that "we" could reduce loss to society by over 30 million dollars over a 5-year period. Bingo—project approved. I believe that the total loss to society that was saved was at least that much, but that's not what made the pitch sell. What sold it was the word "savings" and the 30 million. They'll go for the bottomline results every time.

FINAL WORDS

Having made the last comment, I hope you're not going to go out and cynically use this (or any other information in this book) to pull a slick one, unless it's in self-defense or self-preservation. Your first duty as an American Samurai is to try to use these sorts of tools to save American business. You must use your power with compassion and wisdom.

18

You Can't Do It Alone: Suppliers Are Team Members

Coda 13. **Suppliers are critical team members who must be educated, valued, and treated as equals in the quest for quality. Selection of suppliers based upon price must be abandoned and replaced with selection based upon total life-cycle cost.**

Industries with factory buildings like to think of themselves as manufacturers. "We make things," they proudly proclaim. Yet, if you go around to the back of the factory, you invariably see truck after truck arriving carrying parts and materials. The fact is that most manufacturers don't really "make" all that much from raw materials, they're assemblers—they put together components made by other companies.

Most electronics manufacturers purchase somewhere in the neighborhood of 70% to 90% of their parts (either total part counts or dollar value) ready for assembly. This is true of many industries, including most of our high-tech organizations. Other industries, such as the automotive industry, make a larger proportion of their products' parts. It is generally estimated that the automotive industry makes 60% to 70% of their parts.

The term "make" can be confusing, since it has a connotation that the "maker" is completely responsible for the part quality, since he or she controls the entire process. Not true. Few end-product manufacturers (those who last work on a product before it's usable by final customers) "make" anything, if make is taken to infer, for example, the processing of sand to make glass or the processing of ore to make sheet steel. Yet, a company is generally said to make a part if rather extensive operations are done on the part prior to its use in a product.

For example, a car plant may buy preshaped panels that they weld together to make car doors. In order to use them, the panels must be drilled, deburred, assembled, painted, and hung with handles, glass, and so on. Although the actual sheet metal door parts were not "made" at the car plant, it's generally stated that the car company made the door, rather than bought it.

In the electronics industry, fewer parts are extensively reworked before they are assembled. The nature of these manufacturers as assemblers, and thus their dependence on the quality of suppliers' parts, is more obvious. Thus, they are said to buy, rather than make, more of their parts.

NO ORGANIZATION IS AN ISLAND (EVEN IF IT *IS* AN ISLAND)

There are two points worthy of attention here. The first provides the foundation for this entire Coda.

AMERICAN SAMURAI INSIGHT

The competitiveness of almost all manufacturers' products is at the mercy of their suppliers' competitiveness.

This is not a new concept. John Donne wrote in 1623:

> No man is an island, entire of itself; every man is a piece of the continent, a part of the main; if a clod be washed away by the sea, Europe is the less, as well as if a manor of thy friends or of thine own were; any man's death diminishes me, because I am involved in mankind; and therefore never send to know for whom the bell tolls; it tolls for thee.

So, neither, is any manufacturer an island of competitiveness, apart from his or her suppliers (or the general society of which it is part). If one of your suppliers isn't producing world-class materials, ask not for whom the bells tolls; it tolls for thee. Everything is interrelated, connected, and mutually dependent. The competitiveness of a product is determined by the interaction of quality, cost, value, and availability. Each of these parameters is directly and significantly influenced by the competitiveness of the suppliers who provide a manufacturer with parts and services. After all, how can a company produce a world-class product if 30% to 90% of the constituent parts of its products aren't of world-class quality? It can't. And how can a company maintain a competitive price for its product if it's constantly shutting down a line because parts aren't arriving on time? It can't. It's clear that a company's suppliers must be as good as the company itself wants to be. Either they all do it together, or they'll all be washed out to sea together.

The second insight involves the process orientation we first discussed as Coda 1 in Chapter Six. You'll recall that we described a macro-process as a series of input-event-output sequences, as shown in Figure 18-1.

```
INPUT - - →EVENT - - →OUTPUT
              becomes
              INPUT - - →EVENT - - →OUTPUT
                            becomes
                            INPUT - - →EVENT - - →OUTPUT - - →
```

Figure 18-1. Macro-process chain.

Then, in discussing Coda 6 (Chapter Eleven), we saw that each macro-process (or micro-process) could also be viewed as a series of supplier-customer linkages, as shown in Figure 18-2.

```
SUPPLIER – – →CUSTOMER
           becomes
           SUPPLIER – – →CUSTOMER
                      becomes
                      SUPPLIER – – →CUSTOMER
                                 becomes
                                 SUPPLIER – – →CUSTOMER
```

Figure 18-2. A macro-process shown as a chain of supplier-customer linkages.

The manufacture and delivery of every product and service in the world can be described as such a macro-process. Some consist of thousands of micro-processes, extending from a sand pit in Michigan to the delivery of a replacement car windshield in Florida. Macro-processes know no departmental and/or organizational boundaries. You can show company boundaries on a large macro-process chart, such as the one shown in Figure 18-3, but they're only artificial boundaries in terms of the processes themselves; the processes must be done, regardless of who does them. Every link depends upon every other one.

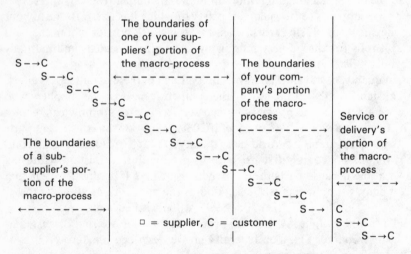

Figure 18-3. Macro-process links with superimposed organizational boundaries.

In Chapter Six, one of the American Samurai Insights stated, "The only people who are in a position to provide accurate information about micro-processes are the workers who do them." If you combine that thought with an appreciation of the diagram we just examined in Figure 18-3, you realize that:

AMERICAN SAMURAI INSIGHT

Suppliers are as much an integral part of your organization's push for competitiveness as your own employees. They must be involved in your processes as much as your employees are.

YOU MEAN WE'VE GOT TO BE NICE TO SUPPLIERS, TOO?

Alas, yes. Traditional business has a tough time with this one. They're often willing to admit that suppliers are important, since they've all seen the impacts of poor quality or late parts. But many executives assume that they can have a positive impact on this process simply by pounding harder on their suppliers to improve quality, as in, "Quality better get world class fast, or we'll kick your heads in and find somebody else." The relationship between suppliers and manufacturers has typically been one of master and servant. Manufacturers have been calling the shots, and suppliers, if they wanted the business, have been forced to keep their mouths shut.

This is about the worst possible approach for developing high-quality suppliers. If the situation in American business is going to be turned around, it's essential that suppliers be included as integral team members in product development and problem-solving decisions. If an organization wants to improve quality, and thus competitiveness, it can't afford to limit its focus to only 30% to 70% of its product. That's what happens when quality improvement attempts don't involve suppliers.

However, simply getting vendors to ship defect-free parts is only half the battle. You can get defect-free parts on time from suppliers and still not get what you need (remember the story of the red shoes in Chapter Eleven). This is where the process knowledge comes into play. In the old system, manufacturers told suppliers what to ship. This assumes that manufacturers know as much, or more, about all of the ways in which the parts or services can be made, used, and/or changed. This, as we know, is totally and completely false. Suppliers *always* know more about their products than the end users.

How many times have you gone to a store to buy something for a project you're working on at home and ended up with something totally different from your initial idea, because the salesperson knew about a better way or a different product? That's because the supplier, the salesperson, knew more about his or her products than you, the end user. That's the way it should be; you can't be an expert in everything.

It's the same with a manufacturer. A manufacturer can't know as much about every part and service it uses as can the suppliers. Even if it were possible to learn, it wouldn't make sense. A manufacturer must concentrate on the competitiveness of his or her end processes and end product, while suppliers concentrate on improving theirs—that's where success lies. Thus, suppliers' knowledge about their own products and processes must be utilized by manufacturers as completely as if the suppliers were employees.

Selection of Suppliers on Price Alone Guarantees
Higher Costs and Lower Quality

It's almost a given that suppliers are selected on the basis of the price of their goods and services in traditional environments. This is an absolute guarantee of higher costs and lower quality. We don't even run our own lives like that, but we run organizations that way. When you need a surgical operation, do you try to find the absolute cheapest surgeon, such as somebody operating out of an old school bus who has already been suspended twice for malpractice? Of course not. You make some trade-off, perhaps subconsciously, between price and what's called the *cost of quality lost*. The cost of quality lost is the total cost impact of a bad decision or a quality flaw over the entire life of the product. You realize, when selecting a surgeon for yourself, that the impact of quality lost could be severe if you choose a quack.

Look what happens when people buy car tires. Does the cheapest tire always sell the most? No. And do people always shop for the place that has the absolute lowest cost, regardless of considerations such as service, reputation for quality, and convenience? No way. When we select suppliers for our personal needs, we balance many considerations. Price is only one of them, and it's often one of the least important.

How many times have you seen a bucket of bargain, less than a buck screwdrivers or a $5.99 mini-ratchet set sitting on the checkout counter in a discount or hardware store? Ever bought one? The screwdriver tips always round off the first time you use them. I even fell for the ratchet ploy once. The handle bent to a 90-degree angle the first time I used it. You always get exactly what you pay for (or maybe even a little less) when you select on the basis of price alone. We all know it.

Yet, go into the typical company's purchasing department and how are buying decisions made? You guessed it: price and price alone. If a bid comes in for red widgets at $1.00 per widget, a second bid coming in at $1.01 doesn't have a chance. That's the way it works. Such a system forces traditionally operating suppliers to cut corners to lower costs, which further reduces quality and service and drives up the manufacturer's costs even though the price of parts and services seems to be decreasing. It's a deceiving situation, if you don't stop to think about it.

IT'S EASY TO UNDERSTAND HOW THIS PRICE
ALONE STRATEGY HAS BECOME A WAY OF LIFE,
ONE THAT WE MUST STOP

It's easy to understand how selection on price has become the sole criterion for most buying decisions. It's easy, it doesn't require management to allow employees to make a lot of independent decisions, and it's supported by decades of tradition and government policy.

First of all, it doesn't take an MIT Ph.D. in Economics to look at two bids for a product and determine which one is the lowest. This makes it easy to relegate purchasing decisions to lower-level, relatively untrained personnel who know little about the processes involved ("Why should they have to understand the process? All they're doing is buying the parts!" is a common refrain).

Second, it's easy to defend a decision based on price against government auditors and private lawsuits. In our volume-oriented, visible costs-only society, all you have to do is wave the lowest price in front of a bureaucrat or a judge and you're home free.

HOW THE LOWEST PRICE CAN KILL YOUR BUSINESS

Remember the story of the red shoes in Chapter Eleven? Our hero Norbert went to Rodeo Drive and got a free pair of expensive shoes, all sorts of foot and neck massages, free drinks, and so on, and lost out big (a large cost of quality lost) because he got just what he wanted. He thought he wanted the shiny red running shoes, but he was wrong. He was an end user, much like a manufacturer, who specified exactly what he wanted, and, horror of horrors, he got it. The same thing happens all the time in business. Suppliers are told exactly what to ship, and, even if they do it on time, right to specification (and we know about those after Chapter Seventeen), and at the lowest cost, disaster can strike. All because the manufacturer doesn't know as much about the part or service as the supplier. Let's look at a few examples.

"Read My Lips" Doesn't Work

A defense contractor asked for bids on 10,000 electronic switches for a missile. It was a simple switch, designed by the best engineers in the company. In the typical imperial manner of a manufacturer dealing with suppliers, the contractor said, "Read my lips, pig suppliers. Here are the specs for the switch. Submit your bids and hold your breath. We'll get back to you." The lowest bidder was awarded the contract. Six months later, all 10,000 switches came in, exactly as ordered, each to spec, each just as they were designed by the manufacturer's wonderful engineers. Great so far.

Thousands of missiles using the switch had been built and delivered to the customer when a problem was detected during a test firing. The missile didn't launch. Upon disassembly, it was discovered that the switch had been put in backwards. Although the wires had been color-coded, an assembly mistake had been made. Somebody not in training as an American Samurai would have immediately blamed the employee who put in the switch. You now know that's ridiculous; nobody, except a malcontent (and guess who hired him or her—management) would do it wrong on purpose. It was a simple, inadvertent error.

The missile maker ended up having to go out and tear down thousands of already delivered and armed missiles in order to check the switch in each one. It turned out that about one in 100 had been put in wrong. This cost the missile company millions of dollars, all of it lost profits. They ended up losing every penny of profit from the sale of 27 million dollars worth of products. This is yet another face of the cost of quality lost.

How was this related to the supplier? Very simple, Grasshopper. The supplier, if he or she had been asked, might have suggested a slight modification of the switch, a modification that was already being used in similar switches they were building for other missiles being made by competing missile manufacturers. The slight modification would have added only cents per switch to the price. What was the modification? Simply design the receptacles on the switch, and the wire connectors leading to it, so that it would be impossible to connect the switch backwards. A very basic, elementary principle of concurrent engineering (which will be discussed in detail as Coda 17 in Chapter Twenty-Two). The supplier had been making switches for all sorts of customers for years and had long ago learned about such problems. The supplier knew a lot more about switches than the manufacturer's engineers. But nobody asked the supplier; nobody considered the supplier an equal.

The only way you learn from suppliers is to ask. And, in this case, the missile manufacturer would have been best advised to encourage two sets of suppliers to work together on a team with the manufacturer's own engineers. The switch suppliers and the connector suppliers would have had to cooperate so that they could come up with the best (and lowest cost) design that would prohibit incorrect connections, allow for efficient assembly, and perform to required levels. As you can see, this is much different from assuming that the manufacturer knows it all and can simply tell suppliers what to do. That approach rarely works.

Another example. Remember the problem with the Hancock Towers building in Boston, Massachusetts? It made all the major news magazines. This was one of the first very tall, "glass tower" office buildings in which the skin of the building is almost all glass.

Each of the thousands of large window panels rests in what's called channel steel, a piece of molding that holds the glass in. The architects for the building specified exactly what they wanted for the windows, both the panes and the channel steel. They then selected the lowest price supplier that could meet the specifications for each part and proceeded to construct the building. So far, so good.

Then the windows started to fall out. Imagine sheets of glass as large as 6 by 12 feet falling hundreds of feet and exploding amidst pedestrians and cars. (If I were an attorney, my mouth would be watering just at the thought.) For months and months, all of the busy city streets around the building were blocked off to protect the public while the Hancock Life Insurance Company (the end customer), the architect, the building contractor, the window contractor, the channel steel contractor, the window manufacturer, the channel steel manufacturer, the city of Boston, and legions of attorneys engaged in a frenzied dance. Tens of millions of dollars were lost to lawsuits, attorneys, repairs, payments to the city of Boston for rerouting traffic, damage to the image of the insurance company (after all, if their windows won't even stay in, what about their insurance?), and so on. All costs of quality lost. All because of selection on price alone.

That debacle might have been avoided simply by having the window and the channel steel manufacturers work together as a team with the architect and the building contractor. And it most certainly would have been avoided if the emphasis had been put first on quality and then on price. Such an approach would have encouraged the additional effort and expense for analysis, research, and modeling of window–channel steel behavior in high wind conditions. But with an emphasis on price alone, such "extras" are unthinkable. No supplier would dare add such expenses to the price because another (lower) bidder would get the business. All of the prospective suppliers were forced to take the low road so that they would win the bid. As a result, everybody lost. The final total life-cycle cost for the windows was hundreds of times more than it would have been if everyone had spent a little more upfront to work together. Stories analogous to this one are repeated a thousand times every day in all industries.

Suppliers Must Be Selected on the Basis of Long-Term Partnerships

So what's the alternative? The alternative is to select suppliers on the basis of their ability to work with a company over the long term; suppliers who can be true partners, not merely lowest bidders. The only good supplier is one who is just as worried about your product as you are. Suppliers who are selected on the basis of lowest bid don't feel that way. And chances are, they won't win the next bid (because somebody will lowball them). Such suppliers have no loyalty to the manufacturer, no sense of teamwork and commitment, and no in-depth understanding of the manufacturers' processes.

A partnership with suppliers means that suppliers will no longer be competing against one another for every part and service. Once a supplier is chosen for a particular type of item, that supplier will always be awarded the business for that item and will know it. This permits the supplier to plan ahead, feel comfortable in investing in more testing and research, and get to know the end-user's product and processes better. Ideally, only one supplier should be selected for each part or service type. This is the approach taken by all world-class companies. Reductions in the number of suppliers will be discussed on p. 212.

Supplier partnerships mean that suppliers are selected prior to the start up of a product design and are included in design discussions (this will be discussed in more detail in Chapter Twenty-Two, Coda 17). In supplier partnerships, contracts contain few penalties, incentives, and conditional clauses; there is a bond of trust between supplier and customer in which each assumes that the other will do his or her best.

The sole supplier approach is often criticized by pointing out that dependence on one supplier is dangerous, since the supplier could go out of business or otherwise stop production. That's a danger that's present no matter how many suppliers are used. In fact, multiple suppliers are an added cost burden of their own due to parts variability and resultant set-up and repair costs. Even companies with ten suppliers for a given product run into continual difficulties with deliveries and quality. Despite the seeming redundancy of multiple suppliers, it's usually difficult for a supplier to bump up production or deliveries of anything other than commodity items on short notice. Most don't keep the stock on hand and/or have the excess capacity to quickly make up for a shortfall on the part of another supplier.

AMERICAN SAMURAI INSIGHT

Multiple suppliers offer very little insurance against short-term shortages. The implied redundancy just isn't there.

The plain fact is that multiple suppliers are used for the sole purpose of playing suppliers against each other in order to get the lowest possible price. We've seen the effects of that approach; it doesn't work. It destroys the incentives for suppliers to take the extra effort to do a really good job.

Another key point is that when business is spread over 5 to 10 suppliers, not one of them is getting enough business to really worry about keeping a customer happy. If the business is concentrated on one supplier, they not only have resources to do better work, they are dependent on the customer and they know it. This fosters an "in it together" mentality.

Many people, especially those who contract with the federal government, have the mistaken notion that it's illegal or impossible or risky to award business on the basis of anything but price. Wrong. The only requirement to avoid trouble, even when dealing with the federal government and its morass of rules and regulations, is that business must be awarded on the basis of a competitive analysis. The competition doesn't have to be on price, it just has to be a competition.

Of course, price is the easiest metric to evaluate, since only two data points must be compared. As you've seen, there lies the road to ruin. Price is easy but essentially meaningless and even dangerous (much like taking the shortest distance to port and not evaluating reefs and sandbars on a chart—the folks who take the longest route get there, while you sink or run aground).

So How Do You Pick Suppliers?

Well, it's not going to be easy, but you don't have any choice. They must be selected on the basis of how well they follow The Code of the American Samurai (or Dr. Deming's 14 points or some analogous system). I suggest that you use a simpler and less stringent version of the Malcolm Baldrige criteria. As you'll recall from Chapter Ten, the evaluation categories for the Baldrige are:

1. *Leadership* The extent to which senior management has been successful in creating and sustaining a quality culture.
2. *Information and Analysis* The effectiveness of the organization's efforts to collect and analyze information for quality improvement and planning.
3. *Strategic Planning* The extent to which quality requirements are integrated into the organization's business plans.
4. *Human Resources Utilization* The success of the organization's efforts to utilize the full potential of all of its employees for quality.
5. *Quality Assurance of Products and Services* The extent to which the organization's systems are effective in maintaining quality control of all operations.
6. *Quality Assurance Results* The degree of the organization's success, determined by quantitative measures, in improving quality.
7. *Customer Satisfaction* The effectiveness of the organization in determining and meeting requirements for customer satisfaction.

What must be done is to evaluate each supplier according to these criteria. This will require on-site visits to each supplier, not only to evaluate them, but also to work with them to coach and teach them (although you'll find that many of your suppliers will be *your* teachers, as they're already on the road to Total Quality Management).

Use of the Baldrige criteria is helpful because it provides an already accepted and established method (supported by the federal government). Of course, there's more to it than simply visiting with a checklist in hand. It's critical to encourage suppliers to learn the necessary philosophy, tools, and techniques for 18 to 24 months before beginning evaluations. Each supplier will have to have training more or less compatible with the training requirements listed in Chapter Sixteen. Otherwise, they won't be equipped to hold up their end of the partnership.

A first step is usually to call all of an organization's suppliers together and announce the new focus and a tentative timetable. At the kickoff meeting (usually more than one, if the number of suppliers is large), the elements of the philosophy are explained. This is generally followed by a mailed survey in which each supplier is questioned about efforts to practice the tools and techniques in this book. This is used as the basis for planning future training and identifying candidates to serve as committee members in some sort of advisory board that provides a forum for obtaining supplier support and feedback. Motorola has a model program for suppliers and gives regularly scheduled briefings about it to outside executives at its Galvin Center near Chicago.

The Number of Suppliers Must Be Dramatically Reduced

Aside from the issue of how to select suppliers, there are other tactics that are an inherent part of a purchasing operation in a world-class company. The first is that the number of suppliers must be reduced as much as possible. World-class companies have reduced their supplier base from thousands to hundreds over the last 10 years. Table 18-1 presents the cost savings one company obtained as a result of reducing the size of its supplier base (the data was shared with an assurance of confidentiality). The data shows the number of suppliers each year, as well as annual and cumulative (cost index) savings on a large sample of common parts.

Table 18-1.
Savings on common parts as a result of reduction
of the size of supplier base.

Year	Size of supplier base	Additional savings on common parts per year	Cost index (base = 100)
1980	12,000	(Start)	100.0
1981	11,200	2.1%	97.9
1982	9,800	2.6%	95.4
1983	8,200	2.5%	93.0
1984	6,775	2.1%	91.0
1985	5,200	3.8%	87.6
1986	3,800	4.3%	83.8
1987	2,325	4.7%	79.9
1988	1,500	4.3%	76.4
1989	1,350	4.8%	72.8

As you can see, the cost of the same parts over a 10-year period was reduced by 27.2% (from 100 to 72.8), even though inflation had been increasing overall costs for all goods over the same period! This is the expected pattern of cost savings that is associated with a reduction in supplier base that's been experienced by scores of world-class companies.

AMERICAN SAMURAI INSIGHT

The price of the same part or service should always go down over time as the supplier learns how to operate more efficiently. At

**the same time, the supplier should also be making more money.
With supplier partnerships, everybody wins.**

THERE ARE ADDITIONAL SAVINGS AS WELL

The reduction of the supplier base has significant, additional benefits in overhead savings. As the number of suppliers decreases, vast amounts of paper work are no longer needed. As the suppliers get better at what they do, there are fewer problems to resolve, fewer invoices, less invoice processing, and less travel. Huge savings result. The company in Table 18-1 realized a net reduction of 432 people in its purchasing department over the course of the 10-year supplier reduction effort. At an average salary plus overhead of $43,500, the head count reduction alone yielded savings of $18,792,000 a year. At the approximately 10% profit margins at which this company operated, those savings represented the profit on sales of 180 million dollars each year—without a single product being shipped. That's the way to make money!

These savings don't even include collateral savings in departments such as finance (which has to do the payables) and personnel (which would have had to recruit, process, relocate, etc. at least 40 people a year to maintain 432 people). As you can see, the benefits of any one Coda sweep through all parts of an organization.

PURCHASING IN VOLUME DRIVES UP COSTS

There is a myth that purchasing in volume drives down costs. Wrong. It drives up costs. The theory of volume purchases is that the supplier can make a huge production run and thereby reduce costs, providing a lower cost per piece. That's often true enough on the surface. The problem is that other costs are buried deep in the system, even if nothing goes wrong. (How often does a product make it to market with no part changes? Hardly ever.) Let's look at the costs hidden in volume purchases.

When material is ordered in bulk, it must be paid for. This requires that money be borrowed (or taken from profits) to pay for the goods until they are incorporated into a product and sold. And then there's the issue of storage space. Storage space must be heated, cooled, painted, and swept, and automatic retrieval systems must be purchased (more profits lost forever) and maintained. Taxes must be paid on the inventory and on the land the storage area is located on. The parts must be handled at least twice, once to store them and once to retrieve them. That costs all sorts of money. If the storage area isn't well organized, the parts may be moved more than twice. Some will be damaged in moving and some will be damaged just sitting in storage.

All these costs are incurred even if nothing goes wrong. Something always does go wrong, of course, and that's when the costs of volume purchases really get you. If an "already stocked to the rafters" part is suddenly found to be inadequate or to have a problem, there are the tremendous costs of rework and repair for existing stock, not to mention the costs of litigation and time as supplier and customer jockey to avoid paying the rework costs. Somebody finally eats the cost. And since the customer told the supplier exactly what to do ("Read my lips, dirt bag supplier . . ."), it's usually the customer. This means that the end-user customer finally has to pay, meaning that the product is now less competitive. There's just no way you can make money on volume purchases. The alternative is simple.

AMERICAN SAMURAI INSIGHT

Commit to a projected amount of material from a supplier and then insist on timed deliveries of parts made only a short time before shipment.

This approach makes it easy to turn on a dime and make changes without having to rework or scrap (not to mention count, examine, diagnose, and ship vast amounts of material). This technique also encourages both supplier and customer to pursue and be open to continued improvements in the product, something that's always held "for the next generation of the product" in the traditional approach. This "time sensitive" delivery of parts is key to JIT (just in time) systems, in which inventories are minimal and parts arrive "just in time."

INCOMING INSPECTION SHOULD ALMOST DISAPPEAR

Another positive impact attributable to supplier partnerships is head count reductions that result from dramatic decreases in receiving inspections. Once suppliers are on board as partners and fully up to speed, they monitor their own processes. Receiving inspection decreases significantly. In world-class Japanese plants, suppliers deliver parts without a customer so much as counting them. Xerox, a Baldrige winner in 1989, has increased the number of parts not requiring incoming inspection from about 30% in 1981 to about 97% in 1988. The number of defective parts discovered on the production line decreased from about 4000 per million in 1982 (0.4%) to about 250 per million (0.025%) in 1988. Almost no inspection and a sixteenfold decrease in defects at the same time. That's a partnership program!

IT'S ALL THE SAME

As you can no doubt surmise, this Coda simply advocates treating suppliers as much like a part of your own company as possible. This is a radical concept compared to the traditional approach of pistol-whipping suppliers for the lowest price, but it's nothing new for a budding American Samurai. In fact, it's nothing new at all. Most wise folks have always known that you can kill yourself by going for the cheapest price. It simply boils down to the well-known, 16th century observation of Gabriel Biel, in *Exposito Canonis Missae*: "You get what you pay for." John Ruskin elaborated on this theme in the late 19th century, when he stated: "There is hardly anything in the world that someone cannot make a little worse and sell a little cheaper—and the people who consider price alone are this man's lawful prey."

It's up to American Samurai everywhere to do what they can to prevent their organizations from being part of the "lawful prey." This won't be easy. If an organization isn't treating its own people with dignity and respect, it sure as hell won't start with suppliers. All we can do is spread the word and hope that a few more executives listen.

19

Why Do We Punish Ourselves?

Coda 14.   **The traditional system of job descriptions, performance appraisals, merit pay, and pay for performance are useless, damaging, and wasteful. They must be abandoned and replaced with a system that encourages and rewards teamwork and group effort.**

In this chapter, you'll discover why performance appraisals, merit pay, and pay for performance systems, as well as their supporting job classifications and job descriptions, are limiting and damaging to maximum productivity. For the purposes of general discussion, I'll be referring to this entire dung heap of insanities as a *performance management system*.

THE ELEMENTS OF TRADITIONAL PERFORMANCE MANAGEMENT SYSTEMS

Before we examine the many failings of traditional performance management systems, let's briefly review the individual components of these systems so that we'll have a common point of reference.

Classifications

Classifications are types of jobs. For example, a company may have classifications for secretarial-type jobs such as Executive Secretary, Administrative Secretary, Secretary, Senior Clerk, and Clerk. With these classifications, the level of job skills and experience required to satisfy the position requirements is highest for Executive Secretary and lowest for Clerk. Similarly, there might be numerous levels of engineers such as Senior Engineer III, Senior Engineer II, Senior Engineer I, Engineer II, Engineer I, and Engineering Aide. Classifications are often broken down on other dimensions as well, such as salaried and hourly. In one company, a Clerk might be salaried, and, in a second company, the position might be hourly.

The salaried classifications are usually also grouped according to whether the position is exempt or non-exempt. This is a legal distinction in which exempt essentially means "exempt from the dictates of the Fair Labor Standards Act." Exempt classifications are generally professional positions in which there is a certain level of responsibility and authority and in which overtime does not have to be paid for work of more than 8 hours a day or 40 hours per week (this is the key driver for the exempt and non-exempt dichotomy; it prevents employers from demanding that lower-level people work more than 8 hours a day without pay). Non-exempt positions are those for which there are no exemptions from the law: overtime must be paid. Generally, secretarial positions are non-exempt. Various state and federal agencies make occasional audits of companies to determine whether their exempt/non-exempt classifications are legal.

Classifications are almost always described in detail in *job descriptions* or *position descriptions* (same thing, different name). A typical job classification for an Executive Secretary is shown in Figure 19-1.

JOB DESCRIPTION

Job Title: Executive Secretary   Category: Non-exempt
Department: Various   Grade Level: 5

Duties and responsibilities:

Provide secretarial services to a Vice-President or the President. Perform executive secretarial and general office work of a specialized and confidential nature. Requires extensive knowledge of a major functional area and companywide procedures.

Exercise initiative and independent judgment in assuming responsibility for routine administrative details. Maintain office procedures in the absence of executive personnel and ensure that urgent matters are directed to the proper alternative authority.

Exercise tact, diplomacy, and courtesy in person-to-person, correspondence, and phone interactions with customers, suppliers, corporate office personnel, and company employees.

Take and transcribe dictation, make meeting and travel arrangements, and resolve calendar conflicts.

Operate typewriters, personal computers, facsimile machines, and other office equipment to facilitate internal and external correspondence and communications. Process incoming correspondence and phone calls and route them to appropriate parties.

Compose routine correspondence of a sensitive and confidential nature. Maintain records and files. Perform other duties as assigned or as required to fulfill position responsibilities.

Experience and Education requirement:

High school diploma. Normally requires 6 years of directly related experience.

Figure 19-1. Job description of an Executive Secretary.

Why we have them. The stated reason for having job descriptions is usually something along the lines of, "We have to have them so that people will understand what their job duties are and so that we can make sure that we hire the right people for each job.'' The problem is, not one job description in 10,000 is written with any substantive input by the folks who do the job. And who is the only one with sufficient process knowledge about a job to write a meaningful job description about it? Right, the person who does the processes, not someone in personnel.

How they really work and are used. Job descriptions are really a game. They're part of a game that provides jobs for all sorts of personnel specialists, in the same manner that the necktie industry provides all sorts of jobs. Neckties don't do anything useful, but they are supported by an entire industry that just validates its existence by promoting their use. It's the same with job descriptions (and the entire performance management system).

Personnel functions have used performance management systems to create a shadow organization that has almost nothing to do with real work but provides a lever for them to tamper with anything they wish, for example, hiring. Nobody I've ever met actually uses a job description to hire somebody. They need a secretary, they know what to look for. But they're forced by personnel to put in a req (pronounced "wreck," for requisition), part of a system that enables personnel to bottleneck everything. (Did you ever wonder why every V.P. in a company has to get the V.P. of personnel to approve every req and all personnel actions but the V.P. of personnel can meddle in everyone else's affairs to his or her heart's content?)

The requisition process allows personnel to "administer" the hiring process. There appears to be all sort of precision, but there really isn't any at all. Let's say a really good person interviews for an Executive Secretary job with his or her new boss (after being "filtered" through personnel), but he or she has "only" 4 years of secretarial experience, although the job description says, "*Normally* requires 6 years of directly related experience." If the hiring manager is tough enough, has enough influence, and/or is willing to create a scene, he or she can hire a fresh high school graduate with no experience for the position. If the hiring manager is powerless, he or she will be forced to take whoever personnel wants to hire.

Job descriptions are also used to maintain the caste system. The Executive Secretary job description in Figure 19-1 was part of a package of job descriptions that dealt with all secretarial positions ranging from Executive Secretary to Clerk. The section in the Executive Secretary job description that said,

> "Operate typewriters, personal computers, facsimile machines, and other office equipment to facilitate internal and external correspondence and communications. Process incoming correspondence and phone calls and route them to appropriate parties."

was written as, "Run office equipment. Process mail and phone calls" in the job description for Clerk. Same exact duties, after you cut through all the verbiage, but the first is written "up" to make it appear more sophisticated. The reason for this "pump job" on the verbiage is that everybody in personnel "knows" that an Executive Secretary is going to get paid more than a Clerk. So they justify the money by making the job description look more sophisticated for an Executive Secretary than for a Clerk. This is a lot easier than really finding out about the processes involved and using the job descriptions to present data that might be useful in hiring and that really discriminates between various types of jobs.

It's just a game. In fact, the catchall phrase at the bottom, "Perform other duties as assigned or as required to fulfill position responsibilities" really sums it up: the person taking the job will do whatever is required to get it done. These things change from day to day. The least important thing to mention is the phone calls, typing, and so on; everybody knows about them already.

Pay Grades

There's a lot more to personnel than the hordes of folks in the classification section. We also have to provide jobs for scores of overhead eaters in "compensation." These are the folks who tell you how much you can pay someone and how much of a salary increase you can give them (even though they know nothing about the employee or the processes). Every company of any size at all (about 250 or more employees) has dozens, if not hundreds of job descriptions. Pay grades, sometimes called job classifications or labor grades if job description is the term used for classifications, are used to reconcile the numerous job descriptions with a smaller number of pay levels.

A pay grade is a level of compensation. For each pay grade, a minimum, midpoint, and maximum is established. Thus, a company's lowest pay grade may be called "Pay Grade G 2" or PG 2. (For some reason, hardly any companies ever start with "1," perhaps because they hope the minimum wage laws will be changed and they want to have room to go "down.") PG 2 might look like Table 19-1.

Table 19-1.
Representative monthly pay grade with minimum,
mid-point, and maximum. Figures in parentheses are hourly rates.

Pay grade	Minimum	Midpoint	Maximum
PG 2	$734	$867	$1040
	(4.00)	(5.00)	(6.00)

The dollar amounts are monthly pay, based upon 40 hours per week and 2080 hours per year (typical assumptions). The figures in parentheses are hourly rates provided for your reference. As you can see, the range of pay, called the "spread," for a PG 2 varies from 4 to 6 dollars per hour. The pay that someone receives when they are hired, the point along the spread at which their starting pay is located, is determined by a subjective analysis of their experience, attitudes, connections, and physical appearance as well as the power and influence of the hiring manager.

Compensation types have an almost religious infatuation with the "midpoint." It's their goal in life to keep the average pay for everybody within a pay grade "at the midpoint." This makes the compensation people look good because they have convinced executive management that keeping averages at the midpoint is good. This is nonsense, of course, since an employee's pay is a macro-process output.

A company's pay scale consists of an entire set of these ranges and midpoints, covering every pay grade. A portion of one is shown in Table 19-2.

Table 19-2.
Representative portion of a pay/labor grade scale.

Pay grade	Minimum	Midpoint	Maximum
PG 15	$9166	$1166	$11666
PG 14	$7916	$8750	$9583
PG 13	$7250	$7667	$8083
•	•	•	•
•	•	•	•
PG 9	$3166	$3541	$3916
PG 8	$2916	$3166	$3500
•	•	•	•
•	•	•	•
PG 4	$997	$1147	$1300
PG 3	$867	$1040	$1213
PG 2	$734	$867	$1040

These scales are developed with a number of procedures. First of all, research is done to determine what everybody else is paying. Many companies participate in voluntary annual surveys in which they share data with a large number of other companies about what each of them pays various job types. This type of effort is often coordinated by a state agency to assure anonymity (so that word doesn't get out as to identity of the lowest and highest paying firms). The ostensible purpose of this analysis is for each firm to "be in the ballpark" on compensation. Nobody wants to pay too much compared to other firms in the area, and nobody wants to end up having recruiting difficulties because they are paying too little. This seems to me like a variant of price setting, which is illegal for products, but apparently employees are fair game.

Consulting companies are involved, too. They claim to provide "expert advice" on adjusting pay ranges to bring things "into line." What they really do is shrink the ranges between the maximums and minimums of the lower grades, add a few dollars here and there to pay grades that are grossly noncompetitive, and then pump the living hell out of the upper pay grades. As a result, over time, the upper pay grades get much wider than a mere regression line would predict (compared to the lower pay grades). This is deliberately done so that executives can continue to get pay increases long after employees have "topped out."

"Topping out" is the consequence of reaching the top amount in a pay grade, meaning that the employee is barred from receiving further increases unless something is done to adjust the pay grade itself. Such systems are routinely manipulated in the interests of powerful interest groups within companies. I was once working at a firm in which the Senior Secretaries had a pay range that extended from a minimum of $2166 per month to a maximum of $2833 ($34,000 per year, or $16.35 per hour). A majority of them were topped out because most of the younger secretaries had been laid off in the past (when factories were closing). The remaining secretaries had been getting merit increases for so many years that most of them had long ago reached the top of their pay grade.

The company had this problem in many pay grades because of past layoffs but insisted that it was not raising the maximums because compensation levels were fair and, in most cases, more than the competition was paying. This was actually true (a rare instance). But we all know who the Executive Secretaries report to, right? Executives. Before you knew it, the maximum of the Executive Secretary pay grade was raised "after much analysis had discovered market imbalances." Right. The old men running the company couldn't say no to their secretaries. No other pay grades were raised. The result was that many Executive Secretaries were being paid more than middle managers with 15 to 20 years of experience.

It's always the same. Pay scales and compensation levels, midpoints, maximums, minimums, and so forth, all sound scientific, but it's just subjective posturing disguised as numbers.

Once a pay grade-compensation matrix such as the one shown in Table 19-2 is constructed, every job position is assigned a pay grade. Thus, there may be two, three, or four positions (or more) at the same pay grade. For example, both a Clerk and a Groundskeeper I may be at PG 2. The top pay grade is, of course, reserved for the President of the company (or a CEO if it's a scale for a corporate office). Whenever a new job is created, it's assigned to the closest existing pay grade that "makes sense" (which means whatever other companies are paying).

Merit Pay and Pay for Performance

Merit pay is supposed to be an income adjustment that's given for performance. This is the traditional 4% to 6% raise that's given annually, if you're lucky (meaning if your boss likes you and the company is doing OK). It's supposed to be directly tied to an employee's achievements and contributions over some period, usually the previous year. Since even American managers have begun to have a dim perception that performance management systems aren't working, they have taken bold, decisive action; they are changing the name to *pay for performance*. Same process, same problems, same system (with perhaps new forms), but with a new name: pay for performance. Pay for performance is touted as more closely tying achievements to merit pay. Unfortunately, it's based upon the same rotten foundations and faulty assumptions. It can't work.

One of the more basic reasons for the move to pay for performance systems is that the almost "automatic" merit raises of traditional systems are not forthcoming under a pay for performance system. When a performance management system has its name changed to pay for performance, the troops are usually told that regular, almost everybody gets them, merit increases are a thing of the past. They are told that good performers will get large bonuses instead of merit pay, whereas poor performers will get nothing (or the boot).

The problem is that the same system is used to determine how and who gets rewarded: appraisals, pay grades, etc. Same rotten system, same rotten results. And, unless management is pursuing a change to a new philosophy of work, the motivation for a pay for performance system is usually financial and has little or nothing to do with performance. In a pay for performance system, merit raises are less and bonuses don't make up the difference. Bonuses are less costly than merit raises, and there's no incurred liability for next year with a onetime bonus.

The Mechanics

"Pay for performance" and "merit pay" work as follows. Each year, depending on how much money the company is making, a certain dollar amount is allocated for compensation increases. The overwhelmingly largest part of this is dedicated to executive "incentives" or bonuses. Those 10 million dollar bonuses routinely awarded to automotive companies' top executives come from this pool.

Once the top guys have dipped into (and pretty much cleaned out) the till, the leftovers are allocated to merit pay for the troops. In a good year, this would amount to enough to pay a 4% average salary increase to everyone if the money were to be evenly distributed. Even if the company is doing great, more than 6% is almost never allocated in a traditionally run organization. The money is allocated on the basis of the results of a *performance review* or *personnel appraisal*.

Performance appraisals. We've all been through these. It's the annual ritual in which the person who hasn't talked to you all year except to yell and scream, who hasn't the slightest idea of what you've been doing, and who doesn't know anything about the problems you've had getting the job done with no support and resources, tells you in detail how you're doing. This stranger is, of course, your boss. He or she gives you arbitrary rankings on various things such as "attitude," "productivity," and "cooperation," perhaps reviews progress toward some objectives that seemed remotely plausible a year ago, and then tells you what your shortcomings are and how he or she is going to help you fix them over the next year.

The whole time, all you care about, all you can think about, is, "How much am I going to get?" Finally, you're told the number. It's always disappointing. You sign the appraisal form and leave, grumbling about the stupidity and arrogance of the boss and the system.

Performance appraisals generally operate within performance management systems in the following manner:

1. Supervisor is given forms by personnel and instructed to pass them out to employees.
2. Supervisor gives material to each employee and asks him or her to prepare a list of preliminary performance objectives for the coming year.
3. Employee completes material, returns it to the supervisor, and then meets with the supervisor to reach an agreement as to what his or her performance objectives will be for the coming year.
4. Forms are submitted to personnel.
5. Nothing happens for about 10 months (supervisors are supposed to meet with each employee regularly, but nobody ever does).
6. Just before the year is up, the forms are sent to the supervisor with an information packet about permissible percentages of "outstandings" and "excellents" (see p. 224), and how much total merit money is available for the area or department. The supervisor is told to rate the performance of the employee in terms of objectives and general characteristics (attitude, energy, etc.). The supervisor also gives a tentative rating to the employee and a suggested merit and/or bonus figure (the money step may be done as a separate step later in more burdensome systems).
7. The supervisor sends his or her package of appraisals to personnel, who review and recommend (demand) changes. The changes and a further review or approval by personnel and several layers of upward management then follow, after which the supervisor is told to "Give the reviews."
8. The reviews are given and merits or bonuses awarded.
9. The cycle starts again for the next year.

The size of a merit increase and/or bonus is based upon the employee's performance ranking. Most organizations have a five-to none-point scale, either using numbers or terms such as Outstanding and Unsatisfactory. Each supervisor is required to rank his or her people on this scale, according to the mandates of personnel. It doesn't matter if all of your personnel are handpicked, workaholic, self-sacrificing, cooperative geniuses, who are saving the company millions per month, or if they're a bunch of lazy, thieving, trouble-making, drug-dealing psychopaths; in either case, you'll be required to rank them according to a predetermined plan. In a company with a seven-point scale, the mandated percentages might look like the ones shown in Table 19-3.

Table 19-3.
A typical mandated performance appraisal distribution.

Performance classification	Recommended* percentages per classification
Outstanding	5
Excellent	10
Very good	15
Good	35
Satisfactory	30
Conditional satisfactory	5
Unsatisfactory	0
Total	100

* This means do it or else.

The mandated percentages in Table 19-3 mean that if you've got 100 people, you'll have to rate five of them "outstanding," ten "excellent," 15 "very good," and so on. You'll be required to jam their performances into such a profile regardless of the actual distribution of achievements. If you send personnel a distribution of ratings that's off by more than one or two in each category, they'll send it back and order you to change it.

JUST WHAT IS A PERFORMANCE MANAGEMENT SYSTEM SUPPOSED TO DO?

Now that we've examined the basic elements of traditional performance management systems, we'll review the objectives of performance management systems and examine how well these objectives are met. You'll see clearly why the systems that have been in use don't work.

Although almost every company has a performance management system, very few organizations stop to consider what they're trying to accomplish. They just do it because it's there and expected—sort of like the necktie. The difference is that a good ties costs 20 to 50 bucks. Operating traditional performance management systems incurs billions of dollars in lost productivity, turnover, and wasted labor every year.

The following are some of the commonly given objectives for performance management systems. Let's look at each one and evaluate how well the typical system satisfies it.

1. Reward Productivity

I don't know what current performance management systems reward, but it's not productivity. I'm speaking here in terms of the entire employee population in a company, not just a specific individual who may luck out or get shafted.

AMERICAN SAMURAI INSIGHT

Traditional performance management systems reward people who set low goals and/or those who play it safe.

Just look at how somebody gets an "outstanding" rating; they reach their goals. If you're in a typical environment, is it smart to reach for the stars, get only to the moon, and then get a horrendous "satisfactory" rating because you failed to reach your objectives? Not if you've got a brain. You'd lose out to some slug who set a goal of jumping 2 inches high, got 3 inches high, and got an "outstanding" for exceeding all requirements. Remember, once the name is changed to pay for performance, not everybody gets a raise. Those who merely do a "satisfactory" job are going to get little or nothing.

The potential for suboptimization is incredible. Each employee knows that he or she must work hard to set goals that are easy to reach and make the boss look good. If the boss is a typical suboptimizer, the process is compounded. A typical refrain is, "We need to make the department look good." All sorts of objectives are set that have nothing to do with real performance. The system rewards people who can successfully play the system, not productivity in its truest sense (which would be long-term improvements in customer satisfaction).

Even if the system did reward productivity, the amount of the typical merit or bonus award isn't enough to really reward anyone. At $50,000 per year, a 6% merit increase (a respectable sum in a pay for performance system) is $3000 over a year, or $57.67 per week ($1.44 per hour) *before* taxes. After taxes, it's around 40 bucks. That's enough to reward 12-hour days, weekend business trips, working through lunch, taking work home, etc., etc., etc.? Of course not. Sure, it's nice to have and you'll take it, but a reward? Not in my book. And, at the same time, somebody who got a "very good" rating got 3%, or $28.56 per week before taxes. This means that the difference between killing yourself and merely working hard is only about 30 bucks a week. Some reward!

2. Motivate Future Productivity

If anything, performance appraisals and merit pay *demotivate* employees for the future. Just think how you feel after a performance appraisal. After busting a gut to get the job done under horrible conditions (that is, you've been working in a traditionally run environment), you get a cursory once-over from the major source of the trouble, the boss, and a lousy few percent increase. At the same time, a bunch of consensus idiots in other departments with more generous (or blind) bosses get better ratings and more money.

The system can't be fair because of the inherent inequities built into it. But even if it was fair, the entire concept of using money as a motivator is faulty.

AMERICAN SAMURAI INSIGHT

People don't work for money; that is, rates of pay, merit increases, and bonuses don't motivate minute-to-minute and day-to-day improvements in productivity.

Many people answer this basic truth with, "Well, (sniff) I wouldn't work for free, would I?" Of course not. At the same time, how often during the day, while you're deciding whether to fight the system, work a little harder, make just one more phone call, or fix one more little thing that nobody would ever know if you let it go by, do you conduct a trade-off analysis between the action and how much you're getting paid? Probably never. That's because our level of effort isn't driven primarily by money.

Consider this. We all have things about our jobs that we hate. We complain about them all the time. Now, suppose that tomorrow your salary was tripled. Same job, but three times as much money. For a few weeks, maybe months, you'd be happy, as you adjusted your life style to the new level of income. At some point, however, you'd be completely acclimated to the new level of income and guess what would happen at work. Right. You'd be complaining about the same old things as before, and you'd be giving pretty much the same level of effort to the job.

As discussed in chapter Nine (Coda 4), people work for a sense of involvement, a feeling of achievement, and a belief that they matter, because they enjoy accomplishment, and because they seek the increase in self-esteem that mastery brings. We all do. The existing systems of performance management work contrary to almost every one of these needs. Sure, a starving, out-of-work person will work hard for money alone, but he or she will soon seek more from the job once the money is coming in. If he or she doesn't get it, the employer gets less than the worker could give.

The system creates losers. Look what happens to employee self-esteem when appraisals are given. A majority of the employees don't get the topmost rating. How do they feel? Like losers. They know others got the highest rating and they didn't. Even if they agree that they don't work as hard and didn't deserve the top rating, they don't enjoy having their noses rubbed in the fact that they're losers. This is especially true when somebody is rated in the middle or lower areas of a rating scale; that's scum-bag territory, and everyone knows it.

AMERICAN SAMURAI INSIGHT

Anything but the absolutely highest performance rating (in all

respects) is damaging to employee self-esteem and sets in motion a pattern of beliefs and behaviors that will damage quality, productivity, and profits.

As discussed in Chapter Nine (Coda 4), when an employee perceives that he or she is considered to be a problem or "not good," it sets up a self-fulfilling prophecy. The employee begins to make adjustments to deal with the negative perception, such as playing it safe, not taking chances when they should be taken, quitting, slacking off, etc. One person I know described her reactions to a recent performance appraisal. Her company uses two scales. One is a five-point performance scale with five being the best, and the other is a five-letter scale as to potential (whatever the hell that is and however the hell it can be measured; I'm a licensed psychologist and I know of no noncontroversial method to do that for 4-year-old children, much less adults).

The potential scale topped out at "O" ("outstanding"—could be promoted to corporate right now), followed by "H" ("high" potential—could be promoted sometime if nothing goes wrong), "G" ("good" potential—further development should lead to opportunities), "S" ("satisfactory"—about where employee should be, could change depending on future performance), to the bottom rating of "U" ("unsatisfactory"—placed about at abilities).

My friend got a five and "H"—the best on one scale and the next to best on the other; only 5% of all management did that well. Not bad, eh? Wrong. She was enraged (but hid it at work). She figured that she had been painted for all time as a divisional hack, not suited for corporate work. And it's not that she wanted to go to corporate. On the contrary, she had contempt for them. But she wanted to be viewed as the best and she hadn't been. She resolved to put in another year to make her resume look good tenure-wise and then leave. She will quit that company in a year or so, and they will have to spend tens of thousands of dollars searching for, recruiting, and relocating someone to replace her and then wait 6 months for them to learn enough about the job to really do it. At least a hundred thousand in lost profit because they told her she wasn't the best. What a tragedy, both for her and for them.

Why couldn't they simply have told her she was great and thus improved her morale, her dedication, and her commitment? Why not tell everybody they're great, they're winners, all the time?

3. Set Objective Standards of Performance and Evluation

About the most nonobjective thing in the world is a performance appraisal rating. The all-time prime, classic example is when you go in for your review and you've been doing great—all year you've been stretching to new lengths of creativity and achievement, even doing enough to make your slug of a boss and his or her boss look good, and you're told, "Bob (or Sally), you were outstanding this year. I'm giving you a four (in a one to five ranking system, with five being the best). You're really a five, but we don't give fives in this department." You smile wanly, hoping that the merit increase will be sufficient to dampen the blow (but knowing that it won't be). Then, you find out that all sorts of just average people in other departments got fives. Some objective standard. And, of course, even in your department, the boss's secretary will always get a five because he or she always does.

There is no objectivity in performance appraisals because people are not objective. A number of judgmental distortions are always operating, even if the boss is honest, objective, and trying hard. Some of these distortions are:

Central tendency. Many people have a belief that everybody should be somewhere in the middle of a distribution. They don't like to use the ends. If they're ranking employees on a five-point scale, they never use ones and fives. Thus, a five-point scale becomes a three-point scale. And since that means that the lowest score, a two, is now the worst, it isn't used very much. As a result, everybody gets rated by that boss as a three or four.

Halo effect. When I was in the seventh and eighth grade, I had a friend named John, who was the classic, all-American boy: tall for his age, muscular, blond hair (I never noticed what color his eyes were, but they must have been blue). We were great friends until he discovered girls while I was still in the kickball, whiffleball, model airplanes phase). He always got straight As, while I was always getting Bs and Cs. I was at least as intelligent and informed as he was, and I studied and read even more than he did.

After a bad week, in which I had gotten a "C" on a history outline on which I had busted a gut (John got an "A"), I decided to do a little experiment. For the next few weeks, I snuck into our homeroom at lunch and copied both his math and history (the outlines) homework word for word and number for number. And what happened? You already know. John continued to get As and I got Bs and Cs for exactly the same work (and my handwriting was neater—in fact, I even typed up one of the outlines I copied and still got only a B while John got an A. The same thing with math. He got As and I got Bs for the same numbers. My math problems would have little notes from the teacher and a few points subtracted here and there for equation reduction steps that the teacher thought could be better: John's, the exact same equations, never got a mark, perfect every time, straight As.

That was a classic "halo effect" situation. John had started out as an A student, looked the part, and was judged "A material." That's all he had to do. From then on, he had a "halo"; everything that he did was viewed as good. I was skinny and shorter, had dark hair, and was probably the classic picture of an underdeveloped, hyperactive young adolescent, everybody's worst nightmare of teenagedom. I was treated accordingly.

What are school grades but ongoing performance appraisals? The same factors operate at work but more intensely, because there's more at stake. Somebody who was great in the past always gets great reviews. Somebody who had a good year last year will probably get the benefit of the doubt this year (and next). At the same time, there are negative halo effects (they should be called the "horn effect," I suppose). Once you screw up, you'll always be rated down.

Part of the halo, or horn, effect occurs because of individual percep- tions and bias on the part of the appraiser, but part is motivated by fear. If someone has been rated well in the past, a new appraiser is often reluctant to change things because he or she will almost certainly have to defend the new rating from attacks by the employee, the personnel department, and other management levels. Nobody wants a lawsuit, and it's easier to repeat the same old, wrong appraisal than to try to do the "right" thing. That's why so many totally incompetent people have great performance ap- praisal histories.

Fear of being "mean". Many supervisors can't handle being critical when they have to directly face the people they're being critical of. So they tone down the criticism or feedback (since they haven't said a word all year until the review, they feel justifiably guilty), thus moving everybody in their area up toward the high end of the scale.

Fear of being nice. As you know if you're already out there working, there are a lot of supervisors who aren't very nice. Some are naturally mean, and some have fallen into that role because that's how they've been trained to supervise. They won't rate people high because they don't believe that anybody except themselves can be that good. As a result, all of their people end up with comparatively lower rankings than the rest of the organization.

Even if all of these biases were not operating to various degrees in every company, how could there be an objective way to rate performances across thousands of different micro-processes across dozens of departments, with hundreds of different supervisors, thousands of employees, and countless different inputs and outputs? How could you compare the performance of an executive secretary working for one boss against the performance of a supervisor in a steel mill who has twenty people reporting to him or her? You can't. It's apples and oranges.

4. Identify and Monitor Performance Objectives

It's often stated that one of the most important functions of a performance management system is to set performance objectives. It also used to be stated that the earth is flat. Both are ignorant and incorrect beliefs. After having read Chapter Fifteen (Coda 10), you realize that the performance objectives of individual employees must be driven by a customer-driven master plan.

AMERICAN SAMURAI INSIGHT

It's better to have no individual performance objectives at all than to develop them based on the suboptimizing goals of individual department heads or section leaders.

You can set individual goals, but they are usually contrary to what the organization as a whole must have. A performance management system can't substitute for a planning system. All it can do is ruin whatever good things are already happening.

5. Make Individual Rewards Proportional to Individual Achievements

There are two aspects to this drawback. The first is related to our previous discussions: nobody has ever devised a system to accurately rate individual employees by a common performance standard. Even if it could be done, it wouldn't be worth it, because performance appraisals are damaging even if they're accurate (self-fulfilling prophecies and all that).

The second is that individuals very seldom have the power, the influence, or the resources to drive improvements in micro-processes, much less the type of macro-processes that are usually listed as performance objectives. "Improve department productivity by 5%" is a commonly seen objective for managers. What about the impact of hundreds of continually changing inputs and supplier parameters? What about the hundreds of customer requirements that are continually changing? What about the impact of a manufacturing problem caused by purchasing, maintenance, personnel, engineering, administration, and so on?

As quoted in the beginning of Chapter Eighteen, "No man is an island . . ." in terms of the work turned out. Therefore, why do we assume that specific, individual contributions can be proctologically exhumed from the past year's achievement and rewarded? They can't. Processes are complex, and it's impossible (and pointless, anyway) to attempt to segregate the contributions of one person from the effects of the group.

6. Identify and Correct Performance Problems

This is the biggest joke of all. We've already talked about how total losers continue to get great performance ratings. One large corporation recently conducted a detailed survey of its almost 100 thousand employees. Seventy percent of the hourly employees who answered the survey were "somewhat dissatisfied" or "extremely dissatisfied" with the company's handling of poor performers. That's the company's handling of Egg Sucking Pigs, the group that routinely is treated the most brutally. If they think things are lax, imagine how bad it really is up in the offices, where tradition protects nonperformers.

For many of the reasons cited in the preceding section, few supervisors are willing to handle performance problems. Performance management systems don't correct performance problems; they hide old ones and make them worse, and they create new ones.

7. Provide a Mechanism for Identifying Employee Development Needs

How can a performance appraisal identify critical employee development needs if nobody understands the exact nature of the micro-processes on which the employee works? The skills and knowledge necesssary to do the tasks, monitor processes, and interact with customers and suppliers should be the driving force behind employee development efforts. At the very least, every employee needs the training experiences outlined in Chapter Sixteen (Coda 11), in addition to critical task skills (such as how to run and maintain machinery). What they get instead is a supervisor's subjective suggestion that they improve their "communications skills" by going to Toastmasters during lunch once a week. Great, that'll really help with the work processes.

In the main, employee development action items are put in performance appraisals simply because there's a spot for them and nobody leaves a spot blank if personnel is going to review the form. So, something gets put in. It's irrelevant and it'll be "checked off" next year on the basis of whether the employee attends or not, and not according to how well the skill is learned and used. And typically, employees can't go to the training, anyway, because of money problems ("There's no training budget") or scheduling difficulties ("We can't afford to have you gone for 2 days"), so they're excused from the requirement and it's "slipped" until next year.

WHY DO WE BOTHER?

Beats me. Just stupidity, tradition, and ignorance, I suppose. As you can see, there's no dimension on which the traditional performance management system makes the grade. There's no dimension on which the system is not doing damage. Traditional American business continues to punish itself and abuse its employees with these systems because they have established performance management systems and personnel as a part of the structure, like loading docks, lights, and desks. It's there, and it's perpetuated because it was there yesterday.

SO WHAT DO WE DO INSTEAD?

Why do anything? If you saw someone sitting in an office stabbing themselves in the back of the hand with a pencil, driving it right through to the desk with every stroke, would you run up and say, "Hey, let's quickly think of something else you can do to hurt yourself so that you can do it instead of stabbing your hand to pieces"? I hope not. Most of us would attempt to completely stop them from hurting themselves. That's what should be done with all of our current, traditional performance management systems. Just stop using them.

AMERICAN SAMURAI INSIGHT

Rather than evolving incrementally less damaging systems of performance appraisal and ratings, the traditional approach should be completely abandoned immediately.

Attempting to make small adjustments to "fix" the current system is analogous to trying to save your carpet from the ravages of a non-housebroken cow through adjustments to its diet. Believe me, no matter what you feed it, you're in trouble. The only answer is to get it out of the house. If we got performance management systems "out of the business house" tomorrow, we would save tens of billions in pure lost profit simply from the elimination of the wasted labor that goes into the process. The ancillary savings from reduced turnover, increased morale, and so on would be just as large.

ARE THERE ALTERNATIVES?

Lots of companies are trying to move to incrementally less damaging systems. They're feeding the cow lawn clippings or grain instead of straw. Good luck with the Shop-Vac. DuPont is trying something new at its fibers department in Wilmington, Delaware.* In exchange for accepting salaries and raises lower than traditionally expected, employees have the potential of earning bonuses as high as 18%, which is 12% higher than the maximum merit increases of 6% under the old plan. Exactly hitting objectives results in a 6% bonus. The article states that performance is assessed by evaluating quantifiable results.

Recognize this system? Sure, it's merit pay dressed up as pay-for-performance, with all of the same old problems. How can one person's performance be "quantifiably" measured apart from the process? It can't. In addition, all of the old target setting, evaluation, and subjectivism problems we've discussed are still there. Break out the Shop-Vac, the cow's still in the living room.

There are alternatives, but they're not merely modifications of traditional performance appraisal systems, they're completely different. There are not

---

The Wall Street Journal, Manager's Journal feature, March 27, 1990.

many of them, because few organizations have the guts to do something different and/or the opportunity to learn a different way. One such company is Anderson corporation, America's largest manufacturer of windows. Although the company is extremely secretive about its operations, some articles* describe aspects of their innovative approaches to performance management, particularly compensation.

The company has been phenomenally successful since it was established in 1914. They were the first to make many window innovations, such as sliding glass doors, awning windows, and vinyl-framed windows. More than 30% of the company's stock is held by employees, and the rest belongs to descendants of the founding family. It operates at profit margins estimated at 30% to 35%.

One key to the company's innovations and productivity is the incentive system. Work groups are given performance standards, and each employee in the group can earn up to 140% of the prior year's pay if the group reaches its goals. In 1986, the average employee at Anderson received a check for 72.5% of his or her earnings of the previous year. In 1987, the average factory worker at Anderson earned more than $60,000.

There are several key points here. First, the bonuses are based on group performance, not individual performance. This motivates positive peer pressure to perform and eliminates the subjectivity of trying to determine individual achievements. There is minimum suboptimization within such a group. There is also little tendency to suboptimize between departments, since the total amount of money available for bonuses is based on overall company profits. If the entire macro-process of the business doesn't do well, nobody does well (a little different from Roger Smith getting his pension doubled to 1.2 million after having led General Motors to an almost 17% decline in market share during his tenure).

Second, the bonuses are directly tied to productivity that is objective. Either the group gets its work done or not. There is little opportunity for "soft" subjective achievements that don't contribute to bottomline productivity, especially since work groups are involved in setting performance standards.

Third, the bonuses are large enough to have an impact. If all you're going to give is 2% to 6%, you're wasting your money if you think that the awards will motivate day-to-day consciousness of key productivity issues. When an employee can earn a really big hit, he or she is cognizant of the profit impact of every wasted paper clip, every bit of trash on the floor that must be swept up, and so forth.

Of course, Anderson Corporation is privately held. It allocates less than 10% of profits to the family; the remainder goes to employees' stock and the bonuses. Not many companies have that type of leeway or the wisdom to realize what it can do for productivity and profits. American firms have

---

*Business Month, September 1988.

become the slaves of stockholders, who increasingly want short-term paper profits that can be quickly gathered. This influence is destroying American competitiveness.

However, many aspects of an ideal performance management system can be implemented tomorrow, if the will to change is there.

THE BASICS OF AN IDEAL SYSTEM

The basics of an ideal system include the following:

1. *Group performance objectives.* Performance objectives must be derived from a customer-driven master plan and given to work groups as group performance objectives. Individual performance objectives are worthless.
2. *Individual rewards must be based on group performance.* All employees in a group must get bonuses or merit pay based upon the group's performance. Whereas there may be some differences in awards based on skill levels and years of service, there must be no large "steps" that set up a caste system, in which some employees in the group get only a little and others get a windfall. The Anderson approach of setting a constant percentage payout and then basing it on the previous year's earnings is acceptable. It gives larger absolute dollar increases to more highly paid employees but permits everyone to get the same percentage. In traditionally run organizations, the higher-ups get larger percentages of bigger salaries, which is unethical, if not morally heinous.
3. *Initial pay determined by market conditions, skill levels.* Many people cringe at any system that makes "all workers the same." They're afraid that if the caste system goes, they'll be a Sub-Human. Well, the caste system must go. But all people aren't equal. It's easier to hire somebody to cut the grass than to hire a specialized engineer. People aren't going to earn the same, that's a fact of life. Initial pay rates should be based on demand, relative levels of experience, skill levels, and so forth.

Ideally, I'd like to see each company pay what it takes to hire the appropriate people and then base *all* additional compensation on profits. Each employee would get the same identical bonus (perhaps prorated for those who had not been there for the entire year of the bonus period), which would be calculated by taking the total money available and dividing it by the number of employees. This would send executives screaming, but they already get six-figure salaries, so I'm not concerned. There is no law that says that every high-level executive must have two to three homes, a large boat, and five cars. They seem to think they are entitled, but they're not.

Now that you've had a chance to think about the failures of our current compensation systems, you can see how they are totally and completely contrary to any principle of improved productivity. Now that you're informed, go out and spread the word. But be careful. The powers that be love the present system because they use it to jack up their pay. Whisper your discontent. There's a whole new generation of managers being bred now, who will soon be sick of seeing their relatives and friends working as chief fry cooks. They may be ready to make a change, if and when they get some power, and if there is anything left of our economy for them to run. All we American Samurai can do is our best. See you in the trenches (the next performance review).

20

The Letter, as Well as the Spirit, of the Code

Coda 15. **Organizations and their policies and procedures must be redesigned to optimize cross-functionality, "flatter" reporting structures, streamlined communications, and accelerated decision making.**

The "structural" features of traditionally run organizations impede productivity and the returns that can be expected from the practice of any one, or all, of the Coda. These structural features are the policies and procedures, reporting methods, formal communication channels or practices with the employees, and the general mode of decision making that is championed by the company. These structural features are the skeleton of an organization, unseen but effecting much of its form and function. In traditionally run organizations, these mechanisms and structures work powerfully to maintain the old way of business. It's difficult to fashion a wolf on the skeleton of a pig.

The old structure will not evolve slowly as an organization changes. Senior executives often tell me, "I want to let the traditions around here evolve as we change. I don't want to create discomfort by just throwing out the old ways." Wrong. If you had a cancer, would you remove it slowly, piece by piece, in operations weeks apart, so as not to "shock" your body? Of course not. You'd have the whole thing taken out as soon as possible, regardless of the effects. It's the same with the structural features of traditionally run organizations: they are evil tumors, causing loss and increased resistance to change. They must be purged from the organizational body as soon as the change effort begins.

Each of the structural features is interrelated, of course, but we'll discuss each area and focus on the most important changes that must be made to fully implement The Code of the American Samurai.

POLICIES AND PROCEDURES

The system of American jurisprudence is built upon traditions, opinions, and precedents. Comparatively few of our laws have been developed on the basis of rational analyses of scientific, societal, psychological, and/or medical data. Our laws are what they are because past practices have become codified. Many of those "legal traditions" originated in repressive and restrictive periods, during which there was extensive racial and religious bigotry, as well as scientific ignorance. Slowly, over much time, the laws evolve, but the pace of change is glacially slow and lags far behind current social practices and trends. This is due to the massive inertia of the thousands of interrelated, existing laws; they form a huge, intertwined mass that cannot be moved quickly. As a result, appreciable changes in policy and procedure are sometimes difficult to observe over a short period of time. This inertia works to prevent social change, since it reinforces old ways that often no longer apply to modern problems.

The situation in regard to the way that traditionally run organizations are organized and operated is almost identical. The behaviors and accepted practices of businesses that are detailed in company policy and procedure manuals exist not because they are most effective in the here and now, but because they reflect accepted practices from some distant time in the past. As long as past practices are accepted and rewarded simply because "they are there," changes to a new way of working will come much more slowly.

Every organization of any size possesses a body of this operating "law" known variously as *Policies and Procedures*, *Standard Practices*, *Organization Directives*, and so on. These rules are generally kept in three-ring binders so that the constant stream of updates can be easily incorporated. In some large, older corporations, these books are thousands of pages long. At the Ford Motor Company, a single set of the policies and procedures takes up almost 5 feet of bookshelf. I sometimes wonder if a vast, world conspiracy of paper and three-ring binder companies is not somehow promoting the development of traditionally designed policy and procedure systems in order to stimulate market demand for their products.

Like our system of laws, policies and procedures (P and P) aren't just there, they're used to dictate what is acceptable and what is prohibited. If nobody every paid any attention to them, the pace of change in American business would be able to move along at a rate that would more closely reflect changes in thinking about the new conditions of world business. But P and P aren't just sitting there idly, they operate aggressively to stifle the very changes that would benefit their organizations.

AMERICAN SAMURAI INSIGHT

An organization's policies and procedures absolutely control how organizations operate, including the hard wiring of inefficiencies and lost profit.

The P and P state how the work must be done, right or wrong. If the

P and P state that the personnel V.P. must approve all requests for special employee recognition awards, that's the way it's going to be, even though it makes no sense (the functional vice-presidents should be free to develop a mutually agreed upon system to recognize excellence). If the P and P state that seven-level review and approval cycle will be used to evaluate all employee suggestions, that's the way it's going to be, even if it ruins the entire system. In large companies, for every conceivable action, there's a detailed P and P regulation, sometimes 100 pages long, outlining what can and can't be done, who can and can't do it, and what individuals (by title) must review, pre-approve, consent, post-approve, and comment on the process.

Nothing Is Allowed to Change, and Not Much Is Allowed to Happen

The end results of having this multilayered bureaucracy of approvals and morass of regulations for every conceivable decision is that nothing ever changes. How could it? Attempting to institute radical changes (such as managing by the Coda) within a traditional system of P and P is like asking a fox to help you work on a chicken protection system; you'll end up with a lot more foxes and damn few chickens.

Of course, the P and P notebooks don't fight for their own existence. The P and P are defended to the last ball-point pen refill and word processor by the hordes of paper pushers that have fashioned entire careers, including professional societies and certifications, around P and P. And since traditional management has been brainwashed into thinking that "everybody of substance has them," management in general rushes in to support and protect P and P even as they personally hate having to fill out all the paper work. Most management doesn't like P and P and knows they get in the way but has had them for so long they don't think about it. They just do them.

What Are They Supposed to Do?

Just what is it that an organization's P and P are supposed to do? The P and P should foster and maximize the long-term success of the business. As we've seen, this requires that there be a focus on processes with a goal of continual improvement in customer satisfaction. The P and P should promote management by facts (SPC), the development and communication of a customer-driven master plan, and an emphasis on valuing and developing employees. The P and P should foster a corporate culture in which quality always comes first and in which group performance, teamwork, and open communication are aggressively promoted. That's all that a P and P manual should contain. It doesn't take 5 feet of bookshelf to get those points across.

Only a handful of companies have P and P that deal with these basic principles. Instead, most organizations have P and P that consist of textbook procedures that foster the traditional organization's Guiding Principles ("Manage by fear," "Don't take chances," etc.).

P and P Evolved to Stop Mistakes

The primary driving mechanism behind P and P is a distrust of lower-level caste members. Since each higher caste considers each lower caste to be somewhat stupid, lazy, and dishonest, it's "obvious" to higher-level castes that P and P are essential to keep the rank and file under control. If you doubt this and work in a medium to large company, take a look at the P and P manuals. You'll find that the emphasis is on control and restriction and that there is far more space devoted to the disciplinary procedures for Egg Sucking Pigs and Sub-Humans than for all other groups combined.

The "blaming" orientation of traditional businesses has been discussed in earlier chapters. In unenlightened organizations, every screw up and mistake is seen as the direct consequence of employee negligence. The response is almost always to "tighten up" the appropriate P and P. The result is that a thousand errors are translated into a thousand new and/or augmented P and P regulations. More signature loops are added, and more approvals are necessary. The book grows ever longer (and the human resources, financial, and legal departments grow, all pure overhead, to provide more review by people who don't understand the processes).

Nobody Knows Them Anyway

Many defenders of traditional P and P contend that the initiative-destroying and mind-numbing detail and control of P and P are essential in order to maintain business operations. They argue that if such details weren't present, nobody would do anything right. Well, I've got news for those folks. Few people have ever bothered to even look at their organization's P and P. In fact, most people do their jobs the way they were shown how to do them, by the last person who had the job. When you bother to look, you find that a large proportion of decisions and actions in most companies are at odds with their P and P.

People do what is necessary to get their jobs done, no more, no less. They don't care what the P and P say; if they want to know how to handle a problem or do something they haven't had to do before, they ask their boss, the next person, or a friend. If they get in trouble for a P and P violation, they're more careful on that P and P area out of fear, but they won't spend their lunch times memorizing other P and P statements (they'll spend it griping about how they get shafted for trying to handle a problem with a little initiative).

After all, who is going to read 5 feet of books? Nobody with anything better to do. The only folks who know this material are the P and P guardians, who have a vested interest (their jobs and power) in maintaining the P and P manual as a focal point of management attention. They are also people who know little about the actual product-related processes of the organization. Everybody else is busting their ass to get the product or service out the door in spite of the P and P; they don't have time to waste to pore through thousands of pages to find answers they know they won't like (more signatures and delays).

One unfortunate result of having these specialists poring over the P and P is that they are forever on the lookout for violations. They have the time, the knowledge, and the incentive to look for trouble. When they find a violation, the violator is abused, time is wasted, and the organization loses even more. Then, a new or enhanced P and P statement is drafted and approved (at an additional huge cost) to prevent that particular violation from happening again. They then return to poring over the books and looking for the next violation so that more time and money can be wasted.

Detailed Policies and Procedures Are Dangerous

Many personnel and P and P types think that the more detailed P and P are, the better, they are. This is the type of myopic thinking you'd expect from nonrevenue producing areas. Even in a government contracting environment (with the most detailed P and P of all time), detailed P and P hurt more than they help. When an organization is doing business with the federal government, they are audited to see whether they comply with the government's P and P as well as their own. Every year, hundreds of government contractors get in more trouble for violating their own P and P (not doing what they said they were going to do) than for not doing what the government said they should do. Why? Stupidity, really. These companies spend millions writing up detailed P and P over the years and then get dinged because their own people can't or won't follow the procedures.

Since nobody reads them, what do they expect? The real irony is that if they had general, looser P and P in many areas, they wouldn't get caught for as many violations. If you don't stipulate a certain behavior, you don't have to do it. The previously cited suggestions program procedures are an example. If a government contractor were found to violate its own P and P by not getting all the required signatures on a suggestion, they'd get a discrepancy. Enough of them and they get in trouble. If the P and P simply said that supervisors would handle suggestions within 48 hours without additional signatures, there wouldn't be as much potential to miss a step and get in trouble. Even though this is self-evident, specialists in many functional areas actually make every P and P as onerous and burdensome as possible for other areas (suboptimization working again).

The incredible detail inherent in most P and P systems has another, more subtle, but even more damaging, drawback. The systems are so intimidating that nobody wants to get involved with trying to do anything, except for the barracks room barristers who use the system to their own advantage.

Since almost anything you do will be in violation unless you spend days reading detailed procedures, a great many people simply give up and just plod along, letting things happen, not trying to fight or improve the system. They sense they cannot win, so they don't try to fight. They try to stay out of trouble as best they can; in a legalistic, P and P ridden system, the best way to do that is to do nothing. The entire organization loses. It's rampant throughout American business.

The Expense of Maintaining the System Is Horrendous

The expense involved in maintaining a typical P and P system is unbelievable. Every time there's a change in the P and P, it must be reviewed by up to dozens of managers, their comments tabulated, and then a new version drafted for review again. Finally, months later, thousands of copies of each change are sent to all corners of the organization. Everyone is supposed to put the new copies in their copy of the P and P. In many organizations, every manager is sent a copy of every new P and P version. Curiously, in some organizations, hardly anyone ever sees the original P and P, much less the revision. How anyone is supposed to be able to follow the P and P is puzzling.

Whereas nobody will ever say it publicly, this must imply that every manager is expected to keep his or her own personal copy of 5 feet of P and P manual. This amounts to hundreds of thousands of dollars of pure profit lost in a large company every year, just for paper and binder costs. Of course, very few employees keep copies of anything (except expense report rules, perhaps), so they simply throw them away. What a waste. All that money and time for nothing but trouble.

And these are the bargain aspects of the losses. The real cost is in the amount of unnecessary work that each modification of the P and P manual adds. Each P and P modification means more labor hours, sometimes hundreds more, to get the same job done. More paper work, more running around for signatures, more uninformed folks who must have the situation explained to them in detail before they'll sign, or tampering meddlers who will insist that it not be done, be done differently, or not done at all (when this happens, it is always about one signature from the end of the process). The drag on an organization's effectiveness and competitiveness is immense, and it's happening in almost every company.

What Is the Alternative?

The alternative is much like the performance management system solution: don't do it. Stop. Every few months, you read of one enlightened chief executive or another simply tossing his or her organization's P and P manual in the trash and substituting a simple document of general guidelines for an enlightened philosophy of management. All that's needed in most cases is a set of guiding principles based upon the Coda. Sounds too simple to be true, doesn't it? That's because you've been in the old system too long.

For example, when Chief Executive Jerre Stead of Square D, an electric equipment manufacturer with about 19 thousand employees, first came on board as president in 1987, he was presented with four volumes of the company's P and P. He has since replaced the more than 750 rules with 11 general policy statements. That's the type of bold action it's going to take on the part of most organizations in order to cut through the profit wasting undergrowth they've generated. Are there enough visionaries like Mr. Stead out there to save us? I hope so.

It's An Executive Responsibility to Destroy the Old Way

Don't expect folks in the P and P area to seize the initiative and pare down the P and P. That's like asking the foxes to escort the chickens safely out of town. I don't know how many times I've seen a senior executive give the lead to personnel to aggressively implement a new philosophy of work or a leaner P and P manual. Forget it. They can't think "new" because they're made of the old. The lead must come from the top, boldly and with vigor. If not, forget it.

MANAGEMENT LEVELS AND LAYERS

A major profit killer is an axiomatic by-product of detailed P and P: multilayered management. Some corporations have as many as 17 distinctly different levels of management between the bare concrete of the factory floor and the extra-plush carpeting of the executive suite (not counting "side branches" of staff specialists and brown nosers). Nobody ever makes a conscious decision to build this type of bloated structure, but it happens almost all the time. It's driven as a natural artifact of rampant suboptimization and the micro-management fostered by a focus on mistakes and results.

Remember the Guiding Principles that are destroying American business, the ones we reviewed in Chapter Four? Just look at how many of those focus on results, mistakes, and keeping people in line:

> React quickly to every situation
> Go for the fast pay-offs
> Employees are a pain in the ass
> Customers are a pain in the ass
> Set objectives and manage to them
> Manage by fear
> Mistakes by others are a chance to look good
> The department or work area comes first
> Decisions are made at the top
> Maintain the caste system at all times

How could you do any of these things with 100 people reporting to each supervisor? You couldn't. People would begin to think for themselves and make decisions. Pretty soon the boss wouldn't know every detail (and wouldn't have time to worry about it).

The short spans of control in American business (few people reporting to each boss) have evolved to enable these Guiding Principles to be maintained. And, once these Guiding Principles, the resulting P and P, and short spans of control are in place, they act as barriers to any changes.

Just think about it for a minute. The whole system is upside down, even if you believe that the traditional system is correct, (with lower-level castes needing more supervision). When I've worked for large corporations, usually only four to six others and I reported to the same boss. You'd assume that since we were all highly trained and autonomous professionals, we could be more loosely supervised. But no, we always got micro-managed; the boss had to do something. When you get up to the Chairman of the Board of a large corporation, the CEO often only supervises his or her secretary and one or two others. Either that president or secretary must be a real problem to require that much supervision!

At the same time, the largest spans of control (the most people reporting to one boss) occur at the lowest level of the organization. The poor first-line supervisor has to supervise from ten to 50 workers. These workers are often the youngest, doing the hardest work, and often need more individual attention and assistance. Yet, their supervisor is hard pressed just to handle routine administration and personnel matters. Even if the environment is an abusive one, a one to 30 supervisor to employee ratio doesn't even permit high quality and frequent abuse.

Research studies have demonstrated that almost half of some organizations' management levels do nothing but massage data, reformat reports, ask for more data, go to meetings, and hand out assignments so that they can get more data and make changes in existing reports. They justify their existence based on how much data they can accumulate and/or how many new data collection schemes they can hatch.

When you see the direct evidence of this waste, it's mind-boggling. Oryx, currently the world's largest independent oil and gas producer, estimates that it will save 70 million dollars in operating costs in 1990 (they had 139 million dollars in earnings in 1989) by eliminating unnecessary procedures and superfluous reports and approvals. How did they do it? Surprise of surprise, they asked the employees and then actually listened. Teams of employees were asked to identify work that didn't need to be done. They ended up eliminating 25% of all internal reports, reduced the number of signature approvals from 20 to four for capital expenditures, and reduced the time it took to prepare the annual budget from 7 months to 6 weeks.

"Flatter" Is Almost Always Better

All other things being equal, "flatter" organizations, those with larger spans of control (more employees reporting to each supervisor), are more efficient. Even if a flatter organization is doing everything wrong, at the very least problems will be discovered more quickly than a traditional organization. Upper levels or management are forced to communicate directly with larger numbers of personnel, and there is a lower probability of distortion, suboptimization, and errors when there are fewer reporting levels. Most world-class Japanese manufacturers have three to five management layers in their plants. In American plants, there can be seven to eight or more.

How do you get to a flatter organization? Well, you don't get there by indiscriminately chopping out management layers and downsizing indiscriminately. That's like losing weight by cutting off a leg; you get some fat, but a lot of essentials are lost as well. More than one company has found out the hard way that reducing management by cutting head count isn't an easy answer to productivity (as The Code of the American Samurai clearly demonstrates, there are no easy answers to anything; there are easy concepts, but implementation is always a killer). It's a lesson that everyone had better pay attention to, because it's been estimated that American companies are still overstaffed by 20% to 30% even after the feverish self-mutilation of the 1980s. Mistakes in downsizing can have severe and long-term effects.

It's gotten so bad that now executives refer to attempts to adjust head count as "rightsizing" instead of downsizing. When done properly (instead of simply hacking away at head count while calling it something new), rightsizing must be based upon intensive process analysis. For example, H. J. Heinz discovered that sometimes it's better to add workers rather than cut them. They added 400 workers, four more production lines, and reduced the amount of work required of each fish cleaner (the people who take the meat off the bones) at StarKist tuna canneries in American Samoa and Puerto Rico. The result was less wasted tuna and a net 10 million dollars per year increase in profits after all additional costs. Simply chopping heads to cut costs would have been disastrous. The canneries chose more people and slower, more careful work standards rather than fewer people and speed. Heinz could have made a disastrous mistake instead of the right move if they had blindly cut personnel instead of studying their processes.

The first requirement for efficiently reducing management layers, and personnel in general, is to adopt the process focus discussed under Coda 1 in Chapter Six. Only by focusing on processes and internal and external customer satisfaction can an organization discover what needs to be done and who can best do it. Once that's been determined, you're halfway there.

The second requirement is to let employees, the Sub-Humans and Egg Sucking Pigs especially, expand their scope of responsibility and do more. Instead of just feeding a machine, they should be taught to make minor adjustments and repairs, keep SPC charts and production records, and so on. Instead of just entering purchasing data into a computer, they could also check for errors and have first-level approval authority. Of course, these types of modifications would require a complete change in management philosophy and a large investment in training and employee development. Once again, you see that all of the Coda work as one. Once employees are doing all that they can do, *then* it's easy to identify what layers you don't need.

ENHANCING COMMUNICATIONS

Many executives believe that better communication means that employees should listen more carefully to orders. Wrong. A business is a macro-process. The more the employees know, the better the job they'll be able to do. They must know about their processes, the general processes of the company, and how things are going. In the overwhelming majority of organizations, most employees know next to nothing about how things are going. Executives think that employees know, but they don't.

The danger here is that if formal communications channels don't do the job, informal ones will. Informal channels are dominated by fear, bad news, and wild extrapolations, which present things in the worst possible light. When people have little news, they imagine the worst. At work, if employees have no real data, they make it up, and it's never good.

If you look at the channels that most companies use to provide information to employees, you'll see that they are dry pipelines. The typical, so-called communications channels in most companies are the company newspaper, notices on bulletin boards, and an occasional speech by an executive. As sources of meaningful information, these are all laughable.

The company newspaper. The company newspaper in most organizations is nothing but fluff and nonsense; "guess who the baby is" contests, blood drives, charity work, the cafeteria menu, retirements, lies about terminations (if they leave under good pretenses, there's a write-up; if they got fired or quit in disgust, you hear nothing), company sports league news, and any good news about the company. All nonsense. It's hard for me to tell the difference between most company papers and the newsletters that retirement homes publish.

There's never anything with real meat on it in a company newspaper. Where's the data on scrap, rework, process improvements, concurrent engineering improvements, better manufacturing processes, and so on? It's never there; "They wouldn't understand" or "They wouldn't care" are the reasons given for not sharing any data. Yet, when things get bad and management wants employees to suck it up, the company paper prints the entreaties to work harder. Why should the employees work harder? After reading the company paper for the last few years, who would know there's a problem?

A real company paper would present real data and real business—costs, performance, improvements, actual data about problems (not blaming but discussions), information on improvements, and so on. The only employee who can take an informed interest in what's going on is an employee who knows what's going on.

Executive speeches. Executives think that employees listen to them, but we know that's nonsense. Most speeches are simply verbal editions of the paper: bombastic exhortations and good news. Nobody cares. Nobody listens. Executives must lead their organization, the first step of which is to tell the truth and do it often and for all employee groups. It's no good to simply talk to the management club once every quarter. The largest segment of employees never go (and, in fact, may not be eligible to join—a great way to foster open communications). Executives must get out and talk to employees at least weekly, in small groups. If an executive isn't spending 25% of his or her time meeting with employees, talking to them, and listening, he or she isn't doing the job right.

Other channels. In most organizations, there are no other formal channels of communications. Nobody tells employees anything. At the very least, every organization that wants performance from its employees must provide the following minimum additional sources of data:

1. Monthly departmental briefings about key events and news from the department manager.
2. Weekly section briefings by each supervisor to his or her employees about problems, improvements, and plans for the next week.
3. Quarterly briefings from a higher-level executive about things in general.
4. Occasional question and answer sessions with senior management that are open to all employees.
5. Monthly breakfasts and lunches to which key executives invite randomly selected groups of employees and then simply visit with them for an hour or two, discussing the business.

These actions, coupled with a decent newspaper, and plenty of communication between each employee and supervisor, will energize the organization and provide both employees and management with a clear idea of what's going on.

YOU CAN START SMALL

If you're a big shot, you can start chopping away at the P and P that are holding your organization back. If you aren't a high roller, all you can do is start communicating with your employees and letting them know what's going on. They may even tell you a few things you need to hear (after a month or so of waiting to see if you can be "trusted"). That's not much, but it's a start. Get started tomorrow.

21

Low Tech is the Right Tech (For Profits)

Coda 16. **Low cost, low technology process improvements must be pursued before technological solutions are implemented.**

There's a perception in much of American business that world-class organizations are world-class because they're on the cutting edge of technology and science; an assumption that the success of these companies is based upon technology. This perception is completely incorrect. It's true that many world-class organizations often possess advanced technology (although many do not; L. L. Bean's superior service is not based solely upon electronic marvels).

AMERICAN SAMURAI INSIGHT

The possession of world-class technology is generally not the cause of organizational success but is most often a result of prior success in more fundamental areas.

Whereas there are organizations that are successful because they alone possess a bold, new technology, they are increasingly the exception. These days, few companies can maintain an exclusive technology long enough to succeed simply because they "have" it.

AMERICAN SAMURAI INSIGHT

World-class organizations are successful with technology because they apply it to efficient processes and because they are sufficiently cost-effective and quality conscious to be able to afford appropriate technology.

Think of the latest technology as an expensive, exciting vacation. People generally get to go on vacations because they regularly do boring and mundane things such as arriving at work on time and going to work when they

247

don't feel like it. Having the latest technology is a lot like the experience of the vacation; you've got to earn it so that you can pay for it. A large part of boring and mundane work that an organization must do is to be cost-effective and productive in all areas, regardless of technology.

This means doing the best you can with what you've got. An organization must squeeze the most it can from existing resources and already paid-for low technology before more money is spent on expensive and often risky advanced technology. And, if an organization's product is technology itself, the company must do the technology development faster, cheaper, and with a higher quality process than the competition if it wants to remain the leader in its field.

In order to achieve this feat consistently over time (anybody can get lucky every once in a while), a Kaizen philosophy, not to mention the implementation of the entire Code, is essential. Unfortunately, the preferred tactic in American business has been, and still is, to go for the quick hit and spend money rather than effort. This technique used to work when the competition couldn't afford to match our spending for new technology. Now that all large competitors are on a more or less equal footing in terms of their ability to spend for technology (except for the Japanese, who are ahead), this technique won't work.

Something more is required. And this "something" is simply more than fixing individual processes. What we need is a strategic approach to management that not only lives by The Code, but one that pursues the optimization of existing processes and techniques from a strategic viewpoint. That's what this Coda will present. We're going to discuss three interrelated approaches that are all "low tech" approaches to optimization of performance. They may be low tech, but you'll see that they can drive performance and profit improvements that are orders of magnitude better than we can get from using high technology in conjunction with the traditional business approach.

These "new" low technology concepts are Just-In-Time (JIT), Single Minute Exchange of Die (SMED), and Design of Experiments (DOE). JIT is an overall approach to organizing processes and work that is 180 degrees different from the traditional approach. A JIT approach assumes the operation of many of the Coda, particularly a micro-process orientation to analyzing work. You might say that JIT is the guiding philosophical ideology of "low tech."

SMED is a specific approach to reducing the cycle time required to change tooling and machining. SMED is easy to implement. It is an absolutely essential component of any true JIT system. At the same time, just the application of SMED alone can save immense amounts of time and money in even the most traditional manufacturing environment. The only reason that traditional management isn't using SMED is because they are completely unaware of the concept (the head in the sand approach to problems). Whereas in traditional working environments millions are spent on all sorts of machines and technology to increase output, the application of SMED (under a JIT system) can often triple machine availability without major capital expenditures.

The final technique, Design of Experiments (DOE), is a specific analysis technique that focuses on the optimization of a specific process. Actions taken on the basis of a DOE analysis are the antithesis of tampering. DOE techniques can be applied at any time, in any environment, although the patience to use them and the realization of their value is often not found in traditional environments.

In each of these concepts, JIT, SMED, and DOE, you find the common thread of making the most of existing processes through careful process analysis and understanding. When you put them all together, you get world-class low tech that, hands down, always outperforms a traditional system using state-of-the-art high tech. Read on, my fellow American Samurai, and learn!

JUST-IN-TIME

Almost everyone has heard about "Just-In-Time" (JIT) systems or JIT manufacturing. To most people who have heard the term but who have not studied the approach in detail, JIT seems to imply that materials are received from a vendor just before they must be used. That is, they arrive "just in time" to be used. This is in contrast with the traditional approach of "just in case" where materials are stockpiled in various inventories or produced in excess "just in case" something happens. Viewing the supplier delivery aspect of JIT as "being" JIT is a gross oversimplification of the concept and misses 90% of the power and productivity gains that can be accrued from true JIT operations.

The terms "Just-in-Time" was first coined by Kiichiro Toyoda, Toyota Motor Company's first president (the company was named Toyota because the Japanese felt that Toyoda sounded "too Japanese"). Taiichi Ohno of Toyota played a primary role in developing and expanding JIT and much of the even more comprehensive Toyota Production System under which JIT operates at Toyota. All of JIT is based on a fundamental asssumption that is not well understood by most American businesses:

AMERICAN SAMURAI INSIGHT

Products should be "pulled," not "pushed," through production systems.

The same can be said of services, but, for the sake of simplicity, we'll keep the present discussion limited to the manufacture of hard goods. That is, a manufacturing system should produce goods in response to customer demand—the "pull"—rather than producing goods and then trying to sell them,—the "push."

If this "pull" concept is extended to all of the internal cusstomers of each micro-process, the result is a system in which successive operations are not provided with input until they ask for it. Parts don't pass down an assembly line or out of a process until they are "requested" or asked for by the next customer.

The flow of goods in a JIT system is regulated by kanban (pronounced similar to the candy "bon bon" with the first syllable pronounced "khan"), which means a "tag." A kanban is a means of communication, most typically a piece of paper inserted into a see-through plastic envelope. Although there is much more to JIT than kanban, the term has almost become synonymous with JIT among those who do not fully understand the concept of JIT. There are many types of kanban: production kanban to authorize a supplier (internal or external) to process or make a certain part, transport kanban to authorize a supplier to "ship" parts to a customer, and withdrawal kanban to authorize a supplier to release parts to the customer, prior to transport.

Kanban serve many purposes besides merely "pulling" goods through the system. In effect, kanban provide both the mechanism of JIT operations as well as the means of locating areas of potential improvement.

The principal rules of JIT demonstrate the integral function of kanban:

1. Defective materials must never be sent to the next process (never knowingly allow a defect to leave the work area in which it is produced).
2. The next process never gets goods unless it asks for them, that is, until a kanban from the subsequent process has arrived. This is the "pull."
3. The supplying process only produces what has been withdrawn, never more. Inventory is *never* allowed to build up at a process.
4. Production must be equalized so that all processes, working at maximum, never generate excess inventory and can always provide what a subsequent process's kanban requests (this is termed "equalization" or "leveling" of output.
5. The careful analysis of problems in meeting kanban allows for the fine tuning. It's easy to see where problems lie when a kanban can't be filled, or when excess inventory is produced before it is requested by a kanban.

Inventory and JIT

It is important to understand the immense philosophical difference between a pull system like JIT and the traditional push manufacturing system. The gap is immense, both in size and character. In a traditional system, the glue that holds everything together is inventory. Just look at the typical manufacturing operation and all the types of inventory that it maintains. Huge stock rooms hold weeks, and sometimes months, worth of raw materials and/or incoming parts, smaller stock areas hold inventories both before and after various processes, materials are often stacked up at work operations, and the largest storage areas of all hold finished products waiting to be shipped (or perhaps to be sold).

As we've already discussed in Coda 13 (Chapter 18), large inventories increase costs for a number of reasons. Yet, large inventories are evil for another, even more fundamental, reason: inventory is used to cover up all sorts of problems as well as poorly understood and/or marginally operating processes. Inventory is used to keep machines busy. American business worships what it considers to be full utilization of machines. Thus, a prime consideration in planning manufacturing work loads is to keep the physical plant running at full capacity. The problem is that this process generates an exceptional amount of in-process inventory in advance of need.

For example, if process A can produce 1000 units in 8 hours, but process B, the customer or pulling process, can only handle 750 units, there is an almost automatic compulsion in traditional environments to run process A at full speed for a regular shift and then operate process B on overtime to "catch up." The entire system is driven by the push at the front end, which is often created by planning that mandates that all machines be kept busy.

A true JIT system does not use inventory to smooth out discontinuities in output between processes. Instead, processes are studied in detail and work is "leveled" so that workers are kept optimally busy while producing only as much output as the next process asks for with kanban. Machines are allowed to stand idle if the alternative is producing "unpulled" output. Inventory is never generated "just in case," output from an operation is never squirreled away for "a rainy day," and machines are not operated simply because of a fear of "lower utilization."

Work and Motion in JIT

An important aspect of JIT is an emphasis on the distinction between work and motion. Motion is wasted energy, labor that is expended to do things that do not add value to a product. Motion is moving inventory, removing wrappers from parts sent by a supplier (Why are they wrapped? You pay double; for putting it on and taking it off!), setting up tooling, and fixing defects. Work is labor that adds value to a product such as drilling a hole or machining a part. A JIT system can be optimized only when motion is minimized. This is expressed by labor density.

$$\text{Labor density} = \frac{\text{Work}}{\text{Motion}}$$

This goal of a JIT system is to eliminate motion so that productive work approaches 100%. This is very different from the concept of efficiency as usually embraced in traditional manufacturing, in which:

$$\text{Efficiency} = \frac{\text{Output}}{\text{Number of workers}}$$

There is a hidden danger in the above equation. As you can see, it is possible to make efficiency look good by simply increasing output even though this improved output may not be required by the next (or any) process. In this manner, inventory is often used as a leveler. All processes are run at full speed to "look good" but inventory piles up at various points. The 45- to 120-day inventories of vehicles that American automotive manufacturers routinely build up in advance of orders demonstrate how inventory is used to make factories look efficient by keeping them running full out as long as possible. The system is made to appear highly efficient, even though total costs are dramatically increased by the excess, unsold inventory. And then there's the human cost incurred when layoffs are required to slow production so that excess inventory can be sold off.

Tact Time

The discussion of this concept begins to get us into areas of complexity that are beyond the scope of this book. However, it's important for you to be familiar with the term and its place in a JIT system. *Tact time* is defined as the time it takes to produce one item, that is, the time it takes between successive units of output from a process (assuming that everything is running smoothly). For example, let's say that 20 workers in a process produce 200 units per 8-hour day. That tact time is:

$$\text{Tact time} = \frac{8 \text{ hours} \times 60 \text{ minutes}}{200 \text{ units}} = \frac{480 \text{ minutes}}{200 \text{ units}} = 2.4 \text{ minutes}$$

There is a big difference between improving tact time in a JIT system sense and improving productivity. It's possible to have the same 20 people make improvements in their isolated work area and produce 250 units in the same work time. This would improve their tact time to 1.92 minutes but would be an added cost unless the customer process can absorb the additional units without building up any inventory.

Assuming that the customer process can use 200 units, true productivity improvement would occur only if the number of workers could be reduced to 19, 18, 17, or less and still produce the 200 units. It's pretty clear that all processes in a chain must coordinate their efforts to simultaneously reduce tact time.

The Overall Goal: The Elimination of Waste

When you put all of this together, a JIT system is aimed at reducing waste, of all types. Taiichi Ohno identifies seven types of waste as the targets of a JIT system such a Toyota's. These seven "sins," which we saw earlier in Coda 5 (Chapter ten), are:

1. The waste of making too many units
2. The waste of waiting time at a machine
3. The waste of transporting units
4. The waste of processing waste
5. The waste of inventory
6. The waste of motion
7. The waste of making defective units

The earlier discussion of inventory, leveling, and kanban demonstrates how JIT attacks these various types of waste.

The Concept Of "One Less"

Of course, no system starts out as a perfect realization of the preceding rules. Even in world-class Japanese plants using JIT, there is often some small amount of inventory in some processes. The key is that process improvement efforts must be ongoing to continually move closer to JIT for every process. A useful method for improving is called "one less at a time." The technique is simple. If process A maintains an input inventory of 100 parts, reduce it to 99 and run the process as before. Continue to reduce the standby input inventory by "one less." At some point, let's say at 50 parts, the supplying process may have trouble meeting demand (the pull) from process B. Part of this problem will be due to the uneven pull of process B which also maintains a "cushion." If the problem solving methods of the other Coda are then applied, the barrier of 50 parts can be broken.

The 50 piece inventory is then reduced to 49, then 48, then 47, and so on. At some point, another problem will surface. Eventually, as "one less" is practiced at each process, hidden problems begin to appear rapidly. These are all of the problems that inventory has hidden. The Japanese use the analogy of high water and hidden rocks. If you maintain high water (big inventories), you'll never find the rocks (process problems). As the water level is reduced, the rocks are found and can be removed. This means that you can operate your boat at high speed in shallow water without hitting a rock. And that's the goal of JIT: a flexible, responsive system with minimal inventory and cost.

As you can see, the implementation of a JIT system will require a profound change in management philosophy. Yet, at the same time, the tools of making JIT work are not complicated. We've already covered many of them in earlier Coda. A prime example of the elegant simplicity of the "workings" of a JIT system is Single Minute Exchange of Die, the second of our "low tech" strategies.

SINGLE MINUTE EXCHANGE OF DIE (SMED)

Shigeo Shingo is the person responsible for developing the SMED methodology. We've already discussed his contributions in Coda 2 (Chapter Seven) when we discussed poka-yoke and source inspection. It's easy to see why he's considered one of the towering giants of productivity and quality.

There's no reason why every company in the United States would not be applying SMED right now. Yet, without a philosophy of JIT, few would understand why SMED is necessary. You'll quickly come to see that SMED is the epitome of low tech process improvement. SMED is essential for JIT however, even in a non-JIT system, SMED practices could save thousands of hours of labor.

A die is a mold, press, punch, form, or other portion of a piece of equipment that can be changed to produce different parts. Examples are molds into which metal is poured, dies in a sheet metal stamping machine, and various tips for spot welding. A given piece of tooling can have different molds, stamps, and/or welding tips, depending upon the exact characteristics required in the finished part.

A time consuming and expensive part of any manufacturing process is "exchange, or change, of die." Change of die involves stopping a piece of equipment after part A is produced and making the modifications to forms, molds, and related "dies" so that part B can then be produced. In a JIT environment, SMED is absolutely essential since production lines must be flexible enough to produce whatever is required without building up inventories.

Let's look at an example of how a traditional manufacturing company handles die change. Suppose a press stamps out car hoods with a tact time of 1 minute (remember, tact time is the time between completed hoods coming out of the press). Let's also assume that it takes 30 minutes to exchange the dies in the press between hood types (this is a very low estimate; die changes can take hours). If we require 20 hoods of each type each hour to meet production requirements, we have a problem. With a change of die time of 30 minutes, the best we can do is 30 hoods (15 of each type) per hour if we make one change of die each hour.

$$
\begin{aligned}
\text{Tact time A (1 minute)} \times 15 &= 15 \\
\text{Change of die} &= 30 \\
\text{Tact time B (1 minute)} \times 15 &= 15 \\
\\
\text{Total time} &= 60 \text{ minutes}
\end{aligned}
$$

There are only two ways around this problem in a traditional work environment, both of which incur needless waste and loss of profit. The first is to use the single press to build up inventory in advance by running it for longer hours (overtime). This means higher labor costs. The hoods would have to be stored, which means additional labor to move them and retrieve them. They would also take up space and incur the risk of system damage. And there's always the danger of producing bad hoods whose defects aren't noticed until they're used. Nothing but waste, waste, and more waste. Yet, this practice is common throughout all of manufacturing.

The second approach, just as wasteful but very appealing to manufacturing techies, is to put in two presses and devote one to each hood type. This would mean no die changes and a production capacity of 60 of each type per hour. Or, instead of two presses, one new, improved, more expensive faster press with a tact time of 30 seconds could be installed. This would permit the processing of 30 A hoods in 15 minutes, a 30-minute die change, and then 30 B hoods in 15 minutes. This approach drives up maintenance and capital costs in many ways. The faster equipment will require more labor for adjustment and maintenance and may actually have a longer die exchange time. The two-machine option doubles capital and maintenance costs and has a hidden danger. As we mentioned earlier in our discussion of JIT, American management hates to see an idle machine. Therefore, there will be an almost irresistible tendency to "keep the machines busy." This means that massive inventories of both A and B hoods will be built up, incurring all of the costs we've already detailed.

SMED focuses on the reduction of the die exchange time. A simple reduction of the exchange of die time to 15 minutes would make it possible to produce 20 of each hood type each hour with some extra capacity (5 spare minutes) to meet future production incrreases. As it turns out, a 50% reduction of die exchange time is laughably easy to accomplish, once SMED is understood.

Benefits of SMED

Shigeo Shingo, in his book, *A Revolution in Manufacturing: The SMED System*, cites numerous examples in which exchange times have been reduced by more than a factor of 15. In fact, the more typical improvements run in the range of 18 to 20 times faster. He cites one example from his experience at Toyota in which he reduced the setup time for a 1000 ton Scheoler press from 4 hours to 3 minutes in a body shop of Toyota's main plant! A 98.75% reduction in time! Dr. Shingo states that it was that experience that first motivated him to formulate his SMED concept.

In our example, a modest but typical reduction of 18 to 1 would reduce the changeover time to less than 2 minutes. This would permit 29 hoods of each type to be built every hour, if necessary, a 93% improvement in output, with no added costs. In fact, if production requirements remained at a level of 20 hoods of each type per hour, 18 minutes of press operator time would be available for other duties, not to mention the savings of maintenance personnel labor (if they were required to do the exchange of die; in many cases, SMED simplifies the procedure to the point at which operators can manage die changes on their own).

A Quick Review of SMED Basics

A detailed study of SMED techniques goes beyond the scope of this book. Refer to Dr. Shingo's book for an in-depth look. I'll review the general features of SMED so that you can appreciate the low tech, process orientation of the approach. There's no magic in SMED, only in-depth process study and insights. (Then again, maybe that is the magic!)

Components of Die Exchange

The typical components of die exchange and representative percent of total time spent on them are:

Component	Percent of time
Getting ready (collecting tools, fittings, jigs)	30
Removal of prior set up parts (jigs, bolts, molds)	5
Taking measurements and installing new die	15
Adjustments and trial runs	50
Total	100

In many environments, the adjustments and trial runs component takes up to 90% of the total time. SMED attacks each of these components and minimizes them.

Internal and External Exchange Of Die

An important distinction in SMED is that between internal exchange of die (IED) and external, or outside, exchange of die (OED). IED procedures are those that are accomplished while the machine is stopped; they happen "inside" the machine. OED procedures are those that can be done in advance of a die change while the machine is still operating with the prior set of dies. Some of these outside procedures would appear to be obvious, such as collecting tools. Others are not so obvious.

The Basic Principles of SMED

1. Convert as many IED procedures as possible to OED procedures. The goal is to minimize the amount of time that the machine must be down. This requires the in-depth participation of maintenance, engineering, and operator personnel. They must carefully study existing processes and determine which must be done internally. The remainder must be moved to OED status.
2. Standardize the functionality of dies. This involves such things as making sure that a standard clamp can fit all dies, regardless of their shape.

3. Eliminate fasteners by using clamps. Bolts are the single most time intensive method of fastening. They must be eliminated whenever possible through the use of one-turn bolts, clamps, and bolts with only partial thread.

4. Use intermediate jigs. While a machine is turning out part A, intermediate jigs are used to prepare the dies for part B. When the change is made, the die and the intermediate jig are installed as a unit. Time that was previously spent placing a jig into the machine (IED) is now OED.

5. Use parallel operations. Instead of having only one worker make a die exchange when the workers must move about the machine a lot, two or more workers should work in parallel, thus eliminating the wasted motion, and dramatically shortening the setup time.

6. Eliminate adjustments. Adjustments are necessary because the process is not well understood. Once the process of the interaction of the die and the machine are clearly understood, it is possible to establish settings for parts and jigs that do not require extensive adjustments. This is one of the biggest areas of potential savings.

Additional Tips

The experts in SMED have found the following to be remarkably effective in reducing exchange times:

1. Color coordination of tool and die sets. A considerable amount of time is used in selecting the correct tools and/or parts for a specific die change from a large assortment of tools and parts. When the color for dies and tools for part A is the same, and different from other die sets, problems are dramatically reduced. Only the proper tools are taken to the work area, and the probability of installation of incorrect clamps and jigs is all but eliminated.

2. Preheating. When a die-cast machine die is changed, residual heat is used to preheat the new die, saving time and energy.

3. Unifying heights of press dies. By using jigs, stoppers, and grooves, adjustment of stroke lengths can be eliminated.

4. Elimination of cranes for IED. Cranes and forklifts are slow. Toyota generally uses specially designed carts that permit operators to slide dies of less than 3 tons into place without cranes and forklifts. Of course, cranes and forklifts are used for OED movements of heavy components.

It's All in the Process Knowledge

As you can see, SMED cannot be implemented without an in-depth understanding of micro-processes, right down to the "which bolt is installed next and why" level. Once again, you can see how all of the Coda fit together, mutually supporting each other and reinforcing the entire philosophy of The Code of The American Samurai.

GETTING THE MOST FROM EXISTING TECHNOLOGY—
DESIGN OF EXPERIMENTS

Design of Experiements (DOE) refers to a general body of experimental approaches and the consequent statistical analyses that are performed on the data obtained in planned analyses called experiments. DOE is the classic approach for optimizing the performance of existing systems.

Although many statisticians have contributed to knowledge in the field, the name of Genichi Taguchi is most often associated with the modern industrial applications of these techniques. In fact, "Taguchi DOE" has become a term in itself. As we explore these techniques, you'll come to appreciate Taguchi's contributions.

Since many people are intimidated by statistics and this is not a statistics text, I'm going to keep the discussion at as general a level as possible. This means that I will be forced to overgeneralize and make broad assumptions on occasion. Those of you who are expert statisticians will have to excuse me. If the discussion gets a little statistically rought for those of you who get hives at the sight of a Greek letter (they are used as statistical symbols), just relax. American Samurai don't have to be statisticians; they have to know what techniques to suggest and where opportunities for improvement lie. There are plenty of people in every organization who will never appreciate the philosophies we are trying to promulgate but who will be able to do the statistics with ease. All you've got to do is bring the people together with the tools at an opportune time.

Let Me Paint You the Story

We'll work through this discussion using a single example to demonstrate both the traditional approach and the DOE approaches to "fixing" a complex problem situation. Let's suppose that we are operating a paint booth in the body painting department of a large truck plant. The paint is applied to the truck bodies with hand-operated spray guns that are powered by compressed air. As the air is sent through the paint gun, a flow of paint is also forced under pressure into the gun through a separate line. The air and the paint come together and the paint is sprayed out. There have been problems with paint thickness, and we have been ordered to "handle it" by the plant manager.

Ideally, the paint should be exactly 2.25 thousandths of an inch, or 2.25 mils, thick. If the paint is thinner than 2.25 mils, the probability increases that the undercoat may show through, meaning that the car will have to be sent back through the paint system. This is costly in lost production time. Thicker paint, up to about 3.0 mils, is OK but costs more because more paint is used. Paint that is about 3.0 mils or thicker has a high probability of running or sagging. If this happens, the paint must be sanded off and the truck repainted, a very costly operation. If you'll recall our discussion in Chapter Seventeen (Coda 12), this means that we have a lower specification of 2.25 mils and an upper specification of 3.0 mils, with our ideal value being right at the lower spec.

There are several other factors involved in the painting process besides air pressure and paint (fluid) flow through the paint gun. One important factor is paint viscosity, the thickness of the paint. Viscosity is typically measured in seconds. Paint is poured through a standard wire sieve, and the time it takes the paint to fall through is the viscosity measure. Thicker paint takes longer to fall through. Viscosity is typically adjusted to compensate for temperature and humidity fluctuations. Additional factors that influence paint thickness include the type of nozzle used on the paint gun, the skill of the operator, variability in the temperature of the baking oven that will set the paint, variations in the condition of the truck surface as a result of changes in the electrostatically applied primer, and changes in the paint itself.

The typical American management approach in the typical paint department, if there were problems, would be for an engineer, a paint department supervisor, a plant executive, or all three, either sequentially or together, to give orders about how to fix the problem. The engineer would be inclined to immediately begin suggesting adjustments in air pressure and nozzle types. At the worst extreme, an influential engineer or engineering manager would push for expensive new painting equipment or modifications. The engineer would be looking at the problem from an "engineering viewpoint" and would be confident that the right engineering changes could fix the problem.

The typical paint department supervisor would be inclined to focus on paint viscosity and/or the skill levels and motivation of the painters themselves. The supervisor would order more or less epoxy to be put in the paint to thicken or thin it, having seen that such adjustments in the past have led to improvements in paint quality. The plant manager might focus on any or all of these factors and give orders to change painters, viscosity, air pressure, or fluid flow through the gun. Workers, if asked (it's not likely in most plants, but it could happen) would focus on whatever inputs they happen to believe are crtical.

Of course, all of these actions are nothing but the most unenlightened tampering. Things are bound to fluctuate between better and worse over time, even if nothing is done. The key point is that nobody really understands the total relationship between all of the factors and paint thickness.

The result, eventually, is that management begins to pound on the painting personnel and tell them to "shape up or else." Of course, what more could the painters do if they're already doing their best? Nothing more that would help. They might try harder, but, not fully understanding the process, they could actually make things worse. Unless they've been given the tools, the training, and the authority to fully work on the problem, they really can't fix the problem. I've worked in plants in which the painters were sent home without pay for 1 to 5 days because of paint defects that nobody could stop. I know for a fact that the painters were doing their best. At the same time, the engineers couldn't explain how to fix the problem, and the painting department supervisors didn't know how to paint in the first place, so they didn't have the slightest idea what to do, other than to threaten the painters and continually tamper with individual factors.

Our Experiment

Let's use DOE to examine how this situation might be scientifically studied.

Let's assume that we have talked with our painters, the appropriate production engineers, our paint vendors, and our quality assurance personnel. We think we have a good understanding of the process inputs and we decide to run a designed experiement, or DOE. Let's say that we decide to study three separate factors: viscosity, paint thickness, and air pressure. As you'll recall, we identified many other factors as being important to paint thickness. It is possible, and probably advisable, to study all of them at once in a DOE, but that would unnecessarily complicate our discussion at this point. If we don't study the other factors, we must deal with them in another way. We must either hold them steady, such as using the same painter for all tests so that painter skill is held constant (this is called an experimental control), or we must vary them much as they would vary in actual situations. Thus, we might use various painters throughout the test so that painter skill is randomly distributed. It's always more accurate to include factors in the DOE if possible, although it may not be possible from an expense or time perspective.

An important consideration in any DOE is to establish *factor levels*. Take viscosity, for example. It's possible to have paint thickness from 1 second to 10,000 seconds; we can't study them all in a DOE. The challenge is to select values, called factor levels, that might make a difference *and* could be used in the real painting process. For example, there's no doubt that 10,000 second paint would perform quite a bit differently than 50 second paint. Finding this out wouldn't do us any good because 10,000 second paint couldn't be used. So we must select paint values to study which are reasonable. Most often, 2 factor levels are studied for each value, particularly in Taguchi type designs. Sometimes 3 or more levels of each factor are used, but not often.

Let's say that all of our process experts have decided to set 2 levels of each factor as follows:

Factor A	Viscosity	Level A1:	50 seconds
		Level A2:	60 seconds
Factor B	Air pressure	Level B1:	50 psi

Level B2:   60 psi

Factor C   Fluid flow   Level C1:   24 ounces per minute
                               Level C2:   28 ounces per minute

A graphic representation of our DOE is shown in Table 21.1.

Table 21.1
Experimental design diagram for a full factorial
2 x 2 x 2 paint experiment.

		(A) Viscosity			
		(A1) 50 Sec.		(A2) 60 Sec.	
		(B) Air Pressure		(B) Air Pressure	
		(B1) 50 psi	(B2) 60 psi	(B1) 50 psi	(B2) 60 psi
Fluid Flow (C)	(C1) 24 ou.	A1B1C1	A1B2C1	A2B1C1	A2B2C1
	(C2) 28 ou.	A1B1C2	A1B2C2	A2B1C2	A2B2C2

This experiment design is called a 2 × 2 × 2 full-factorial design (read as "two by two by two") because it consists of 3 factors, each of which has 2 levels. Each number represents a factor, and the value of the number represents the levels of the factors involved. Thus, a 3 × 4 × 3 design would consist of 3 factors having 3, 4, and 3 factor levels each, respectively.

In order to perform this experiment, Factor A (viscosity) would be set at 50 seconds (level A1), Factor B (air presssure) would be set at 50 psi (level B1), and Factor C (fluid flow) would be set at 24 ounces per minute (level C1). Each combination of factor settings is called a "treatment" or "cell." The one we just described is the A1B1C1 treatment. The paint would then be applied and a paint thickness reading would be collected when it dried. This reading would then be placed in the "box" for treatment A1B1C1. Each application of paint is called a "run" or a "trial run." Each measurement of the quality characteristic is commonly called on *observation*. The process of making runs and collecting observations would continue until the desired number of observations for each unique combination of paint viscosity, fluid flow, and air pressure had been collected.

The manner in which treatments are run must be carefully randomized (to the extent possible) over the period of data collection so that the paint thicknesses are not influenced by outside forces. For example, it's possible that painters are more alert and accurate in the morning than later in the day. Suppose this were true and that all of the observations for one treatment (e.g., A1B1C1) were taken in the morning and all observations for another treatment were taken late in the day. Our paint thickness readings for the morning treatment might look better than for the treatments that are run later in the day. We might erroneously conclude that the difference was due to the specific A1B1C1 combination of viscosity, paint flow, and air pressure, when, in fact, the difference was due entirely to operator accuracy and fatigue.

Arrays

The Taguchi type analyses we'll discuss later in this chapter use something called arrays. Arrays are nothing more than the listing of all of a design's treatments without the A, B, and C designations. Shown in Table 21.2 is a listing of the treatment conditions as shown in Table 21.1 along with the corresponding array. The A, B, and C shown in parentheses at the top of the array are not displayed on arrays when they are displayed. They are shown here to demonstrate that the array is simply another way of listing the treatment levels. We'll see more of these arrays later.

Table 21-2
Listing of Table 21-1 treatments and the
corresponding array for the same treatments

Listing of Treatments	"Taguchi" Array		
	(A)	(B)	(C)
A1B1C1	1	1	1
A1B1C2	1	1	2
A1B2C1	1	2	1
A1B2C2	1	2	2
A2B1C1	2	1	1
A2B1C2	2	1	2
A2B2C1	2	2	1
A2B2C2	2	2	2

Arrays are useful for listing the conditions and results of very large experiments in which a great many factors and levels are studied. Whereas I find pictorial representations such as Table 21-1 easier to understand, they are not practical when designs increase in size.

The Data

Let's assume that we have collected two observations of paint thickness under each of the treatments in a well planned and valid manner. Statistically, speaking, it's always better to collect as many scores per treatment as possible, in order to reduce the effects of random error. If posssible, at least 2 observations per treatment should be taken. More than 5 is probably excessive in terms of time and expense in most industrial applications. It's possible to conduct analyses with only one observation per treatment (as many Taguchi analyses do) but some precision is lost.

Table 21-3 presents all of the individual observations that were collected. You'll notice that it's difficult to capture an accurate picture of what's going on by looking at the raw scores.. The scores seem to vary according to no set pattern.

Table 21-3
Data collected for our full-factorial 2 x 2 x 2
paint experiment.

		(A) Viscosity			
		(A1) 50 Sec.		(A2) 60 Sec.	
		(B) Air Pressure		(B) Air Pressure	
		(B1) 50 psi	(B2) 60 psi	(B1) 50 psi	(B2) 60 psi
Fluid Flow (C)	(C1) 24 ou.	2.40 2.60	1.70 1.90	3.00 2.30	1.60 1.90
	(C2) 28 ou.	2.60 2.40	2.70 2.60	2.90 2.80	2.50 2.40

By using the appropriate techniques to analyze our design, we can evaluate the "pure" effect of each one of the sources of variance shown in Table 21-4. The key point is that we can not only "tell" whether viscosity, air pressure, or fluid flow that have an effect, but we can tell whether there are any unique combinations of any of these factors that have an effect that we might not have expected.

Table 21-4
Sources of variability of Table 21-1 experiment.

Factor code	Source of variability
A	Viscosity
B	Air pressure
C	Fluid flow
A x B	Interaction of viscosity and air pressure
A x C	Interaction of viscosity and fluid flow
B x C	Interaction of air pressure and fluid flow
A x B x C	Interaction of viscosity, pressure, and fluid flow
Error	Variation attributable to all other causes

The "interactions" shown in Table 21-4 are separate sources of variability that can be pulled out of the analysis. The A × B (read as AB) interaction is the effect that a unique combination of some level of factor A and B might have that wouldn't be found just be varying factor A or just B alone. This is the same concept as a drug interaction (that's where the name comes from), in which neither one of 2 or more drugs has much of an effect by itself, but a combination of them interacts to produce a significant effect).

At this point, the statistical procedures get a little complicated for novices, or the uninterested, to follow. In order to spare the nonstatisticians, I'm going straight to the results, with a minimum discussion of how I got there. You'll have to trust me (If not me, who? If not now, when?) to have done the right thing.

Results

In order to examine the impact of each factor, we divide up the 16 scores for paint thickness (2 × 2 × 2 times 2 scores each) according to factor levels within each factor. We do this for each factor, 1 at a time. This permits us to examine the effect of each factor independent of the other factors. For example, let's take the 16 scores and divide them into A1 and A2. That is, we add up the 8 scores that were collected when factor A was set at A1 and compute the average and then do the same thing for the 8 A2 scores. We get an average of 2.36 mils for A1 and 2.43 mils for A2, meaning that more viscous (thicker) paint gives us slightly greater paint thickness.

A similar procedure for B gives us an average of 2.63 mils for B1 and 2.16 mils for B2, demonstrating that higher pressure gives us thicker paint. For C, C1 gives us a mean of 2.18 mils, compared to 2.61 mils for C2. This shows us that greater fluid flow (at least greater up to the levels used in our experiment) give us thicker paint.

The results of the analysis to this point lead us to conclude that:

1. There is likely a main effect for factor B, air pressure. That is, we found that the B1 condition (lower air pressure), leads to thicker paint (but not thicker than 3.0 mils).
2. There is likely a main effect for factor C, fluid flow. The C2 condition (greater fluid flow) leads to thicker paint (but not thicker than 3.0 mils).

A further type of analysis (one that gets a little complicated), leads me to believe that there is a B × C interaction effect. That is, a unique combination of B and C creates paint thickness changes that couldn't be predicted from B or C variations alone.

Analysis of Variance

Most analyses of this type stop here and proceed to take action on the three factors. However, if we wished, we could conduct an analysis of variance

(ANOVA) and determine whether the differences are statistically real. As you know from our discussion of variability, small variations are expected. An ANOVA tells us if we can have confidence that any differences we are viewing are more than expected variability.

What Action Would We Take As a Result of Our Analysis?

Based upon our analyses, we would adjust our paint parameters to maximize paint thickness as long as it would not yield paint thicknesses more than 3.0 mils. Our results shows that:

> B1 yields thicker paint.
>
> C2 yields thicker paint
>
> B1 with either C1 or C2 yields thicker paint than B2.

In order to maximize thickness, we would therefore set our air presssure at B1 (50 psi) and our fluid flow at C2 (28 ounces). This would also net the B1 with C2 benefit. Keep in mind that it is possible to find a situation in which the A1 and B1 factor levels might be "best" at the same time that the A2 × B2 interaction might make statistically significant contribution to "best." This would require a trade-off in terms of which factors might contribute most. You'd probably have to run further experiments.

As you can see, such experimentation requies an in-depth understanding of every facet of the process. If you select the wrong factors, the wrong factor levels, leave out important factors, put in irrelevant ones, or don't control other sources of variability (special causes) that may be present, your experiment will be junk. Worse yet, you could change things for the worse.

A TAGUCHI TYPE ANALYSIS OF VARIANCE

Genichi Taguchi has championed and expanded the development of a particular type of statistical analyses to the point where his name is automatically associated with the technique. Taguchi analyses of variance make a compromise between the power of full factorial designs and the costs of running many trials in the real world. The real benefit of a Taguchi-type design is that it enables the study of many factors with very few scores. In our 2 × 2 × 2 design, we had 8 boxes, or treatments. By sequentially multiplying the factor levels of a full-factorial design, it is possible to calculate how many scores, or measurements, must be taken. Thus, a 2 × 2 × 2 × 2 × 2 (or a 2^5) design would require 32 measurements simply to get 1 score per treatment. Table 21-5 presents a Taguchi design called a L_8 in which it is possible to study 7 factors at 2 levels each (2^7) with only 8 scores. In a full factorial design, 7 factors at 2 levels each would require 128 treatments, 120 more than what the L_8 design requires.

Table 21-5
A Taguchi L_8 DOE array.

1	2	3	4	5	6	7
1	1	1	1	1	1	1
1	1	1	2	2	2	2
1	2	2	1	1	2	2
1	2	2	2	2	1	1
2	1	2	1	2	1	2
2	1	2	2	1	2	1
2	2	1	1	2	2	1
2	2	1	2	1	1	2

As you can imagine, if expensive equipment and/or tooling changes (even with SMED) are involved in the tests, a Taguchi design can save a lot of money and time. An L_{16} design can investigate 15 two-level factors with only 16 measurements. A full factorial design would require 32,768!

Let's say that we were going to do the paint experiment but with 7 factors. Our factors, set at two levels each, might be:

Factor code	Source of variability
A	Viscosity
B	Air pressure
C	Fluid flow
D	Nozzle type
E	Painter skill
F	Temperature of oven
G	P^h of electrostatic primer

Table 21-6 presents these factors assigned to the appropriate columns and a score for each treatment. (Taguchi refers to each set of conditions, each row, as an "experiment" in itself.) The first score of 2.32 was obtained by setting all factors at their "1" level (the first row of the array: 1 1 1 1 1 1 1) and then obtaining a paint thickness reading. The second score, 2.25, was obtained by setting the first three factors, A, B, and C, at 1, and the remaining factors at their second level, 2 (the second row—1 1 1 2 2 2 2).

In order to analyze the scores, the scores are simply divided up into the "1"s and "2"s for each factor (just as we earlier divided up the A1s and the A2s). Thus, for factor A, the "1" level scores are the first four scores in the score column: 2.32, 2.25, 2.19, and 2.17. The level "2" scores for A are the bottom four scores in the score column: 2.27, 2.29, 2.20, and 2.25. The mean of the A1 scores is 2.23, compared to a mean of 2.25 for the A2 scores, demonstrating that factor A probably doesn't make any difference. The same procedure would be done with each of the factors.

Table 21-6
A Taguchi L₈ for a seven factor paint experiment.

A	B	C	D	E	F	G	Scores
1	1	1	1	1	1	1	2.32
1	1	1	2	2	2	2	2.25
1	2	2	1	1	2	2	2.19
1	2	2	2	2	1	1	2.17
2	1	2	1	2	1	2	2.27
2	1	2	2	1	2	1	2.29
2	2	1	1	2	2	1	2.20
2	2	1	2	1	1	2	2.25

The problem with the above design is that it makes no provision for the study of interactions. Unless we know for certain that no interactions are important, or present, the above design presents some risks. If an interaction is present and we do not find it, it will appear as a phony main effect for one of the factors. Interactions can be singled out for special attention in Taguchi designs, but you have to specifically cite which ones are important. They can be assigned to columns only according to very particular rules (called out by what Taguchi calls "linear graphs"). The presentation of these techniques would complicate the scope of this discussion beyond our space limitations (and the tolerance of most people for statistical discussions). Most Taguchi designs are constructed under the assumption that not all interactions are meaningful for analysis. This assumption must be based upon earlier research and expert opinion about the process under study.

Power Tools, But You've Got to Understand Your Processes First—That Means Applying Every Aspect of the Code

As you can appreciate, DOE, JIT, and SMED techniques can be powerful tools to maximize the effectiveness of existing processes. Instead of spending money on new equipment and technology, first fix what's there. This is the essence of the Japanese approach—maximize existing processes by taking advantage of every bit of insight, suggestions, adjustments, and so on before you bring in new technology. How many of us have seen our organizations go out and mechanize or computerize an operation that never worked well when it was manual? All of us. And the result? The same old mess, but now the mess happens faster and costs more money.

Yet you can't maximize what you have unless you find out how it really works. This requires process knowledge and insight. That can come only from the people who do the processes. And they're not going to know how unless the entire organization is moving toward the types of philosophies we've been discussing. It all hangs together.

Fortunately, some of the techniques discussed in this chapter can be "sold" or introduced without a lot of resistance because they seem "technical." American management is willing to do almost anything technical, even if it's the right thing! The problem is that, without the participation of all process doers (the Egg Sucking Pigs and the Sub-Humans), few people will have the necessary process knowledge. But we've got to start somewhere.

22

Everybody on Board the Design Train Early!

Coda 17. Concurrent (or simultaneous) engineering must be implemented on all new products and product modifications (which is simply a process orientation to product development but sufficiently important and specialized to merit individual attention).

There's been a lot of talk about concurrent, or simultaneous, engineering lately. It's gotten so much press lately that it's viewed, even by those who have absolutely no idea about what it is, as one of the techniques that is critical for competitiveness. If you were to apply all of the Coda previously discussed, you'd be utilizing concurrent engineering and you might not even know it. That's because successful concurrent engineering practices require not simply a technique or two but a change to the entirely new philosophy of work we've been discussing. Many traditional managers are rushing to embrace concurrent engineering even as they disdain the "new" enlightened philosophy of work. That sort of concurrent engineering can't work. The Code of the American Samurai and concurrent engineering are both based on the same fundamental assumptions. You can't do the latter successfully without the former, and if you do the former, you'll be doing the latter.

Nonetheless, the intricacies of concurrent engineering and the applied tricks and tools are sufficiently interesting to warrant a separate discussion. First of all, what is concurrent engineering?

Concurrent engineering is the integration of as many sources of relevant information into a product or service design effort as early as possible, using teams of subject experts, with the intent of shortening product development times, lowering total life-cycle costs, and improving customer satisfaction. As you can see, this is nothing more than getting process doers and content experts together to make process decisions.

The benefits of employing concurrent engineering can be phenomenal. Companies that aggressively employ concurrent engineering practices routinely report the following ranges of substantiated benefits:

Product development time	30% to	70% LESS
Engineering changes	60% to	90% FEWER
Product part counts	10% to	70% FEWER
Scrap and rework	20% to	75% LESS
Manufacturing costs	10% to	40% LESS
Time to market span	20% to	90% FASTER
White collar productivity	20% to	125% HIGHER
Quality levels (defects)	200% to	600% LESS
Return on assets	20% to	120% HIGHER

Not bad, right? Let's take a look at the techniques and practices that make such savings possible.

WHAT CONCURRENT ENGINEERING IS NOT

There are many misconceptions about what concurrent engineering is and how it works. Before we get to those points, let's discuss what concurrent engineering is *not,* so that we won't be carrying a lot of excess baggage along with us.

Concurrent engineering is not computer tools or computer systems. CAD/CAM systems are valuable tools, but they are not concurrent engineering. Concurrent engineering is not Design of Experiments (DOE), Statistical Process Control (SPC), Quality Function Deployment (QFD), or any other alphabet soup.

Concurrent engineering is not principal component analysis, configuration management, Manufacturing Resource Management (MRP) II, or project management. Concurrent engineering is not Design for Assembly software, and it's not computer modeling.

All of the preceding can be important tools, sometimes critical tools for a concurrent engineering effort, but they are not concurrent engineering. As already discussed, concurrent engineering is a philosophical approach to managing the design challenge. In that respect, concurrent engineering is no different from managing the entire work environment according to The Code of the American Samurai. There are many who contend that concurrent engineering is a technical problem. It is not. It is a work philosophy/teamwork issue. If it is treated as anything less, it will not produce winning results.

MAKE LOTS OF MISTAKES, BUT MAKE THEM EARLY!

In the late 1970s, the automotive companies were investigating the cost advantage that Japanese automotive companies enjoyed. One of the factors they studied was tooling changes. Tooling changes are the changes made in the equipment that is used to manufacture various automotive parts. The changes are made when initial designs for the parts don't work as planned, that is, when a part that seemed OK turns out to have a problem and must be redesigned. When a part is changed, the tooling that makes it must also be changed.

In the course of the research, they developed a graph similar to the one shown in Figure 22-1. The two curves show the number of tooling changes made by Japanese and American automotive companies from initial concept design to product launch (when a car is first produced from the assembly line) and shortly thereafter.

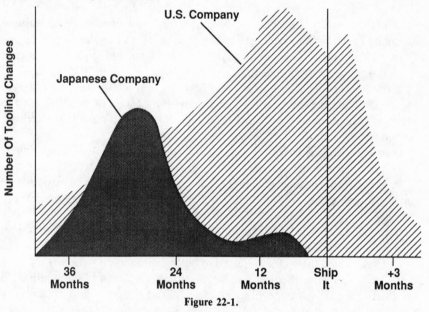

Figure 22-1.

The American car manufacturers were shocked. It was clear that the differences in tooling changes were driving a large part of the competitive advantage that the Japanese possessed. As you can see from Figure 22-1, the bulk of the Japanese tooling changes came very early in the design cycle. The majority of the American tooling changes (and there were a great many of them) came later, peaking shortly before and after product launch.

Just think of the impact of a tooling change once a prototype vehicle has been built. At this point, all of the drawings for the car parts have been completed and most of the parts have been put out to the suppliers for bids. Much of the equipment for making the parts (the tooling) has been designed and ordered, both by suppliers and in the automotive company's own plants. Every change in plans that impacts tooling means that all of the involved drawings have to be changed (including those drawings for associated parts) and all of the involved suppliers have to be notified so that they can change their plans and tooling. It's estimated by the electronics industry that each change in a commercial electronic product that occurs during test production costs at least 1 million dollars.

And that's not the worst of it. The American tooling change curve shows a jump after the first cars come off the assembly line and are being shipped to dealers and purchased by customers. These changes incur not only the costs cited in the previous paragraph, but also require that every dealer's inventory be changed, mechanics notified, manuals updated, recalls performed, and so on. The cost can run into the tens of millions, all cost of quality lost, all pure lost profit.

There's an interesting story that Bart Huthwaite, president and founder of the Institute for Competitive Design, a leading consulting and training company in the field of concurrent engineering, tells about tooling changes. Early in his career, Bart was just getting into the machine tool business in Detroit and had established his own company. He sought out the counsel of a friend, we'll call him Otto, who had built up a large tooling business by working for the automotive companies. Bart asked Otto, "What's the secret of your success? You started out with nothing and now have hundreds of people working for you. How did you do it?"

Otto leaned back in his big chair, took a puff on a giant Havana cigar, and thought for a few minutes. He then said one word, "Changes."

Bart had been expecting a heavy philosophical message or perhaps advice on a business tactic or two. He was a little disappointed and asked, "What changes?"

Otto leaned forward and explained, "When I started out, I used to bid on jobs with the Big Three and I was losing out because I wasn't low enough. Then I discovered the secret. I started to bid the initial tooling orders for 20% below cost. I won all I could handle. Soon, about 2 to 4 months later, I'd get emergency calls about tooling changes, about how they had to have new tooling right away. I explained that such fast response would increase the cost. They'd say OK, as long as they got it fast. I was then able to raise the price to make up what I had lost and then some. It's worked that way for 20 years, like clockwork. I built my business on changes."

Bart notes that Otto has since gotten out of the tooling business because the Big Three have gotten smarter and don't make quite so many late changes anymore. Still many more than they should, but fewer than before. Figure 22-1 shows that the Japanese also made many changes, but they made them early.

AMERICAN SAMURAI INSIGHT

One of the operating principles of concurrent engineering is that mistakes should be encouraged. The more mistakes that can be made very early in the design process, the better.

The electronics industry estimates that changes made during the preliminary design stage, when changes involve only ideas and light pens (on CAD systems), cost only $1000 each. These types of insights led to the current explosion of American interest in concurrent engineering. Let's hope it's not too late.

THE IMPACT OF PRODUCT DESIGN

Product design often gets little attention because it seems like such a small piece of total product costs. After all, total product design costs in a typical company might run from 3% to 5% of total costs. It's not very much. Product design also gets very little attention because there are not typically a great many emergencies or disasters associated directly with it. In the firefighting mode of traditional business, the biggest disasters get the most attention. This means that manufacturing gets the lion's share of attention. The irony is that most of the disasters that show up in manufacturing are caused by poor design decisions that weren't visible when they were being made.

Product design, while driving a small part of total costs to manufacture the product, is a primary driver of the total life-cycle costs.

AMERICAN SAMURAI INSIGHT

It's been estimated by various experts that product design drives as much as 85% of total life-cycle costs.

Figure 22-2 demonstrates this relationship.

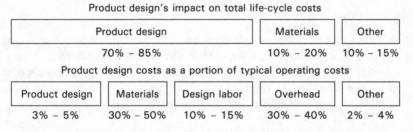

Product design's impact on total life-cycle costs

Product design		Materials	Other
70% – 85%		10% – 20%	10% – 15%

Product design costs as a portion of typical operating costs

Product design	Materials	Design labor	Overhead	Other
3% – 5%	30% – 50%	10% – 15%	30% – 40%	2% – 4%

Figure 22-2. Product design's impact on total life-cycle costs.

Figure 22-2 demonstrates that product design deserves, and had better get, a larger share of attention and resources than it's been getting. Rather than 3% to 5%, expenditures of 5% to 8% would be more appropriate. Let's look at where and how this massive product design impact is generated.

Product Design Drives All Life-Cycle Costs and Performance Issues

The philosophical basis for concurrent engineering is an appreciation that product design drives all life-cycle costs and quality indices. This is difficult for some people to accept, so let's discuss it by examining how product design can impact various life-cycle costs.

Materials Costs

There's been a lot of attention paid lately to materials concepts such as worldwide sourcing (going anywhere to get the best part and having that source supply numerous facilities) and reduction of the supplier base. Yet, much of material's total costs are driven by product design. Consider parts. Just ordering a part, pushing the paper work through the system, is inordinately expensive. Larger corporations routinely find that it takes 1 hour to simply get the signatures, type the paper, and put things into the computer for each purchase order. One hour of employee time, fully loaded with benefits and so on, costs from 25 to 50 dollars, depending upon the organization. Just one multiple-page, NCR paper purchase order can cost from 15 to 50 cents. And this isn't even taking into account expenses to receive the part, stock it, move it, and so on.

Every time a part is designed, it must be ordered. Concurrent engineering routinely reduces part counts by 10% to 50%, sometimes more. Motorola redesigned a battery charger for a two-way radio and reduced the part count from 78 to 11. Just think of the savings in materials processing and paper work. NCR, in its Atlanta plant, recently designed a new terminal for a cash register checkout counter. The number of parts was reduced 85%, compared to the previous model. This directly translates to reduced material costs for labor, storage, transportation, and so on.

Quality Costs

Other than agreeing that product design can make products sturdier and perhaps easier to maintain, it's hard for a great many people to understand how concurrent engineering can impact quality. Stand back, everyone: the scales are about to fall. The first thing to appreciate is that quality cannot be built into a product, it must be designed in.

AMERICAN SAMURAI INSIGHT

Quality cannot be "manufactured" into a product. The maximum quality level of a product is determined during product design; manufacturing processes can compromise this maximum quality but can never improve on it.

In other words, the Egg Sucking Pigs in the plant can only build it as well as it's designed, no better. All too often, they are expected to find a way to "make it work." That's where all the tooling changes come from, and that's where most bad quality comes from.

THE TRADITIONAL APPROACH TO PRODUCT DESIGN

The traditional approach to product design is often referred to as the "over the wall" method. The description refers to the manner in which product designers work in isolation to develop a design and then "throw it over the wall" to manufacturing engineers. I was talking with a senior engineering manager at a concurrent engineering seminar once and he remarked, somewhat wistfully as he watched the young engineers work on a class project, "This reminds me of when I was a young engineer. I remember one time I designed a switch for a motor. It was the best switch design that I've ever seen, before or since."

He even had a little tear in his eye. I asked him, "What motor was the switch used in?"

He replied, "Oh, it wasn't ever used. It couldn't be manufactured."

That's one of the problems with how we train and use engineers in this country. They're taught to do "engineering" and then leave the dirty work to the Egg Sucking Pigs in the plant (which includes the poor engineers who didn't make the cut for product design and got assigned to manufacturing). This isolation of engineers in design departments generates poor designs just as surely as if we asked for them. This is what causes all the late tooling changes; somebody downstream discovers that an aspect of the design either won't work, can't be built, conflicts with an existing process, requires a new process, and/or doesn't meet a customer requirement. All because the product was designed in isolation.

And that's not the entire problem. This "over the wall" approach breeds all sorts of delays and added costs for a bloated bureaucracy. Each department in the design process operates in sequence, cooperating little with departments before and after it. (Suboptimization strikes again; "Mistakes by others are a chance to look good.") Marketing gets an idea, develops it, and "throws it over the wall to design." Product design develops plans and a prototype and then "throws it over the wall" to manufacturing. Manufacturing tries to come up with a way to make it work and then "throws the product over the wall" to field sales and service. If a problem is severe and can't be dealt with by an area, as when a part just can't be manufactured, the design is thrown back over the wall to where it came from, and the battle for blame allocation starts. Meetings, memos, fights, more signatures, and so on, attend each change. This results in more costs and more delays.

In some companies, as many as 25 different signatures are required to sign off each element of a design and any changes. Just think of the delays. In consumer products and electronics, a delay of 2 to 3 months can kill a new product's chances because a competitor will beat you to it. It can sometimes take 3 weeks just to get 25 different people on the phone, much less get them to sign off on something they could get in trouble for. And the overhead expense of this process is immense. All the different functions maintain separate support staffs, equipment, and so on, each of them suboptimizing to make themselves look good in order to justify their cost. This must stop.

THE NEW APPROACH: PRODUCT DESIGN TEAMS

The alternative approach is to form teams and assign to them the responsibility and the authority to come up with a design. These teams are the basic mechanism for successful concurrent engineering—they are cross-functional design teams, often called product design teams (PDT). As I discuss PDT, I'm not speaking of the so-called teams that pursue product design in traditional work environments but teams that are operating as design owners in an organization that is implementing fully empowered concurrent engineering as a work standard. As we discuss PDT in this type of environment, many of you will recognize some aspects of the proverbial "skunk works." In essence, the establishment of a PDT in a concurrent engineering environment is an attempt to formally institutionalize skunk works by duplicating the conditions that allow skunk works to be productive.

Of course, this means that many organizational controls and limits must be removed. This is a very big step for many companies. But it's one that must be taken; we can no longer afford to get maximum productivity in product design from isolated "skunk works" that spring up haphazardly. In order to prosper in the short term and survive in the long term, we must get outstanding product designs from every design effort we conduct.

A fundamental recommendation that successful companies make about PDT is that these teams must be formally chartered and supported. That is, it is not sufficient to simply expect the announcement of concurrent engineering to lead to the formation of effective PDT. The decision to pursue concurrent engineering must be made at the highest levels of management and must be officially announced and supported.

In the same vein, almost all who have been successful say that it is essential to "throw out the old product design handbook." The traditional ways of autocratic, segmented departments simply cannot design products that can make it in today's competitive environment. The PDT must be given the authority and responsibility to come up with "the product design," not simply make recommendations; they must feel as if they own the design. This requires a formal assignment of power from the organization.

A PDT should be formed prior to the first conceptualizations of the product and should receive a formal "buy-in" from engineering and production departments/functions.

Selecting Product Design Team Leaders

It is universally recognized by those who have succeeded with PDT that the most significant variable in determining PDT success is the PDT leader. It's not the technical skills of the leader that are most important; it's his or her personality and interpersonal characteristics. Words most frequently used to describe successful leaders include visionary, driver, persistence, sense of urgency, participatory skills, open to ideas, and flexible. The leader must be of at least equal, and preferably higher, status than the team members. The leader must also be a "hands-on" person who can actually do design work, not simply an administrator. In the words of members of dozens of successful PDT, the leader must get his or her hands "dirty."

Most often, PDT leaders are from Product Design or Product Engineering functions, but it is not uncommon to have a team headed up by a Production Engineer or even a Vice-President of Manufacturing. Remember, the personality characteristics of the leader are more critical than titles or area of expertise.

The Selection of Product Design Team Members

It is absolutely essential that team members be selected by the leader, not the organization. No pressure should be brought to bear to "balance" the team with people from various areas to get a mix of skills or to satisfy "political" considerations. Team members must be doers, preferably from the lowest levels of the organization. This assures that they are hands-on people who know the products and processes.

The most effective teams have no more than eight full-time core members. These full-time members, usually consisting of product designers and process/industrial engineers, generally are supported on a part-time basis by experts in finance, materials, production, research, marketing, customer service, and so on. It is important that all avenues of relevant data be made available to the design team so that critical customer and performance requirements are known from the very beginning.

Teams have been successful with both full-time and part-time members (part-time members are those who work on more than one project simultaneously), although members prefer full-time assignments. It is important that no staff changes in the team or team leader be made during the design challenge unless there are extreme personality conflicts or significant technical skill deficits.

Many companies strongly recommend that vendor involvement be implemented as soon as the PDT is formed. On larger projects in which it is cost-effective, many companies have vendors on the team as full-time core members (the vendor provides the resources in return for an agreement that the vendor will get the business if the design comes in at appropriate and agreed-upon cost and quality targets).

Product Design Team Operating Characteristics

Several key elements of success are:

1. Fast prototyping capability. The team must have the resources to develop and explore iterative prototypes rapidly.
2. The team should be co-located. It is a major, major impediment if the team members do not work in the same area. A driving force in the success of a PDT is its ability to continually "modify and tinker" with an idea by virtue of constant interaction. If team members are not co-located, the number of spontaneous suggestions and iterations decreases and the product design suffers.
3. Informal communications. PDT members must eschew the use of formal communications channels among themselves; they must communicate informally as much as possible.

Setting Product Design Team Priorities/Goals

PDT must be given design challenges that are "embraceable." That is, PDT must be able to get their arms around a project that is clearly definable and do-able. Very large projects will require the team to spend too much time interfacing with experts and not enough time designing. The team must believe that it owns the product design and that it can generate a complete, successful design. Thus, on large projects, there will of necessity be a number of discrete teams, each of which will "completely design" a portion of the final product (e.g., an automobile manufacturer would have separate teams for doors, instrument consoles, engines, etc.)

Management must set broad goals and let the PDT concentrate on specifics. When management sets specific goals, they tend to be much too low. It is better for management to emphasize such priorities as minimizing part count without attempting to set a specific goal. If the team leader and the team are right, the PDT will do the best it can, which is almost always more than management originally thought possible.

Reporting to Management

The consensus is that reporting must be kept informal and relatively unstructured. Odious, formal reporting saps the creativity and the energy of the team and tends to get management into a "manage the numbers" frame of mind that kills innovation and the very risk taking that good product design iterations demand.

Measuring Team Success

Management can easily gauge team success on any number of metrics. The most common and widely used measures are parts count, materials cost, engineering hours, number of engineering change notifications, tooling expense, and time-to-market span. Assembly labor/time was popular but is falling into disfavor because it is such a small part of the total cost picture.

Team members eagerly accept measurement of their performance on these variables, a situation that is not often encountered with the metrics used in traditional performance appraisal systems.

TEAM INCENTIVES AND REWARDS

Although some organizations have tried to reward design teams with cash bonuses, most have avoided monetary rewards for the following reasons:

1. It is difficult to integrate significant monetary award systems into existing compensation systems.
2. The size of monetary awards often cannot be large enough to provide an "order of magnitude" impact on the recipients.
3. It is difficult to determine the magnitude of individual contributions, particularly for employees who support the team on a part-time basis.

In the place of money, most organizations have embraced team recognition and status rewards such as putting team members' names on patent applications, presenting achievement and excellence awards at banquets, recognizing team members on prominently placed plaques, and publicizing the "story" in the organization's media. According to recipients, these types of personal recognition are far more meaningful than nominal monetary rewards.

THE BASIC PRINCIPLES OF DESIGN FOR LOWEST LIFE-CYCLE COST

Every design challenge is different. However, some basic elements of good design are universal. This section presents some of these basic, proven design principles. As you'll see, many of them are common sense dictates. Everybody knows a few of them intuitively, and most engineers "know" the implications, even though they may not have thought about them as a set of design guidelines. They are presented here so that you can appreciate that the central core of concurrent engineering is not arcane, advanced technology but solid, empowered teamwork applying basic design principles. The basic design principles for lowest life-cycle costs are:

1. *Design for reduced part count.* Part count drives all costs upward, all other things being equal.
2. *Design for fewer processes.* Processes drive costs upward as much as parts. Gluing, manual screw fastening, welding, and riveting are separate processes that must be maintained and stocked. Elimination of one in a new design dramatically reduces manufacturing and materials costs.
3. *Design for low-complexity processes.* High-complexity processes cost more to maintain and are guaranteed to have more problems. Design in low

complexity and/or manual processes whenever possible. Make the design tell you when high complexity is necessary.

4. *Design for minimum part and assembly handling.* Assembly labor and systems damage costs are directly related to how often parts and/or assemblies must be handled and reoriented. Design for one axis, top down assembly and minimum handling and movement. As you can see, the only people with this knowledge are going to be from the manufacturing area.

5. *Design for easy access and visibility by operators.* All too often, manufacturing operations are compromised because operators can't clearly see and/or access the area they're working on. The result is missed/poorly done operations and more systems damage. The only folks with this type of insight are the operators themselves. Their input, either directly or via manufacturing engineers, must be incorporated into early design decisions.

6. *Eliminate and/or commonize fasteners.* In the words of Bart Huthwaite, "Fasteners are like spoiled children: they demand so much but give so little." Fasteners are quality sensitive, labor intensive parts. Eliminate them whenever possible. Use snap fits and self-closures instead. When IBM was designing the Proprinter to challenge the then industry leading Epson MX-80, one design goal was to eliminate all fasteners. IBM engineers eliminated all but one screw. (That must have been one important screw!)

    If fasteners can't be eliminated, reduce the number of types. Instead of stocking ten different screws, use only four different types. Commonize head types, lengths, widths, and so on. The only reason most designs have a variety of very similar fasteners is because the last design did. Commonization of fasteners is a quick way to save a lot on materials administration and parts costs.

7. *Design out opportunities for incorrect assembly.* Parts should be designed so that they cannot be incorrectly assembled, especially electrical connectors. Tabs, stops, and projections can be used to prohibit incorrect assembly.

8. *Design for interlocking parts.* Parts should "nest" within each other as they are added to an assembly. The assembly, at any point, should serve as an ideal fixture upon which to place the next part. Positive locking and part identity should be designed to minimize confusion, lost time, and possible incorrect assembly.

9. *Design for easy part handling.* Parts should not be flexible and/or require two hands for orienting and positioning. Instead, design rigid, snap-fit parts. Design parts that have clearly recognizable features so that correct orientation and assembly are self-evident (unless it is possible to design in perfect symmetry, as in a cannon ball, which is impossible to load in an incorrect orientation).

10. *Design the process for minimum transport.* The manufacturing process must be designed so that an in-process assembly does not have to be transported, moved off line, and/or stored between operations. Assemblies should proceed from start to finish without delays. This will obviously require much input from all parties involved in plant operations (it will also most likely require the retirement of 90% of American manufacturing personnel).

THE KILLER PITFALLS OF CONCURRENT ENGINEERING

As you might expect, not every concurrent engineering effort is successful. The failures are not due to failures in the philosophy or methodology of concurrent engineering. They are generally caused by organizations that attempt to half-heartedly implement something that "looks a little like" concurrent engineering but is really the same, old design approach with nothing but fresh lipstick. The following are the most typical reasons why concurrent engineering efforts fall short of expectations:

1. Management expects miracles. There are no miracles, only hard work. PDT can be extremely productive, but they require a lot of effort on the part of management to establish and maintain the conditions that will allow the PDT to succeed. Too often, existing management attitudes are allowed to squash the effort.
2. Assigning the responsibility for the effort to one department. The effort must be mandated from the top to cut across departments. One function/department cannot "make" another do anything; the authority and direction must come from above.
3. Managing the team too closely. You can't expect an explosion of productivity and creativity by employing the traditional "management by the numbers" controls.
4. Assigning team members based on a mix of technical skills. Let the leader pick the team members.
5. Expecting the team to function under the "old" product development routine. PDT using a concurrent engineering philosophy cannot prosper amidst the restrictions of the traditional product design approach.
6. Expecting concurrent engineering to "sell" itself. Nothing requiring change sells itself if the changes involve dramatic alterations of management behavior and employee expectations. Such changes are difficult and must be pushed and supported from the top levels of the company.
7. Focusing on the tools rather than the approach. The tools of DOE, Design for Assembly software, SPC, CAD, and the like are not concurrent engineering; they are useful tools, but no more than that. The successful application of PDT requires a complete change in management philosophy, as does the maximally successful use of any of the previously mentioned tools.

8. Excluding suppliers. Supplier participation is absolutely critical. As discussed in Chapter Eighteen (Coda 13), suppliers know more about their products than the users do. Their knowledge must be incorporated up-front in the design effort.

STEPS FOR SUCCESSFULLY BEGINNING A CONCURRENT ENGINEERING EFFORT

As you can now appreciate, successful concurrent engineering requires a broad range of support systems. If an organization is contemplating the initiation of concurrent engineering, two types of action are required: organizational (to assure long-term, continuing success) and project (to kick off a specific development effort).

Organizational Actions

1. Set up a job-rotation/training system in which engineers actually work (not just visit) in other areas, including sales, customer service, machine shops, and materials, for at least six months. Engineers should never be permitted to work on product design until they have been exposed to at least two other functional areas as a worker.
2. Remove pay/status differences between production and design engineers.
3. Establish a technical career ladder system so that outstanding engineers are not forced into management in order to earn higher salaries.
4. Set up a project management system in which all team members on a design project report on a solid line to the same person.
5. Establish a system that will link all compensation increases for the team members to group attainment of team objectives.
6. Product managers should be held responsible for product costs and performance all the way through manufacturing.

Project Actions

1. Conduct awareness training among key managers, executives, and potential team member populations. This awareness training must involve a hands-on exercise in product design so that all those attending can experience the design challenge.
2. Select a key design project. It must be a critical, real-life problem with high visibility and significant risks. (This will guarantee an enthusiastic response by team members.)
3. Assign a team leader selected for his or her driving, team-oriented personality.
4. Allow the leader to select the core team members (no more than eight with additional content experts available from other areas as needed and with vendor involvement if possible).

5. Make the members full-time and co-located if possible. Provide prototyping tools and design support (such as CAD).
6. Company executives must charter the team and formally announce and mandate the team's responsibilities and authority.
7. Management selects baseline/benchmark metrics and general goals.
8. PDT begins work.
9. Management continuously conducts search and destroy missions for manifestations of the "old way" of product design control, which will invariably appear.

CONCURRENT ENGINEERING MAY BE THE BACK DOOR (OR A TRAP DOOR)!

Because of the attention that concurrent engineering has been receiving in the media over the last few years, it's possible that a great many organizations will begin to explore a new philosophy of work through concurrent engineering efforts. Partially successful efforts may move them to bolder attempts at change. That, coupled with supplier involvement, may be sufficient to show some of them the way to world-class performance.

Unfortunately, many such "toe dipping" excursions will fail for the same reason; you can't do it halfway and expect a lot. All we can do as American Samurai is push as hard as safely possible, talk it up, and hope for the best. I'll be concurrently pushing, talking, and hoping with you.

23

Consensus Decision Making: The Great Unknown of American Business

Coda 18. **All decision making must be reached by consensus decision making on the part of appropriate groups of hands-on process workers.**

You don't have to be a battle-hardened, veteran American Samurai to appreciate that a transformed workplace demands participative decision making. Companies are going to have to encourage micro-process doers to participate in macro-process decisions in order to improve productivity. There's just no other way to obtain the critical hands-on information that will permit continual process improvements.

Consensus decision making involving appropriate personnel is the cornerstone of the participation we've been referring to in all of our discussion. All of Kaizen, process improvements, concurrent engineering . . . everything, depends on an honest and candid flow of properly analyzed information. You receive such data only from unintimidated, cooperative, motivated, and skilled employees. And employees at all levels won't have those characteristics if they're not permitted to participate in decision making and process improvements in their work areas. This involvement can only be fostered by consensus decision making at all levels.

Many managers and executives will actively resist this fundamental truth, secure in their ignorant belief that management knows best (which might compel one to ask why they haven't fixed all the problems). There's nothing to be done about these types. They are millstones around our necks, but we must keep swimming. Yet, many of those who endorse and support The Code of the American Samurai in principle will have difficulty practicing consensus decision making because they don't know what it looks like; they've never seen it. This chapter describes the principles and practices of consensus decision making and how they must be implemented at various levels of the organization. If you're going to be a true American Samurai warrior, consensus decision making must be your new way of working with others.

WHAT IS A CONSENSUS?

A lot of the resistance to consensus decision making and participatory management arises because many executive and managers don't understand what the terms mean. They believe that a consensus means that everybody in the group agrees with the group's decision and feels warm and cuddly toward each other. Sounds horrible, and, fortunately, it's wrong. A *consensus* is a situation that occurs when all members of a group understand a decision, understand the conditions and viewpoints that drove it, have had an opportunity to air their opinions and viewpoints, and, even if they don't wholeheartedly agree with the decision, accept it and will support it.

Consensus Is Not Voting

Consensus is not voting. Voting is a situation in which the majority decides on a course of action that the minority, as much as 49% in some cases, may totally oppose. Voting short-circuits discussion and restricts information flow because it's an easy way out of a dilemma. It appeals to the American emphasis on fast results and ready answers—the old "fast gun" situation. "Let's not waste time here, let's just vote on it now!" is a common refrain from persons who think that they are in the majority and/or who don't think the issue is worthy of attention. The difficulty is that voting leads to poor quality decisions because all participants do not get a chance to share information and influence the knowledge base of other people in the group. In effect, the group is making a decision before it gets all of the information out on the table.

That's why voting is bad even if the vote is unanimous: the group is agreeing too soon, before enough data is present to make the best possible decision. In fact, many early unanimous votes in groups are unanimous because some group members do not want to face the conflict and tensions that they believe a discussion of the issue will bring. They "give in" and vote with what they believe will be the majority in order to avoid problems. Many, many management staff meetings operate in this manner; everybody verbally agrees and nods, the illusion of unanimity. Under the surface, nobody agrees with anything and everybody is upset.

It's Not Everyone Being "Happy" with the Decision

As we said earlier, arriving at a consensus does not require that everybody be happy with the decision. The key element of successful decision making is that all group members participate in the discussion so that they can provide the group with all the data they possess *and* that the group provide all members with enough data to understand how the decision was made. It doesn't matter if everyone is happy (this is nice, but rare). What's important is that they feel that they are a part of the team that made the decision.

This "feeling part of the team" is extremely important for effective group interactions. As groups share opinions and learn about each other as individuals, each person tends to become less defensive, more outgoing, and more confident when working with the group. The group builds up a reservoir of knowledge and a "shorthand" method of communicating, in which every idea and thought doesn't have to be laboriously explained, as it might to a new team member. These phenomena result in increased communications, better quality communication, a willingness to sacrifice for the team, and an unwillingness to let the team down. All of these conditions lead to increased productivity.

Managers will often scoff at this "touchy feely" aspect of teamwork. At the same time, they fondly recall their days of football, fraternities, and so on—all exact social counterparts of the team closeness we are referring to at work.

It's Not "Management By Teams"

Often, when I'm giving my 2-day seminar or a speech, somebody in the audience will make the following accusation: "I suppose all of this teamwork (Kaizen, participation, teams, etc.) means that we're going to have team management of every decision. Sounds like Japanese management to me." This comment is invariably accompanied by a sneer and a look of disgust. Often, the comment is laced with such descriptions as "rule by committee," "sounds like a collective farm to me," and so on. Ah, my fellow Samurai, we have so far to go. Not only to teach our colleagues but to overcome the massive ignorance never addressed by our educational system. Not only do we not teach about variability in our schools, the subject of teamwork is never addressed, except as the exhortation, "Work as a team." How can people work as a team when they don't really know what it is?

Achieving consensus is not a management structure or style (except that a certain style of management would encourage and foster the use of consensus decision making techniques at every level), it is a method for teams or groups to use to arrive at decisions. The team could be the Board of Directors or a group of production employees. Consensus techniques do not imply that a group of blue collar workers will be sitting in every meeting, at every level, participating in decision making, nor does the use of consensus decision making imply that every single decision must be made by a team.

Remember, the basis for everything we do in The Code is the process. We don't want to be taking action on processes without input from the *appropriate* process doers, the folks who make the process go from day to day. If it's necessary to take action to improve the cash flow of the corporation by jettisoning a few unprofitable operations, that's a decision that is best achieved by consensus. The team members who would participate would be the Board of Directors, various operation presidents, and select technical experts. These folks are the ones who are the appropriate hands-on doers for that process. The best way for them to achieve a high-quality decision is to make sure that everyone participates fully. That demands the achievement of a consensus decision.

On the other hand, if the problem is allocation of computer availability to clerical personnel, the hands-on doers would be the clerical personnel, their supervisor, perhaps a computer technician (to discuss file sharing options and so on), and perhaps a computer training person (unnecessary time is being used because computer skills are not adequate). These people run the process; therefore, they should make the decision. The only way to arrive at the best decision is through achieving consensus.

Decision Making Styles and Decision Quality

I've stated several times that the best quality decision requires consensus decision making. Figure 23-1 illustrates the impact of various types of decision making on the quality of group decisions (in cases in which there are objective criteria for determining quality, such as having a group attempt to name all the state capitols in the United States). These findings are routinely replicated with all sorts of groups, from CEOs to high school students.

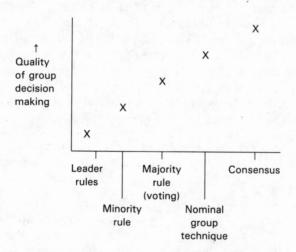

Figure 23-1. The quality of group decision making under different conditions of group dynamics.

As Figure 23-1 shows, the poorest quality group decisions are those in which the boss, or the most dominant team member, makes the decision (with little discussion). Accuracy improves a little when a minority rules and calls the shots. The improvement in accuracy is driven by the fact that data for the decision is coming from several people, instead of just one. Majority rule (voting) is a little better because more people are involved. Next comes Nominal Group Technique (NGT), a more group-oriented, discussion-driven form of voting, which will be discussed later in this chapter. It is better than simple voting because it involves more discussion of the topic. The best quality decisions are generated by consensus decision making. This is because the group shares as much data as possible, thereby minimizing mistakes.

An interesting phenomenon occurs when a group is under stress or pressure to make a decision that is critical or urgent. The style of individual and group decision making they use will be driven to the left side of Figure 23-1, toward more autocratic styles. This explains why executives who are normally participatory will revert to one-person rule if something critical comes along. In emergency situations, such autocratic rule may be essential. (I wouldn't want a group to decide whether or not to yell "Fire!" if the movie theater were burning.) The problem is that there's a tendency for every situation to become an urgent, one-person call; participation and consensus then go out the window. The only way to combat such a tendency is to establish a strong cultural practice of consensus decision making that everyone supports.

Reaching Consensus Is Critical to Commitment

Many studies have demonstrated the importance of consensus decision making and participation to team members' commitment to implement a decision. It's not just enough for a group, or a boss, to arrive at a high-quality decision. Just being "right" isn't enough. It's equally important to arrive at a decision that will be fully supported by the process doers. Many bosses, and even leaders of countries, have come up with decisions that are exactly on target but were not supported by the employees or the general populace. The result: failure to implement the decision and poor process results. The situation can be illustrated by the following formula:

| Extent of process improvement | = | Quality of the decision | X | Commitment of process doers to implement the decision |

If we have the best possible decision, for example, 1.00, but very low commitment on the part of the process doers to carry it out, for example, 0.2, we get a process improvement of $1.00 \times 0.2 = 0.2$. Even if we have a less "correct" decision, such as 0.6, we get a much better process improvement when commitment is increased. As commitment increases to 0.5, our process improvement is $0.6 \times 0.5 = 0.3$, a 50% improvement over the 0.2 that was the result of a perfect decision and low commitment. Of course, as we saw earlier, consensus decision making leads to better quality decisions, as well as commitment, so we benefit in both areas.

A popular method used to illustrate the effects of consensus decision making on decision quality and commitment is to set up an artificial decision making situation and measure both commitment and decision quality. Many of you have probably heard of, or been through, these exercises. Unfortunately, most often they are poorly conducted and explained, resulting in a waste of the experience. The following paragraphs are a description of one such exercise.

A team of six to eight people is given a hypothetical problem. The problems are often "survival" scenarios: the group is asked to pretend that they have just crashed in the desert, in the arctic, on the moon, etc. They are told that they may not be rescued for quite some time and that they have a list of items not destroyed in the crash that they must rank from most important to least important for survival. The team is then told to work on the problem for an hour or two and come up with a ranked list. In these situations, there is a "correct" set of rankings, usually provided by content experts.

A very effective way to demonstrate the effectiveness of participation on decision quality and commitment is to "plant" a few nonparticipants in the group. These are people who are instructed not to say anything or give any opinions unless they are directly asked to do so. Occasionally, there will be a person or two in a group whose natural behavior is to participate very little, but you can't count on it, so it's better to plant them. These nonparticipants are told to answer fully and completely if they are asked a question but then to remain relatively quiet until they are asked again.

After the exercise is completed, each team member is asked to complete a short questionnaire to estimate his or her level of participation in the decision making, level of commitment to the decision, feelings of frustration, and estimate of the quality of the group's decision on a numerical scale from seven (most) to one (least). The questionnaires are sorted into two piles: nonparticipants and participants, on the basis of how they answered the first question about participation. Those who answer three or less are put in the nonparticipant's pile, and those who answer four or more are put in the participant's pile. You can't assume that because you told people not to participate, they won't. Some do, and some people turn out to be nonparticipants who were not so instructed. Each pile is then scored separately for participation, feelings of commitment, frustration, and estimates of decision quality. A remarkably consistent pattern of results is almost always found, shown in Table 23-1.

Table 23-1.
Participation, commitment, and decision quality
ratings by participants and nonparticipants.

	Participation	Commitment	Frustration	Quality
Nonparticipants	25%	48%	91%	86%
Participants	93%	83%	21%	94%
Difference	−68%	−35%	70%	− 8%

The results in Table 23-1 are shown as percentages. The 25% entry for nonparticipants in the Participation column was derived by taking the average rating (from one to seven) of all nonparticipants and dividing it by seven times 100. In the example, the average rating was 1.75. Dividing 1.75 by 7.0 yields 25%. These percentages make interpretation between groups a little easier, since it's clear "how far up" the scale a score is in terms of the maximum available.

As you can see, nonparticipants and participants were markedly different in terms of their participation, with nonparticipants participating 68% less. This is to be expected, given the sorting strategy that was used. However, it's interesting to observe that the people who do all the talking in any group are always pleased with their own participation and will almost always rate everyone else's participation as high, even if nobody else was permitted to say a word. That's why bosses are almost always surprised when their subordinates claim that they don't get to participate; the boss thinks things are fine because he or she is always talking.

Note the large difference in commitment. The nonparticipants feel 35% less committed to implementing the group's decision. Translate that to a work situation and process improvement: every nonparticipant is going to be negatively impacting the ultimate process improvement because he or she won't be enthusiastically supporting the decision.

And look at the frustration levels. Even in a silly little game, which everyone knows is a game with a trivial outcome, nonparticipants are 70% more frustrated than participants. At work, that frustration is real. It concerns careers, self-esteem, and livelihoods. Frustration at work results in grievances, increased absenteeism, turnover, and a host of additional, costly consequences.

The last column is particularly interesting. It's the estimate by each group of the quality of the decision. Note that there's little difference between the two groups, with the nonparticipants judging the quality of the decision to be only 8% less than that of the participants. This is a key point.

AMERICAN SAMURAI INSIGHT

Even if people don't participate in a decision, they make fairly objective assessments as to the quality of the decision. This often leads management to assume incorrectly that participation isn't important because employees "couldn't do any better."

When short-sighted managers see these types of decision quality assessments, they often say, "See, they know that we were right, so what could they have brought to the table? All they have to do is get it done." There's the rub. It's not so much that employees would have come up with a radically different and better solution. The important point is that their participation results in the entire group actively and aggressively supporting the implementation of the decision. That's where the real benefit of consensus decision making lies (although better quality decisions are often a result as well).

TECHNIQUES FOR FOSTERING PARTICIPATION AND ACHIEVING CONSENSUS

The following various tools and techniques, which have been proved valuable in fostering team consensus and participation, should be used whenever appropriate by groups at all levels.

Effective Meetings

Poorly run meetings are almost a foregone conclusion in most organizations. There's no point in attempting to use tools for consensus if every get-together is disorganized and poorly focused (not to mention hostile and unproductive). Since all group activities take place in meetings, it's imperative that the meetings be run correctly. Some basic rules for effective meetings are:

1. Have a coordinator for the meeting. This is not necessarily the leader or the boss but someone (can be different for each meeting) who will set up the agenda (with input from others), arrange for minutes to be taken, arrange for a meeting time and location, and notify other persons who will be attending.
2. Have an agenda. List ahead of time what will be discussed, in what order it will be discussed, and how much time will be devoted to each item. The agenda should be distributed ahead of time to all team members. It doesn't have to be typed or fancy.
3. Have a facilitator. This is an assigned person (can be different for each meeting) from the group who has the responsibility for attending to group dynamics. This person is the one who will manage the consensus techniques discussed on p. 296. The coordinator and the facilitator can be the same person.
4. Start on time. If people don't have enough respect for the meeting to show up on time, they shouldn't be there. This includes upper management, who, in some organizations, demonstrate their power by deliberately arriving late.
5. Minimize interruptions. Unless there are emergencies, there should be no interruptions for outside messages, phone calls, and the like.
6. End on time. This will force the group to deal with meeting management problems rather than simply letting them run wild.
7. Keep minutes. These don't have to be long and formal but should be a synopsis of what happened so that time will not be wasted in the next meeting by rehashing completed topics. Some people have a habit of at-

tempting to bring up issues that were already settled because they didn't like the outcome. Minutes can stop that behavior (although such behavior is an indication that consensus was not reached in the earlier discussion).

8. Evaluate the meeting. Spend a few minutes, as an agenda item, talking about how the meeting went. If things should be done differently, bring them up for discussion.
9. Use the last few minutes to set the agenda for the next meeting. Everyone must participate.

Other techniques of effective meeting management are:

Frequently summarize what has happened. This is up to the facilitator and/or coordinator (if nobody else does it). Whenever it seems that something has happened or a decision has been made, the facilitator should summarize the event to see if everyone concurs.

Make sure that everyone participates. Often called "gatekeeping," it's up to the facilitator (and everyone else) to make sure that everyone participates in the discussion.

Control dominant team members. The facilitator (and others) must control team members who are trying to take over the meeting and/or not allowing others to talk.

Keep things on track. The facilitator must keep the group on the agenda by interrupting if things get off the agenda item that's under consideration.

Listen and ask for clarification frequently. Everyone must do this. If something is not clear, do not make assumptions. Ask for additional explanations. This will bring out more information for the group and permit better decision making.

Brainstorming

Brainstorming is a technique for generating as many ideas as possible in a short period of time. It is a less structured version of some of the Japanese planning tools discussed in Chapter Fifteen (Coda 10), such as the affinity diagram and the interrelationship digraph. The steps of brainstorming are:

1. State a subject for discussion. Very often, the subject can be a quality problem or a goal the team would like to attain. The object of the brainstorming session is to come up with causes and/or related issues. It helps to write the subject on a flip-chart or a blackboard.
2. Give everyone a chance to think about the issues for a few minutes.
3. Review the rules of brainstorming with the group. They are:
   a. Everyone must participate.
   b. No discussion of any ideas as they are suggested.
   c. Write down every idea without evaluation.
4. Decide how the group will participate. Will the discussion be totally freewheeling, or will the group go around the table to each person in turn?

The freewheeling technique lends itself to more spontaneity but may not yield the greatest participation, especially for newer groups.
5. Conduct the brainstorming session.
6. After the ideas are generated, the team then uses other techniques, either those described in the following paragraphs, the Japanese tools discussed in Chapter Fifteen, or both, to analyze the list.

Multi-Voting

Multi-voting is a name often given to a successive ranking procedure in which a group attempts to reduce a large list to a smaller one. For example, if a group brainstormed a list of 100 causes for a problem, it would probably be necessary to prioritize the list for action. It's important to do this in a manner that maintains team participation. The steps of multi-voting are:

1. Number all items for easy reference.
2. Discuss how many items each member will rank order. The object is to have each team member select from the list a smaller number of items than are on the list. Thus, if there are 100 items on the list, each member might select ten to 50.
3. Have each member select the items by writing the numbers of the selected items on a sheet of paper.
4. Tally the votes by hand (or in secret, if the issue is sensitive, by having each person pass his or her list to the coordinator). The items on the board should be noted with the number of total votes each one received.
5. The original list should be kept and a new list constructed, with only the issues that received the top number of votes.
6. Repeat the procedure until a manageable number of items is selected.

Nominal Group Technique

Nominal group technique (NGT) is a more structured form of multi-voting. It is particularly useful in situations in which the group is very large and/or isn't really an intact team (that is, they don't work together all the time). A large number of executives who meet once a year is an example of such a group. NGT allows a large number of issues to be pared down quickly. The disadvantage is that it discourages a lot of discussion, since it's basically a rank-ordering, voting technique.

The steps of NGT are:

1. Outline the procedure of NGT (many people have heard the name, but few know what it is). This brings up the interesting point of who decides that NGT will be used—this is not democratic, usually!
2. Write the main issue on a blackboard or flip chart.
3. Ask each person to privately write down a list of his or her issues.
4. Go around the room and have each person read one item off his or her

list. Write the item on the board. If the item is already up there, have the person suggest another. Keep doing this for 20 to 30 minutes maximum (or until the ideas have all been used up).

5. The group should analyze the list and attempt to group similar items. Usually the facilitator initiates a lot of this (since he or she probably suggested using NGT in the first place).

6. The items on the final list are numbered for reference purposes.

7. Each person is given from three to ten note cards (or slips of paper), depending on the number of items on the board.

8. Each person writes the number of one item on the card and then assigns that item a ranking. If five cards are being used, the top-ranked item gets a five on its card, the next item gets a four, and so on.

9. The cards are collected and the rankings for each item are noted on the board next to the item. The total rankings for each item are added up and the items with the top five to ten scores are the items of choice.

THE GOAL OF CONSENSUS AND TEAM WORK

The tools and techniques described in the preceding paragraphs are approaches and guidelines for effective teamwork. However, do not lose sight of the fact that the goal of teamwork is to improve processes and enrich peoples' lives by allowing them to participate in their work. These consensus building techniques are not themselves the point of teamwork, nor are they the mechanisms by which processes will be improved. The actual mechanisms of process improvement are the Innovate, Do, Check, Act cycle, the Standardize, Do, Check, Act cycle, and the process improvement methodologies discussed in Chapters Thirteen and Fourteen (Coda 8 and 9, respectively). The tools of effective teamwork must be applied to drive these mechanisms. They must work in concert, because neither can be maximally effective by itself.

DON'T WANDER OFF INTO THE
BUSHES OF PSYCHO-BABBLE

I've seen many organizations go overboard with all sorts of team dynamics and effective meeting skills, to the point at which everyone in the place was acting and talking like a social psychologist. People were talking about feelings all the time, and the slightest display of assertiveness was the subject of detailed micro-assessment by a team of amateur shrinks. You can recognize these organizations because they have people who will stop a meeting at a key point and say something such as, "Excuse me, Bob, but I noticed that Sally was reacting somewhat defensively when you made that last comment, and I think we ought to stop and discuss your comment as well as her reaction to it.'' Such discussions have no place at work. Leave the shrinking to the professionals.

The problem with these outfits is that they've gone nuts for team dynamics, but they often don't have the slightest idea about how to investigate a problem with a structured, process-oriented methodology.

On the other hand, there are all sorts of companies that have pursued SPC, DOE, and the like but have absolutely zero awareness of, or ability to utilize, effective consensus decision making. They will never attain their goals because they are not allowing their people to contribute effectively.

CONSENSUS IN THE ORGANIZATION: WHAT IT LOOKS LIKE

So, given all the skills and techniques, what does this stuff look like when it's actually practiced? First of all, it means that decisions, at whatever level, never arrive out of the blue without prior discussion with the hands-on process owners. This doesn't mean that management is asking for permission or that management is required to obtain unanimous approval for every action. It does mean that whoever will be making the decision will also take the time and the trouble to discuss the issues with the people involved.

At the very least, this demands that the issues be laid out in detail in front of people who will be affected and that they be given an opportunity to comment and provide their reactions.

AMERICAN SAMURAI INSIGHT

An open discussion is absolutely essential so that the entire group will feel more committed to whatever final decision is made.

If management decides to proceed with a decision that is contrary to the wishes of the process doers, they must be prepared to explain their logic in detail. People don't expect to get their way all the time, but they do expect to be told why things are done. Of course, I'm assuming that management is acting in the best interests of customer satisfaction and employee participation whenever a contrary decision must be made. If management never solicits employee input and/or doesn't ever really listen, all the explanations in the world won't buy commitment, employees will see through the sham and will react in the same manner as they would in a traditional work environment; they'll resist the changes and hate the system.

IT'S ALL IN THE HANDS (-ON PROCESS DOERS)

Everything boils down to the principle that processes should be run by those who do the process. If management focuses on this truth, there will be few decisions made without the direct involvement (and hence, commitment and support) of the process doers. If management refuses a process orientation and maintains the typical fascination with results and objectives, there will be little emphasis on consensus building and participation and little resulting commitment (not to mention poor quality decisions). The entire Code hangs together (or we'll all hang separately as has-been competitors).

24

Everybody Puts Them on One Leg at a Time

Coda 19. **All nonsalary management perquisites (special dining rooms and parking lots, club memberships, more lenient attendance policies, etc.) must be terminated immediately. No worker is a more inherently valuable human being than any other.**

Perquisites (usually referred to as "perks") are special nonsalary privileges or rewards that are provided to certain management levels and denied to other employees. This is the Coda that really sticks it to the brass. They might put up with a process orientation, they might tolerate some consensus decision making, and they might even sit still for treating suppliers like partners. They might even be able to consider that Egg Sucking Pigs aren't beneath notice (not that they'll start to notice them right away, but a start's a start, right?). But, give up their special perks? "Whoa," they scream in pain, "let's not take this transformation stuff too far!" Well, if it's going to work, that is, if an organization is dedicated to changing to a more effective way of managing, there's no other choice: the perks must go.

TOP-LEVEL PEOPLE DO DESERVE MORE

Let's get one thing straight right away: higher-level people have more responsibility, supposedly more experience and expertise, and should be compensated for it. They should be, and are, paid a lot more for their labors than are lower-level personnel. In fact, they are often paid far out of proportion for their labor. (There's no way any human being is worth 50 million per year, when there are others working their guts out for 12 thousand.) But, within rational bounds, more pay for more value is fine; that's the way it should be. More pay is not a perk.

The other fundamental reward that top-level executives get, and deserve, is more stimulating and enjoyable work. They get to make decisions and have more impact. They have more control over their lives, schedules, and so on. In short, their jobs are more fun. Some of them will contend that this isn't true, but they don't remember what it was like to be at the bottom.

299

The "More" Doesn't Include Perks

Yet, in spite of the fact that higher-level folks get much larger salaries, have more job security, fewer controls on them, and get more satisfaction out of their work, they think they deserve still more as a reward. Nonsense. Perks, too? Where does it stop? They need free coffee? And special parking? Give me a break. Maybe everybody needs free coffee and special parking, but the folks making the most money, with the best jobs, burning the least amount of calories through physical labor, sure don't need the economic support, the free calories, or the shortest walk in from the parking lot. The whole system is backwards; it's the Egg Sucking Pigs who need the freebies and the coddling if anybody does—they're the ones who have it worst.

Perks Maintain the Caste System and Destroy Teamwork

But that's not the primary reason perks must go. The social and economic injustice is bad, but it's not a killer. (After all, the world has never been fair, and everybody knows it.) Perks have long-term, acute, and profound effects on the entire organization. They damage productivity and impede teamwork and participation. That's why they must go.

AMERICAN SAMURAI INSIGHT

Perks have no other purpose than to maintain the caste system and the evils it perpetuates.

How can you have consensus and participation when you divide employees into different social castes, never the twain to meet? You can't. I'll always remember one of my first "professional" jobs in a large corporation. A few up and coming Tiger Sub-Humans and I had been working for weeks on a team with some senior executives, putting together a traveling road show. One morning, after working closely for hours, building what I felt was great team spirit and rapport, the group decided to break for lunch. The executives walked out of their offices and over to the corporate dining room down the hall. We Tiger Subs followed. At the door, one of the executives stopped us, "Sorry, fellas, only grade levels above 15 can use this dining room. See you after lunch back in the office." We were crushed; we thought we were team members, but we were nothing to them, just pack animals. Even though three of us were the key speakers on the road show, we weren't really one of the team. We hated them for deliberately setting us aside as "not as good" and excluding us from the "real team" after sucking us in to believe that we really were part of the team. Even though we continued to work hard, we never again worked quite as hard, or with as much enthusiasm. Why should we? They were on a different team. The same thing happens every time a Proto-Human or Sub-Human or Egg Sucking Pig gets his or her nose rubbed in a perk. A year later, four of the five Tiger-Subs working on that team had quit the company.

EVEN IF EVERYONE SAYS FIRE IS COLD, IT'S HOT—AND IT BURNS!

And one more thing: it doesn't matter whether or not the Egg Sucking Pigs and Sub-Humans notice the perks and/or complain about them. Often, executives will defend the presence of perks with a statement something like this: "I asked a whole group of employees at my monthly lunch if they were upset about the reserved parking for executives and managers and they said it was OK with them. So, it must be OK, right?" Wrong.

First of all, very few people are going to tell an executive something they don't think the executive wants to hear. So they lie and say it doesn't bother them. And then if it really doesn't bother them, who cares? What do they (or the executives) know about the effect of the caste system on productivity? Nothing. Less than nothing. The bad effects of special privilege are operating, even if everybody likes it. Many overweight smokers contend that they are not at risk because of special factors (family history and so on). Wrong. It's a fact that they are at risk. In the same manner, it's a fact of organizational dynamics that perks set up barriers, damage feelings of commitment and teamwork, and negatively impact productivity and costs. So, forget what people think unless they know what they're talking about—perks cause major problems. They must go.

LET US COUNT THE WAYS THAT PERKS CAN KILL (COMMITMENT)

Let's look a a number of common perks and examine the effect they have on building a processs-focused, team-oriented approach to work.

Separate Parking Lots

How would you feel if you were an Egg Sucking Pig and, when you drove up to work in the morning, there was a big sign over the driveway that said, "Gods, Human Beings, and Proto-Humans are better people than the rest of you Sub-Humans and Egg Sucking Pigs. Sub-Humans and Egg Sucking Pigs park in back." You'd be insulted. You'd feel like you weren't a part of the team, that you were an afterthought accessory to the organization; expendable, excess baggage. You'd be having your face rubbed in the implication that you are less than the best.

Well, that's what the Sub-Humans and Egg Sucking Pigs feel when they have to drive by the special parking for the Gods and Human Beings (and maybe Proto-Humans as well). Here they are, arriving for work, usually earlier and for harder jobs with less security, with more micro-management, less pay, fewer benefits, and so on, and the first thing they run into is a slap in the face about where they have to park. If anything, they should get the best parking.

But no, they are put far out in the county, or in back. A farther walk and not as safe, usually. The executives argue, "Special parking is a perk I've earned by my years of service. It's something you earn. If they don't like it, tough." There are two problems with this ignorant reaction. First of all, it doesn't matter if it's good or bad, earned or not. If a practice interferes with the establishment of a participatory, team-oriented working environment, it must be stopped.

Second, what's this claim of "earned by years of service"? What about the years of service of a secretary, or a file clerk, or some poor slob who's killed himself for 25 years just to get to a Sub-Human job? Don't they deserve the same consideration for years of service? Logic says they do.

Of course, giving special parking for years of service visibly rewards simply hanging around. No company needs to send that message. What should be rewarded is long-term process improvement activities, but they can't be measured very accurately. And why bother? The reward for participation and improvement is job satisfaction and the success of the company. Such efforts reward themselves. Parking and other perks don't reward anything but those executives who are willing to sacrifice productivity for their own ego satisfaction and comfort. Parking is simply parking. Dissolve all parking segregation. It's the only thing that makes sense.

Separate Dining Rooms

At Ford, managers of a certain level and above are provided with special dining rooms. In the seclusion of the private retreat, there is quiet, velvet, linen, silver (Ford logo, special order), and waiters. Filthy lucre doesn't change hands; the diners are billed once a month. They are served by waiters and waitresses in little red outfits. It's all you can eat, with special dishes for a nominal fee (2 to 3 bucks). Meanwhile, the Egg Sucking Pigs, Sub-Humans, and Proto-Humans are standing in lines out in the noisy employee cafeteria, having to wait as yet another school bus load of students on a sightseeing trip to the plant is being fed first (talk about a negative message about employee worth). And for the privilege, they get to eat $2.95 grease burgers (fries are extra) from plastic plates with plastic forks out in the employee cafeteria. This sort of arrangement is common in American industry. It makes me sicker than the grease burgers do.

Why is this necessary, you might ask the pampered ones? The almost knee jerk response is, "We need a place to get away and talk." Right. What they want to do is get away from the 97% of workers who do the work and who aren't happy—the very folks they should be seeking out and talking to every day.

This arrangement has a number of damaging effects. First of all, it fosters an "us and them" mentality in the minds of management that runs counter to every thread of The Code. Many discussions take place in these retreats (and they run a lot longer than the usual lunch time given to the troops), hidden from the eyes and inputs of lower-level managers and employees. The pampered ones soon develop a feeling that they and their caste members "are" the company and that the Egg Sucking Pigs are simply "there," part of the furniture. Little input is solicited from the troops because the pampered ones develop a mindset that isolates them from the employees.

The other major drawback is the same old slap in the face about status. The use of special dining rooms means that some people are considered "better" and deserve cheaper but higher quality food and nicer places to eat. If everyone is important because they are a process doer, everybody deserves the same consideration in terms of basic support services. All special dining rooms must go. Almost all world-class organizations have completely abandoned special dining rooms. The CEOs eat with the Egg Sucking Pigs every day and (are still alive and well).

More Liberal Performance Standards

This is a benefit that's not written down anywhere, but it's real and significant. You've all seen it. A factory worker comes in 10 minutes late and gets a "point" (so many and you're out) or gets sent home without pay for the day. An office person comes in 10 minutes late and everybody wonders why he or she is in early. Hourly workers get 30 minutes for lunch, and that's all they get; if they come back late, they're in big trouble. Salaried workers get 30 minutes, but they can take 60 to 90 minutes without a comment.

An Egg Sucking Pig makes a mistake or two in a week and is in major league trouble. I've mentioned the painters at Ford who routinely get sent home for days without pay for errors that nobody can explain. We've all seen the walking wounded of the necktie set who haven't done a lick of work in 20 years and are simply "left alone" to continue not performing. Even as I write this, a friend of mine is working in a large organization in which several lower-level supervisors are only a few days from dismissal for continuing personality clashes with their bosses. That same organization just made a surprise announcement of estimated losses of hundreds of millions of dollars on a large project. The losses had been coming for at least a year but had apparently been "pencil whipped" by project managers so that they would look good. The executives and project managers running that operation are still at work, even though they hid the facts and caused major league losses. What is this but a difference in performance standards? The simple truth is that lower-level castes are held to the rigid letter of the law, whereas upper management is loosely, if ever, held to anything. We've all seen companies in which managers who just can't hack it are shuffled from one job to another. And given real responsibility! It wouldn't be so bad if they just put all these dorks in a building somewhere (else) and paid them to stay out of the way. At least the work could go on back at the ranch. But what usually happens is that upper management doesn't want to embarrass the loser, so they give them "a noncritical area" to manage. "Noncritical"? No area is noncritical; there are valuable employees working there who deserve better and who are working critical processes (if the processes aren't important, why are they being done at all?).

The difference in performance criteria is even more striking when you consider that most hourly personnel are never given formal performance reviews. Of course, we know that such reviews are worthless, but the traditional management system doesn't know that. Traditional management contends that performance reviews are important for the development of potential. What about the potential of the Egg Sucking Pigs? Apparently, not worth worrying about. One more nail in the coffin of American competitiveness. Everyone must be held to the same high standards of performance. Not the same nit picky control and close supervision, but the same standards of excellence.

Larger, More Spacious Offices

This perk is a divisive force among levels of Proto-Humans and some Sub-Humans, mainly. It's a central tenet of the pecking order in American business that as you go up the management ladder, offices and furniture get larger and more luxurious. I've been in executive offices that had more square footage than my house. Why is all the space necessary? To display status and power, to intimidate, to demonstrate authority by square footage, rather than by leadership. To a lesser extent, the same thing goes on down the management ladder.

Now, I'm not an advocate of eliminating all private offices. They aren't evil in and of themselves. And open offices don't automatically engender teamwork, as some office designers would have you believe. Some people need offices. I abhor open office arrangements for their lack of privacy and quiet in which to think. But it's a far cry from having equal-sized private offices to having a 100-page policy statement on who gets how many visitors' chairs (with various degrees of adjustment) in their work area.

One of the hidden evils of this perk is that it generates a huge amount of suboptimization, as greedy and covetous managers fight it out to get to the next level of opulence. If they all had the same basic setup, there would be less infighting for the perks and maybe, just maybe, more attention spent on process improvements.

The Other Extras

These are simply more of the same; little goodies that drive and reinforce caste distinctions and impede teamwork by generating "us-them" perceptions. Some examples are free coffee and goodies for managers and above while everyone else pays, more sick time for office workers than factory workers, free "working lunches" delivered to executive offices while other employees have to hit the machines in the break areas or use the cafeteria, more liberal policies regarding personal leave for office workers compared to factory workers, special parties and social events for executives (paid for by the company), special deals on company products for executives but cheaper or no deals for employees, low-interest loans to senior executives, free or discounted health and golf club memberships for executives, and so on. The list could go on forever, and in some companies it does.

These sorts of perks are given to management at a certain level simply because they've always been given. They are the vestigial remnants of feudal times. They've got to go.

IF YOU'RE IN IT TOGETHER, YOU'RE IN IT TOGETHER

The entire issue boils down to one point: does an organization want the whole team out there pulling together and fighting for success, or does it want various pockets of privilege, layers of management, and castes all struggling in slightly different directions? We saw the impact of participation on commitment in Chapter Twenty-Three. The only thing that will make it these days is to have everyone working as a team: one dedicated, committed engine, all with the same focus, all feeling that they can't let down their teammates. Perks poison that commitment and destroy that teamwork.

Even on a Super Bowl football team, the multimillion dollar quarterback shares the same locker room (with the same size locker) with the rookie bench warmers. The reason: the players must have cohesiveness in their "office" if they are to play as a team on the field. There are few perks. The superstars get rewarded through their paychecks and off-season endorsements. Few perks are permitted because they would estsablish barriers to teamwork and the critical "we're all in it together" feeling. This is even more critical at work because the office is the "field" and there is no off-season.

The perks must go. But beware, this is another one that you can't fight on an individual basis. Things will change as overall organizations change. This is going to be the last bastion of traditional management. The old boys will defend this last parapet to the end. Stand by with the ladders, my fellow American Samurai, we'll go up the wall as soon as they begin to weaken.

25

We March at Dawn (Getting it Done)

Coda 20. **The time for talk is over. It is time for each and every American Samurai to stand tall and be counted, to put this Code into practice today, so that American business and life will be better tomorrow.**

The question is now: what to do. The answer, of course, is: DO IT. GET IT DONE. Now, not tomorrow. There is NO TIME left to dwaddle around, bemoaning our fate and blaming the workers, taxes, the Japanese, and so on. We are up against the wall, and it's getting worse every minute. Every second that we wait we lose capital and resources that are vital to the rebuilding of American competitiveness. Time is running out. We must act immediately to save what's left of American business.

If I could snap my fingers and get it done, I would. But we know that it won't work that way. It never does. It's going to be a long, slow, brutal campaign. While the battle to change the face of American business rages, millions of additional jobs will be lost, tens of thousands of additional careers will be destroyed, foreign companies will buy more of our businesses with the money they make from us (and which we spend on their products), and many thousands of additional acres of manufacturing capacity will be converted to fast-food outlets that pay low wages.

It's up to you, American Samurai—you and I, and the Demings, Jurans, Taguchis, Shingos, and Ohnos of the world. Those of us who know a better way must get out there and fight for it. We must press as hard as we can as long as we can to save what's left and build a better tomorrow. The question is: what's the best way to take the fight to them, to work for change most effectively?

A FRONTAL ASSAULT WILL NOT WORK

The first thing *not* to do is to turn into a raging prophet of self-righteousness and doom at the office tomorrow. That will turn you into a pariah and a "character," and nobody will take you seriously. The Code and its tools and skills are not widely understood. The insights you've developed by reading this book are rare and unique among American business people, believe me. I've been teaching (and raging) about the necessity for transformed management for more than 15 years, and in that time I haven't met more than 50 people who understand how it all fits together; why The Code (or Deming's 14 points or any other approach) is an entire theory and practice of management and not just a bag of skills that can be slapped onto the old management approach like paint on a house.

You must do what you can do as soon as possible, but if only a little is possible right now in your organization, do only a little. Many organizations just aren't ready to accept any large changes, even if they're on the verge of being driven out of business. It's going to be a slow battle in all but a few organizations. With the right executives, ready and eager for change, with just the right amount of competitive pressure in their industry, you could get lucky and be part of an organization that is ready to saddle up and move out fast, but don't count on it.

THE WINDS OF CHANGE ARE COMING, AND YOU ARE THE LEADING EDGE

You can take heart in the fact that you most likely won't be toiling alone very long. There are hundreds of people in every organization who have intuitions about every one of the Coda; they know there's a better way, but they haven't put it all together. There are hundreds who want to do things a better way but either don't know the way or are afraid to even suggest a change. There are dozens of managers in every organization who are ready to change right now. All it takes is a sufficient catalyst to get things moving. There is growing awareness of the horrible state of American business affairs, competitiveness, and educational systems. There is much confusion about what should be done, but people are worried. That is the first necessary step.

There is mounting interest and publicity about the Malcolm Baldrige National Quality Award. As this builds and more and more spokespersons from Baldrige winners hit the streets publicizing their organizations' achievements, interest and action will grow. Change is coming to American business. It cannot be stopped.

The forces of a new business way are going to sweep ashore in great numbers and destroy the fortress of traditional business. Have no doubt, it will happen. The problem is that it must happen soon and in sufficient numbers to effect a complete transformation in a very short 10 years.

Because you are interested and because you know what must be done, you are in the first wave. You will be hitting the beach first in this battle to save American business. Advance commandos like Deming, Taguchi, Juran, and Shingo have done their part by cutting the wire and taking out the sentries. Now it's up to you and I. If we don't weaken the resistance and take out the big guns, the main wave of change will have a tough, slower time of it when they wade ashore. And the final victory will take longer—or may be forever denied. We simply don't have any more time to waste.

PATIENCE IS NOT A VIRTUE, IT'S A WEAPON

Most organizations will move so slowly that it will seem like they are not moving at all. Although it will be monumentally difficult, you must be patient. Your efforts, even if they do not seem to be working, will be having an effect. As Americans, it is hard for us to accept the fact that things sometimes move slowly. Our penchant for the "fast gun, slow bullet" style is part of the problem. Now we all have to face the fact that while we need as fast a turnaround as possible, the change will be a "very slow gun."

AMERICAN SAMURAI INSIGHT

Organizational change cannot be rushed faster than it will naturally move. Change of any type takes time. If it must move slowly, as management style change almost always does, then that's the way it has to be.

You, however, must begin to do what must be done, however slowly it must go, as soon as possible. That is, you must get started now. Lay out a plan and get moving.

Your efforts to "sell" those concepts that the organization and the brass can accept will be preparing the way and providing a slightly more receptive environment for the moment when your organization finally wakes up to the competitive threats that are all around them. It's not glorious and you won't be recognized as a messiah (in fact, if you're not careful, you might turn out to be a martyr), but then, trench warfare and guerrilla fighting (not to mention starting a religious movement) are never, ever glorious.

YOU CAN BAIL OUT, BUT IT'S THE SAME EVERYWHERE—YOU MUST STAND AND FIGHT WHERE YOU ARE

Some of you are thinking, "Why stay with some constipated old bureaucracy and wait for change? Why not go with a champion outfit, a Baldrige award winning company such as Motorola or Xerox?" Well, that would make it easier on you, no doubt. But think about it. Do you want to have to tell your children and future colleagues (and yourself) that instead of being in the first wave on the beach, fighting for American business, that you were a courier who waded ashore with the general's staff 3 weeks after the main assault in a carefully staged photo opportunity? Any true American Samurai would be sickened by such an association.

The fact is, we've all got to stand and fight for the future of American business wherever we are. The most depressing, recalcitrant, hopeless situations are the ones that require the most effort, the most work, and the most sacrifice. It doesn't take much to sell these concepts at a Baldrige winner—they're already on the road to success. There are millions of jobs and careers at risk in the unenlightened companies. They are the ones that need the most work first. And those are the places where most of us work.

I'm not asking you to sacrifice your career to stay with a loser. But don't go running around looking for a place where The Code will sell easily. If they aren't already doing it, it won't be easy, even if they say it will. It never is.

WHAT YOU MUST DO IN THIS EPIC STRUGGLE

Watching Your Back

Although it's absolutely essential that you work for change, it is even more important that you take care of yourself. There are comparatively few American Samurai. Each of you is a valuable weapon, much like a 30 million dollar fighter aircraft. Such aircraft are too valuable to expose to high-risk–low-return missions; they must be used only when the probable outcome merits their possible loss. Each of you American Samurai is similarly precious. You must pay careful attention to your career and your perceived value in each job. If you get reckless and take too many dangerous risks in pushing for change, you may find yourself in deep trouble. The result would be that you could get the boot or lose a critical promotional opportunity. That would decrease your value to us in the future struggle.

Education—Increasing Your Value to the Cause

Education has become the coin of the realm for entrance into a good career. Get as much as you can anyway you can. Keep getting it as long as you can stand it. And, if you can't stand it and don't have at least a Master's degree, choke back your gorge and do it anyway. Things are too competitive in the battle for good jobs and promotions to try and get by with less. It doesn't matter if you think more education is intrinsically useless (much of it is), it doesn't matter if you hate sitting in the boring classes (so did I), and it doesn't matter if you have more enjoyable things to do (everybody does). When you are evaluated for advancement, when you are assessed as a job candidate, when your opinion is sought in everyday business endeavors, your education is like a shield; the bigger and the stronger it appears, the more intimidated your foes will be. You'll win by default many battles that you'll never have to fight because of the intimidation of your credentials.

Is this sort of thing fair? No. Life is not fair, and work is not fair. Is that the way it is, everywhere? Yes. Do you have any recourse but to play by their rules? No. If you think you can opt out of the education game and make it on hard work and brains, you don't have as much insight as you need and you're not as smart as you think you are. There are no exceptions to this basic rule.

AMERICAN SAMURAI INSIGHT

In business, as well as in many social interactions, you are your education. You must be as "much" as you can be.

I don't know how many times I've worked with brilliant, hard working people who, with a little more development early in their careers, could have blown me away. But they'll never have the opportunity to step into that arena because they don't have credentials. Even more tragically (for them), they know it. And what do they do? Instead of setting a plan to go back to school and get what they need, they bemoan their fate (or suffer silently). Instead of paying for school, they go on vacations or buy hot cars. What a waste, for them and for American business.

The traditional management system worships experts and education more than actual contributions. To be accepted, to gain influence, to be granted access to positions in which you can make things happen, all require education. There are exceptions, of course, but they are infrequent, and often holdovers from earlier times.

A key consideration in your early and middle career years is the type of educational support a company can offer. If you don't have a Master's degree (or a Bachelor's degree) and your company offers any kind of tuition assistance, you are a fool if you are not going to school part-time. No excuse justifies not taking advantage of this type of freebie.

AMERICAN SAMURAI INSIGHT

Companies don't care what happens to you unless it messes up their carpet. They only care about you because it helps them.

The only reason people are moved along in a big company is because it's easier and cheaper than "going outside" for fresh meat. Besides, an employee has already has had his or her spirits broken to the company plow and will be pliant and subservient. The company is doing it for themselves. If a company is truly transformed, it will value and cherish each employee as the most valuable resource it has. If the company is a traditionally managed one, it views employees as cannon fodder for profits.

Keep Your Job in Perspective

A job isn't a carefully designed set of duties and responsibilities. It's a hole in the organization that's filled with a person. It changes over time. With you there, it'll be different than it was for the prior pilgrim. Depending upon the company, the boss, and the characteristics of the jobholder, a job can be a source of deep satisfaction and fulfillment, a minimum security, weekend furlough experience, or an ordeal of hard labor, solitary confinement, and occasional beatings. As a jobholder, there's only so much you can do. If the situation is bad, there's not a lot you can do except to work carefully to get by with less aggravation and suffering. You may have no choice but to move your career elsewhere.

Moving on is not giving up. That's surviving and taking care of yourself. No matter how dedicated you are to hard work, no matter what level of sacrifice you're willing to make for the company, no matter how fervently you're working to do your part to save American industry, you may not be allowed to do anything meaningful. There may be no opportunity for significant contributions and/or changes. That's not your fault; it's just one of the many soulless, inevitable, and unfeeling eddies in the entropy of the universe. In other words, that's life. In order to get the most out of a job (and life), you've got to accept that many times you're going to be faced with a situation that you cannot save.

AMERICAN SAMURAI INSIGHT

Companies don't hire people to make incredible contributions. They hire them to do what they want them to do, even if they don't know what that is.

It's up to the smart jobholder to find out what an organization wants and give them as much of it as you can stomach. If what they want is too contrary to your American Samurai teachings, you have a decision to make. Stay and fight, or leave and fight on somewhere else. Do not give up easily, but do not risk your career in a losing struggle; a ruined Samurai cannot help us in the future. If there's a little slack (as there almost always is), you can use it to work for change and make things a little better for the next generation of prisoners. If there isn't any give to the system, you'll have to move the American Samurai Ninja show elsewhere.

Realize that jobs are not permanent. Everybody agrees with the logic of this statement, but they don't believe it emotionally after they settle into a company. There's nothing like a few periods of unstable employment to demonstrate the transient nature of any given job. If you've been tossed out into the street, fired, snuffed, sacked, discharged, booted, canned, turfed, terminated, axed, chopped, dismissed, and otherwise rewarded for years of service by being awarded the late Friday afternoon, "Can I see you for a minute," "Can't look you in the eye," "Would you close the door" back stabbing (with cardboard box clusters), you realize that the job that seemed like a bloodline bond yesterday is less than a used tissue today. It's amazing how many otherwise mature adults don't realize this fact of life.

AMERICAN SAMURAI INSIGHT

You don't own a job; you're a very temporary, month-to-month boarder. As long as there is no noise, no mess, and there's not a more attractive renter on the horizon, you'll be allowed to stay a little longer.

Hopefully, you recognize this attitude as a natural artifact of the small value put on employees in the traditional work environment. Here today (but a pain) and gone tomorrow without a thought (if they need more meat, there's always another warm body stupid enough to take the job). You may have difficulty believing that the nice people at work could be so crass (you'll have trouble with this only if you haven't been tossed out before), but, trust me, it's something they've done before and will do again, with relish, to good workers like yourself (particularly to those people who act like revolutionaries).

YOU MUST NOT APPEAR TO BE A REVOLUTIONARY

As you can see, a large part of any American Samurai's effort must be spent on basic survival skills. That's the way it always is for people working in any revolutionary movement. The open fighting gets the attention, but the real struggle is simply to stay alive from day to day so that you can fight the good fight when the chance for action arrives. This is exactly what you're going to have to do—work quietly for change when you can but don't get reckless and risk major job or career damage by acting like a revolutionary.

This is a problem for many American Samurai; they can't stand the playing along and the waiting. They want action, they want to fight for major changes *now*. This is the path to major problems. You must start working now to change things, but you must work carefully, without alienating the powers to be in the system. You are an American Samurai now, and proud of it. But you're still tainted by the "fast gun" American virus. It will take many years before you are totally cured. In the meantime, keep your impatience under control.

You must survive and prosper so that you can spread the word. This means playing their game, working undercover, until the organization begins to change. Survival means that you've sometimes got to choke back your gorge and pretend to put up with the present system in order to work for change over the long term.

AMERICAN SAMURAI INSIGHT

You've got to "play along" in order to be accepted in traditional business. You've got to appear to be one of them in order to change it.

If you're not tough enough to accept this truth, you won't be equal to the challenge; you'll drop your cover and begin to act like a revolutionary, spouting disturbing new practices and theories to frightened and superstitious managers. They'll cast you out without hesitation, and your opportunity to turn them to the good side will be lost.

GETTING A CHANGE STARTED

The approach you must take is to slowly, very slowly, introduce concepts to managers who have problems and/or are receptive to exploring new methods of work. In effect, you will be applying bits and pieces of The Code to difficulties as they appear. For example, if there is the usual griping about performance reviews and appraisals about that time of the year, sometimes it's possible to suggest an experiment that tests group rewards for an area or department. This suggestion must always be made with the stated motivation to "make the personnel department look good" or "make the division look good" (never drop your guard and admit what you are really trying to do: prove the utility of The Code of the American Samurai). It will invariably take a year or two to get the test under way and completed, but it's a start.

How much you can get done depends on your level of responsibility. If you're a manager or executive, you can begin to use team concepts, flow charting, and SPC with various work groups as you begin to teach people about processes. The results will speak for themselves, and others will be interested (if you are a Human Being or a god, others will do it or play along just because you want it, even if they think it's stupid—which is why the traditional system is still with us).

Always look for ways in which to introduce a new concept without being threatening. What you're looking for is chinks in the armor of the traditional management approach—opportunities to cast some doubt about the effectiveness of the old way, to get people thinking about possibilities. If you're in any kind of "expert" position, you can suggest books from the Bibliography to specific individuals who might be receptive. It's especially helpful to distribute "For Your Information" type magazine and newspaper articles among various members of management whenever you find something that discusses changes at another company. This is particularly valuable if the company is a competitor.

Build Up a Critical Mass

The main objective is to build what's called a "critical mass." A critical mass is a body of people who share similar beliefs and who provide a self-supporting and reinforcing nucleus of energy for the change. Without a critical mass, believers feel isolated, cut off, and threatened. After some time, without support, many will give up and allow the system to reabsorb them.

There are two kinds of critical mass that are required. The first is the nucleus critical mass. This is the group of hard-core believers who will support one another and keep the flame alive in an organization. Not spreading, but alive. It helps if most of them work near each other or in the same department so that they will have more opportunities to support each other.

The second critical mass is the one necessary to initiate and drive overall organizational change. It requires a minimum of about 10% of an organization's head count (assuming they are all at one site or location). Thus, with 1000 people, it will take about 100 who understand and believe The Code (and know how to use some of the tools) to get real change started.

STEP BY STEP, HOUSE BY HOUSE, TRENCH BY TRENCH, CODA BY CODA

What can you do, specifically? The following are specific recommendations for selling and/or promoting each of the Coda in an organization. Remember, use your judgment and don't take chances; there are too few of you to waste in gallant but hopeless battles.

Coda 1.   Management's obsession with outcomes must be abandoned and replaced by improvement activities.

Pick a problem and demonstrate the success of a process focus by fixing it with the 12-step process improvement approach discussed in Chapter Eleven (Coda 6).

Coda 2.   Out-of-process defect inspection must be eliminated and replaced with defect prevention strategies and/or 100% in-process inspection (Poka-yoke).

Read about Poka-yoke (see the Bibliography) and look for applications in your work area or area of responsibility. Demonstrate the success of the efforts with control charts showing before and after process outputs. When discussing successes, always attribute it to the specific tools that were used—this builds interest.

Coda 3.   Process-related decisions must be based upon objective, statistical analyses of micro-process inputs, events, and outputs, not subjective reactions to macro-process results. Policy-related decisions must be based upon The Code of The American Samurai.

Locate several key areas of concern and begin to chart them with SPC charts and pareto charts. This can be done in conjunction with a 12-step process improvement effort. It's always very enlightening to demonstrate to management (the ones who are interested—don't get pushy) that what looks like significant changes in a process are often only normal variation. This is particularly true if you chart something like deviation from plan for cash or sales on an Individuals and Moving Range chart.

Coda 4.   Employees are every organization's most valuable resource; when they do not do a good job, it is almost always management's fault.

You can't sell this one to a traditional manager. Instead, focus on showing, with cause and effect diagrams and Poka-yoke, that the system causes errors, not the employees. Go easy with this one as a philosophy, because management won't want to believe it.

Coda 5.   Quality of product and service, not volume, sales, or profits, must come before all other considerations.

Again, this is a hard one to sell on concept; only results will do it. The best way is to find an area that's really dying with errors and rework and attempt to help them correct a few glaring problems. Don't go poking around if you don't have a reason to be there; you'll get suboptimized out the door for meddling. If you can show that eliminating errors at the source yields more productivity (as it always does), you'll be doing as much as you can to sell this idea. They still may not see it, but it's a start.

Coda 6.   Suboptimization and "management by fire control" must be abandoned and replaced by the implementation of an organized plan for the continuous improvement of key processes with the goal of maximizing customer satisfaction.

Nobody's going to stop suboptimizing in a typical organization until broad changes are apparent (until things change, there's no perceived value in *not* suboptimizing). The best way to start is to focus yourself or your work group on really listening to internal customers (it goes without saying that you'll immediately do what you can to help external customers, to the extent that it's safe in a traditional organization). If another department sees that you, or your people, are really interested in helping them, they'll reciprocate. It could begin to spread if there's any fertile soil at all. (By "spread," I mean grow so slowly that it's hard to see; don't get impatient.)

Coda 7.   Excellence in all critical process outputs must be identified through the use of comparative benchmarks.

Forget about benchmarking for awhile. Until you've got more than a critical mass trained and are implementing most of the other Coda, benchmarks are only going to cause trouble. Traditional managers will instantly turn them into objectives and you're right back to a "results and objectives without a plan" approach. Save benchmarking for 2 to 3 years into the change (if your organization changes that quickly).

Coda 8.   **The role of management is to set policy that establishes and sustains this Code, conduct long-term planning, pursue bold new innovations that generate order of magnitude increases in quality and profitability, and lead through coaching and teaching.**

All you can do here is preach the gospel to those who will listen and do it yourself. It has to start with you. If you're not a supervisor, try to influence your boss by asking for his or her advice and guidance in those areas in which he or she can give it. Start to talk about customers, customer requirements, and so on. If you can "teach" the boss while supposedly asking questions, you may make a small difference. Frankly, it doesn't have much chance of working on the typical boss. All you can do is try. Don't push too hard.

Coda 9.   **The role of employees is to continuously improve their work processes (Standardize, Do, Check, Act), as if the processes they work were their own businesses.**

You can encourage your people to get started on this sort of thing if you can get them sufficiently trained in the basics of processes, customer satisfaction, SPC, and so on. There's nothing you can safely do if you're just a Sub-Human or Egg Sucking Pig.

Coda 10.   **Business plans must be action documents that provide every member of the organization with sufficient detail to clearly understand what they must do in order to help the organization attain its objectives.**

Unless you're a top-level (Human Being or god) type, don't mess with this one on a "let's change the plan" basis. You'll get creamed. If you're a boss, you can start by helping your people understand your objectives and by working with them to develop specific metrics that the area can use to monitor plan-related processes. This will build team spirit and commitment and will help you meet your mandated objectives.

Coda 11.   **All employees must receive extensive skills and knowledge training about their jobs, the company, and the tools of process improvement. Training is a long-term investment in profits, not an expense.**

All you can do here, if you're a boss, is to push for as much development and training for your folks as you can. In the traditional organization, that won't be much. Don't fight too much, or you'll be branded a troublemaker.

Coda 12.   The concept of performance to specification decreases quality and hides costs. It must be abandoned and replaced with an awareness that any variance from the ideal increases costs.

The only way to promote this, unless you're a really high level type, is to look for opportunities to teach and counsel anyone who seems remotely interested. Specifications and the like are the heart and soul of traditional manufacturing and engineering, and it's difficult to do anything specific to turn it around fast. It's seen as an attack. Don't attack; just teach in general.

Coda 13.   Suppliers are critical team members who must be educated, valued, and treated as equals in the quest for quality. Selection of suppliers based upon price must be abandoned and replaced with selection based upon total life-cycle cost.

Again, this one can't be addressed without high-level support. If you're in a small organization and have some purchasing, manufacturing, and/or engineering responsibility, you might be able to do a little something with a vendor or two. If you're in a large organization, there's nothing you can do if you're not a mover and a shaker (except to teach and send out articles).

Coda 14.   The traditional systems of job descriptions, performance appraisals, merit pay, and pay for performance are useless, damaging, and wasteful; they must be abandoned and replaced with a system that encourages and rewards teamwork and group effort.

Leave this alone unless you are a personnel V.P. or higher. You'll be seen as attacking motherhood. Everybody thinks the old way is the only way. This topic is a mine field.

Coda 15.   Organizations and their policies and procedures must be redesigned to optimize cross-functionality, "flatter" reporting structures, streamlined communication, and accelerated decision making.

This Coda will only change over a long time. Do what you can to foster the cross-functional team approach by suggesting such teams for chronic problems and by seeking input from internal customers and suppliers on all cross-functional issues.

Coda 16.   Low-cost, low-technology process improvements must be pursued before technological solutions are implemented.

This is a Coda that you can demonstrate in your own area by improving processes. It won't be immediately apparent to observers that you're supporting this Coda, but that's all right; as you know, they all hang together.

**Coda 17.   Concurrent (or simultaneous) engineering must be implemented
on all new products and product modifications (which is simply
a process orientation to product development but sufficiently important and specialized to merit individual attention).**

If you're an engineer, you can begin applying the principles of effective
design right away. If you're a manager in purchasing, engineering, or
manufacturing, you can begin to promote concurrent engineering by soliciting
cross-functional input on design and manufacturing related process decisions.
This is an especially easy Coda to promote via magazine articles, because
there are a million of them out there all the time. It's a hot topic that may
be easier to sell than you think.

**Coda 18.   All decision making must be reached by consensus decision mak-
ing on the part of appropriate groups of hands-on process
workers.**

All you can do with this Coda is practice it yourself, to the extent that
you have people working with you. Don't try to push upper management
to adopt it until they seem receptive or a golden opportunity reveals itself
(for example, if you are told to solve a problem, put a team together and
then present the "team findings" with the team present). If they don't believe
it, they aren't ready yet. All you can do is teach and model it.

**Coda 19.   All nonsalary management perquisites (special dining rooms and
parking lots, club memberships, more lenient attendance policies,
etc.) must be terminated immediately. No worker is a more inherently valuable human being than any other.**

This is a tough one. Don't throw this up in management's face unless
you're way up there (otherwise, you may end up "way down there" for your
trouble). The brass are very protective about the cookie jar. If they see a
threat to the goodies, you will be branded as a socialist (which is worse than
a communist these days). And you'll have to be careful about giving up any
of the perks you get as a sign of solidarity with the troops. The problem
is that in order to be effective in changing management, you have to be accepted by them first. If you alienate yourself from them, you lose the chance
to change them. Much of what you say will be dismissed as the opinions of
a crazed radical. Thus, you have to balance your belief in The Code with
the necessity to be seen as "one of them." Go slow and take it easy.

**Coda 20.   The time for talk is over. It is time for each and every American
Samurai to stand tall and be counted, to put this Code into practice today, so that American business and life will be better
tomorrow.**

All we can do is our best. It's either that or learn how to flip burgers and say things like, "You want fries with that?" I'll never accept that, and neither will you.

You are now a full-fledged, if somewhat inexperienced, American Samurai (pretenders will not have read this far). Get to work right away, but do not brazenly display your swords of skill and knowledge; they will frighten traditional managers. At first, for years perhaps, you will have to work as a Ninja, springing from ambush to do what can be done to save American business, without sacrificing yourself unless it's a do-or-die matter of honor. It's not as glorious as open combat on a sunlit field of glory, but this isn't a glorious struggle; it's a dirty, stinking, uphill fight against overwhelming odds for our lives and our way of life.

Yet, if there are enough of us who will fight with intelligence and courage, our day will come. In a few short years, the traditional system will be sufficiently weakened by the competition to the point at which it will be more receptive to new ways. Simultaneously, American Samurai will have been infiltrating the management ranks of traditional business, turning thousands to The Code. When that day comes, my fellow warriors, we will cast aside our Ninja cloaks and we will form up in closed battle ranks on a sunlit field of glory. We will march on the remnants of traditional business and we will sweep them aside. With our victory, American business will truly embrace a new way of working: The Code of the American Samurai. It will be the beginning of a business rebirth that will make American business once again feared as the world's premier competitor. And you and I will be there, knowing that our years of struggle made the victory possible.

Until that day of victory, when we stand side by side in the dawn of a new day for American business, we will see each other only occasionally in the shadows. Know that there are many others fighting in the darkness with you. Good luck and good hunting, American Samurai.

Bibliography

The following list is not exhaustive, but it is representative of the types of skills and knowledge that are critical as a starting point in your journey to become totally informed about the challenges we face. For books that are primarily available through mail order, I have provided information for ordering at the end of the Bibliography. All others can be ordered through bookstores.

Braverman, Jerome D. *Fundamentals of Statistical Quality Control,* Reston, Virginia: Prentice Hall/Reston, 1981. ISBN: 0-8359-2197-3.

Camp, Robert C. *Benchmarking: The Search for Industry Best Practices That Lead to Superior Performance,* Milwaukee, Wisconsin: ASQC Quality Press, 1989. ISBN: 0-87389-058-2.

Deming, W. Edwards. *Out of the Crisis,* Cambridge, Massachusetts: Massachusetts Institute of Technology Center for Advanced Engineering Studies, 1986. ISBN: 0-911379-01-0.

Dertouszos, Michael L., Lester, Richard K., and Solow, Robert M. *Made in America: Regaining the Productive Edge,* Cambridge, Massachusetts: The Massachusetts Institute of Technology, 1989. ISBN: 0-262-04100-6.

Monden, Yasuhiro. *Toyota Production System,* Norcross, Georgia: Industrial Engineering and Management Press, 1983. ISBN: 0-89806-034-6.

Ohno, Taiichi. *Toyota Production System: Beyond Large-Scale Production,* Cambridge, Massachusetts: Productivity Press, 1988. ISBN: 0-915299-14-3.

Sandras, William A., Jr. *Just-in-Time: Unleashing the Powers of Continuous Improvement,* Essex Junction, Vermont: Oliver Wight Limited Publications, 1988. ISBN: 0-939246-14-7.

Scherkenbach, William W. *The Deming Route to Quality and Productivity,* Rockville, Maryland: Mercury Press/Fairchild Publications, 1988. ISBN: 0-941893-00-6.

Shetty, Y. K., and Buehler, Vernon M. *Competing Through Productivity and Quality,* Cambridge, Massachusetts: Productivity Press, 1988. ISBN: 0-915299-43-7.

Shingo, Shigeo. *Zero Quality Control: Source Inspection and the Poka-yoke System,* Cambridge, Massachusetts: Productivity Press, 1988. ISBN: 0-915299-07-0.

Shingo, Shigeo. *A Revolution in Manufacturing: The SMED System,* Cambridge, Massachusetts: Productivity Press, 1985. ISBN: 0-915299-03-8.

Tatsuno, Sheridan M. *Created in Japan: From Imitators to World-Class Innovators,* New York, New York: Harper and Row Publishers, 1990. ISBN: 0-88730-373-0.

Walton, Mary. *The Deming Management Method,* New York, New York: Putnam/Perigee, 1986. ISBN: 0-399-55000-3.

ASQC Quality Press, American Society for Quality Control, 310 West Wisconsin Avenue, Milwaukee, Wisconsin 53203.

Productivity Press, P.O. Box 3007, Cambridge, Massachusetts 02140, (617)497-5146.

Index

WANT TO LEARN MORE?